THE HEBREW REPUBLIC

Illustration from the 1700 Dutch edition of *The Hebrew Republic*.

THE HEBREW REPUBLIC

Petrus Cunaeus

With an Introduction by
Arthur Eyffinger

Translated and Annotated by
Peter Wyetzner

SHALEM PRESS
JERUSALEM AND NEW YORK

Petrus Cunaeus (Pieter van der Cun, 1586–1638), Dutch philologist and jurist, lectured at the University of Leiden from 1611 until his death. He was the first Christian scholar to make extensive use of Maimonides' *Mishneh Torah* in his research on ancient Jewish history. In addition to his scholarly work, Cunaeus served the States of Holland as legal counsel in matters of commerce and maritime affairs.

Shalem Press, 13 Yehoshua Bin-Nun Street, Jerusalem
Copyright © 2006 by the Shalem Center

Cover design: Erica Halivni

Frontispiece: Courtesy of the Royal Library, The Hague

ISBN 965-7052-37-8
    978-965-7052-37-2

Printed in Israel

∞ The paper used in this publication meets the minimum requirements of the American National Standard for Information Sciences—Permanence of Paper for Printed Library Materials, ANSI Z39.48-1992

CONTENTS

Introduction   ix

Translator's Preface   lxxi

Chronology   lxxvii

Author's Preface   3

BOOK I

Chapter 1   *The Origins of Law*   9

Chapter 2   *Distribution and Ownership of the Land*   14

Chapter 3   *Reasons for Agrarian Laws*   17

Chapter 4   *The Isolated and Rustic Lifestyle of the Jews*   20

Chapter 5   *Egyptian Farmers versus Hebrew Shepherds*   22

Chapter 6   *The Jubilee and the Sabbatical*   25

Chapter 7   *Laws Pertaining to Cities*   29

Chapter 8   *The Uniqueness of Palestine and the Babylonian Diaspora*   34

Chapter 9   *The Legislative Dominion of Palestine*   37

Chapter 10   *The Focus of Power: Israelites, Judeans, and Jews*   42

Chapter 11   *The Continuity of Jewish Sovereignty*   45

Chapter 12   *Leadership: The Judges and the Sanhedrin*   47

Chapter 13   *Other Courts in Palestine*   53

Chapter 14   *Kings: Their Appointment, Rights, and Obligations*   56

Chapter 15   *Jeroboam and the Division of the Kingdom*   61

Chapter 16   *Corrupt High Priests and Illegitimate Kings*   65

Chapter 17   *The Messiah and the Third Temple*   68

Chapter 18   *The Flaws and Virtues of the Jews*   71

BOOK II

Chapter 1   *The High Priest's Garments*   79

Chapter 2   *The High Priest's Oracular Powers*   83

Chapter 3   *Laws Pertaining to the High Priest*   85

Chapter 4   *The High Priest and the Holy of Holies*   87

Chapter 5   *The Temple Altars*   90

Chapter 6   *Priestly Ranks and Duties*   94

Chapter 7   *The Consecration of the High Priest*   97

Chapter 8   *The Organization and Status of Priests*   99

Chapter 9   *The Functions of the Levites*   102

Chapter 10   *"Anshei Hama'amad"*   104

Chapter 11   *The Organization and Duties of the Levites*   106

Chapter 12   *The Magnificence of the Temple*   108

Chapter 13   *Temple Sacrifices*   111

Chapter 14   *The Sanctity of the Temple*   113

Chapter 15   *The Destruction of the Second Temple*   115

Chapter 16   *The Samaritans*   118

Chapter 17   *Jewish Sectarianism*   121

Chapter 18   *The Prowess of Jewish Soldiers*   125

Chapter 19   *Fighting Wars against Pagans*   127

Chapter 20   *The Seven Canaanite Nations*   130

Chapter 21   *The Army of the Jews*   133

Chapter 22   *The Virtue of Fighting on the Sabbath*   135

Chapter 23 *The Diasporas of Egypt and Babylonia*   138

Chapter 24 *Reasons for the Sabbath and the Ban on Pigs* 144

BOOK III

Introduction   155

Chapter 1 *The Beginnings of the "Jewish Church"* 161

Chapter 2 *Noah and Abraham*   168

Chapter 3 *Melchizedek*   171

Chapter 4 *Slavery in Egypt and the Pagan Lies Told about It* 181

Chapter 5 *Circumcision*   189

Chapter 6 *The Purity of Jewish Worship*   196

Chapter 7 *Prophets*   201

Chapter 8 *Kabbalah: The Secret Meanings of Biblical Passages* 206

Chapter 9 *The Hebrews' Understanding of the Messiah* 212

Notes   221

Index of Sources   278

General Index   290

INTRODUCTION

PETRUS CUNAEUS' *De Republica Hebraeorum*, or *The Hebrew Republic*, is a compelling, evocative, and at moments provocative treatise which, within its class, makes for fascinating reading. This statement may come as something of a surprise. The work recalls, indeed exemplifies, an age when the world of learning seemed as if mesmerized by the unworldly quest for "antiquarian" lore, philological subtleties, and abstruse theological hairsplittings: an age that eminently produced bulky, long-winded volumes which somehow, and as paradoxical as this may seem to us, comfortably made their way from the study into the harsh "outdoor" world of political and social reality. The humanists' dogged vindication of predecessors, their relentless quest to salvage the relics of worlds long lost from the wreckage of time, seems wondrously at odds with their acute social commitment. Still, often enough, it is precisely the spanning of these poles which makes for their rewarding reading. Cunaeus' work is a case in point. Its impact asserts itself on numerous levels. However, without some considerable amount of background knowledge, these aspects tend to elude the modern reader all too easily. This introduction sets out precisely to forestall any such unfortunate outcome.

Cunaeus' *Hebrew Republic* warrants interest on at least three counts. First, its in-depth learning recalls that world of early Leiden humanists who established their university's durable reputation throughout the world of letters. The treatise is in all respects representative of decades of solid biblical research in Holland's bastion of Calvinist orthodoxy. At the same time, it offers much more than that. Within his circle of almost by definition versatile humanists—the Scaligers, Heinsii, Vossii, and the like—Cunaeus is easily identifiable. What made him stand out among his peers was not so much the scope of his learning—his comfortable command of philology, the law, and theology alike—but rather his distinctive approach to all the subjects he addressed. Petrus Cunaeus was endowed with a keen social intellect, an uncommonly critical eye, and a highly creative bent of mind. He was not just another professor of Latin, rhetoric, or the law. As the foremost Leiden

professor of political science, his primary interest was man rather than matter: man's follies, man's superstitions, man's cunning. In his courses at Leiden his subjects were Tacitus and Suetonius, the "political" historians. As a
professor of Latin he read Horace, Martial, and Juvenal, the gem of Roman
satire. He himself authored one of the most biting and intelligent political
satires produced by the Renaissance; in the midst of social upheaval and
political riot in Holland, he made short shrift of the arrogance of university
dons, the imbecility of clergymen and self-acclaimed theologians, and the
fickleness of the mobs.

Among Leiden colleagues and students, Cunaeus also enjoyed a reputation
for his pure, ornate rhetoric. Time and again he was singled out to perform
public addresses, whether at funerals, lustra, or convocations. *The Hebrew
Republic* is written in the lively, argumentative, provocative style which, it
is only fair to say, mirrored his character. Much was written on Cunaeus'
character—and probably much more *not* put in writing—during his lifetime.
Even among our all too polemic humanists, Cunaeus stood out for his readily
inflammable nature. His impatience, his outspoken tenor, his sarcastic wit,
and his merciless criticism of colleagues add a definite flavor to his works,
and likewise to *The Hebrew Republic*. Cunaeus never leaves us in doubt as to
the (want of) merits of an author under consideration. If Maimonides is his
steadfast guide in most matters Hebrew and Jewish, so is St. Jerome among
the Christian apologists. Not as fortunate are the otherwise perfectly repu-
table scholars from all periods whose genius meets with less than respect in
Cunaeus' eyes. Indeed, his verdict on the nation he sets out to describe stands
as perplexingly stern and less than fair. Far from being merely descriptive,
Petrus Cunaeus' *Hebrew Republic* amounts to a thesis, a personal testimony.
But then, in Cunaeus' hands, nothing could ever turn out noncommittal.

Dutch Social Circumstance

A second major element of interest constitutes the acute social context of
Cunaeus' treatise. To be sure, at first sight its title and substance would hardly
suggest any topical relevance. The work sets out to discuss the ancient Hebrew republic and Church. However, its preface to the "States of Holland"
(the civic authorities of that most influential of the "Seven United Provinces"
which at the time constituted the Dutch Republic) makes no allowances for
any misunderstanding. Cunaeus' treatise was meant as an admonition to
the body politic—then in acute peril of losing its grip on society—not to be
trapped by the conniving of religious zealots and political machinators in

the mold of Jeroboam, who neatly undid the unity of the Hebrew Common-wealth. In a way, the treatise belongs to the category of *Fürstenspiegel*—the body of literature designed to instruct rulers in the governance of their countries. Throughout Cunaeus' analysis, records of the corrupting, almost self-destructive impact of power—be this at the hands of kings, high priests, or Levites—and the many pitfalls of religious fanaticism stand out as buoys at sea. Cunaeus felt that there was ample ground for such a warning—and time would prove his analysis right. Within a year of the publication of his work the young, aspiring Dutch Republic was grounded by social cri-sis without precedent and beyond repair, and it was religious friction that had unleashed the forces, *and* the partisan pretexts, that brought about its downfall. With this in mind, the reader cannot help addressing Cunaeus' evaluation of Hebrew circumstance from a double perspective, and will read-ily acquaint himself with the intertextuality and hidden layers of seemingly historical and speculative observations. At this point it comes as no surprise to learn from Cunaeus' correspondence that the treatise actually came about in the context of a major comparative study of models of state, its premature publication hastened at the urging of some of the foremost politicians and theologians of the time.

Whatever impact Cunaeus' plea had at the *Binnenhof* quarters in The Hague, it did not forestall tragedy. In September 1618 the crisis that, slowly but surely, had been building up over the previous decade came to a head in the coup d'état of Prince Maurice of Orange. This political intervention sealed the fate of the struggling aristocratic republic, reorienting it towards a mixed constitution, yet without healing personal rifts or bridging ideo-logical gaps. The purges of the 1620s never came anywhere near to solving the many riddles that had brought the hazardous political experiment of the 1580s to its knees. Instead, they hailed a prolonged period of extremely complex social and political strife that was to seriously impair the balance and efficacy of the Republic's administration until, a full two centuries later, French revolutionary thought finally did away with its outdated program and moldered fabric.[1]

However, the crisis of 1618 did not just rout the shaky balance and faltering synergy of the Seven Provinces; it also questioned the theoretical underpinnings of the Confederacy as such. How had all this come about?

In the previous century and a half, from about 1400 to 1550, Holland had seen its scepter and nucleus of power carried away from The Hague, the time-honored abode of the Counts of Holland, first towards Burgundy, then, by the Hapsburgs' proverbially profitable marriages, towards Philip's proud new center, Madrid—thus to find itself relegated to the very outskirts of that legendary boundless empire. Around 1570, political conservatism, spurred by power-bereft nobility and swept along by religious discontent and anti-clericalism, exploded into the Revolt of the Seventeen Provinces, which spanned the area of what is now Belgium and the Netherlands. A quarter century of desperate, uphill fighting resulted in what proved to be the definitive loss of the Southern Provinces and of the revolt's intellectual heart, Brussels, to Parma and the Counter-Reformation. By the time that, around 1600, a precarious military stalemate was secured, the revolt had grudgingly seen itself reduced to the Seven Northern Provinces. By then, its ideological center had, once more, touched base at The Hague.

Gallant military valor and astounding exploits overseas notwithstanding, the administration of the Confederacy of these Seven United Provinces, which from that time made up the Dutch Republic, was not without its complications. The core of the problem was precisely the absence of any decisive common denominator—be this in terms of policy, religion, or commercial interests—other than the stern renunciation of Hapsburg rule. Toleration was the single pragmatic policy that remained to prevent infighting in the face of acute external pressure, and the growing debate over toleration, notably in terms of religious orthodoxy, became urgent in the years leading up to the Twelve Years' Truce with the Spanish (1609–1621). Ironically, once the truce was in force, it was precisely over this issue that, in the year 1610, debate within the States-General of the Confederacy ended in perfect deadlock. If to many of its protagonists political sovereignty and liberty of conscience were at the heart of the revolt, to others it was Calvinist orthodoxy. What was at stake, in short, was the understanding of church and state, of tolerance and doctrine.

One never stops wondering at the fatal turn events took in subsequent years. Conflict was first triggered by a polemic between two Leiden professors of divinity, Arminius and Gomarus, over issues of predestination and the Lord's grace, a conflict known in literature as the Remonstrant Troubles. When mediation failed and conflict hardened into riots, public authorities intervened to safeguard social order—which then forced the question of their authority to interfere with church matters in the first place. From that juncture the conflict became politicized, placing the slumbering embers of class difference and provincial parochialism at the service of the personal ambitions of the Republic's paramount protagonists. These were the *Landsadvocaat* or Grand Pensionary, Johan van Oldenbarnevelt, that steadfast advocate of the wealthy Holland regent and merchant classes, and the Prince of Orange, captain-general of the Union and champion of orthodoxy, backward provinces, and the lower social strata. The outcome, in September 1618, was a coup d'état and a series of political trials and purges. With proud Olden-barnevelt, that grand old man of Dutch politics, lowering his head to the block, his foremost counsel Hugo Grotius was fortunate enough to get away with a life sentence.

During the years leading up to this crisis, Petrus Cunaeus had grown, step by step, from a keen observer of the political chess game to a serious player in his own right. With time, he became directly involved in the debate and in the genesis of some of the most penetrating tracts issued by leading intellectuals of the period, Hugo Grotius first among them. Now, in the ongoing debate, the analysis of republican models abroad—whether historical or contemporary—was one approach to help clarify issues. Hugo Grotius himself, in an otherwise unpublished tract that dates back to the turn of the century, had explicitly modeled his proposed emendation of the Dutch Republic after the constitution of the old Hebrew Confederacy. In doing so, he had brought all the stock elements of the genre, as developed by Carlo Sigonio and others, to bear on the Dutch situation. Throughout the years 1610–1618 Hugo Grotius and Petrus Cunaeus most emphatically joined forces in an exchange of views to help forestall imminent crisis. *The Hebrew Republic* was Petrus Cunaeus' paramount contribution to that debate.

Dutch-Jewish Relations of the Period[2]

Before focusing on Cunaeus exclusively, there is some reason to further widen our scope and examine a third element which, though mostly on the far horizon,[3] was never fully absent from the scene. To add to the religious patchwork and social complexities of the Republic, after 1600 a new phenomenon presented itself and soon enough further complicated the already elusive issue of toleration. This concerned the influx of Jews to the Netherlands. Shortly before the publication of Cunaeus' *Hebrew Republic*, the States of Holland had, after years of vacillation, instigated a first official memorandum on the position of the Jews and their worship.[4]

Let us briefly review the facts. The few pockets of Jewish life left in the Netherlands after their formal banishment by Charles V in the mid-sixteenth century had been dealt with by Spanish persecution in the days of the Duke of Alva.[5] This is not to say that the Dutch had no dealings with Jews. One can easily think of at least three regular avenues of contact. To start with, throughout the sixteenth century, nearby Antwerp cherished a flourishing Jewish community.[6] Again, Dutch trade with the Baltic was intense. Hugo Grotius' father, who, among other things, kept a brewery in Delft, was among the many Dutch merchants to order his corn and *klaphout* from the cheap Polish markets.[7] Jewish merchants were in complete control of these markets and in exchange, through their Dutch contacts, imported salt, wines, and luxury goods from the West.[8] A third element that came into play were the contacts with the Portuguese (crypto-)Jewish Marranos, the remnants from the wreckage of the 1490s in the Iberian Peninsula who, in subsequent decades, had put up a network of profitable trade routes. These contacts rapidly intensified from the mid-1590s, when the Dutch first ventured out on the oceans to steer towards the Indies. If anything, it is the "historical" chapters of Hugo Grotius' *De jure praedae*, the legal reflection on the contested legitimacy of the capture of a Portuguese *caraque*, which lends us insight into these contacts.[9]

Yet another element came into play. Throughout Europe, the upsurge of atheism and deism, due to the paralyzing stalemate of Reformation and Counter-Reformation, no less than the intellectual skepticism exemplified in the works of Bodin, Montaigne, and Lipsius, reflected a society adrift. In the Low Countries, on top of this, had come the breakdown, in the 1560s when revolt spread, of virtually all central administration. Typically enough, the Dutch Reformed Church, at its constituting Synod of Emden, had been established beyond the control of public authorities—something that would backfire later on. When central administration was finally reinstalled in 1579, the Confederation, at its constituting meeting in Utrecht, explicitly guaranteed freedom of conscience for all religious denominations. Soon enough, the Dutch Republic stood out as a safe haven amidst the bulwarks of clashing ideologies in Europe. Its social stratification was a patchwork of Catholics, Lutherans, Calvinists, and Mennonites, where immigrants, Jews among them, felt immune from persecution or trade guild opposition. All this is not to say that the Low Countries were entirely free from the widespread prejudice against Jewish worship met with elsewhere; far from it. In fact, one has only to single out the reservations regarding the Jews of that great, enlightened Rotterdam scholar Erasmus to appreciate that none of the stock recriminations that were found throughout Europe were alien to the Dutch.[10] Indeed, Cunaeus' own tract prompts the question of how much bias and prejudice still lingered on among Holland's intelligentsia at about 1620. By the same token, however, William of Orange himself, invariably at a loss for how to finance his campaigns against the Spanish, turned from the first to Jewish bankers, with a further view of using their help to kindle the Sultan's opposition against Philip II.[11] In short, if we turn to discuss the first wave of Jewish immigrants into the United Provinces, we will have to bear in mind that, all theory and doctrine notwithstanding, the Dutch and

Jewish communities from the first readily agreed on an eminently pragmatic policy of interaction.

Throughout this period, Antwerp had been by far the largest *entrepôt* and transshipment port in the area. The city boasted a substantial contingent of Sephardic Jews, known as the Portuguese Nation, who were involved in trade, retail, and the diamond industry.[12] When Antwerp was taken by the Spanish in 1585, most Jews were at first hesitant to leave. However, in 1595, with Antwerp eluding recapture, the Northern Provinces resolved on an effective blockade of the Scheldt and all Flemish ports. Two years later, in his dying hours, a repentant Philip II capitulated to Pope Clement VII's unequivocal decree of 1593. Abandoning his previous pragmatic approach, he once more resolved on a formal ban of the Jews.[13] At that juncture, the exodus of the Portuguese Nation towards the North, mostly to Middelburg and Amsterdam, started in earnest.[14] In September 1598, the first resolution of the Amsterdam city council concerning the Jews, while ruling out any form of public worship, granted them citizenship.[15] Their flourishing commerce with Portugal and its colonies (diamonds, sugar, cinnamon, and timber) did not speak against the interests of these Jewish merchants.

In 1600 a new contingent of very enterprising Jews from Venice—half of them Portuguese, half of them Levantine—settled in Amsterdam. Keenly availing themselves of the broad interest that their Venetian and Turkish contacts aroused, they petitioned for the privilege of public worship in a synagogue and the establishment of kosher butcher shops. When these efforts failed, they offered their services to Alkmaar (1604), Haarlem (1605), and finally Rotterdam (1610). On each occasion, highly willing city magistrates were prevented from coming to terms with them by the fierce opposition of orthodox Calvinists.[16]

In the years to follow, a rapidly expanding group of very successful and assertive Jewish merchants, keenly aware of their pivotal role in Holland's booming international trade, adroitly exploited the many loopholes in conflicting local rules and regulations to put increasing pressure on city councils for privileges in terms of religion, handcrafts, and retail trade. In doing so they inevitably invoked the resentment of clergymen and local guilds. At that juncture, it became increasingly clear to city magistrates that more precise instructions with regard to these new immigrants were needed. By 1614, the States of Holland decided on concerted action. By then, Remonstrant quarrels had taken on acute social dimensions. The major dilemma that presented itself now was how possibly to reconcile the granting of public worship to Jews with a formal ban on services by Roman Catholic and less orthodox Calvinist denominations.

To solve this riddle, two major politicians and administrators—Hugo Grotius, the Rotterdam city pensionary on behalf of the (dogmatically more lenient) followers of Arminius, and Adriaan Pauw, the Amsterdam city pensionary on behalf of the (more stringent) adepts of Gomarus—were invited to submit propositions. The outcome, predictably, was inconclusive. No formal resolution of any substance on the position of the Jews was ever passed at the provincial level,[17] let alone at the level of the Union and States-General. As before, Jewish policy was left to city magistrates, a decision that was formalized by resolution of the States of Holland in December 1619.

Still, the substance of the debate is of some interest to us. Whereas Pauw's propositions have not come down to us, Grotius' have, and they have prompted quite some debate among scholars. The least one can say about Grotius' *Remonstrantie nopende de Joden* of 1614–1615[18] is that it presents a competent inventory of outstanding issues by one of the foremost lawyers and politicians of the period. The tract typifies the constantly maneuvering Grotius of the period. Well aware of the sensitivities remaining from the refusal of Jewish merchants in Rotterdam in 1610, he steered a cautious if not ambiguous course. In this one must take into consideration all the prejudices of the period. The pogrom that took place that very year in Frankfurt[19] was symptomatic of the ways in which ministers mobilized rudimentary resentments of the mobs against any dissenters. Reactions to recent incidents in Holland had been very similar.[20]

The core of Grotius' views was the following:[21] The Jewish religion is not even remotely akin to the Christian religion. Still, it is extremely useful to learn Hebrew, if only for biblical research, and to that extent contacts with Jews are helpful. Also, a Christian is bound to proselytize Jews. By the same token, Jews must be forbidden by law to proselytize Christians. To that end, freedom of the press for the Jews should be restricted. Again, public ceremonies in synagogues were out of the question. Intermarriage and sexual intercourse, even with prostitutes, must be prohibited, nor should a Christian be submitted to the ignominy of serving in a Jewish household.[22] Jews were not to be admitted to public offices; however, they should remain at liberty to study at university centers, notably Leiden. Again, inasmuch as Jews served commercial purposes, no restrictions whatsoever should be imposed on them, as long as Jewish shopkeepers observed Sundays and Christian holidays. Ghettoes or restricted areas were not to be imposed.

The tract, clearly, is the product of very peculiar circumstances and conflicting interests. Grotius advocated a pragmatic, considerate approach in which mutual commercial interests and intellectual exchange played a substantial role. Stock elements of similar edicts abroad, as well as in other provinces of the Republic—such as the wearing of special attire, the inter-diction of circumcision—or restrictions in terms of numbers of immigrants, are not found here.[23] In Amsterdam, by a decree of November 1616,[24] Jewish worship, if silent and unobtrusive, was granted, but the bans on synagogues, sexual intercourse, and proselytization were stringently upheld. A States Resolution of December 1619 gave city councils license to open restricted areas, or ghettoes.

All this is of some interest to our purposes. Cunaeus entertained no, that is, no recorded, contacts with the Jewish community of his day and age. However, in the very days in which he was busily (re)drafting his *Hebrew Republic*, he was—witness his correspondence—in regular touch with Grotius on precisely these issues, and his in-depth research will have come to bear on the latter's views. Meanwhile, of all the persistent and obstinate miscon-ceptions, to use the euphemism, concerning the Jewish religion that were found on all levels of society throughout Europe, not a few seem to have made their way into Cunaeus' treatise.

So much is certain, that following Prince Maurice's coup d'état and the edicts of the Synod of Dordt, which defined the orthodoxy, the restrictions imposed on all nonorthodox denominations, whether Arminian, Lutheran, Anabaptist, Mennonite, Roman Catholic, Jewish, or Muslim, became very stringent indeed for at least two decades. These strictures did not prevent the Jews from helping to turn Amsterdam into a cosmopolitan center of in-tellectual and artistic pursuits, commerce, and printing. The various Jewish factions could even enjoy the luxury of endless controversy among them-selves.[25] But that phase, clearly, is beyond the scope of our present topic. It is time for us now to turn exclusively to Petrus Cunaeus, his life and works, and his role in the events sketched above.

PETRUS CUNAEUS (1586–1638)

The name of Petrus Cunaeus is rarely met outside of reference works for specialists in the first half century of Leiden University.[26] Unfortunately so, one may argue, as he was one of the most creative and critical scholars of his day and age. His linguistic talents were fabulous, his rhetorical gifts widely praised. For many years he was the preeminent legal expert at Leiden and, when it came to it, he proved himself a match, and more, for many a theo-logian or minister. Still, acknowledgment is due most of all perhaps to his mordant satire on the vain display of learning and his relentless criticism of hairsplitting ministers.[27] The authority he must have enjoyed at Leiden is perhaps best exemplified by the way in which his biting skepticism escaped punishment during the Remonstrant purges; indeed, it earned him the rectorship of the university in subsequent years. Petrus Cunaeus, in short, was a formidable authority by all standards.

Formative Years

Born the son of a merchant in Flushing in the province of Zeeland, Petrus Cunaeus was, for all the skepticism displayed in his works, of an altogether gentle and polite manner in day-to-day contacts; that is, if his colleague the Leiden professor of medicine Adolph Vorstius[28] is to be believed. In his funeral address for Cunaeus, Vorstius actually calls his friend the antithesis of his reputedly rude and belligerent countrymen from Zeeland. To that extent, Vorstius remarks laconically, Cunaeus reminds one of Hadrianus Junius or Desiderius Erasmus, both of them refined natures, though natives of cities— Hoorn and Rotterdam, respectively—that were not exactly deemed centers of culture. Petrus Cunaeus was first trained in the intellectual center of Zeeland, Middelburg, though not at the public school. He was entrusted to the care of a private teacher of high standing, a Hugo Favolius, before being sent to another teacher of high repute in Haarlem, Johannes Matthisius, in 1599.

In May 1601, at the age of fourteen, he was enrolled in the Faculty of Letters at Leiden. In view of his tender years, he was entrusted to the care of a relative of his mother's, Ambrosius Regemorterus, himself a student of theology, who reputedly taught Cunaeus the elements of Hebrew and Greek. While the story rings true enough, it has been suggested that the influence of the Middelburg minister Herman Faukelius also made itself felt here.[29] It is worthwhile to note that in these years Zeeland produced quite a few Hebrew scholars and Orientalists of fame, such as Adriaen Willemsz,[30] Lodewijk de Dieu, Johannes and Adam Boreel, and Johan de Brune. Middelburg was by all means a major seaport and *entrepôt* in the late sixteenth century, in which a community of Jews had also nestled. Again, it has been attested that well over twenty students from Zeeland matriculated as theologians in Geneva within the first fifty years of the founding of Beza's university.[31] Cunaeus' leanings, in other words, were by no means exceptional among natives from Zeeland of the period.

Ambrosius Regemorterus' father, Assuerus, served the Dutch parish in London. In 1602[32] the two youngsters embarked on a trip to Britain, notably to polish their Greek. In England, Cunaeus' elegance in Greek poetry soon earned him the esteem and friendship of the great Isaac Casaubon, as is attested by their correspondence.[33] In his *Hebrew Republic* Cunaeus eagerly sings the praises of that celebrated humanist. A couple of months later Cunaeus returned to Holland,[34] ready to be entrusted to that inspiring Leiden triumvirate Justus Scaliger, Bonaventura Vulcanius, and Daniel Heinsius, and to become acquainted with men like Dominicus Baudius and Hugo Grotius. In Leiden, Cunaeus found lodgings first with the famous botanist Carolus Clusius, later on with Bonaventura Vulcanius.[35] With time, Cunaeus' interests in theology and the law came ever more to the fore. In 1605, that is, in the very year the Remonstrant Troubles between the two Leiden professors of divinity, Jacob Arminius and Franciscus Gomarus, first surfaced,[36] Cunaeus defended a thesis entitled *De legis et evangelii comparatione*, in which the Old and New Testament were compared, before a committee presided over by Jacob Arminius. This was followed in 1606 by a thesis entitled *De cultu adorationis* under Franciscus Gomarus.[37]

By August 1606, keen to perfect his Hebrew and legal pursuits, Cunaeus was enrolled in the Frisian Academy at Franeker, up north, to follow the courses of the legendary Hebraist and Orientalist, Johannes Drusius.[38] On Scaliger's explicit advice, Drusius acquainted the young scholar with the Chaldean and Syrian languages and with Rabbinics.[39] Here, it would seem, are the roots of Cunaeus' work on the Hebrew Republic, inasmuch as (still according to Vorstius) it was his reading in Franeker of the works of Moses Maimonides that inspired him to embark on the project. It is one thing, as Vorstius observes, to quote a line of Hebrew—any dictionary may be of help there—but quite another to interpret properly the much more complex Hebrew of Maimonides, who for him (and here Vorstius typically echoes the prevailing opinion of that day and age) was the only rabbi worth reading.[40]

The story of Maimonides as the inspiration for Cunaeus' *Hebrew Republic* may well be true. Certainly, he relies on Maimonides throughout the treatise. Still, according to his opening greeting in the 1617 edition,[41] his first acquaintance with Maimonides' treatise came about at a different stage, namely through a text kindly presented to him by a friend of his, Johan Boreel.[42] We will discuss this later in more detail, noting for now that the poor accessibility of Maimonides' *Mishneh Torah* would long preoccupy men like Cunaeus, Selden, and Grotius.[43] When he left Franeker, Cunaeus remained in touch with his beloved teacher and consulted him on varying issues. If Drusius was a father to him, Drusius' son, apparently, was like a brother.[44]

While in Franeker, and again on Scaliger's instigation, Cunaeus also followed courses of that prominent theologian, Sibrandus Lubbertus, the undisputed champion of Calvinist orthodoxy. For many years on end, as another token of his flexibility, Cunaeus entertained the most hearty of relations with Lubbertus, indeed in much the same way as with Drusius. This strikes one as all the more surprising in view of Cunaeus' less than orthodox tenets and his intimacy with those of Hugo Grotius, the formidable opponent of Lubbertus in subsequent years.[45]

The Angry Young Man

Upon his return to Holland in 1608, Cunaeus was once more enrolled at Leiden. In subsequent years, notwithstanding his outspoken legal[46] and theological leanings, he first distinguished himself as a linguist and man of letters, notably by his courses on Horace. In February 1612 these courses earned him the chair of Latin at Leiden. In the following year he was made *ordinarius*, full professor, reading his favorite authors (Juvenal, Seneca, Suetonius, and Tacitus), indeed with great acclaim, as his former pupil Vorstius attests from his own experience. Cunaeus' predilection for Horace's and Juvenal's satire and for the great moralist and political historians of the Silver Latinity is amply reflected in his *Hebrew Republic*. The success of these courses in turn would earn Cunaeus the chair of politics at Leiden in 1614.[47]

Now there would have been nothing special about this, if not for the appearance in 1610 of Cunaeus' first publication, a critical commentary on Nonnus' *Dionysiaca*,[48] in which Justus Scaliger and Daniel Heinsius were also involved. Perhaps this publication should have warned Leiden curators, for in the subtitle of the work the promising young scholar, showing himself the true pupil of Scaliger as far as arrogance was concerned, confidently declared that he had made short shrift of Nonnus' *errores et inscitiam*. This fairly critical approach and his reputation as angry young man were eminently reaffirmed by his laconic publication, two years later, in 1612, of a so-called Menippean satire, entitled *Sardi Venales* (Fools for Sale), a rather venomous attack on the Leiden world of learning.[49] In a way, the satire represented an established Leiden tradition. Cunaeus' *Sardi* emphatically called to mind Justus Lipsius' *Somnium* of 1581, in which the then Leiden professor had reintroduced this classical genre first developed by Seneca.[50] Even so, Cunaeus' move was a lightning bolt indeed, given the tense situation at Leiden University at the time.

By 1612, the vehement pen war that had first been kindled by Leiden theologians over such doctrinal issues as the Lord's grace and predestination was raging among scholars and ministers throughout the country. The States of Holland had added fuel to the fire by the somewhat rash appointment of

Conrad Vorstius from Steinfurt to succeed Jacobus Arminius, who had died in 1609. Vorstius' orthodoxy was no less suspect to the Gomarists than his predecessor's. Accused of Socinianism and many other heresies, he was soon banned from teaching at Leiden and found his works barred from Britain at the explicit orders of King James I. It was his appointment which first made the clergy question publicly the very authority of the States to deal with church matters or university appointments. This controversy, among others, prompted Hugo Grotius' *Ordinum pietas* of 1613, in which he defended the States' policy.[51]

In the midst of all this, Cunaeus undauntedly published his *Sardi*, in which he subtly pointed out that most clergymen and self-made theologians did not understand the first thing about the abstruse issues they were dealing with (a view that was wholeheartedly shared by Grotius),[52] and that the riots now confronting the States were the predictable outcome of their policy of recruiting clergymen from the lower classes. Clearly, this was a distinct thrust against the Collegium Theologiae, the very pride of the university.

To fully appreciate this point, one should realize that from its inception Leiden University was intended, first and foremost, to produce ministers. However, in practice, the low income of the clergy repelled the scions of the well-to-do. In 1591, therefore, to compensate for the shortage of ministers, the States opened a college for bursars,[53] followed in 1606 by a similar college for Wallonian bursars.[54] Cunaeus' pun, therefore, had very deliberate social connotations. On top of this, the *Sardi* equally made a laughingstock of acclaimed university dons such as Dominic Baudius and Daniel Heinsius.[55] The satire was actually coedited with a tract attributed to the Roman emperor Julian the Apostate, which in very similar terms neatly dealt with most of his imperial predecessors. Cunaeus, in short, transplanted a well-established political genre to the academic sphere.

In all fairness to Dutch society of the time it should be said that, in the long run, the satire was a resounding success, in spite of its plainly devastating tenor. It was endlessly reprinted and was translated into Dutch, French, and German.[56] However, initially and especially in Leiden, the publication, which took place around Christmas 1612,[57] roused fierce emotions and prompted severe student riots. In the new year, Cunaeus was twice hooted off by his own students, and university courses were adjourned for a full week. Surprisingly enough, however, Cunaeus was backed by university curators from first to last. The student ringleaders, bursars of the Collegium Theologiae, were suspended, and by mid-January the university senate decided on an official reprimand of students—apparently to no avail, for in the weeks following it required the interference of public authorities to restore order. The matter was finally settled toward the end of January, after the Rector Magnificus himself had made a public address to the students.[58]

The following November, with both Baudius and Heinsius acting as senate members, Cunaeus was elected *ordinarius*, only to succeed Heinsius in the professorship of political science a few months later, in February 1614.[59] In the following October, he was invited to give the prestigious funeral oration for the celebrated Bonaventura Vulcanius.[60] Bygones were bygones, it would have seemed. However, among the victims of the *Sardi* was Daniel Heinsius, a scholar every inch as pompous and jealous as he was brilliant. And although Heinsius himself at one stage called Cunaeus *flos et decus Academiae*,[61] the matter would not rest here.

Years of Controversy

By now Cunaeus' leanings had definitely turned towards the law, the discipline that, according to his intimate Vorstius, probably suited him the best.[62] In 1615, under the auspices of the celebrated Cornelis Swanenburch, he became *doctor utriusque juris*.[63] Subsequently, he obtained dispensation from the Curators for a sabbatical year, to acquaint himself with law practice and the art of pleading at the Hof van Holland in The Hague. Here he was lodged with his fellow countryman Apollonius Schotte, a member of the Supreme Court in The Hague. Schotte was reputedly a man of letters and a personal friend of Hugo Grotius.[64] Cunaeus and Schotte became close, as can be learned from a reference in *The Hebrew Republic*.

Upon his return to Leiden in 1616, Cunaeus was appointed professor of law[65]—still along with politics—and was committed to teach the Digests. In this capacity he would serve his *alma mater* with zest and the greatest success for more than twenty years, up to his death in 1638, showing himself a steadfast representative of the philological and humanistic approach to the law.[66] The repeated references to the Digests in our tract amply reflect this expertise. In 1630 he succeeded his former professor, Swanenburch, and turned to teaching the *Codex*. On 28 May 1616 Cunaeus married Maria van Zeyst, daughter of the Leiden pensionary Niclaes van Zeyst and the granddaughter of a president of the Supreme Court and university curator, Johannes van Banchem.[67] She bore him thirteen children. The eldest of their seven sons, Johannes, was to make his career in the East Indies.[68]

In 1617 Cunaeus' *De Republica Hebraeorum Libri III* appeared. We will discuss the genesis of this treatise in fuller detail below. Suffice it to say here that this publication once more garnered severe criticism (as Cunaeus had anticipated),[69] perhaps somewhat less innocent this time. Within a year of the publication politics in The Hague exploded. Predictably enough, Leiden University was among the first institutes in the Republic to be purged of Arminian and not-strictly-orthodox elements. Even the great Gerard Vossius did not get away unharmed,[70] and neither did Cunaeus. His Remonstrant leanings must have been known by then. Apart from this, through his works he had clearly thrown in his lot with the old regime. His *Dionysiaca* commentary of 1610 had been dedicated to the *Landsadvocaat* himself and to the latter's son-in-law. While the first was beheaded in 1619, the other was expelled. Again, Cunaeus' *Sardi* of 1612 were dedicated to Apollonius Schotte and Rombout Hogerbeets, the latter being the Leiden pensionary who—along with Hugo Grotius—was sentenced in 1619 to life imprisonment in the Dutch Alcatraz, Loevestein Castle. The edition of Julian the Apostate's *Caesares* had been dedicated to his prospective father-in-law, Niclaes van Zeyst, another Leiden pensionary of the old regime, who died in 1617.[71]

Now, clearly, these were the days to settle old scores. The *Sardi* of 1612 had rubbed quite a few academics and clergymen the wrong way, among them the self-acclaimed oracle of the university, Daniel Heinsius. Heinsius and Grotius had been Scaliger's favorites (*ocelli*) and for years had seemed inseparable.[72] However, with time, and notably on account of the Remonstrant Troubles, they had become estranged. After Grotius' downfall, he and Heinsius would serve as principal secretary to the Dordt Synod. Cunaeus and Heinsius had never been on the best of terms. At one point, Cunaeus had severely criticized Heinsius' reference, in an official address, to the Doge of Venice as a functionary entitled to "natural claims" on the Adriatic Gulf, a statement that was indeed curiously at odds with official States policy. At Leiden it was widely felt that Heinsius was the evil genius behind the recriminations now being leveled against Cunaeus.

To start with, Cunaeus was summoned by Leiden clergymen to "clarify" some references in his *Sardi* and *The Hebrew Republic*. In the subsequent interview he felt he had comfortably defended his orthodoxy. However, the South Holland Synod, during its 1619 meeting in Leiden, felt far from satisfied and insisted on a written recantation on Cunaeus' part of "some questionable tenets" he had advanced. Cunaeus replied tactfully by requesting a written inventory of the problematic issues.[73] In 1620, at the Dordt National Synod, his written rejoinders were formally discussed and accepted in general terms. However, some members, allegedly instigated by Heinsius, remained insistent on a public recantation and expression of regrets, which Cunaeus then promised, without, however, intending to fulfill the promise. The issue would continue to haunt him, but he continued to resist all pressure—with impunity.[74] Apparently, university authorities realized that, with quite a few Remonstrant dons purged already, they could hardly do without Cunaeus' genius. Also, the latter's intimacy with the local magistracy, amply represented among curators, must have had a say in this.

The University Don

In November 1620, Cunaeus was invited to inaugurate the newly created Collegium Oratorium with a public address.[75] By that time, his Latin speeches had become famous. In the course of years, he was to deliver the funeral addresses of such famous scholars as Vulcanius (1614) and Aelius Vorstius (1624)[76] and the legal luminaries Bronckhorst (1627), Swanenburch (1630), and Burgersdijk (1636).[77] Vorstius characterizes his style as the pure, succinct, and perfectly clear Latin of the Roman Golden Age.[78] It was perhaps partly on account of his oratorical talents that Cunaeus was repeatedly appointed Rector Magnificus of the university.[79]

His collected speeches were published posthumously by his eldest son, Johannes Cunaeus, and were repeatedly reprinted in Germany.[80] These speeches attest to his ongoing research and personal interests. Small wonder, therefore, if they abound with echoes of his Hebrew and Oriental studies. The opening address of the volume, on the occasion of his assuming the university rectorship in 1624, celebrated the founding day of the university (*In Natalem Academiae*) and included scores of references to the Hebrew lustrum;[81] these make for interesting reading next to his treatment of the matter in our treatise. The second speech, on the necessity and excellence of literature (*De Necessitate et praestantia litterarum*), which was pronounced upon his relinquishing his rectorship a year later, occasioned a long excursus on the preeminence of Hebrew learning and political institutions, which indeed reads as a summary of his thesis from 1617.[82] The fourth address was his farewell speech from 1638, when he laid down the rectorship for what would prove to be the last time. It discussed that preoccupation of the period, to wit, the critical years in the lives of men and states.[83] It resumed the theme of the first speech, then to focus entirely on the Hebrew Jubilee, which again offers an interesting parallel to *The Hebrew Republic*.[84]

Cunaeus did not publish much in later years. His numerous commitments in Leiden, which occasioned regular complaints to his dear friend Adolph Vorstius,[85] must have taken up most of his time. He often mused about editing commentaries on lawsuits, and definitely intended to produce an annotated edition of his beloved Flavius Josephus, the author who was central to his research throughout. That edition was awaited keenly, but in vain, by colleagues at home and abroad.[86] Meanwhile, his renown as a legal scholar and linguist was impressive. His network covered the whole republic of letters, as did his correspondence.[87] Cunaeus, the one-time professor of poetry, clearly had poetical leanings as well. Among the Leiden manuscripts appears a tragedy called *Dido*.[88]

In August 1631, when Gerard Vossius exchanged Leiden for Amsterdam,[89] university curators made sure to commit Cunaeus more firmly by appointing him to the position of university counsel. They were well advised to do so. In September 1625, Cunaeus had been approached by Franeker University for a professorship. In January 1634, when Utrecht University in turn aspired to recruit him and Cunaeus flirted with the invitation, Utrecht curators were strongly advised by their Leiden colleagues not to pursue their efforts and were given to understand that insistence on their part might well be countered by repercussions from The Hague.

To avail themselves of his services further, Cunaeus at this stage was also recruited by the States of Holland to become their legal counsel in matters of commerce and maritime affairs. In this capacity Cunaeus, of all people, was appointed by the States early in 1636 to refute John Selden's *Mare Clausum*, the British reply to Hugo Grotius' celebrated *Mare Liberum* of 1609. On Cunaeus' authority and *Advis*, it was decided against taking further action.[90] In this curious way, the foremost English lawyer and Hebraist of the day was to be linked to his Dutch counterpart of the period. For there can be little doubt that whatever the domain—the law, Hebrew, or Oriental studies (Chaldean, Aramaic, Syriac, and Rabbinics)—Cunaeus at that stage did not have his equal in Holland.

In 1638 the States of Zeeland sounded him out on his willingness to become their historiographer.[91] It was not to be. In early autumn, Cunaeus left for Zeeland to discuss the matter. Along the way he, his wife, and their youngest son contracted high fevers. They were treated well by their physician, but their fevers remitted only slightly. Instead of awaiting full recovery, Cunaeus—typically and against the doctor's advice—decided to return to Holland. Friends who came to visit him upon his return to Leiden in early November were alarmed by his pallor and frail appearance. Still, throwing their warnings to the wind, Cunaeus insisted on resuming his duties. Soon enough, according to Vorstius' vivid description, the fever rekindled.[92]

Two weeks later, Cunaeus suffered from intermittent bouts of delirium. At that juncture, for all the efforts of his medical colleagues, Adolph Vorstius first of all, his health was shattered beyond recall. In the early days of December 1638, Petrus Cunaeus, "the Scaevola, Papinianus, Ulpianus, or whichever reputed ancient lawyer you may call him"[93] of his age, the man whose stoic philosophy is reflected in his lifelong motto *Fata viam invenient*, passed away, at fifty-three years of age, comforted by his minister Abraham Heydanus and with his dear friends Polyander, Walaeus, and Thysius at his bedside. It was reported that, following his demise, rains and storms battered Holland for days on end.[94] During the final stages of his illness, while acquiescing in the inevitable, he showed more concern for his dear wife's illness. In this he was justified. Grief and fevers would bring her down too. She survived him by only two months. Their tombstone is to be found in the Pieterskerk in Leiden.

Reputedly, most of Cunaeus' unfinished[95] works were burned at his explicit orders. In 1749, all remaining manuscripts were bequeathed by his descendants to the Leiden University Library.[96] The impressive volume of obituaries and funerary poetry issued by Leiden University bespeaks his high repute, which is only confirmed by Dutch historiography of later periods.[97] As Hugo Grotius puts it in the funeral poem which opens the volume: "only when Leiden curators go in search of a successor will they appreciate the enormity of their loss."[98]

The physician Vorstius diagnosed Cunaeus' character, in line with the medical idiom of his day, in terms of the four temperaments.[99] From that perspective, Petrus Cunaeus was, most definitely, a hotheaded, passionate man, readily enraged and agitated, but as readily inclined to beg pardon afterwards. He was also melancholic, a combination, as Vorstius maintains with reference to Aristotle, only too often found in men of keen intellect and a serious, judicious nature. Meanwhile, Cunaeus was a *homo pro se*, as it was called at the time, a thoroughly independent mind. As he himself avows in his treatise: "I will not blindly follow someone else's dictates, nor does it suit my character to swear to the truth of another man's statement. The freedom to express oneself is priceless; anyone who considers it to be the very essence of good judgment cannot help but agree with me."[100]

Cunaeus positively hated all frivolity and vanity, luxury and pleasure, as we already had occasion to point out above. Once, in the course of a law faculty meeting discussing the truancy of law students, a querulous Cunaeus whined about the youngsters' exclusive preoccupations with fencing, dancing, and fives ball.[101] He was frugal, economical with food, money, and time alike, a man of few words, who cherished friendship dearly but had only too few friends, due to his ready criticism.[102] Johan Foreest, Simon de Beaumont, Gerard Vossius, and Caspar Barlaeus were dearest to him, as was Claude de Saumaise in later years. A very religious man, he advocated tranquility and peace in the public sphere throughout his life, notably with regard to theological doctrine. For that reason, and inasmuch as he had a perfect command of the French language, he frequented French rather than Dutch divine services. The mildness of Melanchthon had a great appeal to him.

THE 'REPUBLICA HEBRAEORUM'

Hebrew Studies in the United Provinces

By 1600, Hebrew studies had developed considerably from their origins in the days of Manetti and Pico in the 1450s. With the erosion of traditional Christian values in the deadlock of Reformation and Counter-Reformation, and with skepticism gaining ground everywhere, European intelligentsia seemed to drop all previous reserve towards Oriental traditions. Hebrew studies became ever more integrated into humanist research and curricula as respectable disciplines in their own right, in spite of wavering policies in Rome and regular outbursts of Hebrew book-burning. Bodin's keen interest in Mosaic law and the Old Testament is symptomatic of this climate, in which research in Aramaic, the Kabbalah, and the Talmud flourished along with that in Turkish, Arabic, and the Koran.

The greatest Hebraist of his age to many observers was Josephus Justus Scaliger, the celebrated scholar who in 1593 came to replace another *virtuoso*, Justus Lipsius, at Leiden University. Scaliger's biblical research had a predominantly philological outlook.[103] His astounding knowledge of Hebrew was spurred by his relentless search for more reliable texts of the Testaments. His prolonged and stimulating debates with Jews, in both Rome and Avignon, had made him drop prejudice to the point of becoming a veritable advocate of the intercultural debate and exchange of learning. Scaliger's recruitment to Leiden did not fail to have its impact on research in Holland, as is readily attested by the work of his two favorite pupils, Daniel Heinsius and Hugo Grotius. The unbiased, strictly philological aspirations of Hugo Grotius' impressive *Annotationes* on both Testaments, the work of a lifetime, stand out as a tribute to his celebrated teacher.

The name of Hugo Grotius has surfaced repeatedly in our discussion, and for very good reasons. Between 1600 and 1620 he was deeply involved, and increasingly dominant, in most intellectual pursuits in the Netherlands. *Facile princeps* in many domains, Grotius was recommended at a fairly early age to political circles in The Hague by Scaliger himself, who keenly perceived that, given the precarious position of the Dutch, the fairly unique talents of the youngster should be made to bear on politics as well as on learning. Still, thanks to Scaliger, Grotius was involved in Hebrew studies from early on, and although modern commentators have voiced their reservations regarding his in-depth knowledge of the language, his central role as a reference point can never be doubted. More relevant to the present context, the impact of his person and work on Cunaeus' Hebrew studies was momentous, as we will see presently.

Scaliger's influence on Grotius can easily be established from the youngster's early pursuits at Leiden, which cover the closing years of the sixteenth century. In 1601, having by then been called to the bar at The Hague, the eighteen-year-old Grotius published the first of three biblical tragedies, entitled *Adamus Exul*.[104] In an epilogue to this play he proudly intimates to his readers his many projects in progress;[105] of all the titles advertised there none would ever see the light of day, inasmuch as the author's meteoric legal and political career would soon reorient his priorities and interests. Still, reference is made to a dialogue called *Philarchaeus* in which, according to its author, Mosaic law was confirmed from numerous pagan testimonies, Egyptian, Phoenician, Orphic, and Pythagorean.[106] Now this kind of research is typical of Scaliger's approach. In two major treatises, *De Emendatione Temporum* (1583) and *Thesaurus Temporum* (1606), Scaliger dealt extensively with this lore, and the relics of Berosus, Manetho, Sanchuniathon, Abydenus, and so many other, partly mythical, authors, to the point where he unmasked Nannius' fraud.[107] The pinpointing of the primacy of Mosaic law was at the heart of this research. One may perhaps conclude, as Heering has indeed suggested,[108] that if Scaliger's treatise of 1583 had been the major inspiration and reference point for Grotius' research, his tutor's *Thesaurus* of 1606 may well have prompted Grotius to suppress his own *Philarchaeus*.[109]

Scaliger was by no means the only one to have impressed Hebrew studies on Grotius. During his student years, Grotius found lodgings with Franciscus Junius, whom he credits with having left on him an irenical imprint that lasted his entire life.[110] Now Junius was coeditor, along with Tremellius, of a much-used translation of the Bible, had authored a *Grammatica Linguae Hebreae* (1590) and, more than this, a treatise *De observatione politiae Moysis* (1593). For all this, Junius' authority was by no means uncontested in Leiden. If the ever-critical Scaliger did not exactly have high esteem for his learning, neither did Cunaeus, as he intimates in a very revealing letter to Apollonius Schotte from 1611.[111] Junius, Cunaeus argues here, should be read with due reservation. As for his edition of the Bible, rather than being a translation, the work amounts to a personal interpretation, and a rather long-winded one at that. By comparison, Pagninus' translation was much to be preferred. This edition Cunaeus thought excellent and reliable in all its simplicity. In a telling observation he advises his friend Schotte that if the latter would but use Pagninus' edition, there was no reason why he should wish any longer for an expert knowledge of Hebrew.

And then there was that other Hebrew scholar at Leiden, Franciscus Raphelengius, who is on record as having taught Grotius elementary Arabic in 1605.[112] Thomas Erpenius, yet another Leiden eminence, was also a major source of expert information[113] and would prove a tried and trusted friend to Grotius throughout his career.[114] After Erpenius' death, his role as reference point for Grotius' Hebrew studies was taken over by his Leiden successor Constantijn L'Empereur.[115] And, last but not least, Johannes Drusius, the Franeker celebrity,[116] had started out as a Leiden professor.[117]

Still, to return to Grotius' early pursuits, the most relevant testimony by far puts Grotius' studies in Hebrew and the Mosaic law on an altogether different footing than that of his predecessors. Shortly before he took his leave from Leiden University, towards the end of 1599, Grotius conceived a tract entitled *De Republica Emendanda* (On the Emendation of the Dutch Polity).[118] The juvenile work amounts to a critical review of the state of affairs in the United Provinces, with specific suggestions for improving on a situation that is typified as critically urgent.[119] The layout of the tract is that of a parallel of state models, and the reference point is precisely the Hebrew Republic, which is presented here as by far the most recommendable constitution; it is illustrated by a series of arguments which recalls the current literature of the period, e.g., Pagninus, Sigonio, Bertram, and Fricius.[120] The theme also brings to mind the 1593 work by Franciscus Junius on the law of Moses.[121]

As with so many works from Grotius' teens, *De Republica Emendanda* was never published. Petrus Cunaeus, for that reason, could not refer to it in his *De Republica Hebraeorum* of 1617. However, the tract is indicative of the climate in Holland from about 1600. Grotius was among the many political observers in the United Provinces to harbor distinct reservations with respect to the constitutional experiment of the Dutch Confederacy. In the ongoing debate, which started as early as the mid-1580s and would only grow more complex over the decades, the comparison of state models in the Dutch Republic had become a common device to make one's point; so had theoretical expositions on the best forms of government, as exemplified in the Netherlands by Paulus Buys' *De Republica* of 1613 or Paullus Merula's *Commentariolus de statu Confederatorum Belgii* of 1618.[122] Editions of texts by foreign authors also figured in this debate, as exemplified by Ioannes Meursius' critical edition of Porphyrogenetes' *De Administrando ingenio* (1611) and the successive editions of Althusius' *Politica*.[123]

Among the comparisons of state models one should distinguish between contemporary and historical parallels. Prominent in the former category was the Swiss Confederacy, as exemplified by Simler's *De Republycke van Switserlandt* (1613) or François Petit's comparison of the two confederacies from 1615.[124] Venice was another case in point, albeit on a different note.[125] Grotius himself, in some early works, included dedications to the Venetian Doge which leave little doubt as to parallel commercial aspirations and policies.[126]

Turning to the historical parallels, apart from the *Republica Emendanda*, in his late teens Grotius also authored a very ambitious comparison of the Greek, Roman, and Dutch commonwealths. The work dates from 1600–1602 and circulated among friends, but was in the end abandoned and never published in his lifetime. It was lost, save for the third book, which intimates that the previous books had dealt with much material on the Mosaic constitution and Pythagorean lore.[127] Grotius' interests in these matters as well as Franciscus Junius' work of 1593 and the reception of the 1608 reprint in Hanau of Sigonio's treatise *De Republica Hebraeorum* all warrant the conclusion that Petrus Cunaeus' work of 1617 did not come out of the blue, but actually reflected an ongoing debate within what was by then a highly politicized context. There are further compelling reasons to take this view, and to illustrate this we will now inspect Cunaeus' contacts over these years from closer quarters. Hugo Grotius may be our reference point throughout.

Contacts and Correspondence

Cunaeus' first personal contacts with Grotius date from about 1608–1609. At the time Grotius was the States' Advocate-Fiscal (Prosecutor-General) and the leading light of the Hague bar. Their correspondence over the following decade amply attests to their growing intimacy and the gradual evolution of their initially hierarchical relationship to one of equal footing in the academic domain.[128] Cunaeus' friendship with Grotius remained intact, it would seem, even during the latter's long years of exile. Grotius' eulogy, which opens the series of epicedia on Cunaeus in the 1639 obituary volume, is testimony to this. Grotius' brother Willem and his eldest son Pieter likewise contributed to this volume;[129] both were students at Leiden, then to become lawyers in The Hague, and must have met Cunaeus in one or both of these capacities.

Willem actually attests to the excellency of Cunaeus' law courses in a letter from June 1616.[130]

Apart from their shared interests, there was another good reason for Cunaeus' contacts with Grotius, and here our perspective widens. They both belonged to what we may term "The Zeeland Connection." If Grotius was admittedly born in Delft, he was married in 1608 to the daughter of a burgomaster of Veere, Maria van Reigersbergh, and his contacts in Zeeland were legion.[131] Apollonius Schotte, for one, constituted part of this circle, but Cunaeus and Grotius had other contacts in common. The most relevant one for our purposes is Johannes Boreel.[132] He is the scholar who is praised in the preface of Cunaeus' *Hebrew Republic* as the man who first provided him with the texts of Maimonides which may well have been Cunaeus' inspiration to embark on the project in the first place.[133] Certainly, along with the tracts by Pagninus, Sigonio, and Bertram—and, obviously, his beloved Flavius Josephus and, we may assume, Philo Judaeus[134]—Maimonides was a major source of Cunaeus' for his study of the ancient Hebrew Commonwealth.[135]

The reference to Boreel is by no means a matter of chance. Indeed, if Cunaeus refers to Boreel's traveling in the Middle East, this is precisely what had made the latter's renown in the Leiden world of learning. From the mid-1590s onwards, Johannes Boreel—along with the younger Dousa,[136] who died prematurely in 1602—served Leiden University Library as its foremost provider of rare books, prints, and manuscripts, notably from the East.[137] Now, the interesting thing is that Boreel's role with respect to Hugo Grotius was to be precisely the same as with Cunaeus.[138] During his extensive sojourns in the East in the late 1590s, Johannes Boreel had met Meletius Pegas,[139] the Patriarch of Alexandria. This dignitary was to lend his name to the irenical tract that Hugo Grotius produced in 1611 with a view to appeasing doctrinal quarrels in Leiden. Grotius' tract was presented as an "Open Letter" to Boreel, and was inspired by the Patriarch's uncommonly ecumenical ideas, views which Grotius had first become acquainted with through his conversations with Boreel upon the latter's return from the East. Grotius' tract *Meletius*, again not published during his lifetime and only rediscovered in 1983, constitutes an urgent plea to the Dutch to finally close ranks and focus on what united rather than what divided them.[140]

As we have seen, there were compelling reasons for such a plea. If the dispute over religious orthodoxy and the interaction of church and state dated back to 1605,[141] these frictions were merely symptomatic of a deeper, underlying problem, to wit, the essential lack of cohesion among the Seven Provinces. In fact, as Grotius had argued as early as 1599 in his *De Republica Emendanda*, the particularism of city magistrates and provincial authorities and the absence of a central administration had eroded unity to the point of preventing the provinces from ever being welded into a functional union. As early as 1595, Justus Lipsius, himself the victim of professional jealousy and the lack of religious toleration at Leiden,[142] had drawn much the same conclusions, witness a notorious *Sendbrief*.[143] And so had the Spanish and papal diplomats who advised Philip III to open peace negotiations or, as the case might be, to conclude a truce with the Dutch, so as to let internal strife ripen. Grotius, for that very reason, had been opposed to the 1609 truce, as can be concluded from a *Memorie* he conceived in 1607.[144]

Now, on the eve of the truce—much as, for that matter, forty years later, on the eve of the Peace of Westphalia—it was the Province of Zeeland that was the least inclined to curb its sovereignty in favor of the Union and a centralized administration. Actually, as Grotius complains to Vossius on his return from yet another official trip to Zeeland in 1609, nowhere was the internal strife so vehement as in his beloved Zeeland—and the outcome could easily be predicted.[145] It was therefore to address Zeeland magistrates most of all that his tract *Meletius* was composed, and this may be the reason that, before submitting it to the press, Grotius had the manuscript circulate among four tried and trusted friends from Zeeland exclusively. The names of these friends were Antonius Walaeus, Apollonius Schotte, Johannes Boreel—and Petrus Cunaeus.

Walaeus was a major authority to be reckoned with.[146] An influential minister at Middelburg of unsuspected orthodoxy, he had actually been Grotius' personal candidate to fill Arminius' chair upon the latter's demise in 1609. He highly praised the draft of *Meletius*, while pointing out some errors and passages liable to be misinterpreted (which then prompted a learned correspondence), but above all he warned Grotius to be prudent and not to underestimate the tense state of actual affairs.[147] The long and the short of it was that Grotius decided to postpone publication, much to the distress of Schotte and Cunaeus, who both liked the tract extremely well.[148] In early April 1612, Grotius requested his copy back from Schotte. As the manuscript had by then been forwarded to Cunaeus, Schotte contacted the latter that same day and, amidst complaints over the touchiness of theologians, intimated to his friend that Grotius would like the copy back, "not so much because he should distrust your fairness and prudence, but rather because he thinks that an attack from gadflies of this sort can best be warded off by keeping silent for some time and thus removing the cause of their irritation."[149] Cunaeus' reply to Schotte was, as ever, unequivocal: "I am surprised that our ossified theologians have found anything to fault in the *Meletius*. Indeed, Grotius treated the whole matter in such an erudite and elegant way that, even if they combined their efforts, all those illustrious high priests together could not produce anything remotely resembling it, I should think, however great their pains and care."[150]

Certainly, Grotius' *Meletius* stands out as the most unbiased plea for toleration that was to be produced that decade. The tract, incidentally, contains a fairly historic direct reference to the recent settlement of Jews in the Netherlands,[151] as well as scattered references to the Jewish religion, including one in which Judaism is identified as a "true, but less perfect" religion, indeed on the same footing with natural religion, a statement that promptly evoked criticism from Walaeus.[152] Meanwhile, in following Cunaeus' preoccupations over the years leading up to the publication of *The Hebrew Republic* in 1617, we are well advised to focus on his correspondence with Schotte, Grotius, and Walaeus.

In October 1610[153] Cunaeus, in a very elegant letter, invited Grotius to honor the opening session of his public lectures on Horace's *Satires* with his presence.[154] His next preserved letter to Grotius dates from early December 1613,[155] in acknowledgment of the receipt of a complimentary copy of Grotius' *Ordinum pietas*, his apology for the States' policy in matters of church and state. It is the vehemence of this very confrontational tract, based mostly on political miscalculation,[156] which made Grotius lose all credit with die-hard Gomarists and would lead to his downfall five years later. Even so, Cunaeus' reply is, once more, unequivocal in its unconditional support for Grotius.[157] By 1613, the tenor of the correspondence between the newly appointed professor and the politician had become quite openhearted and informal. It is against this backdrop that Cunaeus' next letter, which first introduces his treatise on the Hebrew Republic, is to be situated.

The letter is dated 29 May 1614, and a wonderful and illuminating letter it is.[158] It served, first of all, as an acknowledgment of the complimentary copy of Grotius' commentary on the Latin epic poet Lucanus. Cunaeus expresses his great pleasure with the edition, and indeed intimates that the plans he himself once cherished to prepare a critical edition of the Latin poet were now better shelved. The severe loss the world of letters had suffered in losing Grotius to high politics was made tolerable, he argues, only by the fact that otherwise the Republic itself would have been lost.[159] Still, wouldn't it be marvelous for the world of letters one day to see their own champion, Grotius, heading the state! It was very rare indeed for a nation to see clearly what was in her best interest. Grotius, Cunaeus felt, was in a privileged position, and his age was only to be congratulated.[160] As for Grotius' extreme kindness to himself, one day, Cunaeus felt confident, he would repay this debt. He then continues: "Some time ago I put together a few notes on the Republic of the Jews, which I will now carefully go over once more and perhaps publish, if this may seem opportune. In pursuing these studies, my knowledge of Hebrew has been of great help, as compared to Sigonio's ignorance in these matters."[161] (To Cunaeus, Sigonio apparently was the reference point.)

One wonders who or what may have spurred Cunaeus, some years prior to 1614, to embark upon the project. Was it Boreel? Was it his sojourn with Drusius in Franeker? Could it have been spurred by the 1608 reprint of Sigonio's *De Republica Hebraeorum*? And what made him abandon it, only to resume it some years later? A letter to Apollonius Schotte from February 1615 may be of help to us here.[162] In this letter Cunaeus confesses, in as many words, that the treatise was long finished but that he had recently concluded against publication, upon finding out that he had actually forgotten the most important element: a discussion of the Jewish legal system. This would be a remarkable omission indeed, he admits, in view of the fact that he was now spending all his time precisely on legal research.[163]

This tells us that, in the opening months of 1615, long after its actual completion in first draft, publication of *The Hebrew Republic* was reconsidered on the cusp of the reorientation of the author's career. Cunaeus passed his doctorate in law (*honoris causa*) on 19 June 1615. On 24 February previously, he intimates to Schotte that before publishing the tract he had first to compare the Roman and Jewish legal systems, which would obviously take some time. However, in the third book of *The Hebrew Republic* (the letter continues), he had dealt with the old Hebrew Church and, inasmuch as this constituted a self-contained argument, he now considered publishing that part separately, in advance.[164] He then concludes: "Grotius has promised me to hand that part to you for review purposes."

The letter is momentous for various reasons. Above all, it bespeaks the regular, one might almost call it institutional, contacts between Grotius, Schotte, and Cunaeus on these matters. More than this, it attests to Grotius' direct involvement with *The Hebrew Republic* in the very days that he was elaborating his *Remonstrantie nopende de Joden*. Not that this in itself can come as a surprise to us, given Cunaeus' documented role as reviewer of Grotius' manuscripts of *Meletius* and *Ordinum pietas*.[165] Still, it would be intriguing to know to what extent Grotius' interests as an advocate of the States' policy actually made themselves felt in Cunaeus' decision, the more so as Cunaeus had sent a copy of his draft to Sibrandus Lubbertus as well.[166] What indeed was the "opportune" moment Cunaeus was considering?

From Cunaeus' next letter to Grotius, which dates from 25 August 1615,[167] we can conclude that he was preoccupied with *The Hebrew Republic* all summer. It tells us that, initially, he had planned a trip to France that summer, and to that extent had pocketed letters of recommendation from Grotius to both the Dutch ambassador in Paris and Jacques-Auguste de Thou, the great French historian and a close friend of Grotius'. However, stopping over in Zeeland on his way to Paris, persistent rumors of social unrest in France[168] had deterred him from continuing his trip, which he felt he should let Grotius know. Meanwhile, while in Zeeland, he intimates, he had heard that Walaeus was about to publish his *Ampt der Kerckendienaren*.[169] This work was a solid refutation of the principle of the primacy of secular authorities in church matters as defended by the prominent Remonstrant minister and dear friend of Grotius', Johannes Uytenbogaert[170]—and implicitly a rebuttal to Grotius' own *Ordinum pietas*, although, as Cunaeus indicates, Grotius' name had been discreetly left out of the debate by the conscientious Walaeus.

Cunaeus, being the man he was, then volunteers his own opinion on these issues. As far as the Roman and Greek churches went, he intimates, his mind was readily made up. However, with respect to the Hebrew nation, his perplexity only grew the more he delved into the matter. In fact, in the first version of his *Hebrew Republic* he had dedicated a whole chapter to this issue, but he admits that, quite frankly, "after having remolded and rewritten the text twice, thrice over, I have finally decided to delete the chapter altogether, as I much prefer to remain neutral in the quarrels over this issue and steer a middle course."[171] This, once more, tells us that we must interpret *The Hebrew Republic* within the wider context of topical Dutch social struggle. Cunaeus' intimate, the Amsterdam humanist Caspar Barlaeus for one, concluded from the frontispiece of *The Hebrew Republic* that Cunaeus did indeed fall in with Grotius' so-called Erastian views as to the primacy of state and church—a conclusion which Cunaeus himself apparently deemed premature.[172]

Cunaeus next expounds on his findings regarding the Hebrew religion and ceremonies, and particularly with respect to the position of the Hebrew king as a secular and religious leader, the latter's unction, the role of the Levites, and David's position.[173] There is no denying, Cunaeus notes, that the Jewish nation held very particular and unique views on these issues; but this thorny and inconsequential discussion he would rather leave to the so-called experts, those wiseacre know-it-alls.[174] You, divine Grotius, he concludes, are one of the very few whom nature and reason have endowed with better insight, you *magnum labentis in pessima saeculi praesidium atque columen*. One may conclude that despite cherishing uncompromising views, Cunaeus too had by now become extremely careful and concerned about the state of affairs in the Republic. And one wonders why he insisted on publishing his

Hebrew Republic at all? The planned preliminary edition of Book III apparently never materialized.

Meanwhile, the close friendship that by now had grown between Grotius and Cunaeus is well documented by a most flattering letter from Grotius, dated 22 May 1616, which focused exclusively on personal matters and was occasioned by Cunaeus' wedding.[175]

The next (preserved) letter from Cunaeus to Grotius dates from September 1617, that is, a full two years later.[176] Cunaeus acknowledges receipt of a complimentary copy of Grotius' *De Satisfactione* which Gerard Vossius had handed over to him. Once more, he declares himself sincerely struck by the compelling logic of Grotius' arguments. "Now you have nailed them, these vipers," he writes vehemently. "They'd better come up with some very strong arguments now, or they're finished."[177]

For once, Grotius' reply has also been preserved.[178] It is a most flattering letter indeed, although what has occasioned the letter really becomes evident only in the end. "I must say, your review of my book," Grotius argues, "is not in line with your otherwise keen judgment, which I will therefore gladly attribute to our friendship. But since I prepare a reprint of my *Defensio*,[179] please advise me freely, as becomes friends, as to any possible shortcomings in the work." He then refers to the recent demise of Niclaes van Zeyst, Cunaeus' father-in-law, whom Grotius had admired tremendously for his independent judgment and wisdom.[180] He sings the praises of Cunaeus as a man of letters, volunteers his support with respect to his ongoing research, and attests to his highest esteem. He then expresses his concern about manuscripts of his, notably that of *De Imperio summarum potestatum circa sacra*, which were still in Van Zeyst's possession. His concern was well founded, inasmuch as *De Imperio*, still focusing on the issue of church authority, had finally to be withheld from publication, and was published only posthumously in 1647.[181]

Ten days later, on 8 October 1617, Cunaeus reassures his friend, whom he had just missed in The Hague, that he had identified the manuscript of *De Imperio* among his late father-in-law's belongings, and the delicate matter is resolved. As he recalls, Van Zeyst, on his part, had always put high hopes in Grotius, more than in anyone else, to take over from Oldenbarnevelt in due time. Cunaeus himself felt the same. He recalls their friendship, now of eight years' standing, and calls Grotius an *avis alba* in his sincere concern for the Republic.

In this tenor ends Cunaeus' last preserved personal testimony to the man who, one year later, was to be condemned to a life sentence. The *avis alba* was, by then, becoming not so much a rare as rather an isolated entity in Holland. Two years later, after his downfall, and incarcerated in his Loevestein cell, Grotius would start writing his *Bewijs van den Waren Godsdienst*, an apologetic Christian poem, from which nucleus would grow his celebrated *De Veritate Religionis* of 1627,[182] Book 5 of which is entirely dedicated to a discussion of Jewish religion.[183]

'The Hebrew Republic': Immediate and Ultimate Goals

We have referred above to the device of paralleling state models as a means of suggesting contemporary political reforms. Cunaeus' treatise of 1617 was not such a parallel *stricto sensu*. To all appearances, it was a historic description of a single republic, to wit, that of "the sacred people,"[184] and not by any measure an exhaustive one at that, as Cunaeus insists in his address to his readers.[185] He had left out a great deal which had been treated at full length by earlier writers such as Sigonio and Bertram and, availing himself of Maimonides and others, had focused on aspects related to the Hebrew government exclusively.[186] Nonetheless, in doing so, he had found occasion both to correct and to add to the work of predecessors.[187]

But actually, as Cunaeus himself insists in his preface to Book III, the treatise *did* come within the category of parallel state models, inasmuch as it was only the first step of a much more ambitious project. This project had grown out of his prolonged studies of politics, many years before, and his in-depth reading of—and lecturing on, as we recall—his favorite Roman authors, Suetonius and Tacitus.[188] That project was indeed aimed at comparing states; it was meant, in fact, to focus precisely on those characteristics held in common by all states and republics. A first glimpse of what Cunaeus had in mind may actually be found in his 1638 farewell speech in Leiden on *De annis climactericis et eorum vi in rerumpublicarum et civitatum conversione*.[189] However, as he assures his readers in his preface to Book III, preoccupied as he was these years with his legal and political studies,[190] he was no longer sure whether he might ever be able to accomplish these previously set, loftier goals. In publishing this preliminary tract, he was in fact indulging friends and colleagues.[191]

Meanwhile, his choice of the Hebrew Republic had not entirely been a matter of chance. First of all, it had brought him back, even if only in his spare hours, to his first love, to wit, the study of Hebrew and research of biblical and rabbinic texts, which his current public duties prevented him from pursuing in daytime.[192]

But there was a far more pressing reason to focus on the Hebrew state rather than on any other: there was no state like it. The Hebrew Republic was entirely unique, inasmuch as Moses was unique as compared to other legislators.[193] The latter ones may have instilled virtue and courage in their citizens, but they did not teach them religious faith in the way that the decalogue of Moses did. If anything, it was Moses' religious teachings that held the Hebrew Republic together. It was this comparison of Moses' legislation and the institutions and laws of other nations that would be at the heart of his next major project.[194]

And here we also reach the core of *The Hebrew Republic*, as can easily be distilled from its preface to Book I, dedicated to the States of Holland. The Dedication to the States is in itself symptomatic of Cunaeus' intentions to serve public purposes. The Republic of Moses, he impresses on the States, was not just the holiest, but also the most effective one, and therefore the best to emulate. The Twelve Hebrew Tribes had been extremely successful by virtue of one element exclusively: their unity and cooperation. While indeed, judging by their prosperity, each tribe could virtually pose as a nation in its own right, they all shared the same laws and judges, magistrates and senators, measures and currency, and together they defended the people's liberty.

Then fate struck—the Hebrews experienced what had happened to so many nations: civil strife. There was no other recipe which so effectively brought down nations. In fact, the Romans had made it a principal instrument of their foreign policy—and conquered the world. Once, the Achaean League, just like the Dutch League right now, seemed invincible, based as it was on inner strength, unity, and inviolable laws.[195] Then the Romans, "the plague of the world" as they were once called,[196] interfered.

The technique used by Jeroboam to divide the Twelve Tribes had been very similar: to corrupt true religion and replace it with empty superstition. What had been a battle about freedom and power came to be one about sacred rituals and places of worship. And here Cunaeus has driven his real argument home. No theme could have better summarized the acute problem of the Dutch Republic. From here, not surprisingly, the perspective of the preface shifts from Hebrew history to Dutch topicality. You, State Members, he insists, are aware, better than anyone else, that harmony creates success as surely as disharmony causes ruin. Right now, after a long uphill battle, and thanks to your unity, you have reached the pinnacle of power. I feel confident that this unity will be preserved, and success will be durable. And yet there is reason to draw lessons from the experience of others. Factions and sects have recently multiplied in our Republic, and the bones of contention seem to be rather obscure and fairly pointless issues of religious doctrine, which, most of the time, the rivaling factions don't even understand themselves. The mobs, as usual, are left to follow their whims and passions. From here,

Cunaeus' tenor becomes positively imploring. It is in your interest to apply a timely remedy, he argues. Therefore, study, over and again, the fate of this holiest and best of all republics.

Cunaeus' *Hebrew Republic* was not the major treatise the author had had in mind for so long and which would indeed never materialize, being in a sense superseded by political reality within less than a year. There may be more than just literary convention in his statement that so many people were urging him to publish his *Hebrew Republic*. By now, we can well identify the names he had in mind. *De Republica Hebraeorum* had exactly the same goals in mind as the ones Grotius had aimed at two decades before with his *De Republica Emendanda*. That tract, which tackled the problem directly in a very explicit comparison of the Dutch and Hebrew constitutions, never reached the public domain. Cunaeus' treatise, written at a juncture when tension in Holland had reached its peak and crisis seemed almost inevitable, perforce needed to be more circumspect. The counterpart of Grotius' tract, it urgently held up a mirror, and left conclusions to be drawn by the public authorities to which it was dedicated, the States members it was addressed to. It is tempting to identify "the Dutch Jeroboam," to draw comparisons between the division of the Hebrew Tribes and the Southern and Northern Provinces, and so on. All this has to wait until the full picture of the role of the Hebrew people as a mirror to that of Holland will emerge, one day, from more in-depth research into this fascinating period of two decades (1600–1620), in which Hebrew and Jewish studies became a matter of scholarly, social, and political urgency in the Netherlands.[197]

One may conclude that Cunaeus' *Hebrew Republic* was as bold an enterprise as his Menippean satire had ever been. It was the courageous attempt by a professor of political science to carry what he saw as his personal responsibility into the public domain, and to put all his learning and authority as a Hebrew scholar at the service of his nation's future. Aspirations of this kind suited all too well the university don, who in 1619 intimated, in a letter to his dear friend and mentor Apollonius Schotte, that he was actually considering a move towards the political arena, exchanging Leiden for The Hague.[198] In this, no doubt, his keen social ambitions also played their part. Cunaeus wished to abandon the shadow existence of the academic world and positively longed for the limelight of a public career. Somehow, that ambition never materialized.

Among the numerous literary topics applied in his prefaces by this accomplished expert on rhetoric, there is one element that may perhaps carry more weight than may be apparent at first. Cunaeus was indeed anticipating severe criticism. He realized that theologians would excoriate him for having trespassed into what they considered to be their exclusive domain.[199] To these misers and gnomes who, as he knew quite well, would never accept anything from him, if only out of personal dislike, he had some recommendations to make.[200] But more than this, he was inspired by the motto that is encapsulated in the anecdote of Apollonius of Rhodes found in Longinus.[201] To allow oneself to be constrained by prescribed boundaries will only render mediocre, sterile, and, often enough, pathetic results. This might be a way to avoid criticism, but it could never earn the praise that noble failures did. "There is a kind of grandeur in failing at a great attempt," he concludes. Cunaeus' attempt to stem the political tide, bound to fail as it was, falls into this category. What remains is a fascinating exposure, by a gifted scholar and keen observer, of a virtually unknown culture the Dutch were just about to discover—not this time by dispatching their fleets across the oceans, but by welcoming it into their own centers of learning and its representatives into their own society.

PRESENTATION AND CONTENT

Structure

A final word should address itself to the structure of Cunaeus' work, his overall views, and the merits of his research. Cunaeus' first two books evaluate the Hebrew Republic. In the opening chapters of Book I, its political institutions and matters of legislation are discussed in rather loose succession. Many pages are devoted to the agrarian laws, the "seventh year," and the Jubilee before focus shifts towards city administration, the essence of sovereign authority, and the loss of sovereignty after Jeroboam. There follows the evaluation of the dictatorship, the Judges, the Sanhedrin, and the Assembly of the People, and subsequently, of local councils and courts, notably in Jerusalem. The book is concluded with a discussion of the Hebrew kingship, its nature and changes over time, the rule of the high priests, the reinstatement of the kingdom, the coming of the Messiah, and the awaiting of the restoration.

The second book opens with an elaborate discussion of the role of the high priest, his clothing, his marriage restrictions, his residence, and his entrance into the Holy of Holies. Then follows the discussion of other priestly orders and initiation rites, the historical role of the Levites, the Temple at Jerusalem up to its destruction, and the temple of the Samaritans. Next, Jewish heretics and sects are discussed, followed by the evaluation of the laws of war and peace, Jewish prowess in war, aspects of military service, and the effects of the Sabbath on warfare.

The third book directs itself to the Church: it discusses its origins, growth, and membership, offers a historical survey from Abraham up to Solomon with a substantial excursus on the role and status of Melchizedek, and concludes with matters of circumcision, the religion of the Jews, their alleged worshiping of the clouds, the prophets, the Kabbalah, and finally the Messiah.

Now, the above description catalogues Cunaeus' subject matter in the most general terms. But the real issues to Cunaeus, and the ones that really bring his treatise to life, are found in a series of prolonged debates, at a variety of levels, on the matters which were close to his heart either as a scholar or from a personal or social point of view. Within the context of this introduction we can hardly do more than highlight a few characteristic elements that reflect some of Cunaeus' ideas.

Method

The treatise sets out to analyze and evaluate two issues: the Hebrew Republic and political institutions, and its Church and religious institutions. In his opening chapters Cunaeus makes it very clear that he considers the Hebrew Commonwealth to have been a theocracy.[202] At the opening of the third book, when about to discuss the Church, he makes the sensible remark that, whereas in his analysis it might be better to strictly separate the two, state and church, he felt that in practice it was extremely difficult to handle the subject matter that way. At that stage, this observation strikes the reader as an understatement. From the first, Cunaeus' treatment of the issues at hand is a rather loose one. In that respect, his tract in no way recalls either Sigonio's rigid, crystal-clear structuring, or even that of Grotius in his analysis of similar issues. There is no fault here. In the opening lines of his treatise Cunaeus states quite frankly that such rigid method was never his intention. "In this book, I do not intend to be overly selective or do a painstaking survey. I would rather gather my ideas from here and there as I encounter them, and follow up one thing after another in the order in which these occur to me."[203] Nor did he ever intend to be comprehensive: "This is all I will say on the subject; for though I had determined to give a brief taste of many issues, in my enthusiasm I have said practically everything there is to say" (p. 93).

One must admit, he is true to his word throughout. What he presents are in fact *capita selecta*. He hovers over the surface of the pond, diving into the water whenever he espies a catch; that is, the moment he feels anything amiss in the way Jewish authors, Christian *patres*, or contemporary scholarship have dealt with the issues. Cunaeus never offers the full picture, but focuses exclusively on vexing passages: "...so I won't put any effort into discussing these issues. We will be much better served if I pay particular attention to the things others have ignored or, if they did record them, were careless about. This is what I have tried to do throughout my work" (pp. 99-100).

Neither does he bother about loose ends: "I will leave the rest... to those who may someday follow after me to pick up the remains of this harvest. For I have wanted nothing more than to pique the interest of others; and I think by now I have managed to make it clear to everyone just how many things still remain to be said about Jewish matters in the wake of the studies done by some of our most learned men" (p. 114).

His is never a descriptive approach, but at core an argumentative one. In fact, he would never have the stomach, nor the patience, to work otherwise. To that extent at least, Vorstius' characterization of the author is most certainly to the point: Cunaeus would simply be bored by having to spell out the obvious or to be exhaustive for the sake of method.[204]

There is no doubt that Cunaeus couldn't work otherwise and actually is at his best in the way he proceeds in this treatise. For one thing, it is a very intelligent approach, which bespeaks his intimate knowledge and expertise. It takes some command of this terse subject matter to deal with it in such an offhand way. By the same token, the average reader, who doesn't have his Maimonides, Flavius Josephus, Eusebius, Jerome, or Sigonio at his fingertips, will often find himself taken unawares and wrong-footed. One wonders how the average Leiden student put up with Cunaeus' courses! Cunaeus' approach simply presupposes a considerable amount of prior intimacy with matters at hand.

And then, there is this other thing, what we may perhaps best call Cunaeus' mode of "associative thinking." He is literally true to his opening lines. In the midst of any given discussion, the mere reference to a source, name, or type of error may invite a digression which may easily cover pages or even cross the sacrosanct boundary line of chapters. Consequently, every now and then, the inattentive reader will find himself at a loss, trapped by yet another involuntary detour and unable to decide *if*, and if so, *where* precisely he lost track. Cunaeus himself was well aware of this discomfort to the reader, and on various occasions actually offers apologies to that extent: "But I have wandered farther from my subject than I should; my discussion will grow enormous unless I place stricter limits on myself from now on," he exclaims well towards the end (p. 193).[205] Still, if he is all too prone to undertake excursions and lose himself in detail, this never strikes one as a vain display of learning, and not for a moment does Cunaeus really lose control.

How, then, should we read Cunaeus' work? Perhaps the best way to approach *The Hebrew Republic* is to consider oneself as part of a privileged audience invited to attend a lively debate between Cunaeus on the one hand and (intermittently) Maimonides, Josephus, Eusebius, Jerome, Sigonio, Scaliger, and Casaubon on the other. Cunaeus' treatise is, if anything else, an ongoing dialogue with predecessors. Certainly, the meeting is far from boring! The way Cunaeus tackles his adversaries head-on, the blunt way he calls them names is, for one thing, refreshing. He definitely puts his heart into the matter, and there are not just the recurrent references to Horace's *Satires*, Martial, Juvenal, Petronius, and Lucian to evoke the realm of satire.[206] Still, in spite of occasional outbursts of rudeness, Cunaeus seems fair in his treatment of colleagues. As he states in the preface to Book III, he is only too willing to accept the same criticism from others. It is merely his style, with no offense meant. Indeed, he easily recants, but then again he can't stop wondering at the imbecility, stupidity, or altogether asinine conclusions of normally perfectly sensible scholars he otherwise holds in high respect. He speaks with warmth of his former teachers Casaubon and Drusius, even while questioning their views.

One must not let oneself be bemused by these recurrent invectives. Cunaeus' goal is precisely to confront. As mentioned above, he does not discuss anything exhaustively or even systematically; he restricts himself exclusively to outstanding problems of interpretation, without letting himself be bothered by the obvious, the indisputable, or the issues in agreement. Consequently, he only refers to other scholars within the context of a polemic. He does not make explicit the many instances in which he is in perfect agreement with colleagues. Sigonio must be a case in point here. This scholar is attacked quite severely by Cunaeus on a number of issues. In his correspondence he points out that he actually questions the Italian's knowledge of Hebrew. Still, it would be premature to draw any hasty conclusions here. It would be interesting to verify on which issues the two are in harmony and to what extent Cunaeus actually relied on Sigonio's research. For one thing, Sigonio, in his epochal *De Republica Hebraeorum* of 1582, covered far more ground and worked far more systematically. In his seven books, he fairly comprehensively dealt with the form of the republic, sacred places, sacred days, sacred rites, sacred persons, councils and courts, and the magistracy.[207]

Sources and Authorities

For Cunaeus, by far the highest human authority is Moses himself, whose praises are extolled throughout the treatise (notably pp. 12–13, 15, and 133). His divine legislation and theocratical constitution are of a different nature altogether from any other human effort; they are permanent, stable, independent of so-called human ingenuity, and they are not based on severity and fear (pp. 11–13, 144, 155–156).

For the proper interpretation of Moses' laws Cunaeus accepts just one Jewish source, which is Moses Maimonides, considered by him to be not only "the most distinguished of witnesses," but actually "the first and only member of his nation who correctly understood what it is not to say anything foolish" (p. 15). Numerous indeed are the deprecating references to other rabbis: "I myself would urge this teacher, whoever he was, to go cry among the seats of the students" (p. 145).

All this is not to say that Cunaeus follows Maimonides in any slavish way: "for I am not a schoolboy spitting back his lessons." Cunaeus' veneration has its limits: "Since I respect Maimonides' wonderful qualities, I am hesitant to admonish him for even the slightest of his mistakes. In this case, however, there is no question that this most intelligent of men has left reason behind, and instead favors the opinions of his fellow Jews" (p. 35). Cunaeus' debate with his guide over issues of the Jubilee (pp. 25–28) or the scepter of Judah (p. 38, notice the most charming reference to his studying at the home of his friend Apollonius Schotte in The Hague) are fairly representative in this respect.

Another authority valued highly by Cunaeus is Flavius Josephus, "an unusually careful author" (p. 44), though not beyond rebuke: "I would not have exposed this bit of asinine Jewish stupidity, but even Flavius Josephus—greatest of authors though he may have been—was taken in by the fictions of his countrymen, and indulged in others just as silly or even worse" (p. 51). "I think that he had stepped in something filthy on the day he wrote these things..." (p. 52, cf. p. 81). It will be remembered that Cunaeus for decades on end worked on a critical edition of Josephus that was forestalled by his untimely death (p. 156). Less significant is Philo Judaeus, introduced somewhat as an afterthought as an author "with insight and even inspiration" (p. 91).

If we now turn to the classical pagan authors, we cannot miss the recurrent references to and quotations from Aristotle's *Politics* (pp. 12–13, 21–22, 51, 53, 57), Cicero (pp. 125, 203), and Seneca (pp. 75, 219) in the sphere of philosophy and political science, or to "political" historians like Hecataeus (pp. 14, 21), Plutarch (pp. 17–18, 109, 147–150, 183), Suetonius (pp. 133, 199), and Tacitus (pp. 23, 31, 144–145, 185). Less obviously perhaps, Pliny the Elder is held in high esteem by Cunaeus as a "careful observer" (p. 136) and "the greatest of all writers of history" (p. 146). We have already referred to the Roman satirists, and we could add Aristophanes' plays (p. 198) and references to legal authors such as Ulpian to reflect Cunaeus' law professorship at Leiden (pp. 31, 40–41, 133). None of these authors, however, add in any distinctive way to the core argument of the treatise, with the possible exception of Tacitus. They all fade away next to the Church historian Eusebius. To the latter's interpretation of the prophecy of the scepter of Judah, and in particular "the snares in which this author has carelessly entangled himself" (p. 42), we owe one of the most charming and prolonged discussions of the treatise (pp. 39–46): "Now, with all due respect to Eusebius, all this, whatever it is, is completely pointless."

References to the New Testament are legion, but there can be no doubt that Cunaeus was most impressed by John's Gospel and by Paul's Letters, notably the Letter to the Hebrews, to which he refers in an impressive passage: "In fact, I don't know whether there is any book in the New Testament (aside from the Gospel of John) which contains a deeper and more profound theology" (p. 179).

Most intriguing is Cunaeus' dialogue with the Church Fathers. St. Jerome, in his opinion, is far more reliable than St. Augustine ("wise as he was"), since the latter did not always bring "his sharp and subtle faculties to bear." Witness the discussion over the location of the incense altar in Solomon's Temple: "Come now, unless our senses are being retarded by some stupor or phlegm..." (p. 89). Likewise, Origen, "certainly a great man," was prone to allow himself so much leeway as to overstep his bounds, which he was never afraid to do, as Cunaeus insists in his wonderful comparison of the three *patres* (pp. 209–210). To him, St. Jerome "was the most learned of all the ancient interpreters of sacred scripture because he had mastered Hebrew so thoroughly" (p. 164). Not that this served him much in his erroneous interpretation of Paul's Letter to the Corinthians: "Jerome perverts even this with an insipid interpretation" (p. 192). Truly, next to Gerard Vossius' or Hugo Grotius' reverence in commenting on the patristic legacy, Cunaeus' intrepid style comes as quite a shock.

And this leads us to Cunaeus' contemporaries. They warrant some of the most charming and fascinating moments in the treatise, notably when Cunaeus comments on the way they handle their sources. Most elaborate and intriguing of all perhaps are his extensive comments on the textual criticism of Isaac Casaubon ("the greatest scholar of our age... among the best of our generation"). According to Cunaeus, it is at Casaubon's "impetus that our age has made such amazing strides towards the mastery of every field of knowledge." In his *Baronian Exercises* Casaubon had reviewed the interpretation by Eusebius (here hailed as "one of the greatest authors ever") of the role of the scepter of Judah (pp. 35–46). Perhaps this debate is best suited to illuminate Cunaeus' method. He leaves aside all issues on which both authors agree, plunges straight into the heart of the matter, and emerges with a fresh new interpretation.

Similar, but less sweetened with personal sympathy, it would seem, is his critical review of Scaliger's scholarship, notably with respect to the interpretation by "the great man" of the "laying on of hands," which he reduces in the end to a barren philological exercise based on Scaliger's misreading of a rabbinic Hebrew word (see the explanation of the word *bilvad*, p. 49). In III.6 his offhand dismissal of Scaliger's interpretation of the "heaven-worshipers" (Matthew 5:33–35) almost has a tinge of irony: "Joseph Scaliger, a brilliant man before whose astonishing competence in every branch of knowledge I must understandably bow" (p. 197).

Far more sympathetic is his reference to his old teacher Johannes Drusius [III.5], with whom he disagrees over a minor point: "But he showed how fair-minded he was by giving me his permission to express my natural candor: I am seeking complete freedom to declare, without bias for or against, whatever claims are most correct" (p. 191).

To conclude this overview of authors, perhaps the most vexing issue is posed by Cunaeus' review of Carlo Sigonio. In II.1 one reads: "The learned Sigonio labors under the delusion that Alcimus was from the line of Levi" (p. 79). In II.4, when discussing the entrance of the high priest into the Holy of Holies, Cunaeus tackles both St. Augustine and Sigonio: "I cannot imagine a more pointless line of argument than this interpretation" (p. 87). In II.5: "Though Sigonio also saw this passage, as in the previous case he did not realize that it contradicted his theory... Sigonio will never escape; he is clearly stuck tight" (p. 91). However, in II.11 we read the following: "But both Cornelius Bertram and Carlo Sigonio have explored this question so thoroughly in their learned treatises that I have nothing to add; so instead I will consider some other issues" (p. 107). As we said before, Cunaeus hardly ever mentions his sources except when disagreeing with them. Both Sigonio and Bertram must have been major reference sources to him, at least during the initial stages of his research.

Finally, what strikes one in the perspective of Cunaeus' vivid in-depth debate with biblical criticism through the centuries is his repeated deprecating tenor when referring to merely philological issues or minor details as exercises in hairsplitting which were positively beneath his dignity, again in the most unequivocal of terms: "But all this is the stuff of grammar, and we should leave it to others; we are concerned here with more serious matters" (p. 49).[208] Most surprising of all perhaps are the final lines of the treatise (p. 220), which are the pinnacle of quite a number of similar references (pp. 132, 140, 199).

Opinion vs. Reason, Authority vs. Proof

In view of Cunaeus' entanglement throughout his treatise with sources and authorities that cover some twenty centuries, it is intriguing to be confronted with his plea (p. 163 and again, p. 171) for sound reason and common sense as a more than fit counterpart to all scholarly pretension, and his insistence on the requirement of solid proof and evidence rather than the opinions and testimonies of others to support one's thesis: "Since it is my goal that everything I do is dictated by reason, I have often been surprised that the scholars whose work I have seen insist that they are correct rather than proving that they are" (p. 163).[209] These are quite intriguing, if not revolutionary, statements of principle in Leiden at around 1615.

Of similar purport is his direct attack on Dutch clergymen in III.9: "It is a ridiculous superstition always to worry about definitions, for it is in the nature of certain things that they cannot be properly defined... The result is strife, anger, and a total free-for-all" (p. 216). There is no doubt that Cunaeus entertained very critical ideas throughout with respect to traditional humanist scholarship or biblical studies at the hands of the Dutch clergy. But then again, his overall views on mankind bespeak the astute political scientist rather than the scholarly recluse. Still, one can find a testimony to his clemency in the concluding lines of III.3, where he suggests that anyone who seeks perfection should go to live in a desert. In his introductory note to Book III he puts his critical comments in the right perspective with reference to Marcus Cato who, when found to be drunk, made the people who had caught him blush and feel ashamed instead.

As stipulated above, to Cunaeus, man himself is the ultimate object of study and wonder. Not surprisingly therefore, the treatise abounds with speculations on man's virtues and vices, which clearly mirror his proneness to matters philosophical and political; statements with political or psychological connotations abound: "A certain desire for power is normal among mortal men, and Lord knows it is very ancient and burns more fiercely than all the other emotions" (p. 12).[210] In III.3 we find an observation which recalls his preface: "That we make mistakes and give in to our imaginations is only human; anyone who wants to live in perfection ought to look for a desert. Every man's virtues have to be weighed alongside his vices, and we must take his measure according to which side of his character is the stronger" (p. 180). In a similar vein, he voices his views on the fate of states: "It is part of nature's plan that all great states eventually experience changes of fortune. The Hebrew Republic..." (p. 61). As we recall, the theme was highlighted in one of his official addresses at Leiden.

Some Prominent Themes

Among the plethora of themes discussed in the treatise, the reader's attention may perhaps be drawn, in most general terms, to some clusters which, in a way, reflect the wider interests of humanists and which, in years to come, deserve perhaps to be addressed from that broader context. A first cluster is brought up by Cunaeus in his opening chapters of Book I, in the context of Moses' agrarian concerns and reforms: the conflicting worlds of farmers, shepherds, and handymen go some way, in our author's estimate, in explaining the inveterate hatred between the Egyptian and Hebrew peoples. Closely related to this is his analysis of another stock element of humanist debate, to wit, the role of the vicinity of the sea in explaining a nation's character, its attitude to commerce, its openness to human intercourse, and its tendency towards inventions (I.2–5).

Of special interest to Dutch circumstance is Cunaeus' review of the nature and powers of the Sanhedrin (I.12) and kings (I.14), respectively, inasmuch as these issues were the major preoccupations of Hugo Grotius when proposing his comparison of the Hebrew and Dutch commonwealths at about 1600. Close reading may help us in establishing the eventual influence of the Dutch situation on his analysis. Again, in view of Cunaeus' unequivocal reference to Jeroboam's destructive machinations in his preface to the States of Holland, there is some reason to read chapter I.15 with special interest.

Cunaeus' description of the shameless ambition, perverse deceit, and unrestrained exploitation of power at the hand of the Levites (pp. 65–67, 103) is particularly acrimonious. One wonders to what extent our author is biased from personal experience with the clergy and whether the text implies a hint to contemporary Dutch circumstances, constituting the kind of admonition to Dutch public authorities he had in mind in his preface. No room is left for doubt in this respect when we come to his analysis of the perfectly devastating role of sects and heresies in II.17:

> Their dull human minds wrapped themselves up in their own obscure thoughts. So it became the sickness of an inferior age to dig up controversies and questions from the sacred texts... and when these were combined with the scholars' stubborn zealousness and corrupt ambition, the result was sects and heresies... No mother smothers her own little girl with as many kisses as the fathers of these sects did the children of their invention... Nothing is as deceptive as the devious religion and piety of such fanatics; whenever someone claims that their grandiose plans are God's will, the masses are ready right away to do whatever they are told, and they would much rather listen to their prophets than to their rulers and kings (pp. 122–124).

Petrus Cunaeus' numerous apodictical verdicts on the Jews are perfectly baffling and perplexing reading. One wonders in earnest, with no evidence on record of his personal meetings with Jews in Holland, on what in the world he based these countless references to typical "asinine Jewish stupidity." "This is what passes for Jewish wit! I myself have always been of the opinion that most of the Hebrews' adages are flavorless and tepid" (p. 184). "Of course, we should not expect a Jew to be so strict about his calculations" (p. 54). As to the alleged Jewish hatred of foreigners out of mere envy, he declares in a paraphrase of Horace's *Satire* that "the black venom of the cuttlefish had poisoned their minds" (p. 187). And then we reach his evaluation of Jewry after the coming of the Messiah in I.18:

> Nowadays the Jews are wandering about, pathetically unaware of where they are, there will no doubt come a time when they will be returned to the right path. The sun has not set for the last time: its light will once again shine even on them, and though they have certainly fallen, they have not been extinguished... Its obvious consequence is that we cannot in good conscience continue to shun the Jews as the objects of popular hatred when they still possess such great potential (pp. 71–75).

He contrasts the former glory of the Jews from the days of the patriarchs to their present "slavish and illiberal character," which he interprets as a kind of consequence of prolonged persecution, as "shackles on the soul," so to speak. Then once again he sings their praises as the nation that "has kept the Bible for us, safe and sound... No other nation merits a share in their glory" ("not the Christian scholars"). Finally he concludes on a note of gloom: "If by some miracle they were to get Canaan back, they would change their skies but not their spirit. They bring their own night with them wherever they go" (pp. 71–75).

Clearly, it would lead us far beyond the reach of this introduction to tackle these issues in earnest. The above are just a few isolated references from a wealth of equally controversial and contradictory statements scattered all over the work (cf. e.g. II.12). The relevance of further research into Cunaeus' treatise on all levels seems beyond dispute, inasmuch as the work constituted a *vade mecum* for generations of scholars both at home and abroad, before in its turn being covered by the dust of ages.[211]

Editions

Petrus Cunaeus' *De Republica Hebraeorum* was first published in Leiden in 1617, at the Elsevier press.[212] It was reprinted in Leiden in 1631 by Nicholas Eickhout in what is presented as an emendated edition (*priore emendatior*), which apparently prompted Elsevier to publish an *editio novissima* the following year, 1632.[213] All three seem to have been authorized editions. No further editions appeared during Cunaeus' lifetime. A new edition appeared in 1665 in Hof [Curiae] in Bavaria,[214] followed within a year by a new Amsterdam edition.[215] In 1674 yet another edition appeared in Saumur. Meanwhile, in Cambridge, in 1660, Cunaeus' treatise had been incorporated in the eight-volume edition of *Critici Sacri* which, in 1698, was reedited in nine volumes in Amsterdam.

In 1696, a new line was inaugurated with a Leipzig edition, the first to include an index.[216] This was followed in 1703 by a Leiden edition,[217] which included not just an extended index[218] but also a running commentary on matters literary and theological by Johannes Nicolai.[219] In 1732, this edition was reprinted with an emendated index in Leiden, and in 1745 it was incorporated in Blasius Ugolinus' *Thesaurus Antiquitatum Sacrarum*, which appeared in Venice.

So much for the original Latin text. As early as 1653 an English translation of Book I by Clement Barksdale appeared in London, actually thirty years before a Dutch translation saw the light of day. This Dutch translation was published in 1682, in Amsterdam, by Willem Goeree. The translator was the publisher's son, H.W. Goeree. The edition contained a wealth of annotations and was illustrated with 17 etchings. This edition was reprinted in 1683, 1684, 1685, 1700, and 1704, and saw French editions in 1705 and 1713, in all likelihood also translated by H.W. Goeree. Barksdale's partial English translation was reprinted in 1996, with an introductory note in Italian by Lea Campos-Boralevi.

Nearly four hundred years after the original publication of the book, the first complete English translation is now offered by Shalem Press. The present edition of *The Hebrew Republic*, based on the Latin edition of 1631, seems a timely one, and the editors of Shalem Press must be congratulated on the initiative. It is not a matter of chance that this edition coincides with the launching, by the same research center, of a new journal, *Hebraic Political Studies*.

Arthur Eyffinger
The Hague, Netherlands

NOTES

1. The story has been related in full detail from various angles. See, e.g., Kossmann, *Political Thought in the Dutch Republic*, Amsterdam 2000; Israel, *The Dutch Republic, Its Rise, Greatness, and Fall, 1477–1806*, Oxford 1995; Blom, *Morality and Causality in Politics: The Rise of Naturalism in Dutch Seventeenth-Century Political Thought*, Utrecht 1995; Van Gelderen, *The Political Thought of the Dutch Revolt (1555–1590)*, Cambridge 1992; Leeb, *The Ideological Origins of the Batavian Revolution*, The Hague 1973; Den Tex, *Oldenbarnevelt*, 2 vols., Cambridge 1973.

2. See *Studia Rosenthaliana* (a journal specializing in the field). Recent studies: Van den Berg/Van der Wall (eds.), *Jewish-Christian Relations in the Seventeenth Century: Studies and Documents*, Dordrecht 1988; Bots/Roegiers (eds.), *The Contribution of the Jews to the Culture in the Netherlands*, Amsterdam 1989; Blom/Fuks-Mansfeld/Schöffer (eds.), *Geschiedenis van de Joden in Nederland*, Amsterdam 1995 [English version: *The History of the Jews in the Netherlands*, Oxford 2002]; Israel/Salverda (eds.), *Dutch Jewry: Its History and Secular Culture (1500–2000)* [Brill's Series in Jewish Studies, vol. 29], Leiden 2002. Earlier surveys: Da Silva Rosa, *Geschiedenis der Portugeesche Joden in Amsterdam 1593–1925*, Amsterdam 1925; Brugmans/Frank (eds.), *Geschiedenis der Joden in Nederland*, Amsterdam 1940.

3. Notably in *The Hebrew Republic* I.18.

4. An excellent survey of the greatly troubled history of European Jewry in the late Middle Ages is found in Jonathan Israel, *European Jewry in the Age of Mercantilism, 1550–1750*, Oxford 1985, London 1998[3]. [Dutch translation, *De Joden in Europa, 1550–1750*, Franeker 2003.]

5. The Jews had been formally banned from the Low Countries by Charles V in 1547, an edict that was confirmed by Philip II in 1570.

6. The history of Antwerp Jewry in this period is fairly interesting. The "Portuguese Nation" survived the ransacking of the city by mutinying Spanish soldiers in 1576 and the recapture by Parma in 1585, only to fall victim to the blockade of Flemish harbors by the Dutch a decade later. The successful trade embargo invited the migration of the Jewish merchants towards the North, and the establishment of a first Sephardic community in Amsterdam.

7. It has been calculated that, as from about 1570, some 70 percent of the extremely lucrative trade of barley and wheat, which was in high demand throughout Western Europe, was controlled at this end of the trade route by the Dutch through their Danzig distribution centers.

8. On these issues, see Israel 2003, pp. 34–39.

9. *De iure praedae*, or *De Indis*, was produced between 1604–1608. Critical edition by H.G. Hamaker, The Hague 1868. On its genesis, see Van Holk/Roelofsen (eds.), *Grotius Reader*, The Hague 1983. Grotius' celebrated *Mare liberum* (1609) was a revised edition of a chapter from *De jure praedae*.

10. Indeed, echoes of mystifications as exemplified by the legendary story of Simon of Trente are retraceable even in Hugo Grotius' *Jodenreglement* of 1614–1615: *Remonstrantie nopende de ordre dije in de landen van Hollandt ende Westvrieslandt dijent gestelt op de Joden.* Critical edition by J. Meijer, Amsterdam 1949.

11. Israel 2003, p. 32.

12. They were scattered mostly in the 1576 ransacking of the city by Spanish mutineers, and pockets probably migrated as far as Middelburg in the province of Zeeland, and Rotterdam. See Israel 2003, p. 58. Soon afterwards, with the Union formally warranting religious freedom, most merchants applied to be reinstated in Antwerp.

13. Israel 2003, p. 31.

14. In Amsterdam these Sephardic contingents were actually preceded, at least according to a persistent Jewish tradition, by a group of Ashkenazi merchants from Emden as early as 1593. See Huussen, "The Legal Position of the Jews in the Dutch Republic," in Israel/Salverda 2002, p. 31.

15. By then, as compared to the approximately 400 Jews still registered in Antwerp at about 1600, in Amsterdam we are speaking of dozens amid a local population of about 35,000, to be augmented no doubt by groups of crypto-Jews and Marranos.

16. The Jews then returned to Amsterdam and started building a synagogue of their own accord, once more to be called to order. A first Amsterdam synagogue was opened only in 1639. See Israel 2003, pp. 69–71.

17. With the possible exception of a general set of rules of conduct by resolution of the States of Holland of 4 March 1615.

18. See above, n. 10.

19. In 1614 in Frankfurt. On these incidents, see Israel 2003, pp. 74–75.

20. In Hoorn, Mennonites had converted to Judaism; in Amsterdam a Jew was caught having intercourse with a Christian girl. In 1616 a married Jewish pharmacist was caught committing adultery with a Christian maidservant. See Huussen 2002, pp. 32–33.

21. See Meijer 1949; Rabbie, "Grotius and Judaism," in Nellen/Rabbie, *Hugo Grotius, Theologian: Essays in Honour of G.H.M. Posthumus Meyjes* [Stud. Hist. Christ. Thought, vol. 53], Leiden 1994, pp. 99–120; Huussen 2002, p. 33.

22. As for the interdiction of *connubium*, against the backdrop of similar prohibitions between Sephardic and Ashkenazi Jews, this notion seemed not too far-fetched or reactionary. See Huussen 2002, p. 35. On the other hand, Grotius was never a social revolutionary, as can readily be concluded from his works, e.g. *De Antiquitate* 1610. A stern aristocrat, he never relied on the fickle mobs for a sound judgment.

23. Huussen 2002, p. 30.

24. Huussen 2002, p. 33.

25. Huussen 2002, pp. 46ff.

26. On the life and works of Petrus Cunaeus (Pieter van der Cun in Dutch), see generally M.J.A.M. Ahsmann, *Collegia en Colleges. Juridisch onderwijs aan de Leidse Universiteit 1575–1630 in het bijzonder het disputeren.* Thesis, Leiden University, Groningen 1990 [contains a biographical note and focuses on Cunaeus' career as a law professor]. Willem Otterspeer, *Groepsportret met Dame. Het bolwerk van de vrijheid. De Leidse Universiteit 1575–1672*, Amsterdam 2000, passim. See also *Nieuw Nederlands Biografisch Woordenboek* I, pp. 658–660 (v. Kuyk). The major contemporary source on Cunaeus' life is the funeral address pronounced by his friend Adolphus Vorstius in 1638, enlarged in *Orationes* 1640. See also the various editions of Johannes Meursius' *Alma Academia* [1614, 1617, 1625]. A bibliography of Cunaeus' works is found in Ahsmann/Feenstra, *Bibliografie van hoogleraren in de rechten aan de Leidse Universiteit tot 1811*, Amsterdam 1984, pp. 85–102. On Cunaeus' political studies in Leiden, see Wansink, *Politieke wetenschappen aan de Leidse Universiteit 1575–1650*, Utrecht 1981. On his ancestry, see Roell in *De Nederlandsche Leeuw* 1903, pp. 1ff., 17ff. On his contacts in the province of Zeeland, see Meertens, *Letterkundig leven in Zeeland in de zestiende en de eerste helft der zeventiende eeuw*, Amsterdam 1942.

27. The reference is to his *Sardi Venales* (Fools for Sale), which will be discussed later.

28. Adolphus Vorstius (1597–1663) was a classicist and man of letters who became professor of medicine at Leiden, to succeed his father in that capacity. He was an intimate of Petrus Cunaeus. See Otterspeer 2000, p. 405.

29. Meertens 1942, p. 443. All of these scholars somehow studied Hebrew, Chaldean, Syrian, Arabic, and Persian.

30. Possibly the first Orientalist of Dutch descent and a friend of Casaubon.

31. Meertens 1942, p. 431.

32. That is, according to modern research (see Ahsmann 1990, p. 178), in 1602 in Cunaeus' own memory.

33. Vorstius, *Oratio funebris* 1638, p. 9. On Cunaeus' poetical leanings, see below.

34. Meanwhile, young Regemorterus, who had been a great source of inspiration to Cunaeus and who, as Vorstius insists, was a man of considerable learning in his own right, remained in London to succeed his father and serve the Dutch Church as a minister for many more years.

35. If we interpret Vorstius correctly. See *Oratio funebris* 1638, p. 10.

36. In that year the States of Holland felt compelled to arrange a first conciliatory meeting between the two antagonists.

37. Ahsmann/Feenstra 1984, p. 85.

38. Johannes Drusius (1550–1616) studied at Louvain and Rome. From 1577 onwards he was a distinguished professor of Chaldean and Syrian languages at Leiden.

He moved to Franeker in 1585. Although he considered himself a linguist rather than a theologian, his Remonstrant sympathies and leanings towards Arminius and Uytenbogaert were well known. Indeed, they prompted recurrent problems with his Franeker colleague Sibrandus Lubbertus, the great adversary of Hugo Grotius in the years 1613 and following. Drusius' biblical commentary was widely appreciated.

39. As Vorstius maintains on pp. 11–12: *"Enimvero Syriasmum et Hebraeorum magistros intelligere, non cuiuslibet est, aut vulgaris industriae."*

40. *"Qui solus fere inter gentis Iudaicae scriptores Talmudicos non ineptire censetur."* In general, Grotius showed little sympathy for what he deemed the "spiritual foolishness" of most Jewish teachers, as attested by the "scandalous fictions and ridiculous opinions" that filled the Talmud. Quotations taken from Heering, *Hugo Grotius as Apologist for the Christian Religion: A Study of His Work "De Veritate Religionis Christianae" (1640)*, Leiden-Boston 2004, p. 60.

41. See this edition, p. 7.

42. On Johannes Boreel, see p. xxxi and n. 132.

43. Grotius especially, in the latter part of his life (also witness a letter to Vossius from 1636; *Briefwisseling* VII no. 2885), reveals a singular interest in, and indeed the highest esteem for, Maimonides' impressive synthesis of Jewish law—a businesslike survey in fourteen books that omits all the dialectic and mysticism of the Talmud. Still, Maimonides' textbook was written in a difficult Hebrew and, at the time, only partly translated into Latin, and not too accurately at that. Grotius, for one, preferred working on the basis of the full Arabic translation until, in 1636, the French Hebraist Jean De Voisin presented him with his new Latin version. For a consummate review of these matters, see Heering 2004, pp. 186ff. For the overall background of the problem, see Dienstag, "Christian Translators of Maimonides' *Mishneh Torah* into Latin," in *S.W. Baron Jubilee Volume*, Jerusalem 1974, and Katchen, *Christian Hebraists and Dutch Rabbis: Seventeenth Century Apologetics and the Study of Maimonides' Mishneh Torah*, Cambridge, Mass.–London 1984.

44. While in Frisia, Cunaeus also frequented courses of the lawyers Marcus Lycklema a Nyeholt and Timaeus Faber. Vorstius 1638, pp. 12–13.

45. For more details, see Ahsmann 1990, p. 179.

46. In Franeker he had also followed the courses of Faber and Lycklema a Nyeholt, two prominent law professors. See above, n. 44 and Ahsmann 1990.

47. Vorstius 1638, p. 13.

48. *Notae et animadversiones in Nonni panopolitae Dionysiaca, in quo errores et inscitiam illius autoris persecutus est*, Leiden 1610. (In Ahsmann/Feenstra 1984, pp. 85–86, the title reads *Animadversionum liber in Noni Dionysiaca, in quo quid sit de hujus autoris virtutibus et vitiis habendum ostenditur*.) Nonnus' fifth-century epic deals with the life of the god of wine.

49. *Sardi venales, satyra menippea in hujus saeculi homines plerosque inepte eruditos*, Leiden 1612. Ahsmann/Feenstra 1984, pp. 86–90.

50. The origin of the Menippean satire is Seneca's *Apocolocyntosis*, a biting satire on the deification of the Roman emperors. It was imitated by Emperor Julian the Apostate in his *Caesares*, which made short shrift of many of his predecessors, as did a much similar *Misopogon*. The genre was revived in humanist times by Justus Lipsius' *Somnium* [cf. *Somnium Scipionis*], a very popular satire on the poor state of philology in Europe, published in 1581. In his dream, Lipsius imagined attending a meeting of the Roman Senate presided over by Cicero himself, and discussing the alarming situation. The hilarious tract contained countless innuendos and puns on colleagues. It saw various imitations (Puteanus, Heinsius, Nannius, Bencius), but none nearly as successful as the one by the gifted Cunaeus. Cunaeus' satire presents a similar meeting of the Roman Senate, presided over by Erasmus, and dealing with the poor state of theology, notably in Leiden. For the literature on the genre, see the critical edition of Lipsius' and Cunaeus' satires by Matheeussen/Heesakkers, *Two Neo-Latin Menippean Satires*, Leiden 1980.

51. Critical edition by Rabbie, Leiden 1995.

52. Cf. Rabbie 1995, p. 166: *solentque theologi tantas saepe minutias quaestionum sectari ut eas vix doctissimus quisque, vix ipsi intelligant.* The previous year, in June 1612, Grotius explicitly wrote to Casaubon that unity among Christians was never to be expected as long as theologians were in control (*Briefwisseling* I no. 239).

53. See Schotel, *De Academie te Leiden in de 16de, 17de en 18de eeuw*, Haarlem 1875.

54. See Posthumus Meyjes, *Geschiedenis van het Waalse College te Leiden 1606–1699*, Leiden 1975.

55. Dominicus Baudius, while an eminent philologist, was a notorious drunk, while Heinsius had published an ode to Bacchus in 1614. Cunaeus' attack on Heinsius, a very jealous man indeed, would backfire, and predictably so. On Daniel Heinsius (1580–1655), see Sellin, *D. Heinsius and Stuart England*, Leiden 1968; Meter, *The Literary Theories of Daniel Heinsius*, Assen 1984; and Bloemendal's critical edition of Heinsius' neo-Latin tragedy *Auriacus*, Utrecht 2002. On the *Hymnus* on Bacchus of 1614, see Rank/Warners/Zwaan, *Bacchus en Christus: Twee Lofzangen van Daniel Heinsius*, Zwolle 1965. On Dominicus Baudius, see Grootens, *D. Baudius: Een levens-schets uit het Leidse humanistenmilieu, 1561–1613*, Nijmegen 1942.

56. Ahsmann/Feenstra 1984 list five Latin editions of the *Sardi* published jointly with Julian's satire, nine separate editions, and three editions along with Cunaeus' *Orationes*. A Dutch edition, entitled *Gekken te hoop, of Schimpschrift Op de Verkeerd-geleerden van onzen tijd*, appeared in 1675, after parts had been published the year before in Brandt's *Historie der Reformatie*, Amsterdam 1674, pp. 203ff. A French edition, *La réforme dans la République des Lettres ou Discours sur les pretensions ridicules des demi Sçavans* (1695), and a German edition, *Das Traumgesicht* (1796), were also published.

57. As attested by the dispatching of complimentary copies to Vorstius and Casaubon, among others; *Epistolae*, pp. 118, 121.

58. Matheeussen/Heesakkers 1980, pp. 15–16. Otterspeer 2000, pp. 252–253.

59. On the courses in politics at the time, see Otterspeer 2000, p. 401.

60. First published in Petrus Burmannus' 1725 edition of Cunaeus' correspondence.

61. Otterspeer 2000, p. 252.

62. Vorstius 1638, pp. 13–14: *iurisprudentia semper prae ceteris ei placuit, ac potissima visa est ad ingenii sui explendam magnitudinem et capacitatem.*

63. His theses, defended on 19 June 1616, concerned the *Lex Iulia de Maiestate.*

64. Apollonius Schotte (c. 1574–1639) was born in Middelburg. He studied humanities and law in Leiden from 1591 to become a doctor of law in 1600. Along with his friend Antonius Walaeus, he then embarked upon his *peregrinatio studiosa*, calling at Basel, Bern, Geneva, Lausanne, and Heidelberg. Upon his return, in June 1602, he accepted the pensionary of Middelburg. He became a member of the Supreme Court in The Hague in 1610 and died on 1 November 1639, within a year of Cunaeus. Schotte was held in high public esteem both in Holland and Zeeland and was an authority both in matters ecclesiastical and within the world of letters. Although his Dutch verse is certainly not of the very first order, his poetical rendering of the biblical book of Ecclesiastes was praised in a poem by his friend Hugo Grotius (*Poemata* 1617, p. 362). In his turn, Schotte sent a consolatory poem upon the death of a newborn son of Grotius' (*De filiolo H. Grotii, paucis diebus postquam natus esset vita functo, Poemata* 1617, pp. 522–523). Some thirty-two letters between Schotte and Cunaeus are contained in the Burmannus 1725 edition of Cunaeus' correspondence.

65. His inaugural address was entitled *De Jurisprudentia.*

66. Ahsmann 1990 throughout and Otterspeer 2000, pp. 358–359. On Cunaeus' teachings of the Digests and *Codex* see Otterspeer 2000, pp. 413–415. On the hierarchy of disciplines at Leiden in these days and the policy of successive appointments in various faculties, see Otterspeer 2000, pp. 400ff.

67. Vorstius 1638, p. 15.

68. On Johannes Cunaeus (1617–1673), see *Nieuw Nederlands Biografisch Woordenboek* I (v. Kuyk). He matriculated at Leiden in 1622 without much success, edited his father's *Orationes* in 1640, entered the service of the V.O.C. [Verenigde Oostindische Compagnie] in 1644 and made himself a great career in the Indies. Upon his return in 1658, he settled down in Leiden to resume, but apparently never finished, his legal studies and to serve the city council. Most noteworthy is the report of his diplomatic mission to Persia in 1651–1652.

69. Witness his introductory note, this edition, pp. 157–159.

70. G.J. Vossius (1577–1649), a prominent Dutch humanist and lifelong friend of Grotius', was a Leiden student who became Regent of the States College in 1615, but had to resign in 1619 on account of his Remonstrant feelings. He became a professor of eloquence in 1622, to exchange Leiden for Amsterdam in 1631. See Rademaker, *Life and Work of G.J.Vossius (1577–1649)*, Assen 1981.

71. On Cunaeus' and Grotius' close relations to Van Zeyst, see Grotius' reaction to the latter's demise in a letter to Cunaeus from 1617 (*Briefwisseling* I no. 536, dated 28 September 1617).

72. At around 1600, they used to be referred to as the *gemelli*, the twins, in Leiden.

73. Otterspeer 2000, pp. 282–283.

74. See on these matters also Matheeussen/Heesakkers 1980, p. 17, and the reference to Cunaeus' correspondence with Lydius over 1620.

75. *Exercitationum oratoriarum inauguratio, 1620*. See Ahsmann/Feenstra 1984, p. 96. Cunaeus acted for many years as board member of the Collegium, which was abolished in 1648. Otterspeer 2000, p. 309.

76. Aelius Vorstius had been professor of medicine at Leiden from 1599 onwards. He was the father (and predecessor in the chair) of Adolphus Vorstius, who was to deliver Cunaeus' funeral address.

77. Otterspeer 2000, pp. 322–323.

78. "*Erat illi dictio tam castigata, tam concinna, tam pura ac perspicua, et minime affectata, ut aureum illud Latini sermonis seculum...*" Matters of style were an issue at Leiden ever since the days of Lipsius, who had turned away from Ciceronianism towards a nervous, succinct, "Attic" style. See Vorstius 1638, pp. 13 and 18. Lipsius' satirical *Somnium* of 1581 dealt notably with these matters.

79. In 1624, 1632, and 1637. His addresses prompted by these occasions are invariably held on the *dies natalis* of Leiden University (8 February). They date from 1624 (*On the Idea of "Dies Natalis"*), 1625 (*De necessitate et praestantia litterarum*), 1633 (*Ad authenticam habitam C. ne filius pro patre*), and 1638 (*De annis climacteribus et eorum vi in rerumpublicarum et civitatum conversione*). Cunaeus' address on the fiftieth anniversary of his *alma mater*, in 1624, was particularly impressive. See Otterspeer 2000, p. 442. Other famous addresses of Cunaeus' concern a *Responsum in causa Postliminii*, over a commercial dispute, of June 1631; and a lecture, *Super causa judiciaria Senatus Academici*, dated February 1632 and dealing with the murder of a night watchman by a Polish student in the retinue of the Polish Prince Radzivyl. It was on this occasion, in the middle of university riots, that Cunaeus delivered his *Oratio ad studiosos tumultuantes*, famous for its moral counsel (Otterspeer 2000, pp. 136 and 291–293). Many of Cunaeus' lectures have been preserved, such as the ones on the Latin authors Suetonius, Tacitus, Horace, and Juvenalis. They are found in the volume of collected speeches.

80. *Orationes varii argumenti*, Leiden 1640. The Leiden edition was ever more expanded in the 1643 Frankfurt edition by Buchnerus, the 1674 Leipzig edition by Gesenius, and the 1693, 1720, and 1735 Leipzig editions by Cellarius. On the bibliographical aspects of Cunaeus' various speeches, see Ahsmann/Feenstra 1984, pp. 96–101.

81. *Orationes* 1640, 1–23, pp. 6ff.

82. *Orationes* 1640, 24–45, pp. 33ff.: *Sane Hebraei, cum primi omnium gentium litteras, disciplinasque, et rerum tum coelestium tum humanarum scientiam ab immortali Deo didicissent, atque regundae reipublicae instituta quaedam eiusmodi haberent, quae omnium essent praeceptis potiora, diutissime regionem maximam fertilissimamque tenuerunt per duodecim tribus, quae admiranda foecunditate singulae in magnitudinem gentis excreverant.* The passage, amounting to a summary of his main thesis from 1617, is then elaborated into a survey of the transfer of learning through the ages, from Hebrew to Phoenician to Egyptian to Greek. It concludes (p. 43) upon a rebuttal to Islam, "*triste illud et dirum imperium,*" that flourishes merely by virtue of "*Christianorum et ignaviam et discordiam.*" The *peroratio* consists of a eulogy on the Dutch Republic.

83. *De annis climactericis et eorum vi in rerumpublicarum et civitatum conversione.*

84. *Orationes* 1640, 60–81, pp. 64ff.

85. Vorstius 1638, p. 16.

86. Vorstius 1638, p. 16.

87. Cunaeus' correspondence was first published by Petrus Burmannus in Leiden in 1725 (*P. Cunaei et doctorum virorum ad eundem Epistolae. Quibus accedit Oratio in obitum Bon. Vulcanii*) and was reprinted in 1735 and 1738.

88. UBL [Universiteitsbibliotheek Leiden] Ms. Cun. 7. The work was published in *Humanistica Lovaniensia* 33 (1984), pp. 145–197. Cf. Peerlkamp, *De poetis Latinis Nederlandorum*, pp. 302–303.

89. Upon the opening of Amsterdam University, the Athenaeum.

90. Ahsmann 1990, p. 187.

91. To replace Jacob Eyndius, who had died. In 1642 one of Gerard Vossius' sons, Matthew, was appointed; upon his demise in 1646 he was replaced by his brother Isaac.

92. Vorstius 1638, pp. 25–26.

93. Vorstius 1638, p. 27: *saeculi sui Scaevolam, Papinianum, Ulpianum, aut si quod nomen honoratius est inter priscos istos iurisconsultos.*

94. Poem by Anth. Thysius, *Orationes* 1640, pp. 45–46.

95. "Fate will find a way out."

96. UBL Mss. Cunaeus 1–14. Apart from this collection of manuscripts, quite a few copies and extracts of Cunaeus' courses transcribed by students are extant. Ahsmann 1990, p. 191.

97. Cunaeus' impressive funeral oration was given by the professor of medicine, Adolphus Vorstius. The volume of epicedia opens with a poem by Hugo Grotius, and includes contributions by Leiden celebrities such as Claude Saumaise, Daniel and Nicolas Heinsius, Petrus Scriverius, Marcus Zuerius Boxhorn, and Anthonius Thysius

(on the continuous rains and storms following Cunaeus' demise), and personal friends such as Johannes Foreest, Willem Staeckmans, Willem and Pieter de Groot (Hugo's brother, and eldest son, respectively), Vincent Fabritius, H. Alers, Rochus Hoffer, M. de Vet, and Arnold van Slichtenhorst. See also M.Z. Boxhornius' *Lachrymae* (1638), a collection of six poems.

98. Grotius' poem reads: *Ille tribus linguis toti celeberrimus orbi / Occidit, heu legum regula, iuris honos! / Successor quaerendus erit. Iam mitte, Batave, / Mitte per et terras, mitte per et maria. / Quum bene quesieris, gemina sub cardine, nosces / Quantum in Cunaeo res tua perdiderit.*

99. Vorstius 1638, p. 20. On the succession, see Otterspeer 2000, pp. 334 and 412.

100. III.3, p. 171.

101. Otterspeer 2000, p. 232 and cf. idem, p. 254.

102. Among the dignitaries in the Republic he was close to Van der Myle, de Matenesse, Van Aertsen, and Jacob Cats.

103. As Cunaeus observes, not without distinct reservations, at various instances in his work. See below, n. 208.

104. Grotius' three biblical plays are called *Adamus Exul* (1601), *Christus Patiens* (1608), and *Sophompaneas* [on the patriarch Joseph in Egypt] (1635). Critical editions in *Dichtwerken/Poetry*. On their political implications, see Eyffinger, "The Fourth Man: Stoic Tradition in Grotian Drama," in *Grotiana* n.s. 22–23 (2001/2002), pp. 117–156.

105. *Lectori*, in *Dichtwerken/Poetry* I.1a, Assen 1970, pp. 294ff.

106. "that is, if one may say so of something that is inherently true and not in want of any external support." *Dichtwerken/Poetry* I.1a, ibid.

107. Cf. Grafton, *J. Scaliger: A Study in the History of Classical Scholarship*, 2 vols., Oxford 1983, 1993. Idem, "J. Scaliger and Historical Chronology: The Rise and Fall of a Discipline" in *History and Theory* 14 (1975), 156–185, pp. 164ff.

108. Heering 2004, pp. 169ff.

109. However, this is not to say that the material was not to be used. As a matter of fact, the bulky references to these mythical sources that abound in Grotius' *De Veritate* of 1627 would suggest a later adaptation of precisely this material. Meanwhile, Grotius' keen interest in these matters is also attested by other pursuits over his early years. Prominent among these are *Ghetuychnissen eens seer ouden Wysentijts* (see *Dichtwerken/Poetry* 1.2.3, Assen 1988), an introductory note from about 1601–1602 to a treatise of a very dear friend of his, Simon Stevin of Bruges (1548–1620). Stevin authored a *Vita Politica* (1590). See Dijksterhuis, *Simon Stevin: Science in the Netherlands around 1600*, The Hague 1970; and Vermeulen in *Grotiana* n.s. 4 (1983), pp. 63–66. Critical edition of the works of Stevin by Crone et al., 5 vols., Amsterdam 1955–1966. Here, all the legendary authors referred to above are met. Again, the concept which lay at the base of Scaliger's research, to wit, the cultural transfer of

ideas over time, was at the core of a major eulogy of Grotius' from 1602, in which Prince Maurice of Orange is hailed as the culmination point of many centuries of mathematics. See my comments in *Dichtwerken/Poetry* I.2.3, Assen 1988.

110. Franciscus Junius [Sr.] or François Dujon (1545–1602), professor of theology at Leiden from 1592–1602, was a longstanding colleague of Tremellius, a converted Jew. Their edition of the Bible was, in all likelihood, used by Grotius in preparing his *De Republica Emendanda* in about 1600. On these matters, see my comments in *Grotiana* n.s. 5 (1984), p. 28. The author of a tract *Le paisible Chrétien* and an *Eirenicon* (both from 1593), Junius stood for Grotius as the epitome of irenicism. On Junius' irenicism, see Venemans 1977, De Jonge 1980, and Rademaker 1981, pp. 40–59.

111. Cunaeus *Epistolae* 1725, no. 7, dated 18 July 1611, pp. 8–11 s.f.: *De Junio ita sentire te velim, non esse ei fidem ubique habendam. Mihi ille non vertisse Biblia, sed explicuisse videtur. Non enim Hebraea Latinis reddidit, ut de Scripturae sensu aliis liberum sit iudicium, sed ipse, qua quidem quidque sit ratione intelligendum, praecipit. Tum et sententiam, sive somnium potius suum, involvit miris verborum ambagibus. Pagnini interpretatio praestantissima est, nuda, simplex, plane ad fidem Hebraismi; ea si usus in posterum fueris, non erit cur sanctae linguae peritiam tibi magnopere optes.*

112. Franciscus Raphelengius (1539–1597), professor of Hebrew at Leiden from 1586–1597. On his Arabic lectures to Grotius, see *Briefwisseling* I no. 64, and cf. Lebram in *NAKG* n.s. 56 (1975/76), pp. 317–357. On the Leiden tradition see Juynboll, *Zeventiende-eeuwse beoefenaars van het Arabisch in Nederland*, Utrecht 1931.

113. Cf. *Briefwisseling* I no. 493 from December 1616, among others. Thomas Erpenius (1584–1624), professor of Oriental languages at Leiden, 1613–1624, who applied his considerable linguistic talents to biblical research as well. In 1625 he was succeeded by an equally eminent Orientalist, Jacobus Golius, who acquired a copy of the Samaritan Pentateuch for Leiden University.

114. It was Erpenius who helped Grotius in prison during 1619–1621 by providing him with books through relatives of his. Indeed it was in a book chest of his that Grotius made his legendary escape from prison in 1621.

115. On L'Empereur, see Van Rooden, *Biblical Scholarship and Rabbinical Studies in the Seventeenth Century: Constantijn L'Empereur (1591–1648), Professor of Hebrew and Theology at Leiden*, Leiden 1989.

116. In his *Memorie van mijn bejegening* from his years of imprisonment Grotius reveals that for his research concerning his *Annotationes* on the New Testament he availed himself particularly of the *Annotationes* by Erasmus, Beza, Drusius, and Casaubon. See Posthumus Meyjes 1988, p. 64, n. 163; Heering 2004, p. 4, n. 15, and p. 167, n. 23.

117. All this has caused much speculation among modern commentators as to Grotius' in-depth knowledge of Hebrew and his familiarity with Mishna, Talmud, and Jewish exegetics. From the way he surrounded himself with the most expert Hebraists wherever he lived, one may perhaps conclude that Grotius' keen lifelong interest in all issues regarding the history, religion, and social usages of the Hebrew

nation through the ages was never quite matched by the versatility that would have afforded him ready access to more complex Hebrew texts. A "Hebrew Grammar" is attested in the 1620 inventory of his books, which can of course be explained either way. Certainly, from the 1630s onwards, also thanks to the publications and personal advice of such scholars as Cocceius, Schickard, De Voisin, and L'Empereur, Grotius' intimate knowledge of rabbinical literature, ranging from early medieval sources, through Maimonides, to his contemporary Menasseh ben Israel, grew considerably. On these matters, see Lachs, "H. Grotius' Use of Jewish Sources in *On the Law of War and Peace*," in *Renaissance Quarterly* 30 (1977), pp. 181–200; Rosenberg, "Hugo Grotius as Hebraist," in *Studia Rosenthaliana* 12 (1978), pp. 62–90; Rabbie 1994, 99–120, pp. 113–114. All in all, it is remarkable that no intimate links and personal relationships between Grotius and representatives of the Jewish community, either in Holland or abroad, can be attested. Rabbie is probably right in concluding that his interest was that of the philologist—and literally academic (Rabbie 1994, pp. 118–119).

118. [Provisional] critical edition, Eyffinger et al. in *Grotiana* n.s. 5 (1984).

119. The issue was to be resumed by Grotius, on the spur of circumstance, at various phases in his career, notably in his *De Antiquitate* (1610), chs. 1, 6, 7, and in *Annales et Historiae* (first conceived 1604, published 1657), pp. 107ff. See my commentary on *De Republica Emendanda* in *Grotiana* n.s. 5 (1984), pp. 34ff. and 122ff.

120. On the issue of Grotius' contemporary sources, see my comments ibid., pp. 48–52. Sanctus Pagninus of Lucca was the author of *Hebraicarum Institutionum* (1549); Bonaventura Bertram of Lausanne wrote *De Republica Ebraeorum* (1574); Carlo Sigonio of Modena, *De Republica Hebraeorum* (1565), reissued in Hanau in 1608; Andreas Fricius [or Modrevius], *De Republica Emendanda* (1551). Other likely sources for Grotius were the works of Bodin, Althusius, and Hotman; Henning Arnisaeus' political works; Pierre Grégoire's *Syntagma iuris universi atque legum pene omnium gentium* (1582) and *De Republica* (1591); Bartholomeus Keckermannus' *Systema Grammaticae Hebraeae* (cf. *Briefwisseling* I no. 528, dated 3 September 1617 to Lingelsheim) and probably such well-known works as Bullinger's *Huysboeck* and Wolfgang Musculus' *Loci communes theologici* (1554).

121. Fr. Junius, *De observatione politiae Moysis* (1593).

122. For the broader context, see Van Gelderen/Skinner, *Republicanism: A Shared European Heritage*, Cambridge 2002.

123. The *Politica methodice digesta* (1602) of Johannes Althusius of Emden (1557–1638) was reprinted and enlarged in 1610 and 1614.

124. See my comments in *Grotiana* n.s. 5 (1984), pp. 44ff.

125. Coined as "The Venetian Myth." See E.O.G. Haitsma Mulier, *The Myth of Venice and Dutch Republican Thought in the Seventeenth Century*, Assen 1980; and my references in *Hebraic Political Studies* 1.1 (2005), 71–109, pp. 85ff.

126. Ibid., p. 47. The reference is notably to the *Limenheuretica*, Leiden 1599.

127. On *Parallelon Rerumpublicarum*, see my comments in the introductory note to *Dichtwerken/Poetry* I.2.3, Assen 1988, and in Nellen/Trapman (eds.), *De Hollandse Jaren van Hugo de Groot (1583-1621)*, Hilversum 1996, notably pp. 92–93.

128. The full correspondence up till 1617 is found in Molhuysen (ed.), *Briefwisseling Hugo Grotius*, vol. I, The Hague 1928. Cunaeus to Grotius: nos. 200 (dd. 14.10.1610), 307 (dd. 07.12.1613), 341 (dd. 29.05.1614), 416 (dd. 25.08.1615), 535 (dd. 25.09.1617), 540 (dd. 09.10.1617). Grotius to Cunaeus: nos. 455 (dd. 21.05.1616), 536 (dd. 28.09.1617).

129. *Orationes* 1640, pp. 29, 44–45, and 50, respectively.

130. See Ahsmann 1990, p. 190.

131. See Meertens, "De Groot en Heinsius en hun Zeeuwse vrienden," in *Archief Zeeland* 1949/50, pp. 53–99; idem, *Letterkundig leven in Zeeland*, Amsterdam 1942.

132. Johannes Boreel (1577–1629) was born in Middelburg, where he served as a pensionary from 1613–1619; he then became secretary to the States of Zeeland and the province's Raadspensionaris in 1625. He is attested to have been in personal contact with the Jewish community in his hometown. A gifted scholar by all standards, who studied at Basel among other places (1598), he preferred a career as a statesman. He particularly distinguished himself as a diplomat during embassies to King James I, by whom he was knighted in 1622. Boreel was a most respected member of the Leiden world of learning. His elder brother Adam was a celebrated theologian and Hebraist in his own right, focusing on research into the Mishna in particular.

133. Cunaeus, *De Republica Hebraeorum*, ed. 1632 [Elsevier], pp. *7v–*8r: *Bonam autem partem nobis suggessit Rabbi Moses Ben Maimon Aegyptius, cuius industria sagacitasque omni praedicatione est maior. Eum luculentum autorem transmisit ad nos vir amplissimus Ioannes Borelius, qui potentissimis Zelandiae Ordinibus a secretis est.*

134. Cf. Grotius' many references to Philo in his *De Republica Emendanda*.

135. See also Vorstius 1638, p. 12.

136. Janus Dousa Jr. (*1571) was the eldest son of the famous curator and lifelong patron of the arts in Leiden, Janus Dousa *pater* (1545–1604), and a highly promising scholar whose career was cut short by his untimely death. He became librarian of Leiden University Library in 1593, and it was possibly thanks to him that Leiden obtained the astrological/astronomical manuscripts of Martianus Capella and Aratus which Grotius, with the help of Scaliger and Dousa Sr., edited in 1599 and 1600.

137. From his numerous travels all over Europe and as far as Rumania, Syria, and Palestine from the late 1590s onwards, Boreel assembled extremely valuable collections of manuscripts and rare books. He also treasured an impressive cabinet of medals. At one stage, he presented his *orientalia* to the Leiden Orientalist Thomas Erpenius. The priceless collection was then purchased by the Duke of Buckingham, to end up in Cambridge University Library.

138. Grotius and Boreel had been very close from early on. Both were married in Zeeland in 1608, and Grotius' Latin wedding poem on Boreel's marriage is a gem

in the epithalamic genre. See Rabbie (ed.), *Dichtwerken/Poetry* I.2.4. In those very months, Boreel informed the Zeeland Chamber of the V.O.C. of Grotius' unpublished tract from 1605, *De Rebus Indicis*, better known as *De jure praedae*, and it was this intervention that triggered the publication, the following year, of a single chapter from that treatise, entitled *Mare liberum*. See Fruin, *Verspreide Geschriften*, 11 vols., The Hague 1900–1905, vol. III, pp. 443–445 and Van Holk/Roelofsen (eds.), *Grotius Reader*, The Hague 1983.

139. Meletius Pegas (1549–1601), Patriarch of Alexandria from 1590–1601. Boreel would therefore have visited him in the late 1590s.

140. *Meletius, sive de iis quae inter Christianos conveniunt epistola*. Critical edition by Posthumus Meyjes, Leiden 1988. Grotius was clearly preoccupied with the issue during those years. In 1608 he produced a neo-Latin tragedy, entitled *Christus Patiens*, which in itself was a plea for unity among Christians. In its preface he once more criticized the general discord in the Netherlands and insisted on toleration. The play itself abounds with thrusts at the class of Phariseans (read: Dutch ministers) and the fickleness of the mobs. The play can be read, in a way similar to *De Republica Emendanda*, as a comparison of the inveterate Hebrew and Dutch controversies over matters religious, and the pestilence of all dogma and formalism. See *Dichtwerken/ Poetry* I.5, Assen 1978, e.g., ll. 625–631, and my introductory note. See also my "The Fourth Man: Stoic Tradition in Grotian Drama," in *Grotiana* n.s. 22–23 (2001/02), pp. 117–156. The play was dedicated to the French delegate Pierre Jeannin, a personal friend of Grotius, who had been instrumental in concluding the Twelve Years' Truce (1609–1621). The following year, Grotius would emphatically repeat his point of view in his funeral poem on Arminius' demise; also witness the following lines: "*Iterumque et iterum scindimurque discordes, / Ridente Turca, nec dolente Judaeo!*"

141. As noted above, the States of Holland had by that stage already arranged talks between the two antagonists, Gomarus and Arminius, in a futile attempt to resolve the controversy.

142. On these matters, see my "*Amoena gravitatum morum spectabilis*," in *Bulletin de l'institut historique belge de Rome* 68 (1998), pp. 297–327.

143. On Lipsius' *Sendbrief* 1595, see Blom in Nellen/Trapman (eds.), *De Hollandse Jaren van Hugo de Groot (1583–1621)*; Hilversum 1996, p. 149; and my "Hugo Grotius' *De Republica Emendanda* in the Context of the Dutch Revolt," in *Hebraic Political Studies* 1:1 (2005), pp. 83–84. For the wider context, see *Grotiana* n.s. 5 (1984), pp. 32–52 and, for the early years, Geurts, *De Nederlandse Opstand in de pamfletten, 1566–1584*, Utrecht 1983.

144. *Memorie* 1607: *Ick segge, als men aensiet, dat de Vereenichde Nederlanden nyet en syn een Republique, maer seven verscheyden Provintien* […] *hebbende elcx hare verscheydene form van regeeringhe, nyets gemeen hebbende mit malcanderen...* To conclude: *Want indien wy nyet eene Regeeringe maecken mit behoorlycke autoriteyt* […] *soo moeten wy verloren gaen; want geene Republique kan bestaen, sonder goede ordre in de generale Regeeringe.* The words almost quote *De Republica Emendanda*, pars. 54–56. See on these matters Van Eysinga, *Sparsa Collecta*, Leiden 1958, pp. 489–504.

145. Letter to Gerard Vossius dated 18 September 1609; *Briefwisseling* I no. 170: *consensus caeterarum nationum mediocris, cum Zelandis perpetuae rixae. Fui nuper in ea regione et miratus sum esse homines tam imprudentes—an impudentes dicam [...] Ordinum Generalium auctoritas et communis iustitia contemnitur atque labefactatur, quae quo tendant facilis est coniectura.*

146. Antonius Walaeus (1573–1639) was born at Ghent, as was Daniel Heinsius. A poor bursar from Middelburg, interestingly enough, he was trained at the Collegium Theologiac at Leiden (the institute that was so much criticized by Cunaeus in his *Sardi* of 1612), where he followed courses of Junius and Gomarus. He then turned to Theodorus Beza in Geneva. He was a minister at Middelburg (1605–1619) before becoming a professor of divinity at Leiden (1619–1639). A close friend of Schotte, in 1609 he was Grotius' personal candidate to fill Arminius' chair upon the latter's demise. The interesting thing is that while he and Grotius held very different views on church matters, Walaeus being a firm Contra-Remonstrant, they respected each other's integrity and sincere intentions, in the best spirit of Junius, one might say, which was a rare phenomenon indeed in those days. This circumstance made Walaeus only the more reliable as a reference point and reviewer of Grotius' drafts.

147. Walaeus would react exactly the same with regard to *De Satisfactione*; see critical edition, Rabbie, Assen/Maastricht 1990, p. 21.

148. This would happen to Grotius only too often, for a variety of reasons: *Philarchaeus* (1600>), *Parallelon* (1604>), *De Jure Praedae* (1606>), *De Imperio* (1615>).

149. Quoted from Posthumus Meyjes 1988, pp. 59 and 179; see also *Briefwisseling* I no. 233. Later on, Grotius sent copies of his *Ordinum pietas* and his *De Satisfactione* for review purposes to both Cunaeus and Walaeus. See the introductory notes to Rabbie's critical editions of *Ordinum pietas* 1613 (Leiden 1995) and *De Satisfactione* (1990).

150. Quoted from Posthumus Meyjes 1988, pp. 59 and 180.

151. *Meletius*, par. 2: *aut qui nunc se nobis inserunt Iudaeos respicere liberet...*

152. *Meletius*, par. 12: *Haec illa sunt principia quae communia habet Christiana religio et cum falsis omnibus, et cum veris quidem, sed minus perfectis, qualis est primum naturalis religio, inde Mosaica.*

153. *Briefwisseling* I no. 200, dated 14 October 1610.

154. To summarize: Cunaeus' lectures to students on Horace prompted Leiden University curators on 18 May 1611 to honor him with a gratification; they subsequently made him a *professor extraordinarius* of Latin on 8 February 1612 and *ordinarius* on 7 August 1613. Cunaeus was then appointed professor of politics on 8 February 1614. After receiving his doctorate in law (*honoris causa*) on 19 June 1615, he became a regular law professor on 9 November 1615.

155. *Briefwisseling* I no. 307.

156. Availing himself of his trip to London in 1613 at the head of the Dutch delegation to the bilateral talks with the English on fisheries and colonial trade,

Grotius had a lengthy personal interview with King James I over religious issues. From these talks, he had erroneously drawn conclusions as to James' support for Van Oldenbarnevelt's faction.

157. He typifies the treatise as "*ingenii tui divinum monumentum,*" then adds: "*Iustissimam habuisti causam ea scribendi, quae in Theologos quosdam scribis. Itaque ipsi sibi imputent, Et, si sapiant, admoniti proficiant in melius.*"

158. *Briefwisseling* I no. 341.

159. Cunaeus is not exaggerating. In 1616, in the midst of political uproar, Grotius had his notes and emendations on Lucanus' epic poem *Pharsalia* published in Leiden, another proof of his versatility and relentless philological research. Actually, within a matter of months, towards the end of 1616, Grotius' volume of *Poemata Collecta* appeared.

160. The Latin passage reads: *Saepe irascor laboriosis tuis occupationibus, quas Reip. impendis: intelligo enim quidquid illi das, id omne auferri nobis. rursum, cum video non aliter salvam fore patriam, nisi eam tu et tui similes regant, consolor memetipsum, et iam hac mercede placet illud damnum. Simul cogito apprime illud nostro ordini esse gloriosum, cum tu, qui omnis doctrinae et ingenii princeps es, summum quoque in Republica locum teneas. Rarum enim est, ut iniustus virtutum aestimator populus sua bona intelligat, et magnis viris debitum rependat praemium. Itaque in hac re singulare est tuum fatum: atque id gratulor saeculo nostro.*

161. *Iampridem de Rep. Iudaeorum quaedam collegi, quae ego cum cura iterum lustrabo, et cum opportunum erit, edam. Multum iuvit nos Hebraismus, a quo fuit imparatus Sigonius.*

162. Cunaeus *Epistolae* 1725, no. 10, dated 24 February 1615.

163. *Libros nostros de Republica Judaica ob hanc causam non publicamus, quia cum iam pridem a nobis summa manus operi esset imposita, novissime nunc sensimus tandem id a nobis omissum esse, quod erat in hac re praecipuum. Etenim quoniam omnem operam in iuris pervestigatione ponimus, haud recte atque ordine fecisse videbamur, qui nihil dixeramus de Jure Judaico. Itaque hic restat actus, in hoc elaborandum est.*

164. *Quoniam tamen in libro tertio egimus de veteri ecclesia Hebraeorum, quod argumentum est singulare, ipsum nobis est eum describere* et seorsim edere in antecessum. *Is liber, uti in manus tuas perveniat, Dominus Grotius curabit. Ita enim nobis pollicitus est* [emphasis mine].

165. A role he would resume for Grotius' *De Satisfactione* in subsequent years.

166. On Cunaeus' correspondence with Lubbertus on these matters, see Ahsmann 1990, p. 179 with references to literature. On his contacts with Grotius, see Cunaeus *Epistolae,* 1725, nos. 8–9, Grotius *Briefwisseling* I nos. 214–216, 232, 233 [*Meletius*].

167. *Briefwisseling* I no. 416.

168. The reference seems to be to the awkward position of the Prince de Condé.

169. The core of the rather elaborate title of Walaeus' treatise reads: *Het ampt der Kerckendienaren; mitsgaders de authoriteyt, ende opsicht, die een Hooghe Christelicke Overheydt daer over toecompt. Waerin sekere nadere bedenckingen... maar insonderheyt over het Tractaet des E. J. Wtenbogaerts*, Middelburg 1615, preface dated 25 November 1615. As one can see, the debate at the time had focused almost exclusively on the relation of church and state, and on Erastian policy. Grotius, Cunaeus, and Wtenbogaert were perhaps the most prominent antagonists of the polemic.

170. Johannes Uytenbogaert (1557–1644) was a leader of the Remonstrant faction. He studied at Geneva with Arminius, became counsel to Van Oldenbarnevelt and court minister to Prince Maurice, and was a lifelong intimate of Hugo Grotius'. He fled the country in 1618; in exile he helped found the *Remonstrantse Broederschap* in Antwerp. The work referred to here is the *Tractaet van 't Ampt ende Authoriteyt eener Hoogher Christelicker Overheydt in Kerckelicke saecken*, The Hague 1610. Grotius wrote a moving epigram on Uytenbogaert's return to The Hague many years later, which appeared as legend to a portrait of Uytenbogaert etched by Rembrandt.

171. *Erat in libris nostris de republ. integrum caput huic dissertationi dictum. Sed dicam libere, iam bis terque illud mutavimus, delevimus, interpolavimus. Nunc vero tandem plane visum nobis est illud omittere. Neutri enim parti dissentientium accedo, ac potius medium quiddam sequor....* There follows a literary quote from Varro, found in Nonius (I.228).

172. Ahsmann 1990, p. 184, n. 46.

173. Issues dealt with at some length by Grotius himself in *De Republica Emendanda*, notably pars. 19–27. Cunaeus deals with these matters in *De Republica Hebraeorum* I.14 [kings; unction]; II.9ff. [Levites]; I.11 [David's scepter]. Cf. Sigonio, *De Republica Hebraeorum* VII.3 [kings]; V.4 [Levites].

174. *...illa aspera et inculta magistris quibusdam relinquimus, qui hodie, cum nondum didicerunt quid sit scire, ac nunquam theologum pictum, ut dicitur, viderunt, nullam tamen rem constanti vultu definire, nihil affere parcunt.* The text reminds one of his introductory note to Books I and II, and again to Book III of *The Hebrew Republic.*

175. *Briefwisseling* I no. 455, dated 22 May 1616.

176. *Briefwisseling* I no. 535, dated 25 September 1617.

177. *Iam a multo tempore nullum scriptum in manus meas pervenit, quod magis animum mihi explevit. Ita ubique argumentorum vi atque gravitate lectorem percellit. Utique crucem omnibus fixisti, qui plausibilem haeresin commenti, late iam seculum veneno suo afflaverant. Quare, ni aliud praesidium ad caussam deploratam adferant, actum de illis est.*

178. *Briefwisseling* I no. 536, dated 28 September 1617.

179. The full title of Grotius' treatise reads *Defensio fidei catholicae de satisfactione Christi adversus Faustum Socinum Senensem.*

180. To him too, Grotius admits, the loss transcends the public sphere. Van Zeyst, though many years his senior, had always treated him, Grotius, as a younger brother. Grotius volunteers his willingness to attest publicly to this warm friendship and high esteem, if the occasion would ever arise. Possibly, a volume of obituaries was considered.

181. Critical edition with extensive introductory note by H.-J. van Dam, Leiden 2001. The text was conceived in 1614–1617. The incident tells us of the way manuscripts on crucial political issues were circulating, and the risks involved.

182. *De Veritate Religionis Christanae* of 1627, a great apology for Christianity in the tradition of Vives and Duplessis-Mornay (the two sources explicitly acknowledged by Grotius). On this tradition, see Dulles, *A History of Apologetics*, London 1971. In *De Veritate*, Grotius argued not so much against the increasing atheism and skepticism of his day and age, as against the devastating discord among the endless Christian denominations. In this, he focused on ethics above all: piety, rather than dogma, should inspire Christians, he felt, as should practical toleration, rather than learned doctrine. He then elaborates his theory of necessary and unnecessary doctrines as first developed by Erasmus, and later on by Junius in his *Eirenicon* of 1593. (On the latter treatise, see De Jonge, *De irenische ecclesiologie van Franciscus Junius [1542–1602]*, Nieuwkoop 1980.) Already in 1616, Grotius had ardently advocated the same in his eloquent and impressive, but futile, address to the Amsterdam city council of May 1616. Again, in his *De Imperio*, Grotius argued that theologians would be wise to follow the example of lawyers, who had long since realized the dangers involved in all too strict definitions.

183. Grotius found ample occasion to discuss the religion and position of the Jews, including the history of Jewish learning, in his celebrated treatise of 1627. Book 5 of *De Veritate* deals exclusively with Judaism, and notably with the refutation of traditional Jewish arguments against Christianity, taking up the subjects of Jesus' status as Messiah, his miracles, and his position towards Mosaic law. The book reveals far more sympathy than is shown in Book 6 towards Islam, and enters into much more detail. However, in these references it is never quite clear to what phase of Jewish tradition Grotius is referring. Clearly, the Old Testament is his major reference point throughout. As Heering argues (Heering 2004, p. 146), Duplessis-Mornay's *L'Advertissement aux juifs* (1607) must have been one of his principal sources, and may even have inspired its mildly philo-Semitic tone. Grotius readily acknowledges the debt of Christianity towards Mosaic law and the Jewish tradition, extensively praises the Jewish religion on the grounds of its antiquity (on which see Heering 2004, pp. 106ff.), meanwhile making short shrift of later Talmudic tradition, and ends with a prayer to God to enlighten the Jews and forgive them. Later in life, in his *Annotationes on the Testaments*, Grotius once more discussed many issues relating to Jewish history and customs in full detail. His undogmatic approach would evoke accusations of *iudaizare* by stern Calvinists, in much the same way as he was accused of *papizare*. Cf. Rabbie 1994, pp. 99–101.

184. III: Introduction, p. 155. Book III has a dedication of its own, addressed to a Leiden official, Franciscus van Dyck, an intimate of Cunaeus'.

185. In a reference to the orator Albutius. See p. 7.

186. Ibid.

187. Ibid.

188. III: Introduction, p. 155.

189. See above, p. xxiv.

190. III: Introduction, p. 158. It reads like a valid excuse, considering that he had become a professor of politics on 8 February 1614 and, after receiving his doctorate in law on 19 June 1615, had become a law professor on 9 November 1615.

191. III: Introduction, p. 156. One is reminded that Vorstius, in his funeral address, actually confirms the feasibility of this project; Vorstius 1638, p. 16.

192. III: Introduction, pp. 157–158.

193. Ibid., pp. 155–156.

194. Ibid., p. 156.

195. I: Introduction, p. 5. The Achaean League is a stock reference point of political theory of the time. Cf., e.g., Grotius, *De Republica Emendanda*, par. 58.

196. I: Introduction, p. 5.

197. For recent studies on this ongoing research, see the articles by Kalman Neuman, Arthur Eyffinger, and Miriam Bodian in *Hebraic Political Studies*, 1.1–2 (2005).

198. Cun., *Ep.* 23. Ahsmann 1990, p. 185, n. 54.

199. III: Introduction, pp. 158–159.

200. Ibid., p. 159.

201. Ibid., p. 157.

202. I.1 and 14 ("a kingdom of priests").

203. See I.1, p. 11.

204. To that extent, Cunaeus is the perfect counterpart to his dear friend Gerard Vossius, a great humanist but schoolmaster *par excellence*.

205. Or to give some other examples: "This is becoming tedious... I really shouldn't be cracking jokes in the midst of such a serious discussion" (p. 204). "But come, let us move on to more important matters" (p. 207). "Nothing would be easier for me than to produce all sorts of arguments to prove my position, but I am trying my best to be brief" (p. 208).

206. Such as in II.24.

207. Cunaeus does not intend to duplicate Sigonio, as he states in his opening greeting (p. 7) and only refers to his predecessor when questioning or rejecting a thesis held by Sigonio.

208. Other examples: "It is not for me to investigate this any further; for even after I have conscientiously given it all my effort, I will still be upset with myself for scratching at the dirt with my feet and yet not digging up so much as a single grain" (p. 85). "But I am not going to get into such fine details, or into all the minor issues that still remain" (p. 132). "I have said more than enough about the Sabbath, and I don't have the patience to discuss the other issues…" (p. 146). "Anything more I must leave to those writers who seek to make their names from disreputable kinds of work" (p. 195). "I would like to leave the realm of the philologists and dwell on things of a more contemplative nature" (p. 212).

209. Again: "But because it seems to me that reason itself argues against the accepted opinion, the truth ought to carry more weight than the authority of a scholar" (p. 171). "If I were not dealing with solid proof, it would certainly have been reckless of me to set out to undermine the consensus of so many learned men and so many generations of scholars; but I will hope for the best" (p. 172). "What impresses me is not the cleverness with which we can invent 'solutions,' but the importance of the questions themselves" (p. 194). Or, again: "I am not ready to let my own gullibility make me look like some sort of impetuous fool" (p. 28).

210. "Law is a sort of mind that has no desires" (p. 13, taken from Aristotle). "But it is a law of fate that no one is ever allowed to remain too long at the top" (p. 115). "The soul of a wise man is a precious and noble thing" (p. 169) "People can easily play the part of a madman; it is even easier than being sane" (p. 202).

211. For a full survey of the successive editions and translations of Cunaeus' tract, the reader is referred to the note at the end of this introduction.

212. A detailed description of the various editions in Ahsmann/Feenstra 1984, pp. 91–96. So far, no critical evaluation of the various editions or stemmata has been produced.

213. Or two different editions? See on this Ahsmann/Feenstra 1984 nos. 151–152 and references.

214. Again presented as the *editio novissima* by its publisher, Gottfried Minzl.

215. Provided by Janssonius and Weyerstraet.

216. "*editio novissima indiceque rerum aucta*" by the Wohlfart press.

217. Published by Teering.

218. "*accessit accuratus capitum ac rerum verborumque index.*"

219. "*variis annotationibus, cuivis literato scitu necessariis et ad Scripturae sensum eruendum utilissimis.*"

PETRUS CUNAEUS was a part of the "Northern Renaissance," the revival of classical literature that by the sixteenth century had spread from the Mediterranean to Germany and Holland. As part of this movement, Dutch classicists tried to integrate Greco-Roman ideas and genres with Christian texts and theology. The late fifteenth-century scholar Erasmus, for example, applied his knowledge of ancient Greek literature and language to improving the quality of New Testament manuscripts. Cunaeus brings the same spirit to questions of political theory and organization: he combines classical and biblical political concepts, and is happy to place the Greeks and Romans alongside the Hebrews as the founders, however flawed, of the European political tradition. So, for example, he praises the founders of Greek colonies for the wisdom with which they distributed land to the settlers. And because he believes in the classical idea that the bedrock of social organization is "natural law," the set of unwritten principles that govern human behavior, he claims that it was only the violation of this law that could have moved God to destroy the generation of the Flood, and to order the Israelites to completely wipe out the inhabitants of Canaan.

Although most of Cunaeus' proof texts are drawn from the Bible and from Maimonides, he does refer constantly to classical aphorisms and witticisms, often quoting them verbatim. On the other hand, though he often praises the scholarship and care with which Jewish texts were written, he thinks that their literary style falls far short of the heights of classical literature, which was the Renaissance ideal for both Latin and vernacular composition. Cunaeus' Latin style is, therefore, deliberately and consistently classical. He models himself very closely on a few Roman authors, Cicero in particular, and his vocabulary almost never ventures beyond the prose of the late Republic and the early Empire (first century BCE through first century CE), so much so that he uses Roman political terminology to describe the offices and institutions of his own day. When he does on occasion use nonclassical Latin, he often prefaces it with phrases such as "so to speak." Cunaeus writes in the long and complex sentences, full of dependent clauses, that are characteristic of Ciceronian prose, and he borrows freely from Cicero's stock of rhetorical expressions. In fact, he often inserts specific turns of phrase from Cicero's speeches.

Cunaeus is also fond of quoting classical aphorisms, and he assumes that his readers are familiar with the works of at least the more famous classical authors, whom he often cites without mentioning them or their works by name. In fact, in some cases his allusions will only make sense if the reader can recognize the context from which they were taken. For example, in the course of criticizing Pliny for accepting a preposterous Jewish claim, Cunaeus quotes a line from Horace, Satires 1.9—"I am a little weaker, one of many" (p. 145)—which is spoken there by a Roman admitting to his friend that he follows Jewish customs; and when Cunaeus tells us that the Jews of his day clasped worn manuscripts of the Torah "as though they were balls of amber" (p. 165), we are meant to understand that they are like the superstitious Roman women of whom Juvenal makes fun in his sixth satire for carrying around astrological charts the way other women carried lumps of amber (a fashion at the time). Though judging by such references Cunaeus had a solid command of Latin literature, he will sometimes misquote or misrepresent his texts, presumably because he was citing them from memory, which was also standard practice in the classical world. Sometimes he will even cite the wrong chapter of the Pentateuch.

Cunaeus usually quotes his sources in their original Greek and Hebrew (the text of which has been included in the footnotes of this edition), sometimes translating them into Latin. The only exception is the Old Testament, which he always translates. This seems odd, considering how much emphasis Cunaeus placed on reading sacred texts in their original languages. Perhaps he wanted to spare even those of his readers who did know some Hebrew the effort of having to work through such tedious passages as the laws of sacrifice, which would also explain why even in the Latin he often summarizes and paraphrases. But even when he does reproduce his sources for us, he treats these texts more casually than a modern scholar might think of doing, leaving out the parts that don't interest him without any indication that he has jumped from one point to another. In such cases he will also adjust the grammar of the text to suit the edited version; and when he inserts a quotation into one of his own sentences, he makes the grammatical changes that Greek and Latin require in cases of indirect speech. Of course, compared to his classical models Cunaeus is actually very conservative in his use of citation—in antiquity it was considered a mark of good style to vary as much as possible the specific wording of the texts one was quoting. Cunaeus himself does this only on occasions when he wants to quote the same text more than once (as he often does with biblical passages). When, for example, he repeats a phrase from a Greek passage of Josephus (*Against Apion* 1.12) that he had quoted two pages before, his two translations of this phrase are very different from each other: the first one reads, *regionem bonam incolantes, hanc cum labore exercemus* ("living in a good region, we cultivate it strenuously," p. 20); the second, *terram fertilem habitamus, atque in cultura eius operam sumimus* ("we inhabit a fertile land, and we put our efforts into its cultivation," p. 21). Since Cunaeus is deliberately using synonyms in order to alter the wording, but not the meaning, of his Latin, we are not meant to infer anything new about the interpretation of the passage in question.

On occasion Cunaeus will also use translations to expand upon or clarify the original text as he thinks necessary. Also on occasion, he will deliberately adjust the translation of a passage to make it suit his own ideas better. For example, when he renders Maimonides' statement that outside the Land of Israel "the priests and the Levites were the same as all the Israelites" as "the situation of the priests and Levites is no worse than that of the other Hebrews" (p. 30), it is because, unlike Maimonides, he believes it was to their disadvantage that they did not own land within the nation. Cunaeus takes the greatest liberties in his discussion of Melchizedek in Book III, where in the course of a painstaking analysis of the language with which Paul describes Melchizedek in chapter 7 of the Letter to the Hebrews, he continually re-translates Paul's prose, adds to it, and merges one phrase with another.

There seems to be only one instance where Cunaeus may have deliberately changed the original wording of a text in order to alter its meaning radically: in a citation from Josephus (*Jewish War* 5.236) which describes how the high priest entered the Holy of Holies on the Day of Atonement (p. 81), Cunaeus changes the form of the word *monos* ("only, sole") so that it refers to the day itself (i.e. it was the only day of the year the priest entered) rather than to the high priest (i.e. on that day, he entered alone). The latter is the standard reading of Josephus' text, including the manuscripts and the printed versions that existed in Cunaeus' time. This difference is significant because in another passage Cunaeus has made a point of insisting that the high priest was the only person *ever* to enter the Holy of Holies, and quoted Maimonides and Philo to that end; and this argument would suffer if Josephus is in fact saying that the priest entered alone only on the Day of Atonement.

Sometimes instead of quoting a text Cunaeus will merely summarize it, in which case he will either introduce it as being "something like" a quote, or simply insert it into his discussion without drawing any kind of distinction between his own ideas and those of his source (again, a common practice in antiquity). On the other hand, like many classical authors he often tries to make his source material seem more extensive and varied than it actually is: even though his discussions of Jewish law draw almost entirely on Maimonides, whom he frequently credits as his source, at other times he attributes these same sources to "Rabbis" and "Talmudists." He does the same thing with his classical sources, referring to various ancient books about Jews that he implies he has read, when in fact he has simply read the fragments of these works preserved in Josephus (which is in fact all that remain of them).

Cunaeus varies his own prose by using more than one term for concepts to which he must frequently refer, the most obvious one being "God," whom he variously calls *deus* and *numen*. In the same way he refers to the ancient Jewish scholars indiscriminately as *Talmudici* and *Rabbini*. Because these different terms do not represent any consistent distinctions, in the first instance I have opted to translate both terms as "God"; and in the second I use "Talmudists" rather than "Rabbis" unless it is clear that Cunaeus is referring specifically to "the Rabbis," i.e. the ancient Jewish authorities as opposed to the commentators of the Middle Ages or his own day. There is, however, a case where he reserves a synonymous term for one specific context: when he wants to show his exasperation or frustration over the Jews of his own time, he calls them *verpi*, a derogatory term from Roman satire used to make fun of the Jews for being circumcised. In order to give something of the sense of this term in translation, I have rendered it with the modern slur "yid" (pp. 51, 179, 194, 204).

In another case it is a peculiarity of Latin that makes Cunaeus somewhat ambiguous in translation: he uses the term *Judaeus*—which can mean either "Judean" (i.e. an inhabitant of the biblical tribe of Judah or the Roman province of Judea) or "Jew"—in both of its senses. Cunaeus was certainly aware of the differences between the Judeans of the Bible and the Jews of the post-biblical age and of his own time; but for all the distaste and frustration with which he writes about modern Jews, he still sees them as the direct descendants of the heroes of the Bible, and it was ultimately their failure to achieve their potential (a failure for which he thought Christians shared the blame) that bothered him most. Since, however, both the English language and modern historiography do draw a consistent distinction between Judeans and Jews, I have tried to translate *Judaeus* according to context. Another difficult term to translate is *sceptrum*, which literally means "scepter." This is Cunaeus' translation of the Hebrew term *shevet* in his discussion of Jacob's prophecy at Genesis 49:10 ("The scepter shall not depart from Judah, nor the ruler's staff from between his feet," cf. p. 35). Since, as it happens, both Latin and Hebrew use "scepter" to mean "authority" or "sovereignty," it is not always clear when Cunaeus is referring to the actual symbol of the scepter, and when to the political power it represents.

Cunaeus' treatment of his Jewish sources strongly implies that he had some kind of intellectual contact with the Jews of his day.* As Dr. Eyffinger points out in his introduction to this volume, Cunaeus had studied Aramaic and what he calls "Rabbinism" with Johannes Drusius, one of the great Orientalists of his day. But it seems that he (or his teachers) would also have needed to be familiar with traditional Jewish learning in order to make any sense of Rabbi Joseph Caro's commentary on the *Mishneh Torah*, to which Cunaeus frequently refers: like all post-Talmudic scholarship it uses a mixture of Hebrew and Aramaic terminology and abbreviations that would have been completely unfamiliar to anyone educated in an entirely non-Jewish environment. For that matter, dependent as Cunaeus was on Maimonides, he nevertheless seems to have known about some more recent works which—though totally obscure today—were read by the Spanish exile community of his time.** It also tells us something about Cunaeus' education that when he transliterates Hebrew terms into Latin, he spells them according to the pronunciation used by Spanish-speaking Jews. And yet as a rule he makes use of Rabbi Caro's commentary, which analyzed Maimonides in detail, only to the extent that he points out the Talmudic sources of discussions in the *Mishneh Torah*; and even then Cunaeus' references to this commentary (and sometimes to the *Mishneh Torah* itself) contain some elementary mistakes that show just how limited his grasp of post-biblical Jewish texts could be. It is not surprising then that, as Dr. Eyffinger writes, the Hebraists of Cunaeus' time regarded Maimonides as a difficult author to read, despite the fact that within the Jewish world he has always been considered a model of clarity; but then it may have been precisely his use of Rabbinic concepts and terms, so familiar to Jewish readers, that gave the Hebraists such trouble.

The gaps in Cunaeus' Rabbinic education may, on the other hand, explain just why he found Maimonides (whom he always praises to the skies) so appealing: not only was his Hebrew so clear and concise that it did not require a great deal of help to read; but the content of the *Mishneh Torah* is much more self-contained than that of other rabbinic works. It can be read on its own, and unlike other post-Talmudic books it quotes only from the Bible. While this is precisely what made it so controversial among Maimonides'

---

* Previous scholarship has suggested that Cunaeus did not have any such contact with Jews. See Aaron Katchen, *Christian Hebraists and Dutch Rabbis* (Cambridge, Mass. and London: Harvard University Press, 1984), pp. 37–55.

** See, for instance, Cunaeus' reference to *Michlal Yofi* on p. 160 of this edition.

Jewish contemporaries, and why later commentators like Caro felt the need to expand upon it, Maimonides' silence on the Talmudic sources makes him the only Jewish authority palatable to Cunaeus, who often tells us how much he dislikes traditional Jewish scholarship. The reason is that he sees it as the triumph of casuistry over clarity of thought, and believes that any Old Testament passages whose simple meaning evades us must be understood with the help of the divine inspiration granted to the Church rather than the interpretive traditions of the Rabbis.

Although Cunaeus' style is strictly classical, this does not mean that it is consistently lofty or grandiose. Like Cicero in his speeches and letters, Cunaeus is often pungent, pithy, and humorous; and I have tried to bring this across in translation. This is why the reader is sometimes addressed directly in the second person, just as he is in the Latin. And where Cunaeus uses colorful turns of phrase, I have tried to find comparable expressions in English.

In his introduction to Book III, Cunaeus tells us that he has always tried to be generous about the mistakes of others, and adds: "I can only hope that I am treated as fairly by those who may one day demolish my own observations; in fact, I will regard such treatment as appropriate and admirable" (p. 157). Whatever mistakes we ourselves may find in his work, we should also recognize and apply to Cunaeus the same generosity of spirit with which he approached the scholars who came before him.

Peter Wyetzner
Jerusalem, Israel

CHRONOLOGY

1586   Petrus Cunaeus born in Flushing, Zeeland.

1601   Enrolls at Leiden University. Begins to study Greek and Latin with his cousin, Ambrosius Regemorterus.

1602   Regemorterus and Cunaeus travel together to England. Cunaeus returns to Holland to study with Scaliger and Daniel Heinsius and becomes acquainted with Grotius.

1606–1608   Goes to Franeker to study Hebrew with Drusius.

1610   Publishes a critical commentary on Nonnus' *Dionysiaca*.

1612   Appointed to the chair of Latin at Leiden. Publishes a satire, entitled *Sardi Venales*, attacking the Leiden academic environment.

1613   Appointed professor of politics at Leiden.

1614   Acquires the 1574 Venice edition of *Mishneh Torah*.

1615–1616   Goes on leave from Leiden to study law, during which time he studies *Mishneh Torah*. Appointed professor of law at Leiden.

1617   Cunaeus' *Hebrew Republic* published for the first time in Leiden by Elzevir.

1618   Synod of Dort.

1638   Cunaeus dies.

1653   Barksdale's English translation of Book I appears.

1683   First Dutch edition appears.

1705   First French edition appears.

THE HEBREW REPUBLIC

PREFACE

To the Illustrious and Mighty States of Holland and Western Frisia

FOR YOUR INSPECTION, most illustrious Members of States, I offer a republic—the holiest ever to have existed in the world, and the richest in examples for us to emulate. It is entirely in your interest to study closely this republic's origins and growth, because its creator and founder was not some man sprung from mortal matter, but immortal God Himself—He whose worship, and whose pure service, you have adopted and now protect. You will see what it was, in the end, that preserved the Hebrew citizens for so long in an almost innocent way of life, stirring up their courage, nurturing their harmonious coexistence, and reining in their selfish desires.

There is no doubt that the kinds of rules by which this people governed its republic were more effective than the precepts created by any of the wise men.[1] I have shown that a great many of these rules can be unearthed from the sacred books; it is only their military knowledge of which nothing at all was passed down to the memory of later generations. But as anyone who pays careful attention to the victories and accomplishments of the Hebrews will admit, every one of them was extremely skilled in the arts of war. For after they had left behind the land of Egypt (where they lived for a very long time); and made a long and unplanned journey; and were kept wandering for forty years in the vast deserts of Arabia, they then went on to expel a number of very strong and hostile peoples, and successfully invaded that country where they consecrated their towns and their Temple. Here on this fortunate soil they were incredibly fruitful, because they were able to cooperate with one another. They met as a group to plan for the welfare of all. And though there were many communities, they did not try to set up their own individual fiefdoms; rather they defended with great passion the people's liberty. In order to establish a good and efficient government that would lack nothing, they all shared the same laws, magistrates, senators, and judges, as well as the same weights, measures, and currency. In fact, there was only one thing that kept virtually all of Palestine from coming to be considered one unified city: that its inhabitants were not all enclosed within the same walls. In other respects, both the country as a whole and its various cities were similar and even identical to one another.

Among the towns, however, there was one city in particular which, by force of law, demanded more respect and reverence than all the others. Not, Heaven forbid, so that it might dominate the other cities, but so that people from all over the country (who lived far apart from one another) could gather three times a year for communal rituals and sacred ceremonies. So not only did this city fail to disrupt the harmony of the various communities, it actually bound them more tightly together. The twelve Israelite tribes lived in an extremely fertile area, and because of their amazing fruitfulness they each grew to be the size of a nation. They were in no danger from the power of their enemies, the storms of war, and other evils of that sort. They always emerged from disaster stronger than before, and through defeat and destruction they drew their courage and strength from the very sword that attacked them.

The Republic of the Hebrews remained like this for a very long time, until finally after the death of Solomon—when the high point of its happiness had been reached—its fortunes began to turn in a very different direction. A certain Jeroboam, whose hopes and strength lay entirely in civil conflict, stirred up the people in treasonous assemblies, and when he had drawn to himself ten entire tribes he set up a kind of separate state for himself, whose citadel and capital was Samaria. So there was no longer one republic but two. One of these, which was called Israelite, or the Ten Tribes, lasted only a short time, for the entire nation was soon defeated in war, and followed its conqueror into permanent exile. But the other republic—that of the Judeans, whose seat of government was at Jerusalem—was not completely destroyed until the time of Vespasian Caesar, though its power had been reduced to the point that in almost every conflict it was no match for its enemies. Of course, none of this could have happened if this people, which had conquered so many nations and lands in the past when its power was united, had not been split into opposing camps. It is civil conflict, illustrious Members of States, which presents our enemies with their greatest opportunity. The government of the Hebrews, then, was thoroughly ruined by the very same thing that has destroyed even the most flourishing regimes of other countries.

Review in your minds the history of all the ages, and you will find that it was for this reason that practically all the illustrious nations disappeared. Only rarely does fortune turn its ill will toward one people in order to destroy another, unless that people's domestic troubles have already left it unable to control its own vices and its own power. Certainly the Romans, who were the most clever of men, and of whom Marcus Tullius² says quite rightly that *they became the masters of the entire world in the course of defending their al-lies*, understood perfectly well that the best thing God could do to help them overthrow other states was to disrupt and divide peoples who were joined by treaty. For so it was that the Romans, in the course of giving help to people in trouble or settling local disputes, came to dominate them completely; and *where they had made a desert, they called it peace.*[3]

At one time, everyone feared the Achaeans because the states of the Pelo-ponnese[4] had entered their League, which was based on inviolable laws, the principles of justice, and equality of rights among the member states. And their state was really quite similar to your own, illustrious Members of States, in that it was by far the best: it was rock solid and undisturbed because it trusted in its unity and was supported by its own strength. How many times did the Roman People (who were the masters of the world) try to break up that unity with skill and deceit, because they knew that Greece would be impregnable as long as the Achaean League was left standing?[5] This was the task they gave to the proconsul Gallus; and when it did not succeed, they used a cunning plan. They had the Spartans join the League, but on unequal terms, so that they would always be a source of conflict and argument with the other members. Certainly this was the very thing that brought about the destruction of the Achaeans many years later.

I could mention other examples of this sort—the history books are full of them—but this is not the place for a long recitation. Rome herself, "the goddess of lands and nations" (which Mithridates[6] used to say was founded to plague the entire world), fell apart when her citizens turned on each other and her leaders broke into factions; she grew weary, gave up her freedom, and accepted a tyrant. But since my real topic is the Hebrews, I must save for last what is at the heart of the matter. To wit: the battle of wills and pas-sions that split the holy people into two after Solomon's death could have been resolved, as so often happens, at the very moment it took place, and the people's health could have been restored. But Jeroboam, a man who was thoroughly versed in the shameful crimes men use to dominate each other, and who had been responsible for the secession, made use of a technique which guaranteed that the Twelve Tribes would never reconcile: he cor-rupted the true religion with an empty superstition. So once he had used his glib tongue to foist his fictions on a gullible and apathetic people, what had been a fight about freedom and power came to be about sacred rituals and places of worship.[7]

In my book, illustrious Members of States, I have examined these ques-tions and many more of the same type, and I thought it was quite a worth-while effort to have it published. It is you yourselves, sacred fathers of your country, who are always mindful that *harmony makes small things grow large, and disharmony makes great ones collapse*. The outcome of events has proven the truth of this: through God's grace and your own virtue, and through the auspices of your invincible leader, your republic has grown by leaps and bounds until it has reached such heights that your enemies can complain about nothing but your greatness. I humbly beseech God Almighty, who protects and defends this republic, that the union and harmony that have given you such great success should last forever.

In fact, when I think about your discretion and wisdom, which have always been evident in the way you conduct matters of importance, I have complete confidence that the future will turn out as all good men would wish. And yet, no one today can boast that he has been born into such fortunate times that he does not need to turn his thoughts now and again to the examples set by previous generations. Many of your citizens have already split off into factions of one sort or another, and they have been fighting over these differences of opinion ever since they entered into a pointless conflict over obscure issues of religious doctrine which most of them do not even understand. Then the mob follows its own passions in one direction or another, and every day more and more people are caught up. Since you, illustrious Members of States, are now devoting all your energies to the matter, you must understand that it is in your interest to apply a timely remedy to this problem, before your country, which is flourishing now, is damaged by the kinds of internal evils that have been and will be more destructive to so many nations than foreign wars, famine, disease, and all the other evils that beset the world like so many plagues. But it would be beside the point for me to say anything more about this. There is no way that I could come up with anything so profound that you would not readily think of it yourselves. I ask you, illustrious Members of States, to study over and again the Hebrew Republic—the holiest and best of all—which I have described in this book. It contains ideas that kings, leaders, and the administrators of republics may adopt for their own use. In fact, I was all the more eager to present this information to you because I reasoned that the members of your Senate are the best of the age, and are so learned that they would be able to judge for certain whether anything I have written here might shed some light on antiquity, and on the works of its noble authors.

GREETINGS TO MY KIND READERS

THE ORATOR ALBUTIUS was once taken to task because in every trial he argued he wanted to say not what *should be said, but what could be said*. I will leave it to the judgment of others whether I have discussed what I ought to. But I am sure, and I do not blush to admit it, that I have left out a great deal of what I might have said. In fact, because two very learned men—Carlo Sigonio and Cornelius Bertram—have dealt at length with this subject, I did not want to go over the same ground or to indulge in a tiresome repetition of things they have already said. So in my book I have touched on some other points that have to do with the government of this republic. In addition, after weeding out the information already published by Sigonio and Bertram, I collected in a very loose composition all the material which I could readily get from other books. There was actually a lot of this, and it seemed well worth preserving. Besides, a good deal of it had already been collected for me by Rabbi Moses ben Maimon the Egyptian [Maimonides], whose diligence and wisdom outstrip all the praises he has received. A copy of this brilliant author was passed on to me by a very important man— Johannes Boreel, who is the confidential secretary of the States of Zeeland. But however much I may have enjoyed examining the work of this great rabbi, I owe whatever was pleasant about this experience to the refinement of the man from whom I learned about this exceptional Jewish scholar. There is no one I know these days who is a stauncher defender of Hebrew studies than Boreel; he has also collected from the East a trove of books that have rarely if ever been seen in our part of the world. You who have a passion for such things, be sure to cherish this man's unparalleled erudition and his readiness to adorn the world of letters; and expect unique and brilliant work to emerge one day from his rich library.

Μωσῆς οὐ μέρος τῆς ἀρετῆς ἐποίησε τὴν εὐσέβειαν, ἀλλὰ ταύτης τὰ μέρη τἆλλα συνεῖδε καὶ κατέστησεν. λέγω δὲ τὴν δικαιοσύνην, καρτερίαν, σωφροσύνην, τὴν τῶν πολιτῶν πρὸς ἀλλήλους ἐν ἅπασι συμφωνίαν. ἅπασι γὰρ αἱ πράξεις, καὶ διατριβαὶ, καὶ λόγοι πάντες, ἐπὶ τὴν πρὸς θεὸν ἡμῖν εὐσέβειαν ἔχουσι τὴν ἀναφοράν.

Moses did not make religion a part of virtue, but he saw and he ordained other virtues to be parts of religion; I mean justice, and fortitude, and temperance, and a universal agreement of the members of the community with one another; for all our actions and studies, and all our words, have to do with our piety towards God.

—Flavius Josephus, *Against Apion* Book II, 17

BOOK I

CHAPTER 1

On the institutions of the Hebrew Republic. On legislation.
The empty boasts of the Greeks. Who was the first to make written
law. The seven precepts given to the sons of Noah. What Moses
had in mind in establishing and naming the Republic, and
in passing laws.

IN THIS BOOK, I do not intend to be overly selective or do a painstaking survey. I would rather gather my ideas from here and there as I encounter them, and follow up one thing after another in the order in which these occur to me. The Republic of the Hebrews was founded by Moses, a divine and excellent man who first began the most glorious undertaking the world has ever known. That, at least, is how I see it. Though many people have performed many exceptional acts which were once regarded as the greatest ever accomplished, far more noble still were the efforts of those who dictated rights and laws for those groupings and assemblages of men called states. Nothing is more welcome to Almighty God, who rules this world; but since this pursuit is a source of exceptional glory, many nations have in times past claimed it for themselves.

Certainly the Greeks, when they arrogantly tally up the benefits they have bestowed on all the nations of the world, place their legislation at the head of the list. For they mention Lycurguses, Dracos, Solons, Zaleuces of Locri, and names older than these if they can find them.[8] But all their boasting is pointless, for Flavius Josephus the Jew has made this overblown nation swallow its pride. He wrote an extraordinarily learned apology (which still survives today) against Apion, a man who—though he was hostile to the Jews—deserved even so to be referred to and regarded as "the cymbal of the world" because he was so well-known and lived surrounded by the acclaim of all his teaching. In this book Flavius proves that the Greek lawgivers are, when compared with Moses, scarcely ancient at all, and seem to have been born yesterday or the day before. For as he says, in the time of Homer, father of the Greeklings,[9] the concept of law was unknown, and it does not appear anywhere in his poetry. There were (he says) only some commonly used sayings and brief aphorisms that were used to govern the masses; or, if the need presented itself, rulers would add their own orders and prohibitions, though these were not committed to writing.[10]

The truth is that since Moses, as Flavius correctly notes, preceded Homer by many centuries, he earned for himself the sort of special acclaim that so many later leaders would come to covet; for he was the first to write and publish laws so that the people might learn what was right and what was wrong, and which sanctions might steady the state Almighty God had ordered to be set up in Palestine.[11] Before the time of Moses the world knew nothing of written law. Although the human race had certainly not managed until then without any laws at all, what laws they did have were not preserved on public tablets or on any sort of monument. There were seven precepts of this sort, which the Talmudists[12] say were given to the sons of Noah. Because they included certain rules of equity without which human life could not exist, they were of such broad significance that the Israelites were commanded to kill in battle and to remove from the community of men anyone who did not acknowledge them. And this was perfectly justified—people who had accepted no law were generally regarded as more dangerous than beasts. At any rate, injustice (as Aristotle was inspired to say) is at its worst and most savage when it has been furnished with arms.[13] The arms, moreover, with which nature has provided man—reason and judgment—make him admirably suited to wreaking havoc, once you take law out of the equation.

But let us discuss the arrangements of Moses. Because he wanted to found a republic that would be the most sacred in the world, he handed supreme authority over to God. And though others may apply different names to their states as needed—calling them at various times monarchy, oligarchy, and democracy[14]—Moses understood that none of these would do justice to the natural character of such a wonderful form of government. He therefore established a certain form of rule that Flavius very pointedly says can be called *theocracy* (as one might call the sort of state whose chief and ruler is God alone). For Moses claimed that nothing took place without God's judgment and approval; and that this was so, he proved by his own clear example: although he saw that everything depended on him alone, and that through his speeches he was winning over every last one of the people, he did not seek to exploit such a wonderful opportunity in order to gain power, wealth, or honors for himself. Indeed, his behavior hardly seems human at all—a certain desire for power is normal among mortal men, and Lord knows it is very ancient and burns more fiercely than all the other emotions. As I see it, Moses could not have driven this desire from his heart if he had not seen that God was a part of—and in charge of—all that was taking place, and that it would be utter madness to enter into a joint reign with Him.

Furthermore, in order to strengthen the Republic Moses decreed that everything should be done according to laws, and he wanted his magistrates to be not the masters of the laws, but their guardians and servants. He designed these laws with the greatest integrity, for while even the best of men are sometimes led astray by anger or love, it is the laws alone that speak with everyone and at all times in one and the same voice. And this is what I believe Aristotle meant when he said, rather neatly, that *law is a sort of mind that has no desires.*[15] We should also mention the most important thing of all, i.e. the permanent stability of the laws: to add or take away anything from them was a sin that required expiation.[16] Old laws were not abolished and new ones were not passed; in fact, everyone was strictly required to keep them, even when the Republic was doing poorly. This was clearly not the case in other states. Though they were founded by laws, they were also overturned by them, for many of their rulers altered even decent laws in order to appear to have added something of their own, while many prohibitions disappeared because of disuse and even more out of contempt (which is worse), and in the process vices were made more secure.

But I have never been surprised that states could have such different fates. The laws of other nations, which are the product of human ingenuity, are protected only by the severity of their penalties; and these often fade over time, or because they are neglected by the authorities. But the laws observed by the Jews are the ordinances of the eternal God, and they are not diminished by the passage of time or rewritten as easily as the judges make new statutes. They persist and they remain the same, and even when people are no longer frightened by axes and rods,[17] religion can still scare them.

CHAPTER 2

Hecataeus' unique book about Judea. The lawgiver's wise plan for the distribution of lands. That they should not belong to the people who seize them. On the agrarian law, and its boundless utility. The redemption of lands. The benefits of the Jubilee. The restitution of lands at no cost. Certain further rulings of the Talmudic law on this matter. On Maimonides, and his most brilliant insights. What the occasion of the Jubilee did for slaves. The slaves wore crowns for nine days. A certain likeness to the Saturnalia.

FLAVIUS JOSEPHUS often quotes Hecataeus of Abdera, a very trustworthy and upright man who had at one time accompanied Alexander the Great on his expeditions and campaigns. Though he had visited many countries blessed with all kinds of abundance, he admired Palestine more than any other place. He therefore wrote a unique book about it, from which Flavius quotes many things on behalf of the Jews.[18] Hecataeus' book pertains to our discussion because he says that the Jews inhabited the best and most fruitful of regions, which is three million *arourae* [about two million acres] in size; so it was obviously the place most suited to the Hebrews, and it was through God's kindness that they were brought there from Egypt. In the past they had always lived by agriculture and pasturage, and now that they were on fertile soil they could use these skills to become exceptionally rich and to live well.

When, in the beginning, the holy people had taken Palestine (which had been promised to them long before) by force of arms, Joshua the supreme commander immediately put Moses' instructions into practice. He therefore divided the entire region into twelve sections, on each of which he permitted one of the tribes to settle. He then counted up the families within each tribe, gave each family a set measure of land appropriate to the number of its members, and fixed its boundaries accordingly. In this way he saw to it that everyone would be treated with an equal measure of fairness. This is generally the chief concern of those who govern republics well; in later times, the Greeks and the Romans (the wisest of men) did the same thing when they founded colonies. If on those occasions every settler who first came to an unoccupied territory had seized whatever land he wanted, there would inevitably have been a great deal of fighting and rioting among the citizens; for if a commodity is of the sort that can be turned from public to private ownership, it often leads to such contention that it makes it extremely difficult to preserve the sacred bonds of fellowship.

Since, furthermore, it is the task of the wise man not only to set things in order for the present but to make decisions that will profit future generations, Moses passed an excellent law which saw to it that the wealth of a few men would never crush everyone else, and that the citizens would not change their occupations or turn from innocent labor to new and foreign trades. This was the agrarian law, which prohibited anyone from transferring the full ownership of his property to someone else whether by sale or by any sort of contract. For the right to redeem one's property restored at any time the land even of those who had been forced by poverty to sell it. The law also stated that if the land were not redeemed, it would be returned free to the owner on the occasion of the Jubilee.[19]

There is an excellent author, esteemed by the world, named Rabbi Moses ben Maimon; he successfully collected the Talmud's teachings—and left out its trifles—in that divine work he calls *Mishneh Torah*. I could never say anything so grand about this author that his virtues would not outshine it. For he was, by some quirk of fate, the first and only member of his nation who correctly understood what it is not to say anything foolish. In this book I will often call on him to testify, as he is the most distinguished of witnesses; and even here, in the very matter that I am now discussing, his expertise will be very useful. He has passed on to us a great deal of information about the benefits of the Jubilee, and he says that one of its provisions was that every field should return to its former owners even if it has changed hands a hundred times.[20] Nor does our most learned author exempt those lands which were accepted as a gift: he says that they cannot be kept from their owners.[21] This is also the rule of the Talmud, and it seems to be very just. This rabbi reports another provision of the same law: that the redemption of land was allowed only to those who had been enriched by a chance profit or loan.[22] The reason for this is obvious; for surely those who were borrowing money for the purpose of redeeming their land, or selling one field so that they could redeem another, were perpetrating a fraud against God's law. They and their heirs were supposed to wait for the Jubilee, which would rescind sales of this sort. And yet a poor landowner's countrymen and kinsmen could, in the meantime, retrieve with their own money those properties that he himself could not redeem without borrowing.

The rites of the Jubilee returned every fiftieth year, which began in the seventh month, Tishri. No other occasion was cause for such general rejoicing: not only were those who had given up their property put back on a solid footing, but all the slaves were freed. But none of this could happen until the tenth of the month, which was reserved as a day of fasting and atonement. In the meanwhile, there were nine whole days of public festivities like those of the Saturnalia.[23] About these, Rabbi Maimonides reports information that I believe is worth knowing. He says in the Laws of the Sabbatical Year and the Jubilee: *From the first of the year until the Day of Atonement the slaves were not dismissed, nor did they serve their masters; but neither were the fields restored. So what did happen? The slaves ate, and drank, and rejoiced, and each put a crown on his head. Then, when the Day of Atonement arrived, the senators of the Sanhedrin sounded horns, and the slaves went off on the spot as free men, and the lands were restored to their owners.*[24]

CHAPTER 3

More about the twofold reason for the agrarian law. How social upheavals are often caused by large estates. On the Roman Republic. The law of Stolo. By what methods the ancient Hebrews sustained themselves. How carefully the lawgiver saw to it that they would not be abandoned. Divine laws about farming and cattle breeding.

BUT COME LET ME DESCRIBE the usefulness of the agrarian law, which I said Moses had set forth. I have of course mentioned the first of two reasons for the law: it was in the best interests of the Republic that the greed of a few men could not disrupt the arrangement of properties that had been so well assigned and distributed, for the wealthier man usually drives the poorer one off his property, and as he makes great inroads into lands for which he has no use, he cuts other men off from their basic necessities. This is why changes of regime tend to occur from time to time—there is no question that a state in which most of the citizens have been stripped of their ancestral property, and so hope and pray that their fortunes will be reversed, is full of its own enemies. Because they hate their current circumstances, these men are eager for any kind of change; and they tolerate this unpleasant state of affairs only as long as necessary.

At Rome, in fact, when the most powerful aristocrats were buying up everything, almost to the point that a single man might own the land of three hundred citizens, Stolo passed a law barring anyone from owning more than five hundred *jugera* [about five-eighths of an acre] of land.[25] But the rule of law was immediately flouted by acts of deceit. Stolo himself was the first to violate his own provisions: he was found guilty of owning a thousand *jugera* together with his son, whom he had declared legally independent for this purpose.[26] Later on, many citizens became well versed in various techniques for getting around the intent of the law; they sent others in their place to buy the land, even though they themselves were the owners. Gaius Laelius—a man of remarkable wisdom and a great friend of Scipio Africanus[27]—was aware of these violations and tried to shore up the law. But he proved unequal to his opponents, and when his efforts led to conflict and discord he abandoned them. So people went on doing as they pleased, and there was no limit to the size of their possessions. Eventually it got to the point that a few men were holding all of Italy and the neighboring provinces as though these lands were their personal inheritance. There is no need for me to review here the evidence for this matter; a great deal of it has been preserved in many books.

The other reason for the agrarian law, on which I have already touched, was that the great Moses did not want the citizens' character to grow soft or their virtue to backslide. After all, the most illustrious of their ancestors had led a pastoral life and busied themselves with all sorts of agricultural work, so there was one safeguard and one provision against every sort of sin and misfortune: that their descendants should not someday desert these same pursuits. (These, after all, make human beings much richer, and their beginnings go back to those of the world itself.) Needless to say, those pursuits would have been all too quickly abandoned and forgotten if the law had allowed everyone to buy up everything and merge one field with another. For the usual consequence of this sort of behavior is that those who own endless numbers of pastures and huge estates hate to take on the tasks of honest labor, and hand them over to others; and it usually happens that the people they hire to do this work are foreigners and humble serfs, or slaves bought with money. Then the common citizens, who are unused to farming other people's land, retreat from the fields to the city so that they can take advantage of urban life. There they devote themselves to leisure, and are corrupted; and they lead a lazy life dedicated to soft and undignified pursuits.

The truth is that once the Roman nobles (who were a small minority) had appropriated the lands of most of the citizens, those citizens—and free men in general—became completely unfamiliar with the ways of farming. For fields that had seen the families of Curius, Fabricius, and Cato[28] were now being plowed by men in chains, and everywhere there was the sound of shackled feet. Marcus Terentius Varro[29] complains that the brave descendants of Romulus *no longer use their hands in the fields and vineyards, but rather in the theater and the circus. For those who once divided up the year in such a way that they would visit the city only every ninth day and the rest of the time would look after the farm have put aside the scythe and the plough.*[30] This is how the practices of their ancestors were abandoned, but as long as they had continued to observe them they reaped two benefits: their fields were more fertile, and their spirits braver, than anyone else's.

Moses was a man more skilled than any other in matters both divine and human; and when he framed the laws of land redemption, and beyond these the rights of the Jubilee, his wise actions prevented the great evils that (like a kind of plague) can assault a state when it forgets how to farm. And these laws did not have even a trace of unfairness, or allow the purchasers of land to suffer any sort of disadvantage; for whenever property was sold the calculation of the Jubilee was taken into account, and its value was proportionally increased or lessened according to whether the Jubilee was going to occur sooner or later. This is what it says in Leviticus (25:14–17): *When you have sold something to your neighbor or you have bought something from your neighbor, do not cheat one another. Buy from your neighbor according to the number of years from the Jubilee, and according to the number of years in which the fruit will come forth shall he sell to you. Increase the price of the sale according to how many years there are, and diminish the price of the sale according to how few there are. For he is selling you a number of harvests. Do not, therefore, deceive one another.*

But if in fact the owner should want to redeem his property *before* the Jubilee, the law likewise established (with the greatest fairness) that he could reduce the price he had to pay for it to reflect any profits the buyer had collected from its produce. The obvious result of these measures was that no one ever felt he was taking a loss in the course of restoring his property, and it was very difficult for the citizens to lose their familiarity with traditional practices and honorable forms of labor. There is, at least, no doubt for which people Moses prescribed his teachings and institutions, and what sort of people they were, for although many of the laws he passed concern ceremonies and rituals, and the rules of what is just and unjust, all the rest are interested in nothing but farming; they have to do with the abundance of resources, and with wealth, and with the kinds of work through which profits are made. How carefully in the Pentateuch are the people taught when to let the land rest, and when to leave off the sowing; which rituals they should perform for the wheat harvests, and which for the grape harvests; and in which year it is permitted to take the fruit from the vine! Moreover, how strictly are they forbidden to plant different kinds of seeds in the same field, and then to mix animals of different species or place them under the same yoke! The other laws about cattle breeding, the first fruits, and the tithe are almost too many to count. They are dealt with at great length in the Talmud, where they make up a sixth or more of the whole.[31] In addition, Rabbi Maimonides included all of them in that book he calls "Seeds" [one of the sections of the *Mishneh Torah*], which contains the amazing secrets of mysterious things.

CHAPTER 4

*Into what distress the seventh year forced the Jews. The favor
granted by Alexander the Great because of a certain prophecy. The
Jews' once infrequent contacts with foreign nations. How ignorant
of Jewish matters were the Greeks. Aristotle's comment about the
wise Callani of India. How changes occur in the lifestyle and
behavior of the citizens. Who the best citizens are. That the Jews
were known for not having craftsmen, and that this was meant
as praise. On workmen.*

SUCH WERE THE LAWS and statutes given to the Hebrews. All of their
property and wealth lay in farming, whose success determined whether they
prospered or went hungry. I have the strongest possible proof of this: that
whenever foreign kings demanded money from them, their resources were so
severely strained in the seventh year that they could barely afford to pay it; for
a provision of the law kept them from cultivating the land during that time
and from collecting its produce, which was the entire basis of the economy.
When Alexander the Macedonian had learned in Jerusalem from the Book of
Daniel that the Persian Empire would one day be destroyed by a Greek, he
rejoiced at the prophecy (which he assumed applied to himself) and he told
the Jews to ask him for a great favor. They explained to him that the greatest
gift he could give them would be to release them from paying tribute in the
seventh year; and this they were granted. He then denied this same privilege
to the Samaritans, though they petitioned him many times.[32]

But of all the arguments that we could bring to bear on this subject, none
sheds more light than Josephus' answer to Apion on behalf of his countrymen: *The land we inhabit is not near the sea; nor do we like to conduct business, or to that end cultivate our relations with other peoples. Our cities are
on the contrary far from the sea, and since we live on good land we cultivate
it with care.*[33] It is certainly true that the practice of trade drew the various
nations so close together that once something new appeared in any of them,
it seemed to have sprung up among them all; only the Jews, living in their
own land, and content with the wealth that nature produced there, led a life

free of commerce. They did not cross the sea, nor did they visit foreigners or receive them.

As a result the Greeks and other writers have reported many lies about them, for very few people knew about their affairs. Only Hecataeus wrote what he had learned firsthand about the Jews; the others reported in their writings whatever they had picked up through rumor and hearsay. Just how dangerous this is for a writer of history we can learn, for instance, from the fact that Ephorus (who was once an author of great renown) said that Iberia, which he had never seen, was a single city, which, Lord knows, was the silliest thing he could have said.[34] For it was not a city but a large part of the West, and was inhabited by many peoples. It is an astonishing thing, and one that depends upon a magnificent degree of ignorance, that Aristotle could claim (according to Clearchus) that the Jews were the offspring of the wise men of India but had changed their name. Indeed, he says that the philosophers whom the Indians call Callani are called Jews in Coele-Syria.[35] I am ashamed of this old wives' tale which is completely without value. But Aristotle adds something else besides, which does seem to be trustworthy and is an especially glorious thing to say about the sacred people: that when he was in Asia a certain Jew had come to him, a man of such great wisdom and learning that by comparison all the Greeks who were with him there seemed like bumps on a log.[36] This is certainly a much more valuable statement than his reckless remarks about the origins of the nation. That was a subject he ought not to have brought up at all, seeing as a foreigner would have known nothing about it. In fact, it seems to me that Flavius is actually expressing his pride in the Jews' obscurity when he says that all the areas they inhabit are inland, and that they are cut off from traders and travelers, for this was how they kept their way of life uncorrupted for so many years, and nothing that had to do with wealth or luxury—things that usually lead to the downfall of even the most powerful peoples—could find its way in. Indeed, the rest of Flavius' remarks are such that you might say he is deeply proud that *we live in a fertile land and we occupy ourselves with its cultivation*,[37] as though nothing could be better or more important.

Aristotle records certain edicts that were published by the earliest legislators, and are very much like those of Moses. For Oxylus, the king of the Eleans, made it against the law to borrow money against one's estates or fields,[38] while the inhabitants of Locri were forbidden to sell their ancestral property.[39] Our greatest authority on the laws of nature says the reason for these measures is that the people should not abandon agriculture. This is why he repeats so often in his *Politics* that the best state is one whose citizens live off of agriculture and pasturage. His reasoning is that *such states govern themselves and their affairs according to laws; for they have by their own efforts as much as they need to live on, and yet they have no time to be idle.*[40] He considers other states, which contain a great many workmen and engineers, to be markedly inferior because such men live low and idle lives, and their work has nothing to do with virtue. So we can understand that the criticism commonly made (according to Flavius) against the Jews—that *no member of that nation produced anything new, or any craft*[41]—was an empty and sterile one. It is, in fact, a great compliment rather than a criticism; for how can it be a noble act to invent things that are of no use to respectable citizens? At any rate, all laborers work at filthy jobs, and Aristotle quite properly says that theirs is a kind of slavery,[42] though it is slavery of a limited sort, because we use their hands and the sweat of their brows not, as in the case of slaves, to do everything, but to perform one particular task. Not only is there nothing dignified about a workshop, it is positively evil, because it makes a man's mind and body effeminate. The republics of the past were therefore quite right to decide (as our wise master says) that workmen could not be granted citizenship but would remain outsiders, and were so to speak a body kept in quarantine from the other classes.[43]

CHAPTER 5

The Egyptians' hatred of the Hebrews, and its real reasons. The Egyptians were devoted to ignoble trades and concerns. With what cleverness Sesostris emasculated the vitality of his citizens. The Egyptian law that the occupations of workmen were to be passed down to their heirs. On the commoners of the Nile, who were slaves. On the priests. On the shepherds, who were a third of the Egyptians, and how the other Egyptians were always in fear of them. That the Egyptians' superstitions had nothing to do with their hatred of the shepherd class, and that this is an error in judgment. That the Egyptian commoners did not despise farmers as they did shepherds, and the reason for this.

I TURN MY ATTENTION to a matter that we can now dispose of quite easily: why the Jews were always hated by the Egyptians not only when they were living in Egypt as foreigners, but even afterwards when they had their own community and their own republic in nearby Palestine, the land that (according to Cornelius Tacitus)[44] borders on southern Egypt. The fact is that this hatred stemmed entirely from the differences between the two peoples' ways of life and ideals; every one of Egypt's commoners was engaged in handicrafts, and lived in the shade within the walls of cities. There were even some who perverted their proper role as men, and took to working wool and weaving. And though the natural character of Egyptian men tended to make them effeminate enough,[45] King Sesostris aggravated their condition and sapped their vitality even more; this was his goal, and (as the Egyptians themselves say) he learned his cleverness and his stratagems from Mercury.[46] There was, in addition, an Egyptian law that placed limits on human ingenuity; for no workman was permitted to practice any profession but his father's. In fact, when Juvenal[47] wants to launch a truly impressive insult at Crispinus—a man whose evil deeds, along with Caesar's favor, raised him to the highest levels of power—he calls him *one of the Nile's commoners and the house-boy of Canopus.*[48] For it was believed that the priests of Egypt were free men, while the workers, who were commoners, served as slaves.

But even so, a third of the population was very different from the commoners; these people lived by themselves in the plains of Egypt and near
the swamps. They were the shepherds, and though they were active and
even energetic they were condemned by the entire people, whose sedentary
habits they were always disturbing. They often caused great upheavals, and
sometimes they even set up their own kings. So the Romans (who easily kept
the rest of Egypt loyal to them) were forced to place a fairly strong garrison
in the regions where this group of people lived. When all is said and done,
there was one thing that made the Egyptians of every era hostile to shepherds: they were sedentary types and workmen, who could not tolerate the
shepherds' vigorous strength and vital spirit. Pharaoh himself, when he had
decided to crush and repress the growing numbers of Israelites, said something along these lines to his men: *The Israelites are more robust than we are,
so come let us employ a clever plan so that they do not increase or join with
our enemies when there is a war, or themselves take up arms against us.*[49] I
think that this is right and true; nor can I agree at all with people who claim
that the Egyptians hated the Israelites because of their own superstitions, as
though that nation could not tolerate the Hebrew men—who herded sheep
and cattle—because this group had a taboo against sacrificing sheep, that
group against rams, and still another group against other four-legged animals (which they believed had a kind of divine essence). This explanation is
extremely unlikely; for how really can these people respond when they read
in the Pentateuch that Pharaoh had huge flocks of sheep; or when they see
that so many historical works are being published which make it clear that
(as I have already said) a great many Egyptians lived in pastures and among
livestock? And yet the Sacred Book often tells us that the Egyptians hate the
whole race of shepherds.

It does not say the same thing about farmers, but their virtues, I daresay,
could be neither hated nor feared, because they did not exist. The farmers,
who were the laziest sort of men, placed all their hopes not in their own hands
or in the energy they applied to their work, but in the Nile. The overflowing
river would both nurture and increase their crops; and it not only would en-
rich the existing land but would add to it. Indeed, the current (which had a
lot of mud mixed into it) periodically expanded the existing landmass, and
every year it gave Egypt a constant increase in size. Thus the farmer marveled
at his own wealth and his brand-new fields, which had fallen to his lot even
though he had neither worked for nor expected them.

CHAPTER 6

*When the Jubilees ceased to be celebrated. Why Maimonides
said that they were included in the calculation of Sabbatical years.
Maimonides' opinion rejected.*

I HAVE SAID ENOUGH about the Egyptians, their character, and how different they were from their Jewish neighbors. Now I must return from this detour to the Jubilee, which I had begun to describe. It must, therefore, be understood that once Moses instituted his agrarian law on the restoration of property, it was kept with the greatest reverence until the Assyrians destroyed the First Temple. Palestine then lay abandoned and uncultivated for seventy years (as the prophets had predicted). When, in the course of time, that fated cycle of events had come to its conclusion, the Jews returned to their place and the Temple was completely rebuilt; but the agrarian law was never again revived and the Jubilee was no longer celebrated. For this reason, slaves were no longer given their freedom each fiftieth year, and owners no longer got back the property they had lost or sold.

These matters are skillfully treated and discussed by the Talmudists, and they are considered extremely important. But there seems to be a very complicated and hidden rationale behind what Rabbi Maimonides reports in the seventh book of his *Mishneh Torah*, where he says as follows: *Although there were no Jubilees from the time of the Second Temple, even so it was customary to count them because of the remissions contained in the law.*[50] Unless I can solve this thorny problem, it would seem that I was wrong to say that the Jubilee was abolished; so I must explain this statement of Maimonides. Although it is true that this greatest of the rabbis says that the Jubilee was being carefully calculated even in more recent times, this in no way meant that all the slaves were being freed on that occasion, or that the lands were being returned to their original owners, but rather that the counting of Jubilees was crucial to the calculation of every seventh year, on which (according to the law) certain other rights of remission were to be observed. These rights did not cease until Titus overthrew and destroyed the Republic of the Jews.

It is certain, in any case, that these *shemitot* ("remissions") were of two kinds: first, every seventh year the land lay uncultivated; and second, loans no longer had to be repaid. But we may learn from Maimonides himself why he reasoned that the seventh year depended on the fiftieth. He begins: *The Jubilee year is not part of the count of seven-year cycles—rather the forty-ninth year is the* shemita, *the fiftieth is the Jubilee, and the fifty-first is the beginning of a new seven-year cycle; and the same applies to every Jubilee.*[51] Because trying to translate the Hebrew might reflect badly on the style of my Latin, I will simply summarize the statement of this greatest of rabbis. What he actually says is that the counting of seventh years did not begin from the fiftieth year, but from the year which immediately followed it, and that it proceeded this way one year after the next without interruption until the forty-ninth year was reached, which was therefore the Sabbatical year because it was seven times seven. But then (he goes on) the fiftieth year that followed it was not included in the sets of seven, which began to be counted again from the fifty-first year. It is therefore obvious why the most learned of the Jews said that though the fiftieth year was not observed, it was nevertheless counted, for he points out what would happen without it: the counting of seven-year sets would be continuous, instead of being interrupted (as it then was) by the insertion of the fiftieth year. And this is in fact the opinion of Maimonides, and of others who followed the Talmudists.

How correct this opinion actually is, I will leave to the investigations of those who delve into the subtlest workings of chronology. Some of these men—who do possess great learning and outstanding ability—think that the celebration of the Jubilee fell out in every forty-ninth year; from which it follows that there was no need for two Sabbatical years to follow one after the other, or for the counting of the seven-year sets to be interrupted every forty-nine years. There are also some who claim that their ideas can be proven by the calendar of Rabbi Adda.[52] At any rate, the fact that the Sacred Book calls the Jubilee "the fiftieth year" is of no help to either side of the argument: a very common usage (which agrees with every linguistic norm and practice) calls the seventh "eighth," and the greatest writers of antiquity frequently referred to the Olympics, which occurred every four years, as a fifth-year festival.[53]

It is actually of no particular interest to me which of these opinions is closer to the truth. It was merely my intention to prove, first, that the greatest lawgiver did not establish the Jubilee in vain; and second, that it was never used after the destruction of the First Temple. But as concerns the matter upon which I have touched here in passing, I am firmly of the opinion that there are many legitimate reasons why the incomparable men of our age have defined the Jubilee as a period of forty-nine years rather than a complete fifty. So I not only refuse to reject their opinion, I will even embrace it. In the twenty-fifth chapter of Leviticus, which deals with both the Jubilee and the seventh year, there is an explicit prohibition against cultivating the land during the Jubilee as well. Now, this sanction would in fact appear superfluous if every forty-ninth year, which was itself a Sabbatical year, in fact seven times seven sets, was subject to the laws of the Jubilee. Though I myself have at the ready a very straightforward response to this problem, I do think it is what drove Maimonides to a sort of delusion.

It is absolutely certain that the Hebrews always counted both the Jubilee and every seventh Sabbatical year from Tishri, which was the seventh month of the sacred year; and this was clearly so that each seven-year cycle, and the Jubilees themselves, would begin and end in the same month. From this it appears that we can find no middle path; for it must be either that every fiftieth year was a Jubilee, or that, by God, every forty-ninth year was.[54] But I prefer the second opinion. Nor can I agree in this instance with Maimonides, though in all other cases I embrace his ideas without reservation; for he is, I am certain, a man in whose work a few minor errors of this sort may be balanced against great and divine virtues everywhere else, as well as perceptions of the greatest refinement. And in fact those Jews who say that a period of fifty complete years was necessary for the restoration of lands have carefully recorded the differences between the Jubilee and all the seventh years. Thus Maimonides, who bases himself on their opinion, says in the Laws of the Sabbatical Year and the Jubilee: *The seventh year is distinct from the Jubilee because it forgives debts; while the Jubilee is distinct from the seventh year because it frees the slaves from the power of their masters, and restores lands. Another difference is that the fiftieth year restores the lands at the beginning of the year, while the seventh remits debts only at the end.*[55] His words give the lie to his claim that the repayment of loans could not be demanded during Jubilee years, if in fact it is true that all the Jubilees fell out in the forty-ninth year.[56]

There are other acceptable proofs as well,[57] which seem to be entirely correct; for according to the law of the Jubilees, the forty-ninth year had its own peculiar observances as compared with the other seventh years, and these very observances functioned a little differently than the ones that coincided with the forty-ninth because it also happened to be one of the seventh years. As I have already said, the observance of the Jubilee took its beginning from an ancient and seasonal calendar whose first month was September, which was also the seventh month of the holy year. Therefore, the Talmudists who say that the restoration of lands happened at the beginning of the year (on the tenth day of the first month) are not rejecting the Sacred Book, which sometimes calls that month the seventh. This variation in number is merely the result of the calendar's twofold structure.

Finally, Maimonides has this to say: *The same reasoning applies in every case to both the Jubilee and the seventh year, in respect to the cessation of farming. Whatever forms of cultivation are permitted or forbidden during the seventh year are also permitted or forbidden during the Jubilee.*[58] This is not simply a conjecture of the Jews, or a likely opinion, but an absolute and undeniable truth, which is proven by the lawgiver's own words in the twenty-fifth chapter of Leviticus. But if I were now to accept what I described as the opinion of the Talmudists, i.e. that there were two Sabbatical years in a row, it would certainly be a very strange and unique phenomenon: namely, since it was entirely through the power of Almighty God that in Palestine every sixth year brought such bountiful produce that the seventh—which the law set aside for a Sabbatical rest from farming—would not be a time of famine, this miracle would now have to be much greater still when two Sabbatical years of this sort were happening one after the other. For in neither year was it permitted to sow and to plough. Because, therefore, it says in the Book of Leviticus (25:21) that *I will give you My blessing in the sixth year, and it will produce the fruits of three years*, this act of divine kindness would have had to be doubled, since the Sabbaths of two years—the forty-ninth and the fiftieth—would, for various reasons, have followed one on the other. For it would now be necessary for that single sixth year to provide for the harvests not of three years, but of four; and nothing like this has ever been granted to any other nation or land. Now, I am certainly aware how much Palestine was indebted to Providence, and I will even go so far as to admit that many things happened there that were contrary to the laws of nature. But be that as it may, since neither the testimonies of the prophets nor any historical records have reported so great and so frequent a miracle, I am not ready to let my own gullibility make me look like some sort of impetuous fool.

CHAPTER 7

*The threefold consecration of Palestine and its cities. On the rights
of cities. The law of urban properties. On the city of Jerusalem,
and its privileges. The impious crime of Agrippa, and the Jewish
delegation to Nero which followed it. With which ceremonies
the boundaries of the city of Jerusalem were supposed to be
widened. On whose authority the right to build walls was given.
When the Jews lost their state entirely. On towns which
have the right of asylum.*

THE TALMUDISTS SAY that when Joshua entered Palestine he consecrated all the cities surrounded by walls. This they call *bia rishona*, the "first arrival." [59] But when the Babylonians exiled the holy nation across the Euphrates, its territory was polluted by godless men. This is why, once the Jews had been returned to their place, Ezra the highest chief of the people restored the sanctity of the cities through a solemn act; this was *bia shnia*, the "second arrival." Finally, Titus Caesar, after causing the Jews great suffering, polluted everything again. But at this point the Talmudists are led astray by an appealing misconception; for they are still waiting for the Messiah, who (as they claim) will enter the kingdom of Palestine and sanctify its cities. This, they say, will be the "third arrival." The Talmudists also describe the reasons for the reverence and sanctity that these cities possessed; they then discuss why the villages and farms were not consecrated as well. But it would take me a long time to explain these issues.

When the towns of Palestine were assigned to individual tribes, the Levites also received their own cities in which to live. But the country itself, and its lands and properties, were divided up in such a way that they received no part of it; for they already had the tithes, the first fruits, and all the sacrifices. Hence they had a livelihood, as well as wealth and riches. But Rabbi Maimonides adds a proviso and limitation to these rights, when he says in the Laws of the Sabbatical Year and the Jubilee: *It seems to me that everything I have said applies only to that land which was given in accordance with the covenant to Abraham, Isaac, and Jacob, and which is being held by*

*their sons, and had been divided among them. But in other regions conquered
by certain of the Israelite kings, the situation of the priests and Levites is no
worse than that of the other Hebrews.*[60]

There was a law about a city's buildings to the effect that whoever had
sold his house could redeem it within a year, though once a year had passed
the buyer had it for his own. But the seller's close relations had no right to
redeem it, and the rights of the Jubilee did not apply. Rather, the redeemer
had to give the buyer full price even though the house had been sold and
handed over many months before.[61] The owner could redeem his property
even on the last day of the year; and if he found out that the man to whom
he had sold it was away or was deliberately hiding himself, he went to the
court and there, in the presence of the Senate, he paid out the money he
had borrowed, went out, broke open the doors of his house, and went inside. This is how the Talmudists describe the matter.[62] In the cities of the
Levites the law was quite different; for clearly their houses were governed by
the same laws which (as I said) Moses set down for the fields and country
properties of all the Hebrews. In their case, then, the right of redemption
did not end after a year, and the Jubilee restored whatever had not already
been redeemed.

Of all the cities, Jerusalem alone had a special sanctity that was also
permanent ever since (as the Talmudists tell us) the great King Solomon
dedicated the city for all time. They say, therefore, that there was no real
reason for Ezra to have consecrated it again later on; for it was in no way
despoiled like the other cities polluted by the hands of the sacrilegious. As a
result, the Talmudists report, it was ruled permissible for the Jews to make
sacrifices and to feast on the meat, in the ashes of destroyed Jerusalem.[63] In
fact, the great sanctity of the place was demonstrated by those Jews to whom
the emperor Hadrian gave his permission to visit the twisted ruins of the
holy city once a year, and there to mourn and cry over the wretched fate of
their people.[64] Jerusalem was not assigned by lot to any one tribe, but was
held in common by them all; the Talmudists therefore excluded it from the
law which directed that a murder committed in secret at a border between
tribes must be expiated by the sacrifice of a calf.[65]

Rabbi Maimonides tells us something that was based not on superstition—far from it!—but on an old and respectable custom of the nation: he
says that if anyone had an upper story high enough that they could see the
Holy of Holies from there, they were permitted to go up once a week in
order to keep the roof in good repair; but to do so more often than that,
or for any other reason, was forbidden. These are his actual words: *If a spot
is on an upper floor and faces the Holy of Holies, one may not enter it more*

than once a week, so as to determine if any repairs are necessary.[66] In fact, King Agrippa had severely offended his subjects by repeatedly looking out from the heights of his palace over the place of the holy Temple, and seeing from above what was happening within. The Jews, who thought this was an enormous sin, built a high wall to keep the king from looking at what was going on in the Temple; they then sent ten delegates to Rome (along with Ishmael the high priest and Hilkia the keeper of the sacred treasury) to entreat Nero to approve what the people's piety had compelled them to do.[67] Moreover, what Hecataeus of Abdera (as quoted by Flavius) tells us[68]—i.e. that Jerusalem occupied an area of fifty *stades* [about six miles] and was inhabited by 120,000 people—would hardly be of any interest had there not been a certain unique law about extending the city's boundaries, which Maimonides has quoted from the Talmud. It was along the following lines: When the city was to be expanded, the great Senate (the Sanhedrin), the king, and one prophet consulted the oracle that is called the Urim and Tummim. Then, after they were all agreed about how to interpret the divine response, the senators of the Sanhedrin recited two psalms with which they gave thanks. They then took up two loaves of leavened bread and went out with cymbals, lyres, and citharas, and gathered at the bend of every street and at all the monuments that stood in the city; and they said these words: *I will exalt You, O Lord, because You have exalted me.*[69] Finally, when they arrived at the spot which was supposed to be consecrated because it was there that the new boundary would be, everyone took their places; and there they ate one of the two loaves they had taken after they finished singing the two psalms, and the other one they burned.[70]

This is the account that the Talmudists received from their ancestors and committed to writing, and it is not far from the truth: practically the same account may be found in the memoirs of Nehemiah, in the twelfth chapter. But later on, when the Romans had crushed the independence of the Jews, the decision to extend the city's boundaries was obviously not based on the judgment of the great council, but was made at the behest of the Roman People. In fact, Cornelius Tacitus even tells us that the Jews had to pay a great deal of money for the right to build their walls.[71] It appears, therefore, that Jerusalem—the queen of cities—was in the same situation as all the other towns that were under the Roman sway: the legal scholar Ulpian says in the Digest[72] that they could not repair their walls without the approval of the emperor or the provincial governor; nor could they attach anything to them or place anything above them. Certainly when Claudius Caesar found out that an enormous wall was being built around Jerusalem, he lodged a complaint with Agrippa about his planned alterations; and the king of course was quick to obey the emperor's order, and abandoned the undertaking.

The Talmudists say that Jerusalem enjoyed a distinction shared by none of the other towns of Judea, in that its houses did not belong to their buyers for more than a year.[73] They also say that it was forbidden to plant either vegetable gardens or groves; for what Hecataeus wrote about the precincts of the Temple[74] was, they tell us, true of the entire city. Corpses that were being carried somewhere else were not allowed within the city, so that its sacred rites would not be defiled. There were, however, at least two tombs there—one belonged to David, the other to Hulda[75]—that they say were built by the old prophets.[76] But the Levites were subject to a more stringent piety; they were forbidden to bury their dead not only in their own cities, but even in the fields outside them. God therefore commanded the other tribes to give them a certain amount of land beyond the borders of their own territory, in which they could lay to rest the remains of their departed. In the other towns it was perfectly acceptable to bury someone as long as seven good men agreed to it; but the moment a corpse had been carried from the city it was not allowed back within the walls, even if all the citizens were willing to accept it.[77]

Jerusalem was, as I have already said, the capital of the nation and the seat of its worship and its rituals. When, therefore, it was destroyed, both the civil and the religious government of the Jewish state vanished with it. Certainly Flavius' story that before the city was destroyed, a voice from the depths of the Temple was heard to say, "Let us leave here,"[78] can only have meant that the state was to be annihilated and the sovereignty that had once been given to the sacred nation taken away from it. For soon afterward the class system,[79] the governmental functions, the religious ceremonies, and most of the laws came to an end; and there followed a great deal of confusion, desolation, and dissension. The first thing to disappear was the extremely sacred fellowship of the Hasideans,[80] which traced its origins to the prophets. It had been their custom to go to the Temple every day, and to make voluntary donations for the sacrifices and for the colonnades and walls of the sanctuary. And since Moses had commanded that converts to Judaism had to bring a certain set gift as an offering,[81] this practice began to be postponed until such time as the Third Temple, for which they are still waiting, will be built. Nor, for that matter, do Jews continue to marry the childless widows of their brothers; and from the time of the Destruction the ritual of the paschal sacrifice was no longer observed, since the law had prescribed that it must be performed in that place which God had chosen as the site of His Temple.[82] All this was the consequence of one city's destruction—it changed and upset everything, and brought low the Republic of the greatest of peoples.

I have no particular thoughts about the other towns of Judea, except to say that Almighty God wanted some of them to have the right to provide asylum to people who had accidentally killed someone. These people spent an easy exile there until the passing of the high priest; his death freed them all, and if by chance any of them had died before he did, their remains could now be transferred to their ancestral tombs. There were six towns of this sort. Moreover, the Talmudists say that three more are going to be added to these when the King of Kings, the Messiah, comes to the world; for (they say) not in vain was it written that *you shall add another three cities to these three.*[83] They even map out the territory and the site: they say that three towns are going to be chosen for this purpose from among the cities of the Kenizim, the Kadmonim, and the Kenim. Though God had in fact promised these cities to Abraham when He struck a covenant with him, He never gave them to him. This (they say) must therefore be what Moses is referring to when he says *when your God has expanded your borders.*[84] If anyone should say that the Talmudists have expounded this matter with too much subtlety and care, he would be absolutely correct; but even so it was important to discuss their observations.

In addition to the six cities I have mentioned, the forty-two towns of the Levites were given the same privilege, though the Talmudists say that these towns did not offer any sanctuary to people who did not know about the benefit of this law.[85] I will pass over the other things I could say about the rights of these cities, as well as what the Jews have to say about those towns called *arei hanidahot*, "cities of error," which, they say, included neither Jerusalem nor the cities of refuge, because anything I might have to say about these things would lack both dignity and charm.

CHAPTER 8

Palestine's advantages over other places. That the Hebrew Republic could not have been moved to another location. Maimonides' statement about the Babylonian Jews is explained. Their great power, and the kingdom which they offered to Hyrcanus. On the meaning of the scepter of Judah, an interpretation which disagrees with that of Maimonides. The Jewish Republic is bound to Palestine. The Jewish law about temples which Jews have founded outside Jerusalem.

THE HEBREW REPUBLIC had its beginnings when the holy people were led to the blessed land of Palestine. While they were still in the Arabian desert, Moses, a man of God, had given them very sound laws about religious rites and practices, and about justice and the rights of citizens. But these laws applied to only one location, the place where the tribes were to have their towns, and where one city would be set above them all to serve as the seat of government and to guard the sacred rites. In the last book of the Pentateuch, in which the wisest of legislators sums up the laws he has given, he specifically commands again and again, and in these words, that *these are the laws, statutes, and judgments that you will observe in the land which will soon be given to you as a hereditary possession.*[86] The truth is that Palestine had a certain exceptional quality not found in any other place, which bound the holy nation and its state to this one particular piece of land. If someone had led this people away from its home and set up the very same state with the very same laws, this republic would even so have lost its sanctity, and the people its sovereignty.

A certain saying of Maimonides, found in the fourteenth book of his *Mishneh*, in the Laws of Kings and Wars, is particularly relevant to our subject, and I would like to examine it in passing. It goes as follows: *Just as Jews are forbidden to reside anywhere but Palestine, so they are by no means allowed to move from Babylon to another country.*[87] It is obvious that if I do not put this question to rest, those who occupy themselves with the works of the Hebrews must face some very difficult obstacles. Although Maimonides is talking about "Jews," he does not actually mean all of them, but only those Jews who, having been taken by their enemy across the Euphrates, lived in Babylon and the neighboring regions. Some of these Jews went back to Palestine after seventy years had passed, while the others were persuaded by the generosity of the kings under whom they were living to remain in their communities and colonies in Babylon. There were in fact a great many of these, and they eventually grew to be a nation. It is hard to believe how powerful the exiles became there: they almost offered Hyrcanus,[88] who was rushing from Parthia to meet Herod, a fillet and a crown (that is, a priesthood and a kingdom);[89] and it was to them that the secrets of the Babylonian government were entrusted, and kept by a Hebrew priest in a tower of enormous size that had been built in the Median city of Ecbatana.[90] These Jews had a close and even intimate relationship with the Jews of Palestine—they shared the same institutions, the same way of life, and the same ancestral language. In all respects they were exactly the same. This is the reason God allowed them to live in Babylon, so far from their homeland; it was uncontaminated by any foreign ways which might have infected them. But neither divine nor human law allowed them to move any farther from the land, or to live anywhere else.

This is the insight that Maimonides brings to his interpretation of the verse in Jeremiah: *They will be led to Babylon, and there they will be;*[91] and it is undoubtedly correct.[92] Certain wise men of the first rank have made some lofty pronouncements about the Babylonians, and Maimonides approves of these and supports them. These men believed that after Jerusalem's welfare began (in accordance with its fate) to decline and regress, it was the Babylonians alone who were invested with the communal authority promised to them by the voice of God in that well-known prophecy: *The scepter shall not depart from Judah, nor a ruler from his loins, until Shilo has come.*[93] Since I respect Maimonides' wonderful qualities, I am hesitant to admonish him for even the slightest of his mistakes. In this case, however, there is no question that this most intelligent of men has left reason behind, and instead favors the opinions of his fellow Jews. Now, I am well aware that the Jews of Babylonia took part in a sort of republic, and that they made laws for the others of their nation who lived outside Palestine. I am also aware of the fact that certain leaders, who traced their ancestry directly to David, always held power there.[94] But this does not prove the claims of Rabbi Ben Maimon; for the scepter about which the prophecy spoke can only be the Jewish Republic, i.e. that priestly kingdom whose rites and practices were not, Heaven forbid, some mere afterthought or prop with which to shore it up, but its very soul and spirit.

What is more, the safekeeping of the Republic's practices and sacred objects did not belong to every city but to one in particular, the one in which the sanctuary was located; there the power of God was felt more strongly than anywhere else, as though it were living in its own home. At first this city was Shilo; then it was Jerusalem, in the middle of Palestine. When, therefore, any of the Jewish sects built a temple or altar in another country, they dishonored the authority of the state and its inviolable laws. There is among the documents of the historians[95] a letter that Onias[96] wrote to Ptolemy and Cleopatra[97] in which he indicts his own countrymen because they had founded sanctuaries in the cities of Phoenicia and elsewhere, in violation of the laws of both God and man. Yet meanwhile he himself was no less guilty: for the sake of his own ambitious plans he used a prediction of the great prophet Isaiah as a false pretext for building a temple in the district of Heliopolis. He could not have done this without violating sacred practice. One of the earliest laws of the Jews, which Rabbi Moses (who was himself an Egyptian) records in his eighth book, in the last chapter of the Laws of Entrance into the Sanctuary, was as follows: *If someone has broken the law and built a shrine besides the sanctuary in Jerusalem, it is not to be regarded as a house of idolatry; but even so a priest who has made offerings there can never make them in God's temple in Jerusalem. Even the vessels that he has used may not be admitted to the service of the true sanctuary, but must be hidden away.*[98]

CHAPTER 9

*That criminal trials stayed within Palestine, and were denied
to Babylonian and other Jews. Some light is shed on the whole
discussion of how long the Republic of all the Hebrews lasted, and
when that of the Jews began. That from this we can learn what
the scepter of Judah was. The learned and plausible opinion of
Eusebius, and those who followed him, is refuted. What sovereign
authority is, and to whom it belongs.*

MY DISCUSSION of the Holy Temple gives us the most effective means of
refuting Maimonides; but I must offer other evidence as well, from which
it may be proven that the state, about which the elderly prophet[99] spoke to
Judah at the end of his life, could have existed only in Palestine. This proof
will not be hard to find. I will summon Maimonides as a witness against
himself: does he not frequently remind us that whenever the holy people is
outside its land, it is cut off from most of the laws which the great Moses
gave it?

Particularly important for us is his discussion in the Laws of the
Sanhedrin,[100] where he places certain limitations on the power of Palestinian
judges as much as on Babylonian ones. Now, it is agreed that most of the
Mosaic laws are concerned with those judgments which the Rabbis usually
call *dinei kenasot*, i.e. criminal cases. These cases, says Maimonides, could
not be decided by Babylonian judges in any country, including Palestine.
Palestinian judges, on the other hand, were legally entitled within their own
country to subject their citizens to whatever judgments they saw fit; while
outside it they could not make any decisions about their fellow Jews, unless
given permission either by the Babylonian leaders or by some other heads
of the Jewish exiles. From this I conclude that as long as the Palestinian
judges were on their native soil, their judgments in criminal cases were always backed by the force of law, while at times they also judged cases outside
their land (even if it was only at the behest of others). But the Babylonian
judges could not handle any cases of this sort—not in their own jurisdiction
and not in Palestine; not by the force of law, or even with permission. Now

I ask you, was it to these men that the honor of the "Jewish scepter" was given after the Palestinian community had been shattered? It must be either that the greatest of scholars was not aware of the kind of dignity this scepter possessed,[101] or that he had too high an opinion of some of the Babylonian leaders, who were really straw men who glorified themselves because they were the descendants of David.

But I cannot be surprised that so trivial a misconception appears in Maimonides, when I consider the kinds of fanciful explanations devised by other scholars who wanted to get at the proper interpretation of Jacob's divine oration. I remember that I spoke about this last year with a very respectable man—Apollonius Schotte, a counsel of the Supreme Court. At the time I was spending a delightful holiday at his home in the Hague, and I was rushing, with a great deal of excitement, through the brilliant observations of Rabbi Maimonides. I was so affected by these observations that I almost reversed my pen in order to erase all my earlier notes on Jewish matters. It was on this occasion that the Senator (such was his wisdom and the power of his intellect) remarked to me several times that in his opinion, there was no prophecy in the Holy Book that scholars had sweated over more and yet understood less. Lord knows I was happy to discover that this man shared my beliefs; his authority and reputation were enough to encourage me to discard other people's theories, whatever they might be. I therefore believe, with his support, that it is completely right and proper, given the large number of conjectures about this illustrious prophecy, that I too should publish my own. For any pursuit is worthwhile if it allows a person to make use of his strengths and his natural abilities.

Now, it is certainly true that in this book I am dealing jointly with both Hebrew and Jewish affairs, and that for the most part I describe them without drawing any distinction between the two. But to prevent anyone from being led into error, I will show once and for all that although the holy state—founded by Moses at the command of God—was always the same, and was set up with the same laws, it did not always belong to the same people. For I will prove that though for a long time it belonged to the Hebrews, with the passage of time it belonged no less to the Jews. I will also show that Jacob's prophecy about the scepter of Judah refers only to that time when the state began to be named after the Jews.[102]

It is because people are unaware of this fact that they have failed until now to understand the meaning of this wonderful prophecy. I prefer not to mention here the sad fantasies of Origen, Augustine, Epiphanius, and the others who thought that Jacob's prophecy promised the Jews an unbroken succession of kings from the same tribe and the same family until the time of the Messiah. People who embraced this theory ran into a great many serious problems. They did not know what to say or where to turn when they saw that there was no Jewish kingdom from the death of Zedekiah[103] all the way to the time of Aristobulus;[104] and that from then on, the Hasmoneans (who were only Levites) held the throne until the time of the tyrant Herod. This question recently received a good and productive treatment in the *Baronian Exercises* written by the greatest scholar of our age, Isaac Casaubon;[105] he preferred Eusebius' well-known explanation of this prophecy in his *Proofs of the Gospel* (the first proof of the eighth book).[106]

Rather than go over the same ground, I am going to leave aside all the points on which both Eusebius and Casaubon were correct. I also admit that of all the explanations that have been made till now, Eusebius has devised the best one by far. But it seems to me that neither Eusebius nor the excellent man who has recently succeeded him managed to figure out just what that scepter was about which the elderly prophet spoke to his son at the end of his life, or when it was given to the Jews. I must now, therefore, explain it myself, but not before begging the indulgence of my readers. For I have no desire to take issue with Eusebius, whom I have always considered one of the greatest authors ever; and I so deeply admire that man whom I mentioned, the one who followed the opinion of Eusebius (he is among the best of our generation), that I consider him second to none. It is, without question, at his impetus that our age has made such amazing strides towards the mastery of every field of knowledge. But my natural lack of guile forces me to search without bias for what is right and true. Eusebius' first incorrect suggestion was that the scepter was originally given to Judah in the time of Moses; his reasons are that this tribe had always differed from the others in the unique dignity it enjoyed, and that it had a more honored position in both the layout of the camp and the order in which the people offered their gifts in the Temple.[107] But I find this argument no more convincing than if one were to say that the sovereign authority of Rome or Athens lay not in the Roman or Athenian people as such, but in one particular tribe that was more noble or flourishing than the others. After all, the ancient writers make this point so consistently that it must be agreed that both Rome and Athens contained many different tribes, some of which outstripped the others in dignity, standing, and rank.

So where does this leave us? For my own part, I think that the scepter can only represent sovereign power, namely that which lies in the very republic itself; so whatever can be said of a republic can also be said of the scepter. But from the time of Moses to the reign of Rehoboam, the Hebrew Republic belonged not to the Judeans but to the Twelve Tribes; which proves that the scepter likewise belonged in those days to all the Israelites. On the other hand, this scepter, which was shared for a long time by the Twelve Tribes, was not the one to which the divine patriarch was referring in his celebrated prophecy. He was, in fact, looking at the years that were to follow and the centuries to come, when the people were divided into opposing parts and the tribe of Judah began a state of its own—separate from the Israelites—which had God's approval and love. It was this state He wanted to be called "Jewish" after the land of Judah, until the community of mortal men should receive the gift of that One who was destined to rule over not only the Jews, but all nations.[108]

It is, moreover, my assertion that this sovereign authority remained in the hands of the Jews from the moment they first acquired it, even though the conditions of the state changed from time to time, and supreme power rested sometimes in the hands of aristocrats and priests, and sometimes in the hands of kings and princes. Some very foolish people paint themselves into a corner by claiming that the honor of being called "sovereign" belongs only to kings; in fact, any people that has its own state and lives under its own laws can quite properly take pride in its authority and its sovereignty. History records that even in an age when the people were governed not by princes but by aristocrats,[109] authority resided in Jerusalem with the great council called the Sanhedrin.

This is precisely what was remarkable about that sovereignty which is, according to Marcus Tullius, *a certain greatness of the people in the way it holds fast to its power and rights, which expresses itself in the people's power and dignity.*[110] Not kings and princes, but consuls and senators, governed the Roman Republic at the time when its Aetolian allies were given that treaty from which Livy quotes: *so that they should preserve the majesty of the Roman People without any criminal deceit.*[111] And Proculus the legal scholar bears witness that the same provision applied to every free people who entered into an alliance with the Romans through one or another kind of treaty (though such treaties were by no means equal).[112] In fact, I do not believe it matters at all from which family or tribe came those men who governed Jewish affairs; for even though the Hasmoneans (who were Levites) held the throne for very many years, in no way was the state any less a Republic of the Jewish People. Nero Caesar's wisest teacher[113] told him that the state does not belong to the ruler, but the ruler to the state. Nor did the legal scholar Ulpian believe any differently: he says that a "crime against majesty" is ultimately one that is committed against the Roman People or its sense of security.[114] It is true that Ulpian was writing at a time when the people no longer had either political power or the right to vote—the Caesars had control of the military, and supreme authority. But even so, a stickler for the strict letter of the law would have to say that sovereignty belonged to the people.

CHAPTER 10

*That the twelve Hebrew tribes were never called Judeans. That
the ten tribes which were carried off by Shalmaneser before the
time of Nebuchadnezzar never returned to Palestine. That just two
tribes, and no more, were subject to the Romans, until the time of
Josephus. The mistakes of Eusebius and others are mentioned
here and there.*

I THINK that I will not have disproved Eusebius enough until I have fully
exposed the snares in which this author has carelessly entangled himself.
This is what he says in the book I mentioned above: *You will find, if you
examine the Israelite leaders individually, that even from the time of Moses
some of them were chosen from the various tribes; but that on the whole the
tribe of Judah was in charge of the entire nation.*[115] Thus far he is consistent
and does not contradict himself. But what he then says is ridiculous: *The
following example will make what I have said very clear: in the Roman Empire, the rulers and governors and chiefs of individual nations, and the com-
manders of camps, and the kings who were greater than all of these, were by
no means all from the city of Rome or from the stock of Romulus and Remus,
but all came from countless different nations. And yet all the kings (as well as
the governors and chiefs who came after them) were called Roman; and their
might and power are called Roman, and depend on this name. We should regard as the same thing the arrangements of the Hebrews, as though the single
tribe of Judah bestowed its illustrious name on the whole nation; and though
the leaders and kings of particular areas arose from the various tribes, even
so they were honored with the general name of "Judeans."*[116]

Look at the consequences of this heedlessness! Eusebius has clearly
achieved the opposite of what he wanted to prove: he says that the Judeans
already had dominion in the time of Moses, and his proof is that the state,
the government, and the whole people, which was composed of *twelve* tribes,
took their name from the single tribe of Judah. He takes great pride in this
argument, which he brings in two or three different places; and, but for a
few exceptions, nowhere in his entire discussion will you find him trying

to support his claim with any other proof. Now, with all due respect to Eusebius, all this, whatever it is, is completely pointless; for neither the state nor the government was called by the name of Judah until after the majority of Israelites had seceded at the behest of Jeroboam, who soon secured the kingdom of Samaria for himself through a change in religious practices and ceremonies. I will defend the truth of this against any and all challenges, both from Eusebius, and from all those who had but a passing knowledge of sacred history.

But what, really, is this statement that he makes so frequently and with such confidence, that the Twelve Tribes *as a whole* were called "Judeans"? It is Eusebius' delusion, which he forced upon the unsuspecting; and some scholars of great renown have been found to support it. Well, I say that it never happened, whether you look at the period before the division of the Israelite kingdom or at what happened afterward. And though Eusebius does not give any explicit reasons for his opinion, he believes (if I may hazard a guess) that it happened at the very start of the new government, when the state was founded in the territory of the Canaanites and there were discussions about what to call it.

But since this does not have the ring of truth, that great man whom I called the defender of Eusebius[117] suggests that he had a different idea about when exactly this happened; and he approves of, and supports, what he takes to have been Eusebius' theory. According to this idea, Eusebius remarked that the twelve Israelite tribes took their name from the name of Judah, and that they first began to use this name when the high priests had transferred to themselves the royal power that the tribe of Judah had lost along with Zedekiah. He also says that this event deserves our particular admiration because it was undoubtedly a part of the Divine Plan. For since (as he says) Polybius thinks that there was a serious reason why the Achaeans, a small Greek people, eventually came to give their name to all of Greece, so too in our case we must certainly see it as something rather sublime and grand that when all the sons of Abraham, from all the tribes, came back from their captivity, they were called Jews.

I cannot, and should not, let this mistake pass. It is true that when the kingship of the Israelites was cut in half, two of the tribes—the Levites and the Benjaminites—joined themselves to the Judeans; and since they were smaller and poorer than the latter, they were considered nothing more than its appendages. So not only did the state not take its name from them, but they nearly lost any name of their own; for eventually they were all called Judeans as a group. I admit that this is perfectly true and cannot be otherwise. But the scholars who take pleasure in this fiction[118] should consider what these facts mean and what they have to do with the other ten tribes. After all, from the time when those ten Israelite tribes were led away by Shalmaneser the Assyrian and dispersed throughout Colchis, Parthia, India, and Ethiopia, they never again returned to their native soil or reunited with the Judeans. And trapped to this very day among the realms of the barbarous peoples (if, that is, any of them survived that mess) they continue to work off the heavy penalties for their shameless desertion. Since, therefore, they had no ties with the Judeans and were not at all intimate with them, they could not take part in a state of the Jews or receive the honor of their name. For they were far away on the other side of the world, looking at a different sky and different stars.

There is a memorable passage in Flavius Josephus, who was an unusually careful author, which will more than repay our attention; for it is the best way to settle the issue at hand. Flavius was the first to speak about those who poured into Babylon from all the neighboring lands so that they could accompany Ezra back to Jerusalem. These people were all Judeans, or the Levites and Benjaminites who had joined up with them. But as far as Hebrews from the other tribes, he has this to say: *But all the remnants of the Israelite People remained where they were. This is why the two tribes alone—in both Asia and Europe—happened to fall under the dominion of Rome, while the remaining ten continue even today to live across the Euphrates; there are so many endless thousands of them that they obviously cannot be counted because of their huge numbers.*[119] It is true that those who were taken captive and led off by Shalmaneser suffered a harsher fate than those whom Nebuchadnezzar would later take away; once the Israelites had crossed the Euphrates it forever barred their return, whereas the Judeans, who had also been taken across this river, eventually returned to Palestine. And when Palestine itself became either too difficult or too unpleasant a place to live, they eventually migrated throughout Europe and Asia. This is the reason Josephus said that only two Hebrew tribes were placed under the Roman yoke; for in those days the Roman People, who had subjugated practically the whole world, and could see the sun both rise and set on their empire, had not yet pushed their borders beyond the Euphrates. So our punctilious author has quite properly reported that the ten Israelite tribes, bound by this river in an eternal prison, were not at all subject to the Romans.

CHAPTER 11

The crackpot interpretations of those who say that the Jewish scepter was given to David. That the prophecy about the scepter of Judah was made long before it took place. When the authority of the Jews was taken away from them.

I HAVE SPOKEN candidly about when exactly I think the scepter described in the prophecy was given to the Jews, and then about which citizens were a part of the state that began with the secession of the commoners.[120] Eusebius did not understand these issues at all; but of the many scholars to comment on the prophecy, he was the only one to give it a correct and almost divine interpretation. I am not going to discuss what the others wrote, but most of them say that what Eusebius supposes to have happened at the beginning of the Hebrew state actually took place when David—who came, according to sacred history, from the tribe of Judah—was given the power of a king. Eusebius, however, refuted these scholars so thoroughly and so successfully that no amount of effort could improve upon his work. He tells us that David's descendants ruled the kingdom for a very short time indeed, until the Babylonian Exile, and he very wisely says that the constant references to David's eternal throne are allusions to the Messiah. After Eusebius it was pointless for serious scholars to say more than a few words on this subject; he completed his task so thoroughly that he left them all nothing to do.

In the end it remains for me only to satisfy the concerns of those scholars who wonder why it took so long for the prophecy about the Jewish state to be fulfilled; for as I said, it was finally realized in the time of Rehoboam.[121] But these scholars should be aware that this was exactly what the prophet had in mind. He is an old man who is about to die and is speaking to his sons for the last time, and he says that he wants to describe to them *what is going to happen in the end of days*.[122] The scholars should also bear in mind that prophecies do not hold up well if we try to connect them to specific historical events; in most cases they should be interpreted as broadly as possible. When, for example, it says in this very prophecy that *the scepter shall not depart until Shilo has come*, you might think this means that the nation's scepter was going to be torn from its hands the moment the Messiah had appeared to mankind. But this, of course, did not happen; for the Jews did not lose that honor until later on, when the city was destroyed and the Temple burned. From then on they no longer had any state of their own, and they ceased to govern themselves by their own laws.

This does not mean, however, that the prophecy was not entirely truthful: although the Messiah, the savior of mankind, had left the world a long time before, it is clear nonetheless that these events took place in his time. It has always seemed to me that the Messiah himself referred to this in his public remarks, when he said of the overthrow of the city and the Temple that *this generation will not pass until all these things have taken place.*[123] This should be enough to satisfy every good and intelligent scholar; I am not interested in the others, who always find some reason or other to cast doubts. Of course, since I knew that even the greatest men were not sure which of the answers to these questions were the right ones, I was careful to keep to facts that were solid, and which I could therefore defend in complete security. For otherwise these questions would have constantly hindered the progress of my book.

CHAPTER 12

On dictators and judges. On the senate called the Sanhedrin. On the admission of senators. The laying on of hands. Likewise, the solemn formula. Who was chosen for this council. What sort of jurisdiction they had. On the assemblies of the people. On the drink 'sota.' The Jews' delusion about the use of magic. On the incantations of Eleazar.

I HAVE PROVEN that the republic which is my subject belonged for a long time to all the Hebrews, and then to the Jews alone. It was very important that I clarify this distinction once and for all; and now that I have gotten free of this very troublesome dispute I will go on to tell who was in command of the sacred people, and how we are to understand its courts and its senate. The Lord did not grant Moses the favor of seeing the growth, in Palestine, of the state whose institutions he had founded in the Arabian desert. That distinction was given to Joshua, who after Moses' death became the supreme leader of the people; both at home and on the field of battle, his word was law. He was followed by men who had just as much authority as he did: given their power to command and to make laws they might well have been called praetors and dictators,[124] though the sacred histories call them "judges" for much the same reasons. But Flavius called them *monarchai* [monarchs], which was the same name the Greeks gave to Sulla, Cinna, Marius, and the other Roman dictators.[125] These judges received their powers out of necessity in times of great political strife; and through difficulty and danger they discovered that they were always successful in war, while the rashness of kings often led Fortune to desert them. At times the judges also took an active part in civil matters, and tried cases (though only the more serious ones, for they rarely sat on tribunals). Their task was to give orders, to take command, and to manage the highest affairs of state. The last of these judges was Samuel, who was followed by the kings; as the latter were not content with their power and authority, they also used their style of dress, their badges of office, and the magnificence in which they lived to set themselves above the masses.

Moreover, besides the supreme leaders of the people,[126] the judges, and those who were called kings later on,[127] there were also a number of others who made decisions of state, tried cases, and settled disputes. For several *synedria*[128] were set up whose composition and responsibilities I must now explain in turn. The most obvious place to begin is with the great council, the Sanhedrin, to which seventy councilors belonged. Though this council was set up by Moses, it operated continuously under the judges, the kings, and the priests until the final destruction of Judea; and it stayed in whichever city was the home of the sanctuary and the capital of the state. But since we know so little about the earliest times, and the Holy Book has told us nothing particularly worth knowing about the city of Shilo, I will describe—according to the observations of the Jews—the character of the *synedrium* in the chief city of Jerusalem after the Temple was built there. Then I will discuss the other councils that met at Jerusalem or in individual cities.

The great council sat in the sanctuary itself, where the seventy senators dealt with matters both divine and human. These men were not, Heaven forbid, chosen from the common people; they were all of the noblest descent, and they could boast of the great importance of their ancestors and the ancient honors awarded to their families.[129] Their place of meeting had been given to them by the great Moses, who ordered them to convene in the spot that God had chosen so that the people would honor His name there.

This was the highest court in the land. Within its jurisdiction was every case that could not be decided by the other magistrates and judges in the towns of Palestine and in Jerusalem itself. It had two members whose authority and offices were higher than those of the others—one of these was the head of the whole Sanhedrin, whom the Talmudists call *nasi bechol makom*, that is, the chief in every place; the other one, whose rank was close to his but slightly below it, was called the *av bet din*, the father of the court. All the other members were equal in rank. Since the dignity of these senators was very great, it could be bestowed on someone only by a legal act; this required the laying on of hands which the Jews call *semicha*, but which the Greeks referred to as *cheirothesia*. Thus, Moses put his hands on Joshua and on the senators, and the moment this ceremony was performed a spirit came down from the heavenly throne and filled their breasts. Once they had been initiated in this fashion they were able to authorize others by means of the same principle; but the ritual could not be performed outside the Holy Land, because its force held good only within the boundaries of Palestine.

Rabbi Maimonides writes something very noteworthy in the Laws of the Sanhedrin. He says that although at one time all those who had already been ordained could perform this sacred act whenever they thought it was appropriate, the Sages limited this right; and they drew up a law which stated that from that time on no one could make use of it until they had received permission from the divine old man Rabbi Hillel.[130] He was the head of the great council, and in the post immediately below him was Shammai, who was a fierce and ambitious man. When, shortly after the law was passed, Shammai's followers had risen up against the disciples of Hillel, they stirred up such passions that practically the entire people was divided into factions. Eventually, the laying on of hands, which had been practiced for such a long time, fell out of use. Instead, only a certain verbal formula was recited, which Rabbi Maimonides reports as follows: *Behold, hands have been laid on you, and the power of conducting even criminal trials has been given to you.*[131] The Talmudists mentioned another formula besides this one, whose words were reported in the *Elenchus of the Triheresion* by that illustrious man Joseph Scaliger,[132] who did not, however, grasp them correctly. I will therefore copy over the text here, and explain it as it ought to be understood.

The Talmudists said of Judah son of Baba that he preserved more carefully than anyone else the ancient institutions of his nation. For both criminal trials and the laying on of hands had practically disappeared when this Atlas kept them from falling into oblivion. They then add a statement which I think should be translated as follows: *That solemn act is accomplished not only by the laying on of hands, as Moses did to Joshua, but it is no less valid if done with a verbal formula; and this is how he says it: I lay my hands upon you, and let my hands be upon you.*[133] But the great Scaliger concluded from these words that Judah had found another kind of formula besides the much older one whose wording is given above. This idea does not occur to the Talmudists at all, and it is incorrect. But the great man made this mistake because he thought *bilvad* meant *except*, whereas in Rabbinic Hebrew it actually means something like *just that* and *only*.[134]

But all this is the stuff of grammar, and we should leave it to others; we are concerned here with more serious matters. It was not only the noblest of the citizens who, as I mentioned, were chosen for the great council, but also the Levites and the priests. Maimonides says that the high priest was also admitted *if he was intelligent, and skilled at making decisions.*[135] If not they were required to reject him; for he did not enter the Senate by right, but was admitted on the approval of others. And since it was only proper that all the councilors should be physically sound, people with defects of one sort or another were kept out. But neither converts nor foreigners were received into this order unless they had at least a Jewish mother (Maimonides treats the latter as an exception). This was certainly fair, and the same decision was reached in Roman law: Ulpian says that if a person's father is from Campania and his mother from Puteoli, then he is a citizen of Campania; unless, that is, he should by chance be registered as a citizen according to his maternal origin as a result of some special privilege. In such cases, Ulpian says, the son follows his mother's origin.[136] It was for this reason that the people of Ilium were permitted to enroll as a citizen anyone whose mother was from there.[137] And through the generosity of Pompey the Great, the people of Pontus were able to consider as Pontic anyone with a Pontic mother, and likewise the people of Delphi were given this privilege, which they preserved.

The senators of the Sanhedrin were charged with traveling throughout the land of Judea, holding assizes of the people[138] and setting up magistracies in the towns; and since a certain kabbalah and a secret doctrine had been passed down by hand from the very beginnings of the state, they were in charge of interpreting it and deciding if it was valid.[139] It was also their task to pass laws about sacred matters, and to devise certain principles with which to interpret the law. Maimonides deals with this issue in great detail in the first chapter of the Laws of Rebels. The Talmudists mention many provisions in Jewish law concerning the sage whom they call *zaken mamreh*, the obstinate and stubborn old man. Though at one time he had been learned in the sacred law and the kabbalah, he came to have certain doubts, and he would refuse to approve and to follow the decisions which the senators of the Sanhedrin made as a group. He was then condemned to death by the court of the great *synedrium*. Maimonides addresses this point in the third chapter of the same Law:[140] *The rebellious elder spoken of in the Torah is one of the sages of Israel who has mastered the traditions and both judges and teaches in matters of Torah, just as do all the sages of Israel; when he had a dispute with the Great Court over one of the laws and did not consent to their opinion but disagreed with them and taught according to his own teachings rather than theirs, the Torah condemned him to death.* This is now clear. It was, moreover, in this *synedrium* alone that cases of prophets who had seriously neglected their duties were judged. It was this that the Messiah, the savior of mankind, had in mind when he said in the Gospel of Luke that it could not happen *that any prophet could perish outside Jerusalem.*[141]

They also chose the king, which was the greatest of their powers, and took counsel about waging wars, overthrowing enemies, and expanding the empire. But since these were the kinds of decisions that dealt with the welfare of the entire nation and the highest matters of state, they often consulted with the people before making them: they called assemblies, which were the only occasions when the people took part in governing the state. And in fact the people ought not to have had any other responsibilities, or taken part in any other way. Offices and magistracies are assigned to individuals, and the mob, which lacks intelligence and training, is not qualified to carry them out. But when assembled as a group they do possess some discernment and understanding; for as Aristotle put it so succinctly, every mob has a sort of perception once it has been assembled together.[142] Such assemblies even serve the public interest, because the more intelligent people attend them and lead the others; but as discrete individuals the commoners lack both discretion and judgment. So decrees about kings and wars were sometimes, as I mentioned, passed at the people's initiative, while the senators of the Sanhedrin took care of everything else by themselves. In even the most important matters they were always up to the task, since the only men admitted to the council were those who were by nature both practical and wise. Indeed, the great Moses called them elders not only because of their age, but because they were careful and experienced.

I must nevertheless admit that at times they openly decided the kinds of cases whose solution is beyond the diligence of mere human beings. The Talmudists raise an issue of this sort, which was considered by the *synedrium* alone, in the case of a woman who commits adultery when no witnesses are present. For one of the priests who was a member of the Senate would come forward, and at the order of his colleagues he would compose a terrible curse, and call for judgment against the woman who was on trial. He would then bring her a drink which, if she were guilty, would cause her to burst on the spot, but would make her healthier if she were innocent.[143] The Jewish teachers call this drink *sota*; and since its secret power lay hidden in the formula of a fearsome text, the Jewish teachers believed that all these senators were learned in magic, and that this skill was so important to them that only men who possessed it were admitted into their order.

Even today the yids[144] are of this opinion; but it is entirely without merit. For, as I have already mentioned, once the seventy elders received in a solemn act the laying on of hands, they had a kind of sacred energy; and God Himself, in the Pentateuch, promises them the same spirit that was in Moses. So they certainly did not need the protection of such worthless teachings when they had been given better and more reliable ones from Heaven. I would not have exposed this bit of asinine Jewish stupidity, but even Flavius Josephus—greatest of authors though he may have been—was taken in by the fictions of his countrymen, and indulged in others just as silly or even worse. For he mentions a certain Eleazar, a wise man of the first rank, who supposedly used certain incantations in the presence of Vespasian in order to exorcise the demons of possessed men; these incantations (he said) had been given to the great King Solomon for this purpose by his guardian spirits, and passed on to his descendants. Josephus mentions many other things in that section which are not worth the effort it would take to dismiss them. I think that he had stepped in something filthy on the day he wrote these things; that is how unfortunate, and how uncharacteristic of him, were the ridiculous things he said.

CHAPTER 13

On the other two councils at Jerusalem besides the Sanhedrin.
On the senate of twenty-three found in individual towns. On the
court of three men. What the size of a city ought to be. On the
court of five created to atone for murders. On the courts of seven
and three, which met to intercalate years and months. The calendar
arranged by Rabbi Hillel the Babylonian. How Gabinius cleverly
diminished the power of the Sanhedrin.

IN MY DESCRIPTION of the great senate, I mentioned whatever facts came to mind; it will take only a few words to explain what other councils there were and what they were like. So to begin with, the learned Maimonides mentioned (in the first chapter of the Laws of the Sanhedrin) that there were two others in Jerusalem itself. They are described in the Talmud, in both the Mishna and the Gemara. Both of these courts were composed of twenty-three judges; and just as the great council of the Sanhedrin met in the section of the Temple called the Gazith, these two *synedria* met, respectively, at the gate of the courtyard and the gate that opened onto the Temple Mount. These two courts differed not only in their locations, but in the respect in which they were held: the judges who met at the gate of the holy mountain thought they were being given a great honor whenever any of them was admitted into the senate that met at the gate of the courtyard; and in the same way, to go from that senate to the council of the Sanhedrin was a further step up in rank. Rabbi Maimonides has carefully set out all these distinctions.[145]

Besides these Jerusalem councils, a senate was set up in each of the towns of Palestine to judge trials and take care of public business. It consisted of twenty-three men who judged capital and property cases and decided all matters except for those few that (as I mentioned above) were turned over to the Sanhedrin. Maimonides also describes a council of three men, which he says was found in cities that had fewer than a hundred and twenty inhabitants. But I agree with Aristotle that such a place cannot be called a city;[146] for just as no vessel whose length is either a handbreadth or two *stades*[147] can be called a ship, so no city is worthy of the name unless it is the proper size. One that is too small cannot muster on its own the resources that every city ought to have, and one that is too large is no longer a city, but has become a nation. Of course, we should not expect a Jew to be so strict about his calculations.

The three-man courts judged cases involving damages, money, and moveable goods; defendants in capital cases were remanded to the courts I have already mentioned. Maimonides adds that there were certain cases that did not belong to the seventy elders, or to the court of twenty-three judges, or even to the court of three. Instead, they required a special committee of senators. Maimonides includes among these cases murders committed anonymously within the borders of a town; these, he says, had to be atoned for by five men with the sacrifice of a calf. He mentions more crimes of this type, which I am wisely going to skip over, for I am not a schoolboy spitting back his lessons.

You may well wonder at the fact that judges were selected and placed in charge of arranging the calendar; for Maimonides says that seven judges decided when to have an intercalary year, and three decided how long the month should be.[148] But in later years the entire people was relieved of this concern by a man who was the prince of his age, Hillel the Babylonian.[149] Rabbi Abraham Zacuto[150] pays homage to this man in his book *Yuhasin*: *Rabbi Hillel, the head of the great council, arranged the intercalation of the calendar for all Israel until the time of the Messiah; and he did this before the legal power of the laying on of hands was abolished.*[151] There is no question that if this Hillel had not dealt with the problem in time, the calendar would have become chaotic and confused; for shortly thereafter the ritual of *cheirothesia* ceased to function, and without it the courts of seven and of three were no longer appointed to adjust the calendar. This is according to Maimonides, who says that *all these men were ordained.*[152] But it is time I finished with this, or someone may think that I am writing a thorough and careful work when in fact I am churning out nothing more than a bunch of unfinished ideas.

Another point: Whatever I have said about the councils is meant to apply only to the period before Judea had fallen to Rome, for afterwards the Romans changed many laws and repealed others, not out of lust or cruelty but in order to maintain their control. In particular, Gabinius, the proconsul of Syria, decided to disperse the power of the Sanhedrin over several towns because it was on its assemblies that the stability of the state depended most. So he set up five *synedria* of equal authority at Gadara, Amathus, Jericho, and Sepphoris; the fifth one, which was at Jerusalem, was but a fraction and an appendage of what it had been. Not only were the councils that Gabinius placed in the other cities no less powerful than the one in Jerusalem, but they stood for many more years. In fact, I believe that it is to them the Emperor Justinian is referring[153] when he requires a payment *from the chiefs who were in charge of the synedria of both Palestines*. But I am not going to venture into this period; I have been examining the ancient republic and the pristine institutions of the nation, and it would be pointless to try and examine any of the others. Nothing certain can be said about them because they have undergone constant changes.

CHAPTER 14

On the creation of a king, and whether it was pleasing to God. Why God at first appointed an evil king. The criteria according to which the prophet chose him. The book about the rights of kings which was placed in the sanctuary. The powers which were given to the Hebrew kings. The honors which were paid him by the high priest, the other priests, and the prophets. A verse in Samuel defended against certain commentators. The right to sit in the court of the priests was given to the king alone, not to the priests themselves or to anyone else. What sort of kings the first men obeyed, according to Aristotle. What it was that gave the Hebrew kings more sanctity. That it was not because they were prophets. That only kings and high priests were initiated with oil. That the sacred oil hidden by Josiah was neither found nor used during the Second Temple. Whether the kings of Samaria were anointed.

RABBI MAIMONIDES SAYS in the last part of his *Mishneh*[154] that the Almighty made three demands of the Israelites, to be carried out when they had possession of Palestine. The first was that they should place a king over themselves; the second, that they should wipe out the memory of the Amalekites; and the third, that they should build a Temple. Maimonides then declares that though these tasks were accomplished only after many years and each at a different time, they were all performed in the order in which they were given: the monarchy, he says, was established before the war with the Amalekites, while the construction of the Temple did not begin until that most hateful of nations had met its end. Because Maimonides provides the clearest evidence of this, there is no need to reproduce it all here.

When Almighty God says in the seventeenth chapter of Deuteronomy that the Israelites are going to want a king, His reason (which is certainly correct) is that all the neighboring nations were living under the rule of one man. This is natural to the people who live in that part of the world. Very few of them desire freedom; most want only to have just rulers. Not for nothing does Claudius Civilis say to his Batavians that *Syria and Asia are enslaved, and the East is accustomed to kings.*[155] Seeing that this is so, many people

have wondered why God was unhappy that supreme power was being transferred from Samuel to a king, if in fact He had already given His approval to
monarchy and said that it was going to suit the character of the holy nation.
But for these people Maimonides has a wise response. He says[156] that God
was offended by the people's choice: *since when they asked for a king, their
complaints were disingenuous and their words were rebellious; they asked for
one not because they wanted to fulfill the precepts of the law, but because they
were dissatisfied with the holy prophet Samuel, to whom refers the verse: "It is
not you but Me whom they despised."*[157] This is my opinion as well, and I am
absolutely certain that Immortal God made Saul a king not out of mercy or
concern for the state, but because He was well aware of Saul's arrogance and
cruelty. He wanted to make Samuel seem glorious by comparison with this
man who was so much his inferior, so that the people would come to miss
him when faced with a successor like Saul.

Though the criteria which Samuel used to choose Saul as king (and
which the Holy Book mentions three or four times) may seem random
and trivial, they are in fact extremely important: a distinguished bearing, a
tall stature, and other things that everyone finds attractive and appealing.
These are the qualities that the great prophet praised in the assembly of the
people when he said the words: *Do you see the one whom God has chosen,
that there is none like him among the people?*[158] So not only barbarians but
even men of the greatest refinement revere a magnificent physique, and
think that people whom nature has blessed with unusual beauty are capable
of extraordinary feats. There is a saying of the great author Aristotle, that
if there are people who are by birth as physically superior to others as the
statues of gods are to those of men, then it seems fitting that everyone else
should be their slaves; and that if this is true of the body, it may be considered even more true of the soul (though the beauty of the one is much
easier to see than the beauty of the other).[159] But I will allow other people
to delve into these questions.

The Bible mentions a certain book in which Samuel recorded the sacred
rights of kings,[160] and a copy of which he placed in the Tabernacle. But Flavius
Josephus did not correctly identify the contents of this work; for he believed
that it contained all the evils which God had warned the people to expect
from an unjust king.[161] I, however, think that the book contained those laws
which directed the king how to practice justice and fairness, to administer
the state well and to the advantage of the citizens, not to play the part of
a ruler by indulging in criminal lusts, and finally, to preserve—despite his
great fortune—his sense of modesty (which must not be spurned by even
the greatest of men, and on which God places great value).

The matter of kings is described in Deuteronomy as follows: *Set up a king whom God will choose from among your people. Do not let a foreigner, who is not of your nation, become king. And once he has been made king let him not acquire many horses, or—for the sake of getting them—lead the people back into Egypt. For you have been commanded not to go back that way again. Also, let him not have many wives, for they may lead him astray; nor should he store up gold and silver. But once he has taken the throne let him write for himself a copy of this law, from the scroll that belongs to the Levite priests; and he should keep it with him and read it his whole life, so that he may learn to fear his God and to observe His laws, and so that he should not become arrogant or despise others.*[162] The wording of this law is perfectly clear, and it seems to contain the gist of the book that the greatest prophet of all time hid away in the sanctuary.

I said before that the Jews had the kind of state that the Bible calls a kingdom of priests. This must mean that their kings not only governed the citizens in peace and in war, but were also in charge of religious practices, holy objects, and ceremonies; for they were considered *hieromenai* [sanctified], and their authority, honor, and power were supported by both divine command and prophecy. But just as the kings were in charge of the sacred rites and had supreme power and the right to judge others, so it was the Levites—that is, the high priest, the regular priests, and their assistants—who claimed as their own right the management and care of these sacred duties. They were in charge of offering sacrifice, making atonement, reading the divine law before the people, and performing the other duties in the Temple. The Talmudists are quite right to point out how much greater the king was than everyone else, including the priests and the prophets. I shall record in passing what Maimonides has to say on the subject. He writes more or less as follows:[163] *There was a law that the high priest should defer to the king, and give up his seat to him, and stand whenever the king came to him. But on the other hand, the king does not stand in the presence of the high priest unless he is consulting the Urim in the solemn rite. Moreover, so great is the king's dignity that even a prophet humbly lowers himself to the ground whenever he is in the king's presence; as it is written, "Nathan the prophet came before the king, and as a show of respect he prostrated himself down toward the ground with his face forward."*[164] Not only that, but David himself, once the prophet had anointed him king, was so unconcerned about usurping the honor of the high priest that he put on his sacred cloak (which is called the ephod) and asked the Lord whether it would go well if he attacked the enemy.

This is a famous verse in the Book of Samuel[165] which recent translators have completely misinterpreted. Though they are very learned men indeed, in this case they seem to have dozed off or to have turned their attention to something else. I summon as my judges all those who are even slightly familiar with this text: the translators have rendered the words *vayiggash evyatar et ha'efod el david* as *applicavit sibi Ebiathar amiculum Davidis causa* [*Ebiathar put on the cloak for David*], when clearly the verse means what I said: that David took the sacred garment from Ebiathar and consulted the oracle. But let me quote some more of the things I have collected from the writings of the Rabbis. The king's unmatched dignity lay as well in what Rabbi Maimonides tells us in the second chapter of the Laws of Kings and Wars, and in the seventh chapter of the Laws of the Temple: *No one was allowed to sit in the courtyard of the Temple except for a king who was of the family of David.*[166] This is why a little before this he says something similar: *If he enters the courtyard, and he is of the family of David, he may sit.*[167] The courtyard was in fact divided into several areas. Part of it was designated for the priests and part for the people; and yet the priests remained standing even within the areas set apart for them. Maimonides says that the senators of the Sanhedrin also had the right to sit, but *in the middle of the area occupied by the profane masses,*[168] while in the more sacred areas of the courtyard no one sat but the king. So this set him above the priests as though he were closer to God, or a more important religious figure than they themselves were. And as for the other nations, Aristotle says that the earliest men more or less considered the same person to be both king and priest. I cannot see anything the least bit wrong with this. Those men were still living innocently according to nature, and the closer they were to their origins and their divine ancestry, the better they understood what was right.

But to return to the Hebrew kings, their sanctity was greatly enhanced by the fact that they were anointed with oil; for according to the Talmudists this practice was peculiar to them and to the high priests. There was also among the priests the one whom the Talmudists call *meshuah milhama,* "anointed for war," because he was anointed as a guarantee of divine protection, so that the wars would turn out well. The act of being anointed gave the kings a kind of divine stature and majesty, so that men would treat them as holy and they would have a closer relationship with God; but if the kings of that age did from time to time establish ceremonies and rituals or restore them to practice, it was certainly not because they were prophets. Though some people have this mistaken idea, it is completely groundless; for with the exception of David and possibly Saul, none of the others predicted the future by means of divine inspiration. Solomon, and Jehosaphat, and Hezekiah, and Josiah, and the others had power and authority over sacred matters only because they were suffused with the power of the sacred oil.

The types of spices with which Moses was ordered to mix this oil are described by Maimonides in the first chapter of the Laws of Vessels of the Sanctuary;[169] and according to the Talmudists it was kept for use in anointment and consecration until the time of Josiah. He then hid it in the Temple under the earth, in a secret spot that King Solomon had carefully prepared many years before when he learned from the prophets that one day the Temple would be leveled by the Assyrians. In the same hollow (the Talmudists say) Josiah put the Ark of the Covenant and the staff of Aaron, as well as the Urim and Tummim stones and the remains of the manna; and they say that the Jews got none of these things back when they returned to their land from Babylon and built the Second Temple.[170] So from that time on kings and priests received nothing like the same grandeur from the rites in which they were initiated, and most of the ceremonies and rituals did not receive divine favor, as they had before. The Jews commonly make a claim which Rabbi Zacuto reports in his book *Yuhasin*: *The fire used to lie upon the altar like a dog, because its power was extinguished after five things were missing from the Second Temple. But in the First Temple, the fire was like a lion.*[171] This most learned author says that the five things that were missing were in fact the ones I just said were hidden by King Josiah in such a way that his descendants never found them again.

I will put last a matter that almost escaped me because it is so trivial. The Talmudists think that the kings of Israel who made Samaria their seat of government after the split with the Judeans were never anointed with the oil that Moses had compounded in accordance with God's command; and this is why Elijah used nothing but common balsam to anoint Jehu the son of Jehosaphat. But they add that *this tradition was only passed down by the Sages.*[172] So I do not want to expend a great deal of effort to determine if it is true.

CHAPTER 15

*The methods which Jeroboam used to worm his way onto the
throne. The decline and fall of republics. The wisdom and modesty
with which Scipio held the lustrum. The lustral prayer on behalf
of the Roman Republic. The natural character of the commoners.
Why Jeroboam withdrew to the city of Samaria. Changes in
worship and ritual are the secret behind a shameless tyranny. All
the evils that arose from the secession of the Ten Tribes. Herodotus'
incorrect story about Sesostris. The overthrow of the kingdom of
Samaria. Why the victors in war transplanted nations. The exile
of the Judeans. The temple of Bel and the fortification of Babylon
came from the spoils of Jerusalem. The hanging gardens of Babylon,
and its brick walls. Berossus proves the ignorance of the Greeks.
The Judeans' return to Palestine. Power wound up in the hands of
the Levites. They fought each other for it.*

THROUGH THE EFFORTS of Jeroboam, who was a very energetic and passionate man, the unity of the Hebrew nation and the fabric of its magnificent state were torn in half. He was the sort of person who, as that Thessalian says in Aristotle,[173] felt hungry as long as he was not in command. When he was the military commander of the tribe of Joseph[174] and a prophet led him to hope that he might become king, he reasoned (correctly) that rulers are appointed by fate; so he turned his insatiable appetites towards getting absolute power. First he shook the loyalty of the soldiers and tried to switch them from Solomon's cause to his own. But when he saw that his plans had been discovered, he avoided execution by escaping to Egypt. When he returned home after Solomon's death he found a change of circumstances that suited his grand designs: he used the tribute with which the commoners were burdened and the unfair demands made upon them as an excuse to stir them up; he turned everything on its head, and he was the cause of the terrible calamities that Palestine went on to face.

In fact, it is part of nature's plan that all great states eventually experience changes of fortune. The Hebrew Republic had just reached the height of its happiness—it was entirely safe and peaceful, it was overflowing with riches, and the nearby kings and chiefs (and even the distant ones) were friendly. The state had also expanded to its geographical limits. So, its growth at an end, it remained only that, as fate decrees, it should start to shrink and decline (which must be the saddest thing about the human condition). When Scipio Africanus, who was then a censor, performed the lustral sacrifice,[175] a scribe recited before him during the ceremony that prayer which asked the immortal gods to make the lives of the Roman People better and greater. But Scipio said they were already good and great enough; so instead he prayed that the gods should keep them that way forever, and he ordered the public record of this prayer to be revised at once to reflect the change. This very wise man, then, understood that the grace of God never consistently favors one people with its gifts, or makes these gifts exclusive to that people alone. He feared the vicissitudes of fortune, and he was aware of all the factors that often come from within a state, and disturb or corrupt it without any help from abroad.

Thus, even Jerusalem—which flourished more than any other city, and was given a deep and secure peace by David and Solomon, two kings of the greatest virtue and wisdom—could not remain at rest for very long. For though after Solomon's death it did not have any enemies abroad, it did discover them at home. For that Jeroboam whom I have already mentioned made his appearance. He was a very restless man, and though his first criminal attempt failed, his second met with better success. He called a mass meeting where in front of the commoners he criticized the people's condition, the state of current events, and the king's actions; he knew that these commoners always bore something of a malicious grudge against their rulers. He himself was pretending to offer them "freedom" and other empty slogans of the sort, when what he really wanted was to make them slaves and subjects to a usurper. By this time most of the people were inflamed by his powerful words, and (as so often happens) allied themselves with the greater of two evils. There were plots and civil disturbances, which are usually the reason why the most ancient kingdoms and even the greatest republics tend to collapse or to change their character.

Then this turbulent leader took the Ten Tribes—which he had whipped up into rebellion—beyond the borders of Jerusalem, and chose the city of Samaria as a secure location for his government; from there he would rule everything. But in order to give his plans an even firmer footing he altered many of the ancestral practices; and he created a somewhat different form of divine worship and a new set of sacred rites. In establishing the worship of calves, he revived an old superstition[176] by adding a new twist, and since he could not keep the people loyal to him with the justice of his cause he won them over by religion, which is the glue that holds states together. So from then on the ten Israelite tribes, drunk on the sweet nectar of their rites, refused (as though at God's command) to develop any ties with Jerusalem, or to have anything to do with it. And whatever else may have been behind their hostility, the ultimate cause seems to have been their religious loyalties.

So this is how the Israelite kingdom began. From then on it was separate from the kingdom of the Judeans, whose citadel and capital was Jerusalem; and this, then, was the reason for every misfortune that befell the Hebrews, for the same people, who in the past could not be disturbed or defeated by the entire world and all its peoples banded together, became easy prey for foreign nations once it had grown weary and lost its vitality. Sufacus the Egyptian[177] immediately plundered the Holy City and the Temple; and so that he might spare the city no indignity, he had columns put up in various places on which (I shudder to mention) were engraved the female genitalia. For though Herodotus reports that this was the act of Sesostris he had the wrong name, as Flavius correctly realized.[178] And though this was certainly a trying experience, after many years both peoples—the Judeans and the Israelites—came to suffer far worse. The state of the Ten Tribes was completely destroyed and overturned by Salmaneser the Assyrian,[179] the entire people was carried off to Media and Persia, and their territory was left to the Chutaeans, a godless people whom Essarhaddon had immediately sent to Palestine from Persia in order to settle the Israelite country. Kings are generally in the habit of moving nations from one place to another as the fancy strikes them, just like the flocks that shepherds lead from winter to summer pastures. This helps them to break down and change the natural character of conquered peoples; and though these peoples might offer resistance while they are on their own soil, they are calm and cooperative on someone else's.

From that time on the Israelites never had a chance to return to their homeland or to revive their state, for they had so entangled themselves in the snares of their impious idolatry that not even the many years of their exile, or the passing of the ages, could satisfy God's wrath. Once the Israelites had been led off into exile it remained only for the Judeans to pay the penalty for their actions. Though this certainly did happen, it took rather a long time. During the reign of Zedekiah,[180] Nebuchadnezzar defeated Egypt and Syria with his enormous forces and reduced to ashes both Jerusalem and the Temple, which was extremely opulent. While this was happening he received word of the death of Nabolassar, and since he had to make great haste to take up his father's throne, he gave his officers orders to lead the Judeans to Babylon and the areas surrounding it. There he assigned them the settlements and lands on which the new colonists could make their living.

In the history of Berossus there are ancient documents which tell us that Nebuchadnezzar used the spoils he brought back from Jerusalem to build a temple to Bel, and that he enlarged Babylon to suit the grandeur of his empire, and surrounded it with walls of brick.[181] He also made aerial gardens and hanging groves to please his wife, who had been raised in the mountains of Media and loved to look at woods high up, as they were there. So even though the Greeks were all agreed that this amazing accomplishment was the work of Semiramis, their claim is worthless. They have been refuted by an author of incomparable quality who is quoted in Flavius' work—Berossus the Chaldean, whom everyone believes to be extremely ancient and to have preserved for all time, and with the greatest reverence and fidelity, the history of his nation.

The penalties that Almighty God visited on the Judeans were not heavy, nor did they last very long: though in exile, they lived comfortable and easy lives, as if still in their ancestral home. Then after seventy years had passed they returned to Palestine, built Jerusalem and the Temple, and reestablished their state. But their circumstances were very different from what they had been before; for the government which had once been under the control of the descendants of David was now taken over by the Levites (though they did this on several different occasions, and in different guises, nonetheless they were all Levites).[182] Once these men had acquired supreme authority they made the republic as wealthy and powerful as it had ever been, but they violated the distinction between sacred and profane by competing for power, honor, and glory. So the fact that the Levites were considered "religious" (and therefore sacred) did nothing to assist their piety or self-control, even though God had chosen them long before and set them apart from the citizen body to live lives free of ambition, among the sacred rites and ceremonies.

CHAPTER 16

The republic ruled by high priests. Their sins and their shameless machinations. On the sons of Eliashib. The impiety with which the temple of Gerizim was built. The loathsome crime of Onias. The magnificent leader Mattathias the Hasmonean. The prince Judah Maccabee. On Alcimus, the most worthless man on two legs. Judea again under kings. On Herod. On the Idumeans and their god Qos. The accurate prophecy of Sameas. The injustices of Herod's rule. How he corrupted the laws of the Jews.

OF THE MEMBERS of the Levite class, it was above all the high priests who were in charge of the nation's affairs after the restoration of the Temple, even though they were not called chief or king. These men kept to themselves every bit of influence, power, and wealth, or gave it to whomever they wished. All the other priests were part of the crowd, and had neither honor nor authority, so those who were regular Levites stopped at nothing to win the honor of this important position. Some tried to achieve it by force, many more by deceit and trickery, and only a few by doing what was right. But the most shameful of all was what the two sons of the high priest Eliashib did after his death: Joshua was planning to use underhanded means to seize the priesthood from his brother Jochanan (who was morally and legally entitled to it) with the help of a barbarian[183] general named Bagoses, while Jochanan, hoping to keep what he had been given, committed an even greater crime. He murdered this same Joshua with his own hands in the temple of God, in the middle of the sacred service, and sprinkled the altars with his brother's blood.[184]

Not long afterward, Jochanan was succeeded by Jaddua; and once again his brother Manasseh hoped to take the high priesthood from him. But because Manasseh had unlawfully married the daughter of Sanballat, who was a gentile,[185] the people rebelled against him, and he realized that he either had to break off his relation to his powerful father-in-law or else (Heaven forbid!) give up any hope of attaining the high priesthood. Once he had carefully weighed his options and discussed his plans with his father-in-law, he finally settled on an infamous course of action that has been talked about ever since, though never with approval. He decided to build a temple on Gerizim, the highest mountain of Samaria, and Alexander soon gave him the necessary authority, at Sanballat's request. So this man who had been unable to perform the highest office in Jerusalem, because he had violated the law, became high priest the best way he could—in a fraudulent temple—and having achieved this distinction he thought he was in Heaven.

Such is the character of a truly worthless human being: you can't say which is greater, his ambition or his sinfulness. And yet Manasseh's actions pale in comparison with the things the fourth Onias[186] did to satisfy his lust for power. After he became high priest he realized that he was no match for the supporters of Jason.[187] So in order to win over Antiochus Epiphanes, whose protection he needed, he abandoned the laws of Moses, and in their place he adopted the beliefs and rituals of the Greeks. Then he had a foreskin surgically attached so that he would not have to bear the marks of circumcision, and he had all his people do the same. In the end this high priest became an instrument for the impiety of Antiochus Epiphanes, who subverted all the practices of the Jews.

There was nothing left of the ancient and pure ways when Mattathias the Hasmonean—the great restorer of the nation—took up arms, returned the Jews' laws to them, and took control of the state with the title of prince.[188] After his death the title of prince was taken up by Judah, who was called Maccabee. But the high priesthood still possessed great power and authority, so some time later, Antiochus Eupator[189] used deceit to gain entrance to Jerusalem and made Alcimus high priest in place of Onias. (Antiochus no longer trusted Onias, because he realized that both the people's behavior and the turn of events hinged upon him.)[190] But once Alcimus obtained the sacred office he acted much more immorally than Onias ever had.[191] He went immediately to Demetrius the son of Seleucus[192] and made accusations against Judah the prince, whose authority he could not bear. Sinfulness disturbs even itself; it is never satisfied with only one crime. So Alcimus had Bacchides, the king's superintendent, attack his own country with an armed regiment; and when Bacchides went back to the king with his mission unfulfilled, Alcimus gathered together a group of criminals and added them to the troops he had already gotten from Bacchides. Parricides, godless men, and adulterers, driven by shame and guilt, came from all over to Alcimus' side; and he used flattery, encouragement, and bribes to get them to do his bidding. In the end, this model of a high priest was even prepared to tear down the walls of the sanctuary, which had been built by the prophets and the Hasideans, in order to add it to his list of accomplishments. But death took him while he was making his plans, and the people appointed Judah high priest in his place; this made him the first man to serve as both priest and prince. Jonathan, Simon, and Jochanan went on to do the same thing, and finally Aristobulus put aside the title of prince and called himself a king.[193]

So for the first time since the death of Zedekiah Judea once again had kings, if only Levites; the last of these was Antigonus. After he was driven out and killed,[194] Herod ruled the kingdom, which he had already received from the Romans. His origins were not at all royal, and he did not come from a priestly family; he was a Jewish convert from the Idumean people. Though the Idumeans were not really Jews, they had been considered and called Jews ever since Hyrcanus forced them to adopt the beliefs and observances of the true God.[195] Before that they worshiped some god named Qos, whose rites had always been in the custody of the Costobars, an illustrious Idumean family. There was a well-known prophecy of Sameas,[196] who had predicted, long before it happened, that Herod would be made king of the Jews, but as a plague and a punishment; and this is exactly what happened. For this Idumean immediately did away with Aristobulus the high priest, who was only a young man; then with Hyrcanus, whom he had lured away from the Parthians;[197] and finally with whatever remained of the line of the Hasmoneans. Their fate was shared by the seventy elders who were members of the great council called the Sanhedrin. Once Herod had gotten rid of anyone who might frighten or endanger him, he gradually began to increase his power, and from this position of supreme authority he started to do entirely as he pleased: he changed the ancestral practices of the Jews, introduced new ones, and did many things forbidden by the laws. Let us see what Josephus has to say about it: *With his foreign enthusiasms he corrupted the ancient teachings, which had never before been tainted by innovations. This is why in our own times, which followed his, we have suffered serious harm. For we have neglected everything which used to lead the masses to piety.*[198]

CHAPTER 17

On the Messiah, king of the Jews and of all nations. The mystical spelling of a word in the text of Isaiah. The Jewish interpretation of the prophecy of Balaam. What is unique about this kingdom. Rabbi Abraham's observations on Maimonides. Ezekiel's obscure prophecies about the Temple and its rites in the time of the Messiah. That these have been subjected to incautious questions.

SO THIS WAS HOW it happened that after the Jews returned from Babylonia, the government came to be in the hands of those who had the weakest claim to it: first the high priests, next the Hasmonean princes, who were Levites, then the kings from that tribe, and finally Herod the Idumean. It was during his reign that the Messiah, the King of Kings, was born to the family of David; and it is to the Messiah alone that we should apply God's promise to David that his throne would be eternal, and that his offspring would sit upon it.[199] Certainly this promise cannot have referred to Solomon or his descendants: after they had lost the kingdom, not once in the period after the Babylonian Exile did they get it back. If this were God's pledge, it must have been empty and false (and to think such a thing would be the grossest kind of impiety). This is why we must understand "the offspring of David" to be the Messiah, the guarantor and defender of our freedom; it was about him that the angel proclaimed, in the passage from St. Luke, that *his kingdom will be without end.*[200] The angel took those words from the ninth chapter of Isaiah,[201] about which Rabbi Yarhi[202] has commented that the scribes once *used a subtle method of analysis to determine why—contrary to normal practice—the prophet placed a final "mem" in the middle of a word.*[203] It was certainly not for nothing that the scribes gave in to such anxious ambiguity[204] and the Talmudists believed that it signaled some great mystery which was neither freely available nor open to all, but hidden away and shut up in a secret shrine.[205]

Though the Holy Book contains many prophecies about the great king Messiah, the Jews consider none so worthy of their admiration as the one that God inspires Balaam to speak in the twenty-fourth chapter of Numbers.

But after thoroughly examining the meaning of this prophecy, they came to the wise realization that not all of it refers to one and the same king, and that the prophecy must therefore be divided up in such a way that part of it refers to David (who was the first member of the tribe of Judah to occupy the throne) and the rest to the Messiah (who, though the last king of that line, was greater and more powerful than all the others).[206] Maimonides described this with great care at the end of his *Mishneh.*[207] Our great master likewise refuted those who think that in the Messianic Age nature will wear a different face and its course be permanently changed. He says these people did not understand Isaiah's words in the eleventh chapter of his book.[208] In that chapter are certain riddles which mean to tell us that every pious and good man will live in peace among the wicked and the criminal, so that he will have nothing to fear.[209] The verse with which Rabbi Abraham son of David[210] reproves Maimonides, which he quotes from the book of Mosaic laws, i.e. *I will remove the wild animals from the land,*[211] is completely irrelevant and does not apply to the times of the Messiah. But then, this sharp and thorough critic of Maimonides' faults tends to select proofs of this type, which have the appearance of solid reason rather than any real power, and fall apart when you test them.

Whenever I examine the sacred rites, practices, and religious ceremonies that the holy prophet Ezekiel described in the last part of his book,[212] I find myself thinking about what they mean and to what they might refer. They are so different from the ones that Moses commanded, and the Jews (as they themselves admit) have never adopted them. But the proper way to understand these verses was set forth in the Talmud, in Tractate Menahot.[213] Moreover, Maimonides touches briefly on this matter in the *Mishneh*. It will be worth our effort to quote his words here: *All the quantities for libations described in the Book of Ezekiel, and whatever is written there about the numbers of sacrifices and the order of the sacred service, are only peace offerings*[214] *which were not adopted by the generations of men and did not become part of the general custom. Moreover, the prophet instructs and explains how the peace offerings should be carried out during the dedication of a new altar in the times of the Messiah, when the Third Temple will be built.*[215]

This is not a fantasy of the Jews or a figment of the Talmudists' imagination—it is an absolute fact. The prophet has described a different Temple and different rites, which would exist in the age of the Messiah; and he has also measured the Temple's structure—its courts, gates, and other features—according to the specific criteria necessary for its construction. This is why the Jews say that its form cannot be clearly understood,[216] and that although Ezra was building the Second Temple to be a copy of Solomon's structure, he also followed Ezekiel's instructions for the Third Temple, but only as far as this holy man could understand the prophet's vague and complex description. This is what our great rabbi meant in this quote from the Laws of the Temple: *The building of Solomon was already clearly described in the Book of Kings; but though the building of the future is described in Ezekiel, it is not clearly set out or explained. And when the people of the Second Temple period built in the days of Ezra, they did so according to the building of Solomon, and along the lines of the things set out in Ezekiel.*[217] But the Jews have nonetheless indulged in a serious delusion: they expect that the Messiah will build the kind of temple that can be seen, entered, and walked upon. Of course, we who have been born into the kingdom of the Messiah know that this is not so: everything that the prophet says about the building's design and its parts has a hidden meaning, and it is hard to say exactly what these specific details signify or how they ought to be explained. In fact, I will offer everyone the same suggestion that Xenophanes of Colophon makes in the work of Marcus Terentius Varro,[218] that *people should write in terms of what they believe and not what they are sure of; for it is man's part to suppose, and God's to know.*

In any case, when the Jews label certain parts of the Bible *genuzin* [hidden], which bans children and young men from reading them, they place into this category Ezekiel's prophecies at the end of his book. I believe they made the right decision, for that whole section is harder to understand than Plato's theory of numbers. Let those who would have themselves be known as masters of divine wisdom marshal their resources—they will do their share of sweating before they can uncover even the tiniest bit of the knowledge that has been hidden there. *The man who guesses well I will call a great prophet.*[219] But I also think that no good can come of too much guessing; at least we can agree that this prophecy and some of the others are of the sort that God did not want human beings to understand. For though the light shed by the Gospel has helped us to make great strides in our understanding and knowledge,[220] there are still things we can only wonder at. This is why, in the case of prophetic secrets, it would be nothing more than foolish audacity to reach beyond what the Holy Spirit has put within our grasp.

The place of the Jews after the coming of the Messiah. On the restoration of the Jews, which they are still awaiting. What makes that nation respected even today. How much our religion owes to the Jews. Whether they have rewritten or corrupted the Holy Book. On the diligence and dependability of the Masorites.

IMMORTAL GOD wanted the Jews to be called a kingdom of priests and a chosen people, and to be the only caretakers of His rites and worship until the day should dawn when the Messiah would be presented to the world. From that moment on, the son of God wanted his heavenly gifts, which for a long time had belonged to only one people, to be shared by everyone; and though the news was spread to peoples everywhere, it benefited only those who believed. Here was a truly astonishing turn of events: the gentile nations received with joy and awe the One who was entirely devoted to their welfare, and who left the kingdom of Heaven in order to rescue mankind when it had stumbled. The Jews, on the other hand, did not understand that this man, who more than one prophet had indicated was going to arrive at a set time and place, had now done so and was there among them, so strong was the power of their incomprehension. Their eyes were blinded because their minds were on other things and refused to see what was right in front of them; so they were disowned and spurned by God, and *even now they eat lentils, and cry over their lost birthright*. The prophet Jeremiah says that their crime was recorded *in hardest steel*.[221] In fact, they did not even try to avoid their punishment: they said, *may his blood be on us and upon our children*.[222] St. Paul wrote something very noteworthy in the letter he sent to the Romans. There he says as follows: *I do not want you to be ignorant of this mystery—a hardening has come upon part of Israel, until the full number of the Gentiles shall come in*.[223]

Though nowadays the Jews are wandering about, pathetically unaware of where they are, there will no doubt come a time when they will be returned to the right path. The sun has not set for the last time: its light will once again shine even on them, and though they have certainly fallen, they have not been extinguished. Ezekiel also produced some prophecies about this, which are found in chapter 36 of his book. The prophet says that in the future God will give them a new heart, and a better understanding will occupy their breasts. Then the veil that Moses placed on his face will be lifted,[224] for they will turn to God, who allowed them to live in darkness and the profoundest ignorance so that the day would finally come when He could show them exceptional mercy. This is the proper interpretation of the words of St. Paul: *And when Israel turns to the Lord, the veil will be lifted up.*[225] Many people have found this verse to be extremely murky, and it has taxed the efforts of a number of scholars.

This matter of which I am speaking is very significant, and its obvious consequence is that we cannot in good conscience continue to shun the Jews as the objects of popular hatred when they still possess such great potential. Certainly St. Paul reveres them, and despite their errors he lavishes praise on them. For he says: *It is they whom God chose, and theirs is the glory, and the Covenant, and the Law, and the sacred worship, and the promises; theirs are the patriarchs, and from them came Christ in his corporeal form.*[226] What greater nobility could there be? They can count so many patriarchs, prophets, and kings among their grandfathers and great-grandfathers; in short, so many excellent men of divine virtues whose names God has sanctified!

It is true, I must admit, that all of today's Jews have a slavish and il-liberal character, and if you were to examine their way of life and their pursuits, you would find nothing at all worthy of a great and proud spirit. The reason for this is not hard to imagine, for such pursuits are (like other phenomena) cyclical in character. Just as the times change, so does human behavior. Certainly, on the day the bright light of their freedom was taken away from them and their power was torn from their hands, their noble spirit was also broken, so that today nothing remains of their energetic vigor. As good Eumaeus is inspired to say to his king Ulysses in Homer, *Zeus, whose voice is borne afar, takes half a man's worth away from him when the day of slavery comes upon him.*[227] Just as the boxes in which slave dealers tie up dwarves while they are growing not only keep their little bodies from expand-ing but even shrink them, so slavery of any sort places shackles on the soul itself and suffocates a man's noble characteristics. How high can they aspire when for so many years and throughout the world they have been wearied by such terrible injustices? Haven't boys dragged them by the hems of their garments, and men by their beards? And wasn't the rage of every Caesar vented upon them? Tiberius sent their young men out to provinces where the climate was unhealthy, on the pretext of assigning them military service.

He sent four thousand to Sardinia, which was especially plague-ridden, so they would meet with a horrible death.[228] Titus threw nearly as many to the animals when he put on shows at Beirut and Caesarea.[229] Even Trajan, who was the most lenient of all the emperors, forbade the Jews to read the Law, and later emperors often did the same. This was the worst kind of affliction, and Rabbi Zacuto includes it among the *shmadot* or persecutions. He says that *they decreed a persecution, so that the Jews could not read the Law.*[230]

But all these things were done by the pagans; since we have much closer ties with the Jews our two groups should show affection for each other, and should consider it a common bond that we obey the commands of the same God. So deeply does St. Paul love this people that he actually wants to give up his life for them; he also says that *if the first fruits are holy then so is the lump;*[231] *and if the root is holy so are the branches.*[232] I am not going to indulge myself now by singing their praises, since I despise nothing more than silliness; and yet it is perfectly obvious, as far as the more recent past is concerned, how much our religion owes to this nation. For who if not the Jews has kept the Bible for us, safe and sound? How many scribal errors would have crept into the Holy Book if it had been entrusted only to the care of men like Lactantius, Augustine, Gregory, and Chrysostom, who—holy as they were—knew nothing of Hebrew? Among the Greeks and Latins who governed the early Church,[233] only Origen and Jerome[234] knew Hebrew (and this is an overstatement). Others did not even know the alphabet. When, therefore, mistakes were made because of the carelessness of the copyists, it was not the Christian scholars to whom the men of that age looked for help or support.

The Jews, on the other hand, had one interest and one concern that they all shared: to protect the books of Moses, the Prophets, and the Writings from the dangers of the times. They alone are to be congratulated for this; no other nation merits a share in their glory. Rabbi Abraham of Salamanca[235] has a very important passage in his book *Yuhasin*, from which we learn that all the copies of the biblical text had been corrected according to an extremely ancient manuscript which Rabbi Hillel had once written with his own hand. (He was the greatest leader of the Jews, and came from Babylonia to Syria[236] sixty years before the birth of our Lord God Christ.) Rabbi Abraham's words are well worth quoting here:

In the kingdom of Leon[237] *they uncovered the book of* arba'a ve'esrim [twenty-four, i.e. the number of books in the Hebrew Bible] *which is called "Biblia," and which was written down by Rabbi Hillel; and they corrected all their copies against it. And I have seen a part of it which was for sale in Africa, and it had been written nine hundred years before my time.*[238] *And Kimhi*[239] *says in his Grammar, on the verse "that you may remember,"*[240] *that the Pentateuch was in the city of Toledo.*[241]

So at that time the Jews had the good judgment, the intellectual power, and the set of rules needed to correct the text of the Bible. How easy it would have been for them to rewrite those passages that seemed to contradict their delusions,[242] since the Christians hardly knew three words of Hebrew! But their piety stood in the way, and kept them from changing any of the sacred text. And yet there were some who believed that the Jews had deliberately misrepresented many passages, though Origen gave a brilliant response to these people in the eighth book of his explanations of Isaiah. I myself am astonished whenever I think about the tireless efforts of the Masorites,[243] for after carefully examining and comparing every part of the Hebrew text they marked it with certain signs.[244] This happened after the destruction of the Second Temple, around the year 436. They recorded not only how many verses and words were contained in each book, but even how many letters; so even though the world later descended into complete barbarity, thanks to them not a single mark of that wonderful text was lost. With good reason did the Rabbis say that *the Mesorah is a sort of walled enclosure for the Law.*[245]

Rabbi Zacuto, whose testimony I just now praised, includes in his book some Jewish foolishness from which, Lord help us, he concludes that the accents and punctuation marks existed in the time of Ezra.[246] I have mentioned this theory only so that those men of our time who say it was not the Masorites who invented the system of marks can add it to their other frivolous arguments. I would also like to criticize another theory that appears in this rabbi's book. Using the same argument as before,[247] he dates the Targum of Onkelos[248] to the time of Ezra. Although this argument has no value, and readily shows us how little the first conjecture is worth,[249] it will no doubt find its defenders, if only as a reason not to reject the other theory. For a long time now, many scholars have been motivated by a zeal so stubborn that they will latch on to anything at all which supports their opinion, and it is not of the slightest interest to them what it is or what they are doing with it.

If the text of the sacred scriptures is not in doubt and is unlikely to undergo any further changes, I give the credit to the Jews who lived in more recent times, after the destruction of the Second Temple. For once their great and wealthy state had been destroyed, they began to take measures so that despite extreme misfortune they might salvage from the wreckage at least this one plank, whose value was priceless. Though I love them for this, the rest of their activities deserve only pity. They busy themselves with marks and letters and books, but no more than that. They neither examine nor seek out the sacred and true perceptions, so what they themselves say in their own language fits them to a tee: *They made the essential trivial, and the trivial essential.*[250] And the worst of it is that they have no idea how childlike and clueless they really are, for even though all their misfortunes have occurred because they know nothing of God's law, they claim that it was because they lost their homeland, and their kingdom was snatched away from them, and other things of the kind which cannot make us happy when we have them or truly unhappy when we lose them. Seneca mentions a foolish friend of his wife named Harpastes, who suddenly lost her sight *and did not know she was blind, and kept asking her pedagogue*[251] *to take her somewhere else, saying that her own home was dark.*[252] The same thing has happened to the Jews. They carry around within themselves the cause of their own misfortune; and if by some miracle they were to get Canaan back, they would change their skies but not their spirit. They bring their own night with them wherever they go, and it will not lift until they have paid the heavy penalties for their foolishness and their stubbornness.

BOOK II

CHAPTER 1

The family of the high priest. Alcimus judged to be bad.
Who was responsible for choosing the high priest? The privilege
which Claudius gave to the king of Chalcis. The duties of the high
priest. When the high priest carried out his noble duty. The clothes
he wore on that occasion. The mistake which Flavius Josephus
made out of haste, and which has till now misled everyone. Its
refutation. The correct opinion of Maimonides.

AFTER THE KINGSHIP, the most distinguished office was the high priest-hood. The Rabbis had an old saying that Israel had been graced with three honors—crowns as it were—the kingship, the priesthood, and the Law.[1] Since in my treatment of the kings I discussed whatever issues happened to come to mind, I am going to examine the other topics in the same way, casually and at random. Though Moses established twelve priestly families and David then established twenty-four, only one was the family of the high priest, and its grandeur outshone that of all the others. According to Flavius, Onias the son of the third Onias,[2] who was a young man of the high-priestly family, fled in his indignation to Egypt, where he established a temple. The reason was that he saw his office transferred to Alcimus at the whim of Antiochus, and though Alcimus was born to a priestly family he was not part of the succession to the high priesthood. I am pointing this out only because the learned Sigonio labors under the delusion that Alcimus was from the line of Levi, though not of Eleazar or Ithamar.[3] That this is a mistake is clear from what Flavius says about Alcimus in the twentieth book of his *Antiquities*, in the eighth chapter.[4]

After Alcimus, Judah Maccabee likewise received the high priesthood, even though he was an outsider with the wrong lineage, who did not have the right of succession (although he was from a priestly family). By now it should be obvious that not all of Aaron's descendants could achieve this distinction through legitimate means, but only a select few. It was the high priest who was in charge of all the other priests,[5] a distinction conferred on him by the unanimous agreement of the seventy elders, to whose judgment and power everything was entrusted, however important it might be. This is how Maimonides has described it for us, with great accuracy, in the fourth chapter of the Laws of Vessels of the Sanctuary.[6] But though Herod did a few things for good and honorable reasons, as a general rule he violated both the law and time-honored custom; and he made it his practice to install and remove high priests as the fancy took him. In the end, the right to choose the high priest was granted by Claudius to King Herod Agrippa of Chalcis,[7] and his successors kept this right until the end of the Jewish War.

The functions of the other priests were divided among them all. No one could perform the offerings on the altars or slaughter the sacrifices until he had been chosen by lot. Only for the high priest was it completely legitimate to perform any of the rites, and anytime he wished; he was not made to wait his turn, and he did not keep to a set duty or post. The high priest's duty was a noble and distinguished one—to enter the Temple enclosure, which in Hebrew is called the Holy of Holies. This he did only once a year, on the solemn Day of Atonement, and only at the hour set aside for the ceremony of atonement. (I will soon have an opportunity to discuss this in detail.) Until now no one has analyzed the clothes that the high priest wore when he entered the awesome enclosure of the Temple on the most important day of the year; for they have all assumed, with great self-assurance, that on that occasion he wore two cloaks—one of them called the Humeral[8] (*efod*), and the other the *hoshen* or Rational (because it was tied around the seat of intelligence and reason, i.e. the breast).[9] I am not going to discuss here the great skill with which these two garments were made. It is certain that they were crafted of gold, and purple, and scarlet, and gems, and they were obviously made according to the instructions given in the twenty-eighth chapter of Exodus.

But now I would like to assert that the high priest never wore these cloaks in the enclosure of the Temple. I must therefore reject a theory that for a long time was supported by the greatest scholars, and is now universally accepted and gains strength every day. I wish that at least I did not have to part company with Josephus: we know that he belonged to a priestly family and performed the highest offices in Jerusalem, and that he left for posterity a record of things he had seen with his own eyes, or about which he was well-informed. But what person is so perfectly diligent that in the course of a long meditation he does not doze off from time to time? Or how can he avoid haste and sloppy thinking, which is reckless and blind even when dealing with matters that are crystal clear? So I cannot accept what Josephus says in the fifteenth chapter of the fifth book of his *Halosis*[10] about the *efod* and the cloak called *hoshen*: *The high priest wore this garment only when he entered the enclosure; at other times he naturally wore something less precious. Moreover, he entered only once a year, on the day when ancestral custom commanded everyone to worship God through fasting.*[11]

No one has dared to say a word against this; they have all accepted it, every last one. But this author, great as he was, really ought to have remembered that one of the oldest laws of the Jews was that there were four special garments that were white and woven entirely from linen, and that these were the only things the high priest wore when he performed the ritual of atonement once a year in the enclosure.[12] This is why the Jews gave these garments their own name, *clothes of "laban,"* i.e. *white.* Maimonides says about them the following, in the eighth chapter of the Laws of Vessels of the Sanctuary[13] (which comes from the Talmudic tractate called Yoma): *The clothes of white were four garments in which the high priest dressed when he performed the rites on the day of fasting. They were white in color, and made entirely of linen: the tunic, the trousers, the belt, and the fillet.*[14] The day of the fast was the tenth day of the month of Tishri, when the high priest would go into the Holy of Holies. The Talmudists were the first to investigate this issue, and on this point I have absolute confidence in their findings.

I also wonder at the laziness with which Flavius Josephus and the others have ignored the edifying words of the sixteenth chapter of Leviticus, which prove beyond a doubt the truth of my statements. It will be useful to us to copy out this passage. These are God's instructions to Moses about the day of fasting and atonement: *Tell your brother Aaron that he should not go at any time into the sanctuary, behind the curtain, so that he may not die. With these things he should enter the sanctuary, with a young suckling ox to serve as a sin offering, and with a ram which will be a holocaust.*[15] *He will wear a holy linen tunic, and linen trousers will be on his flesh; and he will be girded with a linen girdle, and covered with a linen fillet. These are the sacred garments.*[16] Then at the end of the chapter it adds: *Let the priest make atonement and let him put on the linen garments, the holy garments.*[17]

It is now a simple matter to describe the other mantles, which the high priest wore outside the enclosure of the Temple. The Talmudists call these *golden clothes,* not of course because they all had gold woven into them, but because they were rather ornate. Now there were eight garments of this type, four of which were worn by both the high priest and the other priests: *an ankle-length tunic, trousers, a girdle, and a fillet.* The other four were worn by the high priest alone: a *purple cloak* with bells and pomegranates; a *shoulder cloak* or *efod;* then a *pectoral garment* or *hoshen;* and finally a gold *plate,* which was placed over the fillet. Let no one say that of these eight garments, the first four appear to be identical with the ones that, as I said above, were used exclusively in the Holy of Holies, for the clothes that the high priest wore outside the enclosure were made of expensive linen, and the girdle was of Phrygian workmanship.[18] This will be obvious to anyone who compares what is written in the twenty-eighth chapter of Exodus to the sixteenth chapter of Leviticus. Though the garments described in both places are made of linen, *bad* is common linen, while *shesh* is the most exquisite kind of byssus.[19] Nor is my opinion contradicted by the fact that in verses 29 and 35 of the twenty-eighth chapter of Exodus, Aaron is commanded to enter the sanctuary wearing the *efod*, the *hoshen*, and the purple tunic. For it is generally agreed that the sanctuary had two distinct parts: the outer part, which is always called Holy, and the inner one, which the Sacred Book calls (not always, but usually) the Holy of Holies. To be unaware of these facts would be the height of ignorance. Besides, what I said about the *clothes of white*—that the high priest could not wear them outside the enclosure—was so true that even on the tenth day of the month of Tishri, when according to custom he used to enter the enclosure, he had to put on the *golden clothes* in order to carry out the rites that he then had to perform outside the enclosure. This is accurately described in the Talmud, in the third chapter of Tractate Yoma.

CHAPTER 2

The sacred clothing of the high priest was kept at times by the Romans, and at times by the Jews. On the high priest's cap. On the hats of the priests. The Urim and Tummim stones, which had the power to prophesy. When they were lost. Why others were made and used, though they no longer had any power. The method of consulting the Urim and Tummim oracle. The kinds of questions to which the high priest gave a response.

THE BEAUTIFUL and remarkable craftsmanship of the garments that the high priest wore outside the enclosure is obvious from Flavius' remark that *the sacred clothing of the high priest*[20] was very carefully preserved in a well-fortified tower which the Hasmoneans had built in the northern precincts of the Temple, which Herod later named Antonia after Mark Antony.[21] In any case, to look after this clothing was a very prestigious honor, which is why the Romans repeatedly claimed it for themselves; they did give it back to the Jews, but only as a favor.

I said that of the eight garments that the Talmudists call golden, there were four that the high priest wore along with the other priests. Among these was a cap or fillet. Both high priests and regular priests were forbidden to perform the rites with their heads uncovered, just as the Roman *flamen*[22] was not allowed to do so. The Jews report that the high priest's cap was not entirely the same as the hats worn by the other priests, and Maimonides says that a kind of band was wound around his head, just like a worn or broken limb is wound up.[23] The priests' hats, on the other hand, were shaped like helmets. This, he says, is why they are called *migba'ot*: they rise up like hills.[24] Rabbi Abraham ben David disagrees with this in his commentary on Maimonides. He says that although the priests' hats were like helmets, the high priest's fillet was much taller, with the band wound around in a circle like the headdresses of the Arabs today. Rabbi Joseph,[25] who is a very careful author, says the same thing. (His commentary, whose title is *Kesef Mishneh, The Crown of the Mishneh*, is priceless.)

As I said before, the Urim and Tummim stones, which were set into the clothing of the high priest, were hidden by Josiah in the time of the First Temple, and were not recovered in the time of the Second. But other stones were made and placed on the cloak called *hoshen*—not because the high priest was still using them to prophesy the future, but in order to complete the inventory of objects that the great Moses had decreed to be the proper ornament of the high priest. In fact, if even the smallest item was missing, the high priest was declared *improperly dressed*[26] and could no more perform the rites than if he were one of the profane masses (whom God's law condemns to death for making such an attempt).[27] But what is the reason that in the Second Temple the high priest was not consulted[28] and did not give prophetic responses? This question has been debated by the most intelligent Jews, who believe that it was simply because the Holy Spirit and the Will of God[29] were no longer a palpable presence in the Temple.[30] They also said that the human mind can know nothing about fate or destiny unless it has been inspired by God, an opinion which is absolutely correct.[31]

Maimonides mentions all this in the Laws of Vessels of the Sanctuary, where he also describes the method with which the oracle had been consulted in the past:[32] the high priest used to stand and turn his face toward the Ark, while the person asking the question was at his back. Once he had asked about the outcome of the course of action he was considering, the high priest, roused by the Heavenly Spirit, examined right away the cloak called *hoshen*; and from the letters that swelled up on it by some miraculous means he learned what was going to happen and answered the question. This method of learning about the future was not used by private citizens or commoners. It was reserved for kings and the most senior judges, or for men who were sent by the people on public business. Whenever a matter of importance arose it was dealt with there, while the business of private individuals was left to vows and prayer, so that the sanctity of the oracle would not be cheapened.

How much the high priest was permitted to rip his clothes. How much the other priests were. On Caiaphas. The laws of marriage treated the high priest differently than the others. Marriage with a virgin, a widow, a blemished woman, and a divorcée. Polygamy. The high priest's residence. On Augustus Caesar.

NOW LET US DESCRIBE some of the other laws pertaining to the high priest. One of these was that he was forbidden to tear his clothing out of grief,[33] but the Talmudists restricted this prohibition to the *way* he tore it: the high priest was allowed to rip his clothes, but only at the bottom around his legs; above that and up to the breast, he could not.[34] On the other hand, they say that the other priests were allowed to tear their clothes from the top part downwards.[35] This is how it is set out at the end of the tractate called Horayot, and if it is true, we may arrive without any need for discussion at the conclusion of the commentators that Caiaphas[36] violated the law when he tore his own robe because he could not endure the majestic words of the Messiah, as St. Matthew tells us in the twenty-sixth chapter of his gospel.[37] It is not for me to investigate this any further; for even after I have conscientiously given it all my effort, I will still be upset with myself for scratching at the dirt with my feet and yet not digging up so much as a single grain.

In the twenty-first chapter of Leviticus the high priest is commanded to marry no one but a virgin. The reason is somewhat obscure; after all, this rule did not apply to regular priests, who were allowed to marry widows and were only forbidden women who had made a living from their bodies, or were divorced from their husbands, or had a visible flaw.[38] The Talmud (in the first chapter of Tractate Yoma) tells us that the high priest was forbidden to marry two women at the same time,[39] but if he did he had to divorce one of them before the tenth day of the month of Tishri.[40] Otherwise he was unable to perform the ritual of atonement in the Temple enclosure on that solemn day. His situation was in fact unique; other Jews were legally permitted to marry more than one woman. I will show this later on, at the appropriate point in my discussion.

It is written in Tractate Middot that there was a small chamber in the Temple for the high priest where he usually stayed during the day; this was called *the high priest's chamber.*[41] As to the house he owned outside the sanctuary, Maimonides tells us that it had to be located in Jerusalem, and within the city itself.[42] Roman law, on the other hand, ruled that the *pontifex maximus*[43] should live in a publicly owned house; so because Octavius,[44] who had obtained the distinction of this office after the death of Marcus Lepidus, refused out of modesty to accept a public house from the Senate, he ordered that a part of his own house should be made public in order to satisfy the law.[45]

CHAPTER 4

The high priest's entrance into the Holy of Holies examined, in conflict with the theories of St. Augustine and Carlo Sigonio. A passage in the Letter to the Hebrews which Sigonio misunderstood. That the incense altar was not in the Holy of Holies, despite the opinion of St. Augustine.

I WOULD LIKE to turn back to the topic from which I was diverted. I said that the high priest entered the enclosure of the Temple on the solemn Day of Atonement, which was observed every year on the tenth day of the month of Tishri. All the Jews, as well as the greatest scholars of the Greeks and Romans, have reported this fact in exactly the same way, and I myself have come to the same conclusion: at no other time, and for no other reason, was the high priest allowed to see this mysterious place. And yet among the learned men of antiquity, there was one, Augustine (a man of great holiness and learning), who thought that the high priest entered the Holy of Holies every day, in order to burn the incense. As to the statement that he entered only once a year, Augustine thinks this refers to the annual expiation that was performed with the blood of purification.

Carlo Sigonio, who applauded this theory, added more support to it. He proposed that the high priest went into the enclosure every day, though in the company of the other priests, while once a year he went in by himself, i.e. without the priests. But I cannot allow it to seem that I have let pass without comment such a crass mistake; and let me be the first to say that Sigonio, in fact, either wanted to deceive us with outright sophistry, or (I daresay) was himself unwisely deceived. He was obviously thinking of what the Apostle[46] said in his letter to the Hebrews: *The high priest entered the second tabernacle once a year on his own, and carrying blood.*[47] These words really mean that the high priest could enter the enclosure only once a year, and then only by himself; but Sigonio has twisted them to mean something else, as though to say he went in once a year by himself, and every other day with the other priests. I cannot imagine a more pointless line of argument than this interpretation.

I will leave aside the weighty judgments of all the Talmudists and Rabbis, to which intelligent scholars everywhere have always paid the greatest respect whenever they examine the ancestral rites and ceremonies of the Jews. Maimonides reports the gist of these judgments in the Laws of the Temple: *The Holy of Holies is more sacred than the rest of the Temple, since no one goes in but the high priest on the Day of Atonement, at the very time of the sacrifice.*[48] The evidence that this statement is true is so clear that the Jews had no need to embellish it: I say that there is no place in the Holy Book from which it can reasonably be concluded that anyone but the high priest was permitted to enter the secret place. Besides, we have learned how often the high priest himself went in from what is written in the sixteenth chapter of Leviticus: *Tell Aaron that he should not at any time enter the sanctuary, which is behind the curtain and before the propitiatory cover*[49] *above the Ark, so that he does not die. For I will appear above the cover in a cloud. But let Aaron enter the sanctuary with these things: a bull-calf and a ram for the holocaust. And from the assembly of the Israelites he should take two goats for a sin offering and a ram for a holocaust. And when he has offered up the bull-calf, and has prayed for himself and his house, he should stand the two goats in the presence of the Lord, at the entrance of the Tent of Witness; and he should cast lots on both the goats, one lot for the Lord, the other for the goat to be sent forth.*[50]

Notice that the sanctuary, which the verse says is "behind the curtain," is none other but the Holy of Holies, which contained both the Ark and the cover of propitiation. Moreover, everything that Almighty God orders to be done there belongs to the category of rituals performed only on the tenth day of the month of Tishri, on the famous Day of Atonement. From this it follows that the high priest entered the enclosure only on the day those ceremonies took place; for this is clearly what the law commands. So away with Sigonio's soothsaying; it doesn't suit the gifts of this great man whom in other respects I have often admired. (The fact is that he wrote well and auspiciously about Jewish matters, which was too much to hope for given that he knew no Hebrew at all.)

But how will we respond to Augustine, who thinks that the incense altar was *inside* the enclosure, and that it was there that the high priest offered incense every day? This man, wise as he was, has nonetheless made a serious error; and in this instance he has not brought his sharp and subtle faculties to bear. The place where the incense altar stood was definitely separated by a curtain from the enclosure itself;[51] this is why in Leviticus 16 the enclosure that lies *behind* the curtain is called the sanctuary,[52] whereas Exodus 30 says of the altar used for smoking incense that it was *in front of* the curtain.

So clearly the curtain hung in the middle, between the enclosure and the incense altar. I will quote the words of Exodus 30, so as not to leave the reader hanging. It says there: *Make an altar for incense from shittim-wood and cover it with gold, both its sides and its horns. And place it before the curtain which is before the ark of testimony and the propitiatory cover, so that Aaron may burn fragrant incense upon it every morning.*[53] Come now, unless our senses are being retarded by some stupor or phlegm[54] we can see that the incense altar was before the curtain, and the curtain itself was before the ark of testimony; this means that the curtain separated the incense altar from the ark of testimony and the seat of propitiation. I will admit that in the fortieth chapter of Exodus, verse 6,[55] it is commanded *that a gold incense altar should be placed before the ark of testimony*; but what is not said there about the curtain that came between them is added shortly afterwards: *a gold altar was placed in the tent of meeting before the curtain.*[56] So that argument carries no weight at all with me.

CHAPTER 5

Certain passages of Philo the Jew are examined and explained. A mistake of Philo's, and of the author of the First Book of Maccabees. That after the Jews returned from Babylonia, they did not keep closely to the law in the way they built the Temple. Certain opposing arguments are rejected. The privileges which Moses was given above the high priests.

IT IS ONLY out of carelessness that I have not yet quoted here that famous passage of Philo the Jew[57] which could have warned Sigonio, who knew about it, as to just how ill-advised Augustine's doubts[58] really were. In the book called *On Sacrificers*[59] this esteemed author says: *The law commanded two altars to be built, which were made of different materials, stood in different places, and had different functions. One was built of stones that were carefully chosen and yet unfinished, and it stood in the open near the Temple courtyard; it was used for burning the sacrifices. The other altar was made of gold, and stood behind the first curtain in an inaccessible place; and no one was allowed to see it but the priests, and only when they were pure. It was made for offering incense.*

Philo is obviously saying that this altar was behind the *first* curtain, which was hung before the Holy; so he clearly means that there was a different, second curtain, which separated the Holy from the Holy of Holies. In any case, just as priests (except for the high priest) were not admitted to the Holy of Holies, so the Holy—where the incense altar stood—was closed to the masses; even the priests could go in only when accompanied by the high priest. In fact, in the Gospel of St. Luke[60] Zacharias,[61] who had the rank of priest rather than high priest, burns incense at this very altar. And about the commoners Luke writes: *The entire mass of the people was praying outside at the time of the incense offering.*[62] And yet again: *The people were waiting for Zacharias, and were surprised that he was taking so long.*[63]

Since I have already started to quote Philo as a witness, I would like to mention some of his other comments. For though he said that no one but the priests entered the Holy which was behind the first curtain, in other places he says explicitly that the Holy of Holies (which stood behind the second curtain) could not be entered by the priests, but only by the high priest, and then only once a year. His statement on this matter is found in the second book of *On Monarchy* (though Sigonio also saw this passage, as in the previous case he did not realize that it contradicted his theory): *No praise of the Temple could do it justice, as we can conclude from those parts of it that are visible; for as far as the things contained in the innermost areas are concerned, no one sees them but the high priest.*[64] Sigonio will never escape; he is clearly stuck tight.

In the same passage Philo adds about the high priest: *And yet he was allowed to see everything, though he was permitted to enter only once a year.*[65] This is a weak and half-hearted statement which looks as though it wants to correct what has just been said. This it completely fails to do, for what is different about this, and how does it oppose what came before?[66] But it is no great effort to restore the meaning of the passage and read it as follows: *And though he was permitted to enter only once a year, nevertheless he was not allowed to see everything.*[67] This is of course very different. After he has said that only the high priest saw the Temple enclosure, he then qualifies his statement by saying: *And though he was permitted to enter only once a year, nevertheless he was not allowed to see everything.* Then Philo gives the reason for this statement, which is certainly noteworthy: *For he brings in a censer full of burning coals and incense, and the entire place is completely filled with smoke, which naturally rises up. Then of course the sense of vision is obscured, and is inhibited, and cannot penetrate very far.*[68] So this is the reason why Philo says that even the high priest could not see everything in the enclosure with his own eyes.

Up to now Philo has described these things with insight and even in-spiration, but what I quoted before from his book *About Sacrifices* was not entirely without error, i.e. that the other altar—which stood in the open near the courtyard of the Temple, and received blood and sacrifices—was built, *as the law dictated*, from *whole, unpolished stones*. Actually, in Exodus 27 God wants it to be made of wood and covered in bronze, which Moses then does in chapter 38. A long time later, when the great king Solomon founded the Temple, he did the same thing (Second Book of Chronicles 4:1 and First Book of Kings 8:64). In fact, the command in Exodus 20 that the altar must be made of soil or stone applies to the days when the holy people was wan-dering through desolate regions and hostile territory, and did not have a set location for its rites, or a fixed home.

I am aware that this altar was also made of stone in the time of the Second Temple; but how many other such cases can I name, in which the instructions of the ancient law have not been observed? It was certainly a harsh and fearful time for the Republic, when things were often made uncertain by fears of foreign enemies and by civil conflict; even the holiest men did not follow the law completely when they built the Temple.[69] The passage in the First Book of Maccabees, chapter 4—*they found whole stones in accordance with the law, and a new altar was built on the model of the old one*[70]—is not a very strong proof; for I am no more afraid to accuse this author (whoever he was)[71] of making a mistake than I am in the case of Philo. Both were misled by the passage I quoted from Exodus 20.

But there was no need for me to go off on this tangent; I would like to finish my discussion of the incense altar, once I have discussed the most important point of all. In Exodus 30 Immortal God orders the horns of this altar to be sprinkled once a year with the blood of a calf, on the day set aside for fasting and atonement.[72] But first the high priest had to carry this blood into the Holy of Holies, and then he had to go out and sprinkle it on the horns of the altar (this was commanded in the sixteenth chapter of Leviticus).[73] So I have already settled the matter beyond the need for further discussion; for if the high priest had to leave the enclosure in order to sprinkle the horns of the altar, obviously it could not have been inside the enclosure. Though these arguments contradict the opinion of St. Augustine (and of Carlo Sigonio who agrees with him), they had to be examined so that everyone would be persuaded by the testimony of the ancient Hebrews—and the wise men of Greece and Rome—that the high priest entered the Holy of Holies only once a year. It is true that the Talmudists say what I mentioned before, that when the high priest was consulting the oracle with the Urim and Tummim gems, he stood with his face turned towards the Ark.[74] But he could have done this in any part of the Temple; let no one be under the inadvertent impression that the high priest went into the enclosure whenever he consulted the oracle.

This is the method of consultation described in the Book of Judges, chapters 1 and 20,[75] and in the First Book of Samuel, chapter 10.[76] The case of Moses should be treated differently, i.e. that he conversed with God at the ark of testimony, near the cherubs themselves, and at the cover of propitiation; this is clear from both Exodus 25:22 and Numbers 7:89. But what kind of madness would it be to associate with Aaron and the other high priests what applied to Moses alone? There is no question that once God deemed Moses worthy enough to speak openly with Him, to be together with Him, and even to be seen by Him, He exempted him from the norms of the human condition. The Holy Book comments that none of these things was granted to anyone else.[77] This is all I will say on the subject; for though I had determined to give a brief taste of many issues, in my enthusiasm I have said practically everything there is to say.

CHAPTER 6

A substitute was appointed for the high priest on the tenth day
of the month of Tishri. The grades in rank which separated the
high priest and the other priests. In the time of the Second Temple,
a solemn oath was demanded of the high priest once a year. The
reason for this. The appearance of a heresy about burning
the incense in the Temple enclosure. A goat was sent into the
desert. The mountain of Azazel. Certain laws of the
Jews on this subject.

SINCE I HAVE SAID that the noble calling of the high priest was connected
with the events which took place on the tenth day of the month of Tishri, it
seems appropriate to discuss several issues related to this subject. Maimonides
writes in the Laws of Service on the Day of Atonement that the high priest
alone performed all the rites that took place on that day, even including the
ones that were not specific to the holiday;[78] this (he says) is the reason that
on that occasion, the high priest was also in charge of those offerings which
were normally performed by the other priests. Maimonides also says that
around the time of the holiday the high priest was very carefully guarded
in public for seven whole days, so that he might not accidentally become
contaminated[79] and therefore ineligible to perform the sacred rites. We know
this from the beginning of the Talmudic tractate called Yoma.

Our great rabbi then says something worth quoting about the high priest's
substitute, who was appointed every year on the eve of the fast. I will give
the sense of this passage: *It was established as a practice*[80] *that a second high*
priest should be appointed to the first; for if anything had happened to make
him appear impure, the other one would perform the ritual in his place. But
though this substitute was going to enter the enclosure instead of the high priest,
he did not need to be initiated,[81] *whether the high priest happened to become*
contaminated before the daily morning sacrifice,[82] *or whether it happened after*
the offerings had been made. As soon as the Day of Atonement had passed, the
first high priest returned to his duties, and the second one gave up his position.
But if the first one died,[83] *the second was put in his place.*[84] More or less the

same thing is reported by Flavius in *Antiquities* 17:8.[85] He mentions a Joseph son of Ellemus who served as high priest for a single day when the regular high priest, Matthias, had defiled himself in his dreams with an impure vision on the very night before the Day of Atonement.[86]

In the Laws of Vessels of the Sanctuary, Maimonides calls this sort of substitute *s'gan*; and he says that all the other priests answered to him.[87] He also tells us that there were two priests who performed the same duties for the substitute that he himself performed for the high priest; and these Maimonides calls *katikolin*, "controllers."[88] He then defines another rank below this one, in which he places the seven functionaries who were called *amarkalin*, "officers," and kept the keys to the courtyard (which none of these men could open unless they were all present). Below them were the three *gizbarin*, "treasurers," or the men in charge of the sacred depository. After these was the *rosh hamishmar*, "head of the watch," who commanded the Temple guards; then the one called the *rosh bet av*, literally, the *head of a father's house*, i.e. one of the twenty-four units into which the priestly families were divided. And finally (says Maimonides) after them came the rest of the rank-and-file priests.

This is more or less the way the Talmudists defined the various grades of priests, except that there is a different kind of priest whom they rank between the high priest and his substitute; they call this priest the *meshuah milhama*, i.e. *anointed for battle*. But I will discuss him later on. Right now I would like to add something that occurs to me about the Day of Atonement: according to Maimonides, a delegation was sent every year by the Senate[89] to secure from the high priest a solemn oath on the day before he was to perform the ritual of atonement. They used to do this because in the time of the Second Temple a certain heresy had reared its head, which gave birth to the sect of the Sadducees. According to this heresy the incense that was used to fill the enclosure with smoke should first be put on the fire, and then brought into the enclosure, whereas the Jews had a tradition (handed down from the time of Moses) that it should be lit only in the enclosure itself. This is proven by the wording of the law in Leviticus 16:12–13.[90] The new interpretation, on the other hand, was motivated by the wording at the beginning of this same chapter: *I will appear in a cloud over the place of propitiation.*[91]

This verse, however, does nothing at all to help the Sadducees' claim, as we can clearly see from the wording used (as I have said) in verses 12 and 13. And yet unlikely as their opinion was, it gained more followers every day and thoroughly swayed men's minds. So the Sanhedrin, which was very concerned that the high priest himself might give in to this mistake, decided that their representatives would make him swear a solemn oath on the day before the tenth of Tishri. Maimonides says that the formula was as follows: *We order you to swear by Him whose name dwells in this Temple that you will not change a thing of what we have told you.*[92] Then they mentioned some other decisions that had been made for everyone's benefit.[93]

The most significant aspect of the festival's celebration was the ritual casting of lots, which marked one of two goats for the altar; the other was sent off to the nearby desert, to a mountain called Azazel, so that it would fall straight to its death. The Jews write that this goat was led into the desert by a foreigner, with great effort, and was then thrown down from the top of the mountain.[94] They also say something or other about the shelters that were placed along the way from Jerusalem to the desert, to house the men who were feeding the goat. Then they also describe the cord, one end of which was tied to the goat's horns and the other to a rock; they even describe the color of the cord and many other things of this sort,[95] about which they know no more than I do. So I will leave these questions open-ended; there are no better theories or conjectures that might explain them, and they are certainly not going to draw any strength from what meager information there is.[96]

CHAPTER 7

The two ways in which the high priest was initiated, and their character. When one of these ceased. When the high priest was not bound to offer the young ox prescribed by the law.

THE CONSECRATION of the high priest consisted above all of two things—his clothing and his anointment. God commanded that whoever was going to serve as high priest should wear the holy tunics and cloaks for seven days, and that he should be anointed with the oil produced for this purpose by a unique process. The Talmudists called this kind of high priest *increased and inaugurated by clothing,*[97] and *increased and initiated by anointment.*[98] They called the solemn act itself *the increase of majesty through clothing and anointment.*[99] But in fact, once the holy oil disappeared—Josiah (as I said) had hidden it away in a hollow at the time of the First Temple, and neither Ezra nor anyone else ever found it in the time of the Second—the high priests were initiated without anointment. It was enough to inaugurate them with clothing alone.

Their clothing was of the kind described by the Talmudists in the first chapter of the tractate called Yoma. There were eight cloaks that the high priest wore for seven whole days, though only in the morning; in the evening he took them off. And before the holy oil was lost, he used to be anointed for the same number of days. It is written in the last chapter of Tractate Horayot that there was no difference between a high priest who was consecrated with oil and one who was initiated with clothing alone, except that the anointed priest was commanded by the law to offer a young ox to God if he had sinned in such a way that his individual fault would cause the entire people to be held guilty.[100] The priest who was initiated with clothing, but not with oil, was spared this requirement; but in all other respects, both types of priest were the same. The Talmudists' observations about the sacrifice of a young ox were derived from the fourth chapter of Leviticus.[101] In fact, the essence of everything I have said in connection with the high priest's initiation can be found in the wording of our great Egyptian rabbi:

And they appoint the high priest, who is the head of all the priests, and they anoint him with the oil of anointing; and they dress him in the clothing of the high priesthood. And if there is no oil of anointing they exalt him with the priest's clothing alone; just as he is exalted with the oil, he is exalted with the clothing. How do they exalt him with the clothing? He wears eight garments and takes them off, and puts them on again the next day; he does this for seven days, one after the other.[102]

Then a short while later: *There is no difference between the priest anointed with oil and the priest exalted with clothing, except for the ox which the anointed priest brings if he erred in regard to one of the commandments for which a sin offering is required.*[103] I don't want spend the time and effort it would take to translate this, because I have already described its contents in great detail.[104]

CHAPTER 8

The divisions of the priests, and their daily tasks. Those who judged
the priests' flaws. The situation of priests who had been convicted.
The "woody chamber." Antigonus' crime against Hyrcanus.

THOUGH TILL NOW I have discussed the high priest, who was the
leader of the other priests, the two categories are extremely close; so obviously I could not avoid touching on many issues that concern the priests
themselves and their duties. Of course I have no intention of going back
over these same issues. The priests were chosen from among the Levites to
perform offerings and sacrifices. Moses set up eight divisions, four of which
were descended from the family of Eleazar, and four from that of Ithamar.[105]
Later on the great King David created twenty-four such divisions, sixteen of
which were descended from Eleazar and eight from Ithamar. According to
Flavius Josephus, all these divisions were preserved intact until the destruction of Jerusalem; the family lines that defined them were never confused.[106]
This actually proves to be true if you follow them back, starting with Judah
Maccabee's rededication of the Temple, from one generation to the next. And
this is truly a thing almost beyond belief, when we consider that the condition of the Jews was always changing from good to bad and back again. Let
the author be responsible for the truth of his words.[107]

These twenty-four divisions came to Jerusalem one at a time and in
their turn, and each performed the Temple rites for one week; so after one
hundred and sixty-eight days each division returned to its place in the order. (During the three famous festivals the Jews call *regalim* [the pilgrimage
festivals], all the divisions were permitted to serve in the Temple at the same
time, on the condition that the voluntary offerings and the daily sacrifice
were performed only by the priests whose turn in the rotation had come
around.)[108] These are the divisions that St. Luke, discussing Zacharias, calls
ephemeriai [daily].[109] All this was handled wonderfully by the illustrious Joseph
Scaliger in his *Isagogic Canons*, which he published to refute Eusebius; so
I won't put any effort into discussing these issues. We will be much better
served if I pay particular attention to the things others have ignored or, if

they did record them, were careless about. This is what I have tried to do throughout my work.

The Talmudic tractate called Middot[110] records that the power and judicial authority of the senators who belonged to the great council lay above all in the fact that they held court (in the part of the Temple called Gazith)[111] over the cases of priests whose membership in their family or clan[112] was disputed. If one of these priests lost his case he left the Temple court in shame, dressed in black and stripped of his office; but if he won he appeared in public wearing white, and went right back to performing his sacred duties along with his fellow priests. In the second chapter of this Talmudic tractate, it is written that these senators also made decisions about the physical flaws and illnesses that (as though they were evil omens) made any priests they afflicted legally unfit to serve. Priests who were judged unfit then stayed in the part of the Temple called *lishkat ha'etzim* ("woody," as it were), and there they chopped the wood that was piled on the altar. But though they were stripped of their priesthood they still enjoyed exactly the same rights as the other priests of their division, including the right to eat from the sacrifices. Flavius Josephus says the same thing in Book 5, chapter 15, of his *Jewish War*.[113] In addition, everything I have just said about the account in the Talmud is also reported by Maimonides, as follows: *The great court would meet in the Chamber of Hewn Stone, and their daily activity centered around judging the priesthood and checking the priests' lineage and their defects. Every priest whose lineage is found to be invalid dresses in black and wraps himself in a black shroud, and he leaves the court. And all who are found to be whole and kosher put on white, and come in and serve with their fellow priests. He who is found to be kosher but has a physical defect sits in the Chamber of Wood and chops wood for the offerings, and he shares the meat of the sacrifices with the members of his house, and he eats.*[114] As the meaning of this passage is obvious from what I have already said, there is no need for me to translate it.[115]

The law ordered that not only the priests had to be physically perfect, but the high priest himself. Flavius, at any rate, reports that Antigonus captured Hyrcanus and cut off both his ears,[116] which made it absolutely certain that he would never be able to administer the holy office. His friends kept reminding him of this fact when he tried to return from Parthia to Judea because of a foolish notion that with Herod's help he could regain his former position.[117]

The subject at hand seemed to call on me to discuss which marriage rights were given to the priests, what was the system of casting lots used to assign individual priests their daily tasks, and into which classes they were divided up (so that some were *katikolin*, others were *amarkalin*, and still others were *gizbarin*, while all the rest were part of the rank and file). But I have already touched on these issues in the course of my discussion of the high priest. I also discussed in that context the four garments worn by both the high priest and the others, for they did not have any special clothing of their own. I am therefore leaving this issue aside.

CHAPTER 9

That the priests and the Levites were a part of the great council called the Sanhedrin. The Levites were entrusted by the people with both the king's and the citizens' business. They represented the ideal of virtue. That once the Republic of the Hebrews was split in two, they joined the better half and the more righteous cause. How much they then declined from their upright character and ancient integrity. They acquired complete command of the state, which they exploited without self-restraint.

MAIMONIDES SAYS in the Laws of the Sanhedrin that Levites and priests were elected to the supreme Senate in Jerusalem, which consisted of seventy-one men; and also among its members were the most distinguished of the other Israelites.[118] From this we may conclude that some of the Levites and priests seem not only to have taken care of the sacred rites but also to have administered civil suits, and—along with the prince or the chief leader of the people—to have deliberated on matters of state. For the Senate called the Sanhedrin was appointed by the king, or the prince, or whatever else they called the man who looked after the public interest, and Flavius Josephus listed among the rules established by Moses *that the king should do nothing without consulting the high priest and the senators.*[119]

Nor am I surprised at this form of government, since God Himself (as I have often mentioned) refers to it as priestly.[120] Certainly in chapter 19 of the Second Book of Chronicles, when king Jehosaphat placed Zevadiah in charge of all the business of the king and the people of Judah, he also assigned the Levites to him as satraps[121] who would take over some of his responsibilities. And long before this the great David ordered Hashaviah and seventeen hundred of his kinsmen to take charge of the inhabitants of Benjamin, Simon, and Judah, and to administer both religious and royal affairs.[122] David also gave Jeriah and twenty-seven hundred of his kinsmen power (and obviously the same twofold authority) over the inhabitants of Reuben, Gad, and half the tribe of Manasseh. The proof of this is found in First Chronicles, chapter 26.[123] There is no question that Hashaviah, Jeriah, and their kinsmen—who (according to the author of Chronicles) served in the highest offices in the state, and altogether numbered forty-four hundred men—were Levites, and members of that tribe which was the guardian of all the sacred rites.[124]

In addition, the Levites claimed it as their special privilege to have supreme knowledge of all the laws, and of matters both divine and human. They passed this knowledge on to the people in congregations throughout the towns of Judea; so it is understandable that they were regarded as the source and inspiration of every expression of genius, every work of scholarship, and all the fine arts. It was therefore to the Levites that the people turned as paragons of piety and virtue. In fact, while some of them saw to the ceremonies and rituals, others directed their efforts to teaching, and many more tended to their civic duties and took part in the deliberations of state, they all lived lives free of ambition. But when the tribes split into two factions and the Israelites broke away from the Judeans, the Levites left behind the cities they had held in Israelite territory, and embraced that faction[125] which preserved the religious rites untouched and uncorrupted according to the custom of their ancestors.

But nothing lasts forever, and after the Babylonian Exile and the building of the Second Temple, the injustices of the age and the wars that raged provided (as the laws of fate decreed) the motive for a new scheme of government: for the first time there were Levites who dared to serve as high priest even though the law did not allow them to accept this honor. This was, so to speak, the source of all the evils that followed—their exceptional good fortune made them greedy, and they did not restrain their desires to the point of settling for what was already within their grasp. Their position went from great to even greater, and men who had gotten things they dared not hope for were driven by shameless ambition to obtain the highest office. Finally, as if all that were not enough, they assumed the title of king and placed crowns on their heads. After that they plotted against one another, practiced deceit and the ways of aristocrats, and did nothing to restrain their desires. From that time on they considered it to their advantage to place themselves above the state, and it didn't matter at all to them how they got there, as long as they did. So men who had once yearned for the rarest kind of compliment, one which has never yet been granted to any ruling class, i.e. that they were harmless, eventually changed their goals; and the arrogance and pride of monarchic rule caused them to blur the difference between God's place and man's.[126] But I have already discussed this issue.

CHAPTER 10

*Who the 'anshei hama'amad' were. The sort of mission they
performed. Sacrifices performed on behalf of the people. That these
delegates also performed their duties outside Jerusalem, in their
congregations. On their fasts. Why they did not fast on the days
before and after the Sabbath.*

THE TALMUDIC TRACTATE called Ta'anit discusses those men who were
sent by the people or by the entire community[127] to take part in a public
delegation in order to attend the sacred rites. I really do not think I should
pass up the chance to examine this institution, because it is quite unique.
The law decreed that whoever wanted to offer God a sacrifice or gift had
to be personally present at the ceremony; but some of the offerings were
made in the name of the entire people, and of course such a huge number
of citizens, who lived in many different locales and cities, could not present
themselves at the Holy Temple. So the earliest prophets decided that men
of the greatest integrity and piety should be chosen from among the Israelites[128] as representatives of the entire community, and should be present at
the sacrifices in place of the people. The Talmudists call these men *anshei
ma'amad*, which might be translated as something like "station-men"; they
were enrolled into twenty-four divisions, just as I have already said about the
priests and Levites. Each division was led by a man called the *rosh hamishmar*,
the *head of the watch*. In addition, the law did not permit any of the community's representatives to decline this solemn duty, when the week of their
particular division's turn in the order arrived.[129]

Now, those among them who lived in Jerusalem or close to it had to
gather in the Temple together with the two divisions of Levites and priests
whose turn it was that week. On the other hand, those who lived in distant towns far away from the Holy City were spared the difficulty of making the long journey; it was enough that they gather together in their local
congregations and direct their minds and thoughts towards the Temple in
Jerusalem.[130] So even though they were absent from the actual performance
of the sacred rites, they kept up with them at the very time they were taking

place, and even in public. While these representatives were performing their weeklong duties they had to fast four times, and on fixed days; Monday, Tuesday, Wednesday, and Thursday had been set aside for this purpose. It did not matter whether they were gathered at the Temple in Jerusalem or in the congregations of their towns; in both cases they were obligated to fast. In honor of the Sabbath, they were freed from the obligation to fast on Friday; and for the same reason they did not afflict themselves on Sunday, *so that the joy of the Sabbath should not give way to the sorrow of the fast.*[131] But I have said enough about this; the rest of the Talmudists' description of the prayers of the representatives and the reading of the Law[132] may be found in their own work.[133]

CHAPTER 11

On the Levites who ministered to the priests. Their divisions, and
their various duties. 'Netinim.' When the law on the Levites' term
of service ceased to apply. That Levites were not rejected from
service as the priests were. How serious a violation it was for
Levites to perform each other's duties.

IT FOLLOWS that I should say something more about the Levites, whose
title had a double meaning. It is true that all the members of the tribe of
Levi were called "Levites," and my remarks in chapter 9 of this book apply to all of them. But at the same time the term "Levite" was also used of
those who took turns performing the sacred duties in Jerusalem, and these
duties were very different from the functions of the priests. I should briefly
describe this matter here, as I do not want to seem to be neglecting the
role these men played. The function of these Levites, then, was to serve the
priests and perform all the tasks that were beneath them. For Jewish practice and law clearly assigned to the Levites the same jobs that the Romans,
at the sacred rites and in the temples, handed over to the sacrificers, their
servants, the temple stewards, the heralds, and the flute players. Not, to be
sure, to all the Levites, but only to those who were the descendants of Levi
but did not trace their ancestry to Aaron. Though Aaron himself was, of
course, of the same stock as they were, the honor of the priesthood rested
in his family and his descendants; so the Holy Book does not generally refer
to his children as Levites.[134]

At first, in fact, the Levites (in accordance with Moses' law) did nothing
but assist the priests in their work, carry the Ark on their shoulders, and
look after the sacred vessels. Then David organized the entire group into
twenty-four divisions, each of which took its turn in the Temple for a week
(obviously they were organized just like the divisions of the priests). But
with the same law King David also set up an additional twenty-four families
of Levites—some to sing during the rites, and the others to play harps and
lyres.[135] He also organized yet another twenty-four divisions of temple war-
dens. Finally, just as the Levites would minister to the priests, so the Levites

themselves were assigned others to fetch wood and water. At first these were
Gibeonites whom the great leader Joshua had spared in war.[136] Then in the
time of David and Solomon, others were added from among the conquered
nations; these were all called *netinim*,[137] what we might call "surrenderees" or
"enrollees."[138] But both Cornelius Bertram and Carlo Sigonio have explored
this question so thoroughly in their learned treatises that I have nothing to
add; so instead I will consider some other issues.

In the Talmudic tractate called Hullin (at the end of the first chapter) it
was remarked that the divine law which releases Levites from their service
at the age of fifty was not meant to be permanent—it applied only to the
time when the Holy Tabernacle had to be constantly moved about. But once
the rites and ceremonies were firmly established in the Temple at Jerusalem,
even Levites who were older than fifty did not retire from their sacred duties.[139] It is also reported at the end of that chapter that the Levites were not
examined for physical flaws, because there was no flaw that would make them
unfit for their sacred task. This is why my earlier discussion about the high
priest and the other priests does not apply to them. Yet at the same time,
the Talmudists exempt from performing singers whose voices were affected
by their advanced age, and who would therefore spoil the performance.[140]
Maimonides writes that it was a capital crime for a Levite to take over the
duties of a priest, or even to take over a task which, though it belonged to
the Levites, was not the kind of work to which he had been assigned. (Just
imagine the results if a Temple steward were to switch places with a singer!)
But if a priest undertook the task of a Levite he did not receive the death
penalty; rather he was doing a thing *against the command of God*.[141]

---

CHAPTER 12

*The Jerusalem Temple. Why it contained so much gold. On
the temples of the ancients, to which gold was not brought. That
this was not against the custom of the Jews. A mistake made
by some scholars is refuted. The Talmudic law regarding those
who came to the Holy Temple. What 'ta skeua' are in the Messiah's
statement. The industriousness with which Solomon built the
Temple. How quickly the work was finished, despite its enormous
size. How expensive, and how slow, was the construction of the
temple of Diana at Ephesus. Why it was built on marshy ground.
The Jewish fiction about Mount Moriah.*

NOTHING THE JEWS have ever done was as wonderful, as magnificent,
and as celebrated in every work of history as the incredibly extravagant
Temple that Solomon built and dedicated in Jerusalem. Since there is a brilliant description of it in the eighth book of Flavius Josephus' *Antiquities*,[142]
I am not going to give a full account of its grandeur, or of the techniques
and methods used to build it. I *will* say that though the innermost shrine
of this Temple was covered in heavy gold and countless vessels of pure gold
were produced for its ceremonies, we should see this not as the lavish ex-
travagance of a king who had more money than he knew what to do with,
but as the order and command of God. The Almighty does not weigh the
value of the gifts He receives, and He has no need for earthly riches. To Him
belongs whatever we see and whatever we do not see; and yet He delights in
the piety that men show whenever they offer up the things they most dearly
love, and those they regard as their greatest possessions.

Plutarch says in his *Political Precepts*[143] that there were once temples that
no one could enter until they left all their gold outside. Some of the greatest
scholars have concluded from this that the men of antiquity (whose judgment
was beyond reproach) had condemned shrines that glittered with magnificent
gifts and large amounts of gold. But these scholars are completely mistaken.
This is not what Plutarch meant to say, and he immediately adds that people

who wished to enter the temple also put aside their iron. I think the reason for both these prohibitions is obvious: people who came to a holy place to humble themselves before the gods were supposed to appear without gold, or coins, or finely crafted ornaments; and they stripped themselves of their iron and weapons because they understood that all their strength lay rather in God. I myself believe that when Plutarch wrote this he was thinking of the ancient Temple in Jerusalem; for practically the same thing is said in the first chapter of the Talmudic tractate called Yevamot. From there Rabbi Maimonides quotes the following, in the Laws of the Temple: *No one may enter the Temple Mount with a staff, or with shoes on his feet, or with a wallet or money wrapped up in a cloth.*[144] In chapter 11 of the Gospel of St. Mark, when the Messiah, the Savior of men, wishes to bring back an ancient and vanished custom, he declares *that no one should go into the Temple with any vessels or equipment, or burdened with baggage.*[145] And I have heard that the meaning of *skeuos* is a chest or pack, or one of those containers that overflows with its burden. It was no doubt for the same reason that the Messiah drove the moneychangers, and the merchants who were trying to sell their wares, out of the holy precincts: the ancient prohibition had been forgotten because of the exceptional sinfulness of the age.

The impressive bulk of the Temple looked down upon the city from above, for it was located at the base of the mountain whose area King Solomon expanded by heaping up earth at the lowest point of the valley until it reached a height of about four hundred cubits. Despite the enormous amount of work that went into its construction, it was completed in seven years. This may seem almost beyond belief. After all, the Greeks took much longer to build things; they barely finished the temple of Diana at Ephesus in two hundred and twenty years, even with all the wealth of Asia at their disposal.[146] But then, that project was made difficult by the topography of the site—they decided to build the temple on marshy ground so that it would not be shaken by earthquakes.

Rabbi Eliezer mentions in his work[147] an idea that was the general opinion of the Jews, though it is completely worthless and deserves nothing but contempt—that the mountain on which the Jerusalem Temple stood was the very one on which Adam, the father of mankind, first offered sacrifice. Later on (he says) it was on this same spot that Cain and Abel offered their gifts to God, and there again that Noah built an altar when he emerged from the ark; and it was there that Abraham traveled at God's command to sacrifice his son. Along the same lines, it says in Genesis Rabba (on the verse *Vayitzer*),[148] and in chapter 23 of the tractate of the Jerusalem Talmud called Nazir, that

Adam was formed from the dust of that mountain,[149] and that the Sages were right to say—as the ancient expression goes—*man's creation took place in the same spot where he received atonement for his sins.*[150] None of us is so stupid as to believe this; and yet the Jews still cling to their old delusion.[151] But it is not my task to say anything more about such fancies.

CHAPTER 13

*Certain amazing facts about the Temple, and about the large
numbers of sacrificers and priests. A unique and almost
unbelievable fact about Passover. On the three piles of wood on
the altar. On the eternal flame. 'Korban ha'etzim,' the wood-
offering, and the festival set aside for it. The disagreement between
the Talmudists and Flavius Josephus. A superstition of those
who entered and left the Temple.*

IT WOULD be difficult to say just how many types of sacrifices the Jewish
religion had, and how many different occasions for offering them. Certainly,
since Flavius says that each of the divisions that performed the rites in the
Temple for one week at a time contained more than five thousand priests,[152]
there must have been a pressing daily need for huge numbers of sacrifices to
keep all those hands from being idle. The same author writes that on a single day of Passover 255,600 animals were sacrificed.[153] And as I have already
said, on the festival of Passover (and on the other two festivals besides) all
the divisions of priests came to Jerusalem, and by joining their forces they
performed the rites together, so that 120,000 priests had to perform their
duties on the same day and at the same time. But even if we figure that
of the total number of sacrifices which (according to Flavius) were offered
on that festival, every priest slaughtered two, this still leaves 15,600 whose
slaughter is unaccounted for.

Moreover, all these sacrifices were burned on one altar; Rabbi Moses the
Egyptian says that three piles of wood were made on this altar every day.
He discusses each of these piles separately in the Laws of Daily Offerings
and Additional Offerings:[154] *The first pile was large, and on it they placed the
daily sacrifices and the other offerings. The second pile (which was at its side)
was smaller, and from it they took fire in a censer for lighting the incense on
the other altar, which stood near the Holy of Holies.*[155] *The third pile's only
purpose was to fulfill the command of God's law, which says about the fire,
"You will light a permanent flame."*[156] Flavius writes in Book 2, chapter 31, of
his *Jewish War*[157] that Jerusalem had a festive day he calls *ta xylophoria* [*the*

wood-carrying festival] because all the Jews brought great loads of wood from the forest to the Temple to light the sacred fires. According to the divine law, these should burn all the time and never be extinguished.[158]

Here, however, there is a slight disagreement between Flavius and the Talmudists, who say not that everyone did this all at once, but that individual families were chosen to do it, each on a set day. I agree with this opinion provided it means that on each of these scheduled days, several families— say twenty or thirty—gathered together to carry out their obligation. These families, of course, did not come from the inhabitants of the other parts of Palestine, but only from the Jerusalemites.[159] The Talmudists add that those families whose turn it was to gather wood offered a voluntary holocaust[160] called the *wood-offering*, because it was in addition to the gathering of wood.[161] And during this time they were forbidden to mourn,[162] to put on sackcloth, or to afflict themselves with fasting. Maimonides summarizes the opinion of the Talmudists as follows, in the Laws of Vessels of the Sanctuary: *A time was set for the families to go out to the forests to bring wood to the altar. And on the day that the members of a family were to bring the wood they would make voluntary holocausts, and this is the wood-offering; and for them it was like a festival day.*[163]

Moreover, a practice was introduced (not from the laws of Moses, but from the old customs of the Jews) that whenever people entered the Temple they would turn to the right, and walk around it in that direction; and they would leave by the same entrance, which was now to their left.[164] This was done in order to strengthen the people's veneration of the Holy Temple. On the other hand, people who were in mourning or who had been excommunicated from the Jewish people by the type of banishment called *niddui* had to walk around from the left to the right. Even the priests themselves walked backwards to the gate of the courtyard after they had made their offering, almost in the way that crabs walk, but turned a little bit to one side.[165] The Talmud describes this and many similar things, which we must explain as the product of a time when superstition—which is a kind of madness—had invaded men's minds.

CHAPTER 14

How faith was augmented by magnificence. The Talmudists' opinion about the wall which divided the enclosure, and why it was not rebuilt in the Second Temple. On the Temple watches. Whether Maimonides reported correctly that the watches were commanded by the Law.[166] *Why the priests frequently fell ill.*

IT WAS THE WISE SOLOMON (rather than any of his later descendants) who instituted separate courts for priests, Israelites, and women. This was a very proper provision against the sort of mixing that would have polluted the pure worship. In fact, even the rule that the priests themselves were not allowed access to the innermost parts of the Temple served only to increase its majesty (a quality made more impressive by secrecy). And though in the past there *had* been a wall one cubit thick between the Holy and the Holy of Holies, when the Jews who returned from Babylonia were building the Second Temple they were unsure about the proportions and the placement of the wall that had stood between these two sanctuaries.[167] Since they could not reach a decision, instead of a wall they hung two curtains separated by the space of a cubit, where in the First Temple there had been only one curtain.

This is the account of Rabbi Moses the Egyptian, in the Laws of the Temple,[168] and from it emerges clearly the painstaking piety of those men. But there are even more proofs of this piety. Our great rabbi says that the twenty-four divisions of Levites and priests stood watches every night in and around the Holy Temple, not because they were afraid of enemy soldiers or vagabonds, but to show respect for their faith. The laws also specified that the priests would stand guard inside and the Levites outside, and that three of the divisions would be drawn from the priests and the other twenty-one from the Levites. Finally, while the Levites stood watch all night, the priests were permitted to get some sleep.[169] But they had neither pillows nor cushions to make their rest comfortable; they had to sleep on the ground. This was something they had in common with the priests of Apollo at Delphi, whom Callimachus,[170] in a very elegant turn of phrase, called *those who sleep on the ground, attendants of the noisy cauldron.*[171]

I think that the Temple watches I have just described were not instituted until very late, when the Republic was in the process of decline. Many other innovations were made around the same time, of which not the slightest trace had existed before; for though our great Egyptian rabbi quotes some scriptural evidence for these changes, his arguments are faulty at best.[172] Whatever the second and third chapters of Numbers may command about laying out the camp that was to be set up around the Tabernacle in the desert,[173] it would be very unwise to apply it to the city of Jerusalem, which was the established seat of the rites and ceremonies.[174] What are we to make of the fact that after the Babylonian Exile there were fifteen duties performed in the Temple that the previous kings of Judah, who were from the house of David, had known nothing about?[175] These duties are mentioned in the fifth chapter of the Talmudic tractate called Shekalim; they included the sacred festivals, the water, the drawing of lots, the watches, the clothes, the showbread, the cauldrons, the mixing of the incense, and other things which are not worth reviewing.[176] Over each of these tasks was appointed a chief, called *memuneh*, and he had under his sway a huge number of functionaries.

Maimonides says that the priests fell victim to many illnesses. They ate mostly meat, and they performed their sacred duties dressed only in linen clothes which they had to put on and take off whenever they set aside their jobs or went back to them. Besides, they were always standing on the pavement, and they were forbidden to sit anywhere in the courtyard where they performed the rites. All of this led to weakness, and swelling of the veins, and a thousand other problems.[177] Juvenal[178] describes this condition very skillfully, in a case that is clearly similar to our own: *the* haruspex *will become varicose*.[179] Men were therefore appointed to look after the health of the priests at public expense, and the one put in charge of these men was called the *memuneh al haholim*. But enough about this—I will leave the rest of the information about the Temple, so admirably handed down to us by the Talmudists, to those who may someday follow after me to pick up the remains of this harvest. For I have wanted nothing more than to pique the interest of others; and I think by now I have managed to make it clear to everyone just how many things still remain to be said about Jewish matters in the wake of the studies done by some of our most learned men.

CHAPTER 15

On the destruction of Jerusalem and the Temple. What pushed
the Romans to perform such a savage act. Certain amazing
coincidences which the Jews have mentioned regarding the
destruction of the First and Second Temples. Titus' compassion and
tears. On the Third Temple which the Jews are still awaiting. Aelia
Capitolina was founded on the ruins of Jerusalem; and Hadrian
Caesar added something which made sport of the Jews.

WE WILL NOW TURN to other things. In every age, the city of Jerusalem, the site of the Temple and the home of the faith, had been shaken by
powerful storms. First the Assyrians and the Babylonians, then Antiochus
Epiphanes and the other kings,[180] and finally the Romans sent their armies
against it. Its citizens were taken captive, its walls were torn down, it was
entirely desolate and forlorn. The First Temple was burned by Nebuchadnezzar and rebuilt by Zerubabel.[181] But the new building's height fell sixty
cubits short of its predecessor's, so many years later, Herod, who had more
than enough wealth, and materials of every sort, restored the Temple to its
unparalleled glory. Now it was among the wonders of the world—there was
no nation so distant or barbarous that people did not come from there to
Syria in order to see it.

But it is a law of fate that no one is ever allowed to remain too long
at the top. God decided to scatter the great accomplishments that the Jews
had painstakingly amassed, and since He did not want His invading armies
to be defeated, He allowed the recklessness of a few men to stir the people
to defect.[182] The mob unwisely listened to its leaders and threw off its fear
of the Roman emperor. Thus error turned to guilt; and though it was the
leaders of the rebellion who were responsible for all this madness, the entire
nation paid the penalty.

Jerusalem was besieged and destroyed by Titus. He did not even spare
the Temple, which until then had survived unharmed through a great many
disasters. The Rabbis, who zealously compared ancient and recent events,
and pored over everything with the greatest care, made an observation that

is both a remarkable thing and a unique sign of divine judgment. I will quote the text from the chronicle called *Seder Olam*,[183] the sense of which is as follows (though I have taken some liberties in the translation): *Rabbi Yose*[184] *said: Just as the reward for a virtue occurs on the same day of the year on which it was performed (even after a long time has passed) so it is with a sin. This has been proven by experience. When the First Temple was destroyed it was the end of the Sabbath and the end of the seventh year; it was also the week of the division of Yehoyariv and the ninth day of Av. All these were exactly the same when the Second Temple was destroyed. On both occasions, moreover, the Levites were standing at the lectern and reciting this psalm: "He will revisit on them their iniquity."*[185]

Josephus describes the destruction in great detail. He says, in fact, that at the time the sight looked so bleak that even the enemy was moved to pity: when Titus saw that everything was destroyed he let loose a sigh of pain; and he became furious with the men who had instigated the rebellion, because their terrible crime had hastened the city's fate.[186] He would not have applied so harsh a remedy unless he had been given no choice; and certainly he did not have a vicious temperament, which among the gentiles was a constant evil. On the contrary, he was considered the darling and beloved not only of the Romans but of the entire human race. So why did he act this way? He had to be savage for the sake of the state,[187] and the illness was so severe that the doctor could not afford to be gentle.[188] A city was lost whose loss served even the people who were lost along with it.[189]

The Temple lay in ruins and burned to ashes; it had taken the returning exiles forty-six years to complete, and after that Herod had restored it so well, and made it so incomparably gorgeous, that the only fault his enemies could find with it was that it was too beautiful. The Messiah certainly spoke the truth when he said in St. Matthew's Gospel that *not one stone will be left standing atop another.*[190] It took only a moment for unparalleled magnificence to become shapeless ruin; everything was overturned in an instant. While nature uses its forces sparingly when it comes to creating things, it is at its most violent when tearing them down.

The Jews are still waiting for a Third Temple, and they say that each of the three patriarchs—Abraham, Isaac, and Jacob—merits his own. They derived this belief from several misunderstood passages in the Holy Book. Thus these unfortunates comfort themselves with their hopes; like the Sabines, they can dream whatever they wish.[191] There were hardly any traces left of the Temple and the city when, many years after Titus, Hadrian Caesar[192] built his city Aelia on the same spot, and in place of the Temple of the true God he built a temple of Capitoline Jupiter.[193] Not only that, he placed a marble sculpture of a pig in front of the gate that opened on to the Bethlehem road, so that the Jews would be badly upset whenever they saw this hated animal (a fact recorded by the learned Eusebius).

CHAPTER 16

On the temple of the Samaritans, which is on Mount Gerizim.
Who the Cutheans were. How they came to be settled in Samaria.
How much worse off they were than the Jews. A few words
about their religion. That they were originally idol worshipers; and
that although they later put aside their idols, they then
fell into heresy.

THE JERUSALEM TEMPLE (which I have just described) was venerated only by the Jews; the Samaritans had a different temple on Mount Gerizim. This had been built by Sanballat—who wanted to bestow a high priesthood on his son-in-law Manasseh—with the permission of Alexander the Great. So even though the rivalry between the Jews and the Samaritans had already led them to develop completely separate cults a long time before, this new building made their old hatreds burn a great deal hotter. As it happens, not even the destruction of this temple by Hyrcanus two hundred years later was enough to calm these hatreds.

It will be enough to say a few words in passing about the Samaritans, who are mentioned very often by writers on Jewish affairs.[194] They were not a true offshoot of the Israelites but a confused mass of colonists, whom the king of Assyria had gathered from the territories of the Cutheans, the Babylonians, the Chamatites, the Sepharvaimites, and the Avites.[195] These he resettled in Samaria after all the Israelites (who had seceded from the Judeans) were sent off to their distant exile and dispersed throughout Colchis,[196] Parthia,[197] and Ethiopia, so that they never again returned to Palestine. So the Samaritans, who were now sent to the region that had been cleared of its Israelites, were nothing more than human refuse and beggars, just like the men described by the Sicilian poet:[198]

> Of no account, not in the reckoning,
> Like the wretched men of Megara, in the most dishonorable
>   of circumstances.[199]

Of course, we can get an idea of their worth from an old saying of the Jews mentioned by Rabbi Elijah:²⁰⁰ *Whom did King David resemble? A Cuthean begging for money from door to door.*²⁰¹ I think this statement was made about the greatest of kings because he had sullied himself with mud and filth in the court of Achish,²⁰² so that the contempt he aroused would keep him safe in a place where the law gave him no protection at all.²⁰³

Even during the Roman Empire, when conditions in Palestine had sunk to their lowest point, and both Samaritans and Jews kept or lost all their rights at the whim of the conqueror, the Samaritans were infinitely worse off. For they did not have the right to make any of their acts legally binding; they were only allowed to make wills—which consist of final declarations or agreements—for the sake of the general welfare, so that people would have the freedom to document their financial arrangements.²⁰⁴ Now, it is true that the Jews did not have the right to testify against Orthodox Christians in court; but when they thought there was a need for a lawsuit among themselves they had recourse to a mixed pact,²⁰⁵ and could even introduce witnesses as long as the litigants agreed. This was the arrangement recorded much later by Justinian in *Codex* 1.5.21 ("On Heretics and Manichaeans"). Moreover, Justinian says the same thing in *Novella* 129: *The Samaritans of long ago were savage and overbearing toward the Christians; but in recent times their arrogance has outstripped all that came before.* It should therefore be obvious to anyone why *Novella* 144 ruled that adults who had adhered to the superstition of the Samaritans could not be admitted to baptism until they had been taught the basics of Christianity for two years.²⁰⁶

There is no simple way to describe their religion, for it has changed more than once in the course of time. At first the Israelites—who had withdrawn from the Judeans because of civil conflict, and settled in Samaria—were idolaters, and worshiped golden calves in imitation of the Egyptians, whose chief god was Apis. After that, each of the peoples that had been settled in the area left vacant by the Israelites observed their own national rites: the Chamatites worshiped Ashima, the Cutheans Nergal, the Babylonians Succotbenot, the Avites Nibhaz and Tartak, and the Sepharvaimites Adrammelech and Anammelech.²⁰⁷ This was the tactic used by Essarhaddon king of Assyria when he settled new colonists on the lands of Samaria: he thought that nothing would make his subjects easier to control than the differences in their beliefs, which kept them from coming to any sort of consensus.²⁰⁸ Later on, however, a new set of evils began to besiege those lands; so the king, moved by the entreaties of representatives sent by the colonists, released an Israelite priest from exile, in order that he might quickly set about teaching them the ancestral rites and placate God's anger.[209] In this way they adopted the rituals of the original inhabitants; and yet they all kept their own national superstitions fixed in their hearts.[210] However, in the course of time (quite late, in fact, though somewhat before the time of Sanballat)[211] they completely abandoned every form of idol worship, and practiced the faith commanded by the divine Moses. This is, in fact, the very reason for their unusual heresy: while the Jews accepted three volumes into the sacred codex—the Pentateuch, the Writings, and the Prophets—all of which they believe are inspired by God and have a special sanctity, the Samaritans decided to accept only the Pentateuch. They reject the other two volumes, alleging that they are less significant, and the product of human ingenuity.

CHAPTER 17

*On Jewish heresies and sects. When they first appeared, and
the real reasons behind them. Why the Jews fell into idolatry before
the Babylonian Exile, and into heresy after it. Why it is difficult
to go from idolatry to heresy. On Banus, and the Galileans, and the
Zealots. On certain false prophets, who used religion as an
excuse to foment revolution.*

THE SAMARITANS' perverse beliefs about the Writings, which (as I said)
were widespread among them, developed only when they had given up their
pagan superstitions; so they did not become heretics until they had stopped
being idolaters. In fact, it is clear that the very same thing also happened to
the Jews, which gives me a good opportunity to say something about their
sects. It is, of course, beyond dispute that the Jews turned more than once
from the proper worship of God to foreign cults and false gods; this is why
the prophets harangued them in so many harsh speeches, which even today
are so widely read that they have been enshrined among our greatest works
of literature.

But be that as it may, I have noticed that although the Jews of the Second
Temple period were completely free of idolatry, they were guilty of a different
sort of sin: from that time on they fought one another over their conflicting
interpretations of the Holy Book, and their disagreements about doctrine
and matters of ritual. So another evil, and a serious one at that, emerged at
that time—sects and heresies. Men whose religion was excessively zealous
split themselves into opposing factions, and once divided by a single mistake
they disagreed on everything and came to be entirely at odds with one another. Now, for the first time, a great many people embraced the Sadducees'
insane idea that the soul like the body is mortal, and that after this life good
and evil men receive neither rewards nor punishments. At the same time,
the Pharisees (who were far too argumentative) used their imaginations to
broaden the scope of divine law far beyond anything Moses had intended.[212]
After these two sects a third emerged,[213] the Essenes; they scrutinized every

aspect of religious purity with somewhat more care than the others, in accordance with certain anxious superstitions of their own.[214]

The grounds for this sectarian conflict did not appear until the time of the Second Temple, when there were no holy prophets and the Jewish people was no longer accustomed to the worship of idols. It is true that the age before this—the time of the First Temple, when the voices of the prophets rang out all over Palestine—had been a time of idolatry, but there were never any sects, or any stubborn and perverse arguments about faith.[215] The reason for this is obvious: as long as the prophets were communicating with God or receiving from Him in some other way the news He wanted mortal men to know, there could be no debates or controversies over the performance of the sacred rites, or over the divine laws and teachings. People had at their disposal men who could put an end to their foolish ideas, and to the disputes that sometimes erupted among them. Armed with superhuman authority, these prophets would declare the intent of the sacred law and of God Himself. So because they were unable to make a bad decision, whether out of poor judgment, error, or even ignorance, it was inevitable that those who did not want to obey them became stubborn and contentious; throwing off their piety, they gave themselves over to idolatry. There was no middle ground: either the demands of the prophets had to be promptly obeyed, or the fear of God had to be set aside.

But during the Second Temple, when there were no longer prophets driven by a greater power or by divine inspiration, things were very different. Since there was no longer anyone well versed in the sacred laws and the mysteries of Heaven, whose words could be accepted with complete confidence, mortal men—who were not satisfied with knowing what the prophets had already told them—wasted no time in applying their mental energies to burrowing into every area of knowledge, and their dull human minds wrapped themselves up in their own obscure thoughts.[216] So it became the sickness of an inferior age to dig up controversies and questions from the sacred texts.[217]

The Talmudists say that there were eighteen points of contention between the schools of Hillel and Shammai, which not even Elijah could resolve.[218] But this is hopelessly naive—the two leaders of these opposing sects devised such thorny and intricate problems that the Talmudists ought to say rather that not even a prophet or a divine oracle would have been of any help. Besides, during the First Temple only the Levites could read the Law to the people, and even at home it was read by individuals;[219] and teachers did not interpret the text or comment on it. But since under the Second Temple there were no longer any prophecies, it gradually became the general custom to explain the words and the meaning of the biblical text, and men of learning applied their ingenuity to this pursuit. So disputes and conflicting opinions developed, and when these were combined with the scholars' stubborn zealousness and corrupt ambition, the result was sects and heresies.[220] I know, of course, that before the Babylonian Exile there were groups called Nazirites, Kenites, and Rechabites,[221] but they differed from the rest of the people only in the set of rules according to which they lived, and not in their ideas or beliefs. So they have nothing at all to do with the matter at hand.

Moreover, it is now easy to understand why it was that although there were heresies in the time of the Second Temple, idolatry had no place among the Jews. After all, this is in the nature of things—people observe with the greatest dedication the ceremonies and beliefs that they adorn and elaborate with their own fantasies and fictions. Everyone loves what he has invented himself, and applauds his own genius; no mother smothers her own little girl with as many kisses as the fathers of these sects did the children of their invention. Thus in recent times, the Jews have kept the Mosaic faith on the condition that they could add to it something of their own.[222] Since in the past the prophets had not permitted this to happen, Jews often abandoned their people and turned to the idols.

I said that there were three principal sects—Pharisees, Sadducees and Essenes. Flavius Josephus says that he visited them and tried them all out, so that he could discover what was most worthwhile about each one.[223] He then writes that when he could no longer restrain his burning desire for knowledge, he spent three whole years with a man named Banus who lived in the desert, wore tree bark, lived off the land, and immersed himself day and night in freezing water in order to live a purer life.[224]

Flavius also mentions several other sects, but to discuss them would take us too far out of our way. Some of these were more splinter groups and conspiracies than sects; though they used religion as a pretext and spoke in high-sounding words, they were attacking the very essence of the state and its government.[225] The Golanites,[226] at least, were men of uncompromising piety who claimed that God was the only king of the world because they wanted to throw off the yoke of Caesar. On the other hand, the movement of the Zealots, which threw practically all of Judea into chaos, was not restrained by such considerations, and it now became common for troublemakers to drum up hollow excuses for chasing after their own ambitions and desires. Their actions were no longer the result of divine inspiration, but only of their lust for power.[227]

When Cuspius Fadus was procurator[228] a fraud named Theudas convinced a huge number of Jews to pack up their belongings and follow him to the Jordan. He claimed that he was a prophet, and promised that he was going to cross the river without getting his feet wet.[229] The Egyptian[230] did something just as crazy—he called the people to the Mount of Olives (ostensibly at the command of God) and was going to go from there to Jerusalem and knock down the city's walls with one word, so that everyone would have a clear and safe path through the ruins.[231] In fact, when Flavius is describing in general the situation of the Judean people at the time of Felix,[232] he says (almost dismissively) that *the entire region was filled with robbers, and even more with sorcerers who bewitched the masses*. And then he adds about these men that *they would say that they were going to produce clear signs and wonders, which would come about because of God's concern and providence. And though most of the people trusted them, they paid the price for their madness and stupidity.*[233] Nothing is as deceptive as the devious religion and piety of such fanatics; whenever someone claims that their grandiose plans are God's will, the masses are ready right away to do whatever they are told, and they would much rather listen to their prophets than to their rulers and kings.

CHAPTER 18

The Jews' prowess in war. How much it was valued by foreign kings. Flavius Josephus misunderstood the words of Choerilus. Who were the inhabitants of the Solymi mountains in Choerilus' poem. A style of haircut forbidden to the Jews. What Choerilus says about the language of the Phoenicians.

IF WE WANT TO DISCUSS the society of the Jews we must also consider the character of their military affairs, because a people's well-being is entirely dependent on how it cultivates and guards the arts of warfare.[234] But the old Rabbis devoted so little energy to studying this aspect of the Hebrew state that practically nothing I am going to say on the subject is drawn from their thoughts. The proof of this people's unmatched military strength is that they managed to conquer Canaan—which contained nothing but the most warlike of peoples[235]—in no time at all, even though they were exiles who had been driven out of Egypt and were then, in the deserts of Arabia, worn down by endless wandering and by forty years of misfortune and utter deprivation. In fact, whenever Flavius talks about the character traits of the Jews, he describes a nation that from the very beginning has been tough, heedless of death or danger, and so resistant to hardship and hunger that it could almost be accused of obstinacy.[236] This is why even foreign kings often made use of Jewish soldiers whenever they had to import auxiliary troops from abroad; and the exceptionally difficult trials through which they put these Jews showed them that the courage and strength of this people could accomplish great things.[237] Indeed, though Alexander the Great with his small band of troops was conquering endless numbers of nations scattered all across the world, it was the Jews whom he made a part of his army. He wanted to give them a share in the glory he was earning by conquering the entire world.

At that time, as Flavius points out to Apion, *if they wished, they could join his army while still adhering to their ancestral customs and living according to them.*[238] He obviously means this as a point of honor for the Jews, for at the time it was extremely unusual. Flavius also thinks that when Xerxes was launching his celebrated attack on the Greeks[239] he included Jews among his auxiliaries and allies, and as his proof he quotes a passage of Choerilus.[240] I would like to discuss this for a bit, because I have never been able to believe that Flavius correctly understood the sense of this ancient poet's words. The passage Flavius uses to refute Apion is as follows:

> The next camp in line[241] was a people of remarkable appearance
> Who spoke the Phoenician language;
> They lived in the Solymi mountains, near a huge lake.
> They wore their hair in a round cut, and the crowns of their heads
>   were dirty;
> The hide of their horselike heads was hardened by fire.[242]

Flavius says at this point that the Solymi mountains are the ones in Palestine where the Jews live;[243] and he thinks the passage refers to the Dead Sea, which is the widest and largest of all the lakes in Syria. But however grand this passage may be, it is worth nothing: what reason does Flavius give, or what explanation does he offer, for why Choerilus said that the Jews *wore their hair in a round cut*?[244] There is no question that the Jews to a man despised and practically condemned this sort of haircut; for a strict law forbade them *to cut around the corners of the head*. God's word on this subject is found in Leviticus 19.[245] Now, as for the proof Josephus brings from the famous poem of Choerilus about the Solymi mountains and the nearby lake, I can dispose of it without any trouble. Homer often mentions another set of mountains called Solymi which were located far from Palestine, as when in the *Odyssey* he says as follows about Odysseus' voyage:

> But as the glorious Earth-shaker[246] came back from the Ethiopians
> He beheld him from afar, from the mountains of the Solymi: for
>   he saw Odysseus
> As he sailed over the sea.[247]

The greatest and most ancient authors report that these mountains belonged to the Pisidians,[248] who inhabited them. They also place a lake in this region; so everything fits with Choerilus' description. Moreover, we must suppose that the Phoenician language (which Choerilus says was spoken by the inhabitants of those mountains) was a widely used idiom, and that practically all the peoples who lived in that region spoke various kinds of Phoenician dialects; so there is no need to assume that this applied to the Jews alone.[249]

CHAPTER 19

On wars that were proclaimed by the Law, and those the Hebrews fought voluntarily. What were the laws of accepting peace from an enemy. What the Talmudists say about the seven precepts that all nations had to observe. How soon after its creation was the world taken over by idolatry, and how completely the minds of men. The Hebrews' important ideas about Abraham, and when he initiated the proper worship of God.

I WOULD LIKE to put these matters aside, and turn next to whatever it occurs to me to say about the Jews' military affairs. The Talmudists declare that the holy people fought two kinds of wars: those *that were undertaken at the command of God and the Law* they call *wars proclaimed by the Law*; while *wars of discretion* are, they say, *the wars fought by the Israelites for the sake of their empire and to expand their state.* About the first type Maimonides says in the Laws of Kings and Wars: *A war which is called "proclaimed by the Law" is one that was fought with the seven peoples and with the Amalekites; or if it was necessary to supply help to an Israelite tribe that had been invaded by an enemy.*[250] The seven peoples to whom Maimonides refers were the Hittites, the Girgashites, the Emorites, the Canaanites, the Hivites, the Perizzites, and the Jebusites; God orders the Israelites to invade their territory in Exodus 24[251] and Deuteronomy 7.[252] It is also clear from God's edict in Deuteronomy 25[253] that the Amalekites were to be wiped out without a trace. As for the second type of war, we should mention what Maimonides adds in the same passage: *A war that is called "fought for empire" is one that the king has declared on other peoples in order to expand the Israelites' borders, and increase their greatness and fame.*[254]

In chapter 6 of the same book[255] Maimonides examines certain provisions that Almighty God wished to be observed in both types of war; these are written down in Deuteronomy 20, and their sense is more or less: *When you come to a city to attack it, first invite it to make peace. If they answer that they do want peace and they open the gates, let them pay you a tribute, and let all who live in that city serve you. But if they will not enter into peace with you and prefer to challenge you to battle, besiege the city. And when God has handed it over to you, put every male to the sword, and take for yourself the women, the children, the cattle, and whatever else is in the city, and all of its spoils. Then enjoy the booty of your enemy, which God has given you. In this way you will achieve victory over those cities that are far away from you in other lands. But you must treat differently those cities that your God is giving you to inhabit with full rights of inheritance; be sure not to leave anyone alive there.*

The Talmudists (based on the ancient traditions of their ancestors) say that when the supreme lawgiver tells us here that the Israelites are to spare those nations that accept the peace offered to them, we must understand this to mean that these nations also had to accept the seven precepts that had been given to the sons of Noah before the blessed age of Abraham.[256] Otherwise, they say, the Israelites would hardly have left alive people who were impious and did not serve God.[257] For according to the wisest of the Jews, there were six matters concerning which the original father of mankind received an edict from God: he learned from Heaven that he was to declare the majesty of the divine name, and that men should establish courts; and he was forbidden to shed human blood, to worship idols, and to commit robbery. And then (once the human race had increased its numbers) he was told not to pollute himself with incestuous marriages.[258] The Jews also say that although this was a kabbalistic teaching[259] that was handed down through the generations from the time of Moses, our own human intuition—and the words of the Pentateuch in general—tell us that these precepts were given in this way to the first man.[260] Finally, Noah was ordered by divine command not to eat the limb of a living animal; as it is written in Genesis, *do not eat the meat with its soul, which is its blood.*[261] Thus (they say) seven precepts were given by which the entire race of man was governed, until Abraham received the law about circumcision. The opinion of the Talmudists I have just described is quoted by the learned Maimonides as follows, in the Laws of Kings and Wars: *The first man was commanded about six things: idolatry, blessing the name of God, bloodshed, sexual immorality, robbery, and judgments. Though all of these have been handed down to us from Moses our teacher, and they seem sensible to us, it may be proven from the text of the Torah that he was commanded to do them. Noah was given the additional commandment of the limb of a live animal, as it is written: "but do not eat the meat with its soul, its blood." Altogether there were seven commandments; and this was the case throughout the world until the time of Abraham. Ever since Abraham we have also been commanded about circumcision.*[262]

Before I return from this small digression to the subject at hand, I would like to explain what I said before—that (in the opinion of the Talmudists) one of the seven precepts given to the first human beings was a divine sanction against the worship of idols. Maimonides, for one, demonstrates brilliantly in the Laws of Idolatry and Heathenism [263] that sinful beliefs appeared even at the very beginning of the world. Already in the time of Enosh men were led by a superstitious notion to start holding the stars and planets in great regard (a practice which was not, it is true, entirely removed from the worship of the true God).[264] And since mistakes go on to bear their own fruit, men soon came to dedicate temples and images to the stars, until eventually they rejected God entirely and worshiped only the planets as gods.[265] Even so, our great rabbi singles out a few individuals—Enoch, Methuselah, Noah, Shem, and Eber—who revered only one God who they thought was truly the best and greatest, and whom they worshiped with thoughts and words that were always pure, innocent, and uncorrupted.

Maimonides is speaking here about a mistake made by the entire human race, and about the failing of that age. Even Abraham, he says, did not acknowledge God as his Maker until very late in life, when he was already forty years old. For he was in Ur of the Chaldeans where his mind was sunk in darkness and fog, and where he was surrounded by superstitious and idolatrous men, and suffered from the same madness they did.[266] Eventually, though, God taught him something better, and he was eager to free the Chaldeans from their ignorance of the truth. But since the king tried to ambush him [267] he left for the territory of Haran; and from there he went to Canaan, where he so successfully established God's teachings among his family and friends that Maimonides is quite right to call him *the pillar and support of his age.*[268] It is because our author is so intelligent that he treats this issue [269] with such great discernment; and I was happy to refer to his discussion because it was able to shed light on the Talmudists' teaching (which I described above) about the seven precepts they required of Noah's descendants, i.e. that if any people refused to observe these precepts as part of a peaceful settlement the Jews were commanded to completely destroy them, since their savagery had as it were turned them into wild beasts.[270]

---

CHAPTER 20

*That, contrary to what is generally believed, fetials were sent
to offer peace even to the seven peoples of Canaan. Why the
Gibeonites needed to resort to trickery in order to obtain peace.
Why the seven peoples of Canaan were completely annihilated. Why
the Ammonites and Moabites were not offered peace. On the priest
who was anointed for the sake of battle.*

I WOULD NOW LIKE to proceed to the other contributions Maimonides has
made to the interpretation of the passage I quoted above from the twentieth
chapter of Deuteronomy. Our Egyptian proves beyond a shadow of a doubt
that God's command that the Jews should first send an embassy of peace to
the nations they are preparing to attack also applies to the seven peoples
whose well-favored territory God had promised to the Israelites. Though
this claim does in fact contradict the opinion of scholars who say that God
ordered those nations to be wiped out without making any such qualification,
and that there were no exceptions to this law, these scholars have been dealt
a heavy blow by the remarkable evidence our Maimonides quotes from the
Book of Joshua, chapter 11, where it is written more or less as follows: *The
only city to make peace with the Israelites was that of the Hivites who inhabited the town of Gibeon. All the others were captured in battle, for God had
hardened their hearts so that they would fight with the Israelites. In this way
He could completely kill them off, and they would be shown no mercy.*[271]

From this we may conclude that the seven nations were destroyed because they preferred risking the fortunes of war to making peace in accordance with the laws of the Israelites; if, on the other hand, they had obeyed
the fetials,[272] their survival at least would no longer have been in doubt.[273]
Maimonides then goes on to ask why it was that the Gibeonites decided to
obtain peace through trickery and deceit, and pretended that their nation
lived far away in another land,[274] when it was perfectly obvious that they
could have gotten what they wanted by being straightforward.[275] To this the
prince of rabbis responds that the Gibeonites, like the other six nations, had
already been sent an embassy, which they had rejected; so from then on the

divine law that called for the massacre of the seven nations applied to them as well. When, however, the Gibeonites later found out about this law,[276] and grew terrified of the Israelite armies that were winning one battle after another, they took measures against the disaster that awaited them. And since they had already rejected peace once, and thus given up the chance of an aboveboard solution, they turned to deceit and trickery. This is more or less how Maimonides frames his argument.[277]

Moreover, a victory against the seven Canaanite nations called for different measures than one against any other nation: in the latter case the law said it was enough to kill only the men for the sake of expiation,[278] while after a victory against one of the seven peoples, men, women, and even children had to be exterminated. The only reason for this distinction is that the seven peoples adopted certain disgusting and criminal practices which the community of men were led to flee and to shun, both because of reason and because of human nature; the Canaanites performed these practices all the time and at every opportunity.[279] When, therefore, God Almighty says in Leviticus, chapter 18 (after He has listed all the sins of this sort),[280] that *the land has been polluted, and I have repaid it for its sins, and the land has vomited up its inhabitants,*[281] it is as though He were suggesting that these peoples were the object of the world's hatred and its cross to bear. In Deuteronomy 23[282] there is a unique provision about the Ammonites and Moabites which decrees that the Israelites should never seek to make peace with them. The reason for this is similar to the one we have just seen—the two peoples did not supply provisions to the Israelites when they were coming from Egypt, and they also paid the prophet Balaam a great deal of money to foretell all the misfortunes that would befall them.[283] Yet Maimonides adds a certain provision which I ought to write out here: *Even though they*[284] *did not send embassies of peace to them,*[285] *if they nevertheless sought peace right away on their own initiative, they did not reject this overture.*[286]

In chapter 7 of the Laws of Kings and Wars (which I have mentioned several times) our Egyptian says many things about a type of priest who was publicly consecrated for the purpose of battle. He says about this priest: *In both wars fought to expand the empire and wars commanded by divine law, they appointed a priest to address the army at the hour of battle, and they anointed him with the sacred oil. This is the one called "anointed for the sake of battle."*[287] His speech, which he delivered before the people, is recorded in Deuteronomy 20[288] and went as follows: *Come and hear, O Israelites! Today you are going out to battle against your enemies. Do not let your hearts weaken, and do not be anxious or afraid because of them; for your God is setting out alongside you on the march, and is fighting your enemies to save you.*

Maimonides also mentions[289] the words that this priest read in public from a tablet or book,[290] not, of course, at the battle itself, but while the people were going out to war. But I am not going to get into such fine details, or into all the minor issues that still remain.

CHAPTER 21

Who was exempt from military service. The severity with which
Saul recruited his army. The penalties leveled against men
who refused to serve. Why Flavius wrote that in war, Jews were not
to violate foreign gods. The praiseworthy piety of the Jews when
Alexander restored the temple of Bel.

THE BOOK OF DEUTERONOMY lists a number of exceptional circumstances because of which certain men were granted temporary exemptions
from military service. Among these men were those who had recently planted
vineyards, or built a new house, or were engaged or newly married.[291] From
this we can confidently conclude that military service was performed not only
by men who voluntarily enlisted, but by whomever the king or the nation's
leader called up; their service was entirely a matter of necessity rather than
of choice. When Saul, at least, wanted everyone to take up arms, he sent
the limbs of two cows cut up into bits to all twelve tribes of Israel, by way
of threatening to do the same to the cattle of anyone who refused to follow him into battle.[292] So the Romans did in fact have a precedent for their
severity—it was their practice at one time to reduce to slavery anyone who
had not answered a call for recruits, on the grounds that such men were
traitors to liberty, while if a man had withdrawn his son from service he
was beaten with clubs in peacetime, and in wartime he was punished with
exile and the loss of part of his property. This is how it is described in the
work of Arrius Menander in Digest 49.16.4.10–11ff. ("On military matters").
In fact, the divine Augustus[293] had a Roman knight[294] and his property put
up for auction because he had cut off the thumbs of his two teenaged sons
to keep them from entering military service;[295] and there was an edict of the
divine Trajan that such a father should be exiled.[296]

Moses, the greatest legislator of all, ordered the Israelites on more than
one occasion to attack enemy territory and destroy every image, temple, and
altar of those gods whom the other nations mistakenly worshiped. Even so,
Flavius says[297] that according to the Law of Moses, *no one should mock the*
gods who are figments of the other nations' imagination; nor should anyone

speak badly of them. We should at least pay them the respect due to this great name.[298] I can't imagine from what part of the Pentateuch Flavius might have taken this idea; I think it was actually a product of his own imagination, and that he misunderstood the passage in Exodus chapter 22, which reads *you will not curse gods.*[299] In fact, the real meaning of this verse is that the leaders of the state—who function as God's representatives on earth—are considered sacrosanct.

On the other hand, in the same discussion Flavius brings a piece of evidence against Apion which has more truth to it, and which proves how insistent the Jewish soldiers were about observing their ancestral laws. He quotes a story from the account of the great writer Hecataeus[300] which says that once, when Alexander was in Babylon and ordered all his soldiers to pile up earth for the reconstruction of the temple of Bel (which had collapsed), only the Jews refused his order; and they were severely punished for it until the king finally forgave them and promised to leave them in peace.

CHAPTER 22

*Keeping the Sabbath always hurt the Jews in wartime. People
were relieved of this superstition by Mattathias the Hasmonean.
The feverish piety of Stratonike. How Meshullam, a very bright
Jewish soldier, debunked the power of signs and omens. That
portents and omens were not beyond the control of human beings.
Flavius misunderstood a divine law about the different styles of
dress required of the two sexes. Among the Romans, adulterous
women wore the toga, and Charondas had a soldier wear dresses.
The effeminacy of the Medes and Persians.*

SINCE I AM on the subject, I ought to discuss Maimonides' comment that
*the Jews lay siege to the cities of the pagans on the Sabbath, and even engage
them in battle.*[301] This had not always been their practice—Mattathias the
Hasmonean, the brave commander whose strength saved all of Judea, was
the first to persuade his countrymen that it was not against God's law.[302]
Until then everyone was under the terrible misimpression that any actions
a person took on the Sabbath, whether for himself or for the state, would
be ill-favored and make God angry. When, in fact, Agatharcides[303] (who is
quoted by Flavius)[304] makes fun of Stratonike[305]—who was captured and
killed by Seleucus because she could not bring herself to flee after being
spooked by a silly dream—he adds that a similar kind of madness afflicted
the Jews. Jerusalem, he says, was captured by Ptolemy the son of Lagus[306]
because the entire people was keeping the Sabbath and was forbidden to
defend the city. As I have said, Mattathias the Hasmonean freed them from
this misconception; and yet the very same superstition came to infect men's
minds once again—we know that many years later, Pompey got control of
Jerusalem because everyone was resting on the Sabbath.[307]

I myself happen to think that this Mattathias was a man of exceptional
character and flawless judgment, who understood that there are times when
it can actually be admirable to set aside the painstaking observance of ritual.
Certainly no laws are required to be kept in a state of emergency; the idea
that they are has always been the greatest source of human stupidity, and

whatever laws it has forced on us it continues to defend. Plus, it is typical of men, and especially leaders, that they take advantage of whatever fortune brings their way, and turn to their advantage the circumstances that have been offered them. Though this is true of all human affairs it is especially true of wars, in which events unfold not according to agreed-upon rules but because all sorts of unexpected things happen without warning and can erupt into a crisis if they are not dealt with immediately. Now, to me it is nothing short of a miracle to have found a Jew whose exacting piety did not keep him from following through on his plans, and dedicating himself to winning God's approval.[308]

Hecataeus has a story about a certain Jewish soldier; and though it is on a completely different topic I will mention it here nonetheless, because it shows that within the Jewish heart was a remarkable contempt for superstition. This author says[309] that he took part in Alexander's campaign, and that he journeyed towards the Red Sea with a number of Jewish cavalrymen who were in his company. One of these men was named Meshullam; he was a very high-spirited man whose skill with the bow was unmatched by any Greek or barbarian. When an augur[310] was trying to halt the army, which was rushing to arrive at its destination—he had seen a bird perching, and wanted to find out where it would fly so that he could predict whether or not their journey would be successful—Meshullam immediately took a large arrow and ran the bird through. So besides making a rather harsh joke, he was able to demonstrate the foolishness of people who believed that a poor bird could know anything about the fate of others when it was unaware even of its own fate—after all, it had not known how much danger it was in from Meshullam the Jew. A person can learn about the future not by relying on the responses of priests, or the unfavorable song of a bird, or how the chickens eat their food,[311] but by taking the initiative and being watchful, and thus getting the better of such absurd and empty omens. Certainly Pliny the Elder, who was a careful observer of such things, says that even within the discipline of augury itself, it is agreed that *neither evil omens nor any other signs have any effect on those who have said from the start that they will not pay any attention to them*;[312] and he believes that nothing is greater than this gift of divine kindness.

Anything else I might say about military matters is hardly worth mentioning. According to Flavius one of the rules of military practice was that in wartime, men should not dress like women or women like men. In fact, he has given us a fairly free and daring interpretation of a passage in the twenty-second chapter of Deuteronomy,[313] as follows: *Take particular care that in battle women do not wear the accouterments of men, or men those of women*.[314] But he has obviously misunderstood God's word in the passage in Deuteronomy; this divine law has to do not with the battlefront but with the home and peacetime, and with every other part of life. Immortal God did not wish the clothing and accouterments of the two sexes to be perverted or confused, because this would be completely at odds with the dignity for which He created and formed us. This is why no other nation has ever followed such a practice except as a form of humiliation or a punishment. Among the Romans, at least, the way women convicted of adultery went about dressed to fit their lack of virtue[315] inspired many jokes among their writers; of these Martial's stands out: *Numa saw Thelys the eunuch in a toga and said she was a convicted adulteress*.[316] As for the Greeks, Charondas—who was a very harsh general—actually made his men, who had abandoned the line of battle, stand before the assembled troops for three days dressed in women's clothing. I am aware that the Medes used to go around in robes that went down to their ankles like women's dresses, and that the Persians (as Xenophon tells us in the eighth book of his *Education of Cyrus*)[317] imitated the style of the Medes. But since these peoples lived in a warm region, the very climate made them effeminate.[318] This is why their softness was notorious among the other nations, and was always considered a vice.

CHAPTER 23

*On the Jews who lived outside Palestine in foreign kingdoms. The
migrations of many nations, and voluntary exiles. On the
Jews of Asia and Babylonia, and on those of Egypt and Alexandria.
The money they sent to Jerusalem. How much wealth there was
in David's tomb. How Darius was tricked by Semiramis. The hostile
rivalry of the Greek-speaking and Palestinian Jews. The rights
and status of the Jews of Rome, after the destruction of the
Holy City. On polygamy.*

MARCUS[319] ANNAEUS SENECA mentions, in the consolation he wrote
for Helvia,[320] a number of peoples who had left their ancestral soil and their
own territory, and moved to a new home: there were Greek towns in barbarian areas, and one could hear the Macedonian tongue spoken in India and
Persia;[321] the Achaeans[322] built cities on the shores of the Black Sea; Tyrians
lived in Africa,[323] and Phoenicians inhabited Spain.[324] Seneca calls all these
cases nothing less than group exiles, some of which were brought about
by uprisings at home, others by the destruction of the exiles' own city, and
still others by wanderlust or for some other reason. But there is no clearer
illustration of this phenomenon than the Jews, who settled far away from
Palestine, throughout Egypt, Greece, and all of Asia and Africa,[325] and who
lived successful and prosperous lives in those places. They received such great
benefits from kings and princes that they preferred to live their lives among
strangers than to practice their faith and revere their Temple from close by,
on the blessed soil of their homeland.

Of all the Jews who lived in Asia, it was in fact the Babylonians (whom I
described in Book 1, chapter 8) that were the most worthy and noble; while
among the Greek-speaking Jews it was the inhabitants of Alexandria who
were in the forefront, not only in Egypt but in all of Greece. At any rate,
when Ptolemy the son of Lagus had witnessed the great loyalty and bravery of
these Jews, he entrusted to them all the defenses and fortifications of Egypt.
He also established many Jewish colonies in Cyrene and the other cities of
Libya, so that he might keep these places firmly under his control.[326] Later

on, Philadelphus[327] was so taken with the Jews who lived in his realm that he wanted their sacred laws to be translated into Greek and made freely available to all. Finally, Philometor and his wife Cleopatra[328] put these Egyptian Jews completely in charge of the entire kingdom; and they put Dositheus and Onias (who were also Jews) in charge of those resources on which the country's very existence depended.[329] Moreover, all the Jews of Egypt enjoyed such freedom that they even had a temple in the district of Heliopolis, which they attended with great fervor. This was not at all a makeshift work of the kind the Babylonian exiles had slapped together in their desperate haste, and as circumstances allowed. King Ptolemy had authorized its construction, and it stood solidly for three hundred and forty years. But it was finally closed and desolemnized under Vespasian.

Be that as it may, the Egyptian Jews and the Greek-speaking Jews in general, as well as all the others who lived outside Palestine, felt a strong love and affection for the Jerusalem Temple. They sent regular contributions there, and their donations were of enormous size. Flavius Josephus quotes from the letters sent by Octavius Augustus, Agrippa,[330] Norbanus Flaccus,[331] and Julius Antonius[332] to the inhabitants of Cyrene, Ephesus, Sardis, and other places, in which they are ordered not to prevent the Jews who lived among them from sending gifts and money to Jerusalem for use in the Temple and the sacred rites.[333] In fact, the Jews who lived in Mesopotamia and Babylonia used two of their cities—Nehardea and Nisibis, which had both natural and artificial fortifications—as a sort of treasure house for all the wealth that was periodically brought to Palestine at the proper time by a huge squadron of men (assembled because of the Parthians, whom they feared would attack the convoy). It is no accident that the opulence of the Jerusalemites reached its peak at the very time when their fellow Jews—who lived all over in very distant communities—were sending them so much gold.[334] But even in earlier times, before civil conflict had led the ten Israelite tribes to secede from the Judeans, they were incredibly wealthy. David is known to have possessed amazing storehouses; none of the other kings, whether Hebrew or foreign, could compare with him. This is why his heir wanted even his tomb, his bones, and his ashes to overflow with riches, which were hidden in a series of chambers. We can easily get a sense of the amount of wealth contained there if we bear in mind that when Hyrcanus[335] was being besieged by Antiochus the Pious[336] thirteen hundred years later, he entered the storehouse and took from it three thousand talents.[337] Likewise, when Herod opened some of the other chambers many years later he found that they contained more than enough to cover his great expenses.[338] No doubt the great king had all this wealth buried with him so that it would be, so to speak, out of reach and protected by the sanctity of the place; for we know from history that other kings often did the same thing and for the same reason. In fact, Darius became a laughingstock when he entered the tomb of Semiramis, whose inscription promised vast treasures, because there was nothing inside but a tablet that called down curses on the godless man who had committed the terrible crime of defiling the resting-places of the dead.[339]

But I was discussing the wealth of the holy people that was to be found in Jerusalem before the tribes were carried off. Though this was great enough in the time of David, it was far greater still under Solomon who succeeded him, for every three years he was brought the most valuable objects of the East,[340] and the generosity of the local rulers increased the holdings of this wisest of kings. Accordingly, Flavius Josephus says with open-mouthed wonder something that has always amazed me—that *the king saw to it that Jerusalem had as much silver as it did stones*.[341] There could be no better proof that the king had come to the pinnacle of good fortune.

Since I need to keep to my theme, I cannot discuss these issues in too much detail. I must return to those Jews who, as I said, lived under foreign kings. We should not place them all in the same category, nor should we draw the same conclusions about them all. Though the Babylonians lived outside the Holy Land they did nothing against law or custom, and they enjoyed that unique privilege I mentioned earlier.[342] But the disgrace of those who left the territory of Palestine, whether before or after the Jewish nation was exiled, to settle in the other countries of the region, has been passed down over the generations; and the general consensus is that they showed their contempt for the Holy Land. The Talmudists mention a very harsh divine edict that prohibited every Jew from leaving his native soil of his own free will.[343] There is also a teaching to the effect that *anyone who lives outside the Holy Land is regarded as though he were a worshiper of stars and planets*.[344] They prove this from David's words to Saul, which have been recorded by Samuel as: *If it is men who have stirred you up against me, may they be cursed before God; for today they drive me away so that I will have no share in the land that God has left to us, and they say, "Go and worship other gods."*[345] There was only one reason why people could leave without incurring serious guilt, and that was a superior force such as famine, barren land, and other such things that turn on the anger of God, which is, so to speak, the ultimate tragedy.[346]

We should take note of what the learned Maimonides writes in the Laws of Kings and Wars; for after mentioning some of the extreme circumstances under which Jews were permitted to move temporarily to foreign states, he makes Egypt the only exception to this proviso. He says it was banned by three divine prohibitions to prevent anyone from going to Egypt with the intention of living there. There were no obligations, opportunities, or circumstances of any sort that could justify this. It would be a waste of time to quote the evidence; let the author be responsible for the truth of his words. Of course, Maimonides himself offers the most obvious explanation for this law, *since this nation's behavior is worse than that of the other nations.*[347] Rabbi Maimonides then adds something found nowhere else: *This prohibition includes even Alexandria.*[348] Although the most respected and most successful of the Egyptian Jews were those who lived in Alexandria, our learned author is quite right to put them into the same category as the others; for they violated the letter of the law no less than the others did.[349] Besides, it was these very Jews who were enticed by Alexander's good will to move far away from Jerusalem of their own accord, and to settle alongside some of the Macedonians in the city that this king was founding in his own name. Later on, there were also many people who descended on the city because of the upheavals in Syria.[350] And finally, quite a few accompanied Ptolemy the son of Lagus, including the high priest Hezekiah.[351] In this way they settled throughout the whole of Egypt.

Although the Jews of Egypt came to Jerusalem every year or sent people to attend the sacred festivals, they were held in contempt by the Palestinian Jews and were considered traitors. And though they brought an enormous number of offerings—practically beyond our ability to calculate—for use in the Temple and its ceremonies, it was not enough to persuade the Palestinians to admit them into their community. Another reason they disliked the Alexandrians was that they had stopped speaking their ancestral language, and most of them could not even understand it. This is why the Jews living in Egypt were called Hellenists no less than the ones who left them to go settle in Greece and the neighboring regions (almost all those communities were offshoots of the one in Egypt). None of this applied to the Babylonian Jews, whom the Palestinians held in the greatest respect—they saw them as blood brothers and as their legitimate offspring, who were greater than themselves. And yet we must give just as much credit to *all* the Jews who lived outside Palestine, since they always kept the practices of their fathers with perfect piety even though they were living among godless gentiles. It is not only the Babylonians who deserve the credit for this; it belongs equally to the Jews who settled in Egypt starting in the time of Alexander.

In fact, in the years that followed even the Jews living under the rule of the Caesars in various places throughout the Roman world continued to carefully observe the laws laid down by the divine Moses. This of course was not at all difficult for them, since the people in whose communities they had settled treated them with kindness, consideration, and honor. But after the destruction of the Temple and the city, their standing among the gentiles took a definite turn for the worse, and wherever they lived they lost all sorts of privileges. The imperial legislation, at any rate, *ordered that they shall remain undisturbed only in cases in which their worship is in danger of being polluted* (Digest 27.1.15.6, "On the excuses of guardians and curators").[352] In fact, it was against the law for them to build new synagogues, or to burn crosses on the holiday of Purim in commemoration of the punishment (*Codex* 1.9.11, "On Jews and Heaven-worshipers").[353] Finally there is a provision that *they shall not continue to keep their marriage customs; nor shall they arrange marriages in accordance with their law,*[354] *or contract more than one marriage at the same time.*[355] From this last provision we may be certain that until then they had been legally permitted to marry more than one woman. This is what I said before[356] when I was discussing the high priest, who according to the Talmudists was the only man forbidden to do what was permitted to everyone else. Certainly, when Almighty God speaks to King David through Nathan the prophet, He says that it was He who had given David Saul's wives;[357] and there is a divine edict in Leviticus 18[358] which prohibits the Jews from marrying two sisters at the same time, for the simple reason that the competition between two sisters in such a marriage is usually fierce. In general, though, women who are not related may live together blissfully alongside the same husband.

I know, of course, that the first parents of the human race were commanded to do the exact opposite; and that the Messiah, our God and Lord, ultimately restored this command and made it our law once again.[359] And yet there is no question that in the Republic of Moses, the Jews were legally permitted to marry as many women as they wished; and that for a long time during the Roman Empire this ancient and widespread custom continued to be practiced by those Jews who had not yet begun to revere the Messiah. But Theodosius, Arcadius, and Honorius[360] eventually decided that the marriage practices of the Jews should be exactly the same as those of the Romans.

It was in this same era that many of their other practices were made obsolete. In fact, from that time on they used the same body of law as the Romans:[361] *They appeared in court according to the usual custom, and they litigated and settled all their suits according to Roman law, both cases that had to do with their own superstition, and those that concerned the bar, the laws, and the rights* (*Codex* 1.9.8).[362] Thus their freedom of choice was covered over and buried, and hardly a trace of it was left. Their only remaining privilege was that *by common consent they could try lawsuits, using their fellow Jews as a kind of arbiter; and they were permitted by public law to abide by the judgment of these men* (*Codex* 1.9.7). Of course, this was done *only in civil cases*, and though the decisions of the arbiters were executed by judges, those judges were Romans. It does appear, though, that the Jews enjoyed somewhat greater privileges in their ancestral homeland. In *Codex* 1.9.16 the emperors Theodosius and Valentinian indicate that the Jews had chiefs *who were in charge of the synedria of both Palestines*. But I think that their power and jurisdiction had almost nothing to do with matters of state.

CHAPTER 24

*On the Law that Moses wrote for the Jews. The beliefs of some
of the ancients regarding the Sabbath are refuted. The reports of
Pliny, Rabbi Maimon, and Flavius Josephus on the sabbatical river
are disposed of. Why did the Jews avoid pigs more than other
animals? Plutarch's explanations are rejected. On the diseases of the
Egyptians. The Jews were not worshipers of Bacchus, despite
the opinions of Plutarch and other Roman writers.*

ONE OF THE THINGS that set the holy people apart was the Law. This
had been written by Moses and was greater than any of the institutions and
laws of the gentiles; and it was certainly more distinguished, since its author
was God. It fills up five whole books because it contains many different kinds
of material, it goes on at great length, and it is often repetitive. But the gist
of it has been summed up in ten principles;[363] of these, the first half have to
do with divine matters, and the second contain what Marcus Tullius[364] calls
the duties of men. Now, every act of service to God takes one of two forms,
either thought or worship. "Thought" is contemplating God in a reverent and
proper fashion. It would be pointless to say anything more about this, since
right now we are primarily concerned with the facts of history. "Worship,"
on the other hand, consists of ceremonies and rituals. One of these ceremonies—the Sabbath—is laid down explicitly in the Ten Commandments. It
was created at the beginning of the world and has always been kept by holy
men; then it was commanded once again when the Law was given. Though
the real reason for the Sabbath is spelled out in God's choice of words in
the text of the Ten Commandments,[365] the Jews see a mystical explanation
for it in Rabbi Elijah's famous statement in the books of the Talmud:[366] he
divided the history of the world into three distinct periods of equal length,
such that after six thousand years had passed a new state of nature and a
new order would appear, and the human race—which had long since grown
weary—would then receive a better fate and a wonderful rest.[367]

Cornelius Tacitus came up with a different explanation for the origin of
the Sabbath.[368] He thinks that the Hebrews kept it in honor of Saturn, *either*

*because they had received the principles of their faith from the Ideans, who we
are told were driven out along with Saturn and were the founders of this nation;*[369] *or because of the seven planets which govern the lives of men, Saturn
is believed to have the highest orbit and the greatest power. And the planets in
general derive their celestial force and their courses from the number seven.* In
fact, Tacitus is not the only one to have said this. Rabbi ibn Ezra[370] quotes
the ingenious argument of a certain sage who links the nine headings of the
Law[371] to the corresponding number of celestial orbits.[372] And to refute the
idea that the seventh day was chosen as the Day of Rest for no particular
reason, he says that Saturn and Mars are ill-favored planets; for on the day
they are dominant none of our efforts turn out well.[373] I myself would urge
this teacher, whoever he was, to go cry among the seats of the students;[374] he
was overly ingenious when there was no need for it. But since I am merely
a minor and second-rate figure, I will settle for drawing conclusions that
speak for themselves.

The proper observance of the Sabbath consisted of sanctifying whatever
one said or did, as well as serving God and praying. Rabbi ibn Ezra writes[375]
that it was also on the Sabbath that oracles were consulted. The husband of
the woman of Shunem says to her regarding Elisha:[376] *Why are you going to
him today, when it is neither the new month nor the Sabbath?*[377] On the other
hand, everyone was ordered to forgo their usual activities on the Sabbath, so
that profane activities would not be mixed with sacred ones; whoever did not
was committing a capital crime. In fact, the people were taught that sacred
rites were not to be carried out too hastily; the mind must be completely
given over to contemplation when it worships God, who is the purest mind
of all. Both Pythagoras[378] and Numa[379] were aware of this; and it was quite
proper that during the Roman rites, a herald solemnly proclaimed *Pay attention.*[380] But the Jews, whose practice it is to pervert every one of their sacred
institutions, have made many additions to the body of the Law that Moses
had never asked for; so the observance of the holy day has declined into an
anxious superstition, and at times has even brought about their deaths.

But let us move on to a new subject. If we are to believe Pliny, Nature
herself (the ultimate source of things) seems to have approved of the sacred
rest of the Sabbath: he says that a certain stream in Judea dried up on every
Sabbath.[381] But begging Pliny's pardon, I could never believe this. *I am a
little weaker, one of many.*[382] Even so, I will explain the mistake that misled
this Roman writer: for a long time the Jews have indulged in the fantasy
that the ten captured Israelite tribes were being held near a river they call
Sambatyon. They also say that during the week this river ran with currents
so rapid that no one could cross it, while on the Sabbath it rested and was

passable. This was meant as a punishment for the Israelites: the current only slacked off when they were prevented from crossing the river by their respect for the Sabbath; thus the path to freedom was placed before their eyes in order to make them suffer all the more. They see their freedom, and having seen it and yet left it behind they continue to yearn for it. Pliny could not have embarrassed himself any more than he did by swallowing whole such a worthless Jewish fiction.

Flaccus says that painters and writers have the license to say whatever they like,[383] and he is right. But to these two groups I want to add the Jews, who make up contradictory and absurd things. They are governed not by a sense of dignity or modesty, but only by their intellectual desires; they do it merely for the joy of making them up. Nor do I care that Rabbi Moses ben Maimon, whom I have quite rightly praised to the skies, identifies this river as the Goza.[384] I say that he is crazy, and I am throwing Josephus in with him, because in Book 7, chapter 13, of the *Jewish War*[385] he mentions things that, while they may contradict the claims I just mentioned, are no less impossible.

Certainly Pliny happened to be taken in by other writers more than once. Generally speaking, his comments in that same chapter (about springs, rivers, and bodies of water) are just as worthless. I can put up with such tales of unbelievable and unnatural phenomena in Julius Obsequens[386] but not in Pliny, who is the greatest of all writers of history.[387] Nature rarely departs from her customary habits, and it is easier for miracles to be believed in than to actually happen. And yet most people suffer from a kind of seductive insanity, and they make unwise and self-indulgent leaps in judgment; we swap one old wives' tale for another, and we do it not carelessly but intentionally, and as though such tales were to be taken seriously.

I have said more than enough about the Sabbath, and I don't have the patience to discuss the other issues having to do with the Ten Commandments. After the laws of the two tablets (including the law of the Sabbath) were enacted, Moses was given a broader interpretation of these laws; and God added other ceremonies and rituals, and explained to the people the offerings He wanted to receive and the manner in which He wanted to be worshiped. The reason for this[388] is obvious: the simple worship of God laid down by order of the Ten Commandments was not enough, because all the Israelites had quite readily turned to the idols of Egypt. There was, accordingly, an obvious need for many outward symbols that would keep their minds trained on the real faith. After all, it is very difficult for human beings to worship an invisible God with their minds alone. Unless their eyes also have something to focus on, they are seized before they know it by an irrational kind of sinfulness.[389] Of course, even before then—in the first age of man—the sacred rites were performed according to certain laws and ceremonies: Noah learned from God the differences between clean and unclean animals, and a severe prohibition forbade him to eat blood. But the Law given by Moses defined all these restrictions with much greater care. There is, at any rate, a long list of animals in the eleventh chapter of Leviticus that the Hebrews could not eat or touch without becoming impure.

Many of these were placed on the list of unclean animals not because nature or reason demanded it, but because God wanted it so for His own purposes. We cannot, therefore, explain clearly the reasons for such prohibitions, and they cannot be comprehended. Who among us is so arrogantly self-assured that he thinks he can explain all the institutions of the Hebrews?[390] At one time, the Ephors[391] were strictly forbidden by the laws of Sparta to let their sideburns grow once they had taken office; and a law of Solon publicly dishonored men who had refused to take sides in times of rebellion or civil conflict. Though Plutarch is sure that the Greeks had perfectly good reasons for passing both these laws, nonetheless he says that *the intentions of the legislators are unknown to us*.[392] So I would suggest that the same thing applies to the commands of God, the greatest of all lawgivers—can anyone tell me why God decreed that four-legged animals whose hooves are not split are unclean? While every other nation considers it perfectly permissible to eat rabbits and hares, only the Hebrews do not.

But since in the same chapter of Leviticus there is also a law about pigs, I should take a moment to ask why the Jews have always avoided this animal more conscientiously than any of the others declared by the Law to be just as hateful and repulsive. It is worth mentioning what Plutarch has to say.[393] He claims that far from regarding the pig as taboo the Jews hold it in the highest honor; in fact, they worship it as the patron saint of agriculture. This, he says, they first learned in Egypt, where the fields are never ploughed; instead, the moment that the Nile's seasonal flooding is over and the river has retreated back to its banks, the natives let their pigs loose in the fields so they can dig up the rich soil with their snouts and plant the seeds in the earth. This is why (according to the most likely derivation) the Greeks also call a plow *hyne*. And why (Plutarch asks) should it surprise us that a superstitious people like the Egyptians worships such a filthy animal,[394] when they also pray to the cat, the griffin, and the crocodile? Finally, he says that he knows of no reason why, if the Jews consider pigs an abomination, none of them dares to kill this beast they supposedly hate more than all the others.

After all, the magi (who were first established by Zoroaster) consider nothing sweeter or more glorious than to kill a great many water-mice,[395] which they all despise because of some ridiculous religious principle.

I can dispose of these arguments without much difficulty. The Egyptians had no religious scruples about *touching* any of the beings they worshiped. To bite into a leek or an onion was a great sin, and Flaccus says as a joke *if you should slaughter a leek or an onion*, as though he were talking about murder;[396] and some other poet cries indignantly *O holy peoples, whose gods are sprung from the vegetable patch!*[397] And yet they used to pull these very same gods from the ground with their own hands, and store them up in cellars and chests so they could serve the other necessary functions of life. The Jews, on the other hand, were defiled simply by touching pigs, which would not have been the case if the reason for their superstition was that they cared for and worshiped them. And since they did not consider pigs worth touching they did not want to kill them either; so Plutarch's remarks are completely baseless. Nor should we be any less skeptical about the joke Petronius makes in this witty epigram: *And let the Jew worship his porcine god / and call on the highest ears in heaven.*[398] His words stem from a misconception that was common among the Romans, who firmly believed in this notion.[399] And yet here I am changing my mind: though at one time I proposed that the text of Petronius should be corrected to read *and let the Jew* abhor *the* name *of pig*,[400] this has proven to be a mistake. If he *had* written this, he would have been perfectly right; but since as it happens he did not, it makes him a fool. But I would rather that Petronius *had* made this mistake than that I had relied on a complete conjecture just because it suited my purposes. Of course, at the time I was moved by the best intentions to invent the emendation I am now rejecting; and that is how things stand.

The Jews consider the very name of this animal to be an omen of future disasters, and even when they do discuss it they don't actually name it—instead they follow the traditional custom for averting an evil omen, calling it in their ancestral language *davar aher*, "another thing." The Romans could not express this concept effectively;[401] if you were to say *res alia*, you would be translating word for word but you would not understand the sense of the expression. The Greek phrase *pragma allokoton*, "an abnormal thing," would be much closer to the mark. On the other hand, on the Passover holiday they are also very careful not to use the word *bread* when they speak, and for the same reason—they believe that during the holiday, anyone who has caused someone else to think (however briefly) about leaven has committed a great sin.

But it is high time I explained the reason why the Jews avoid this one animal more than all the others. The people of Israel were at one time extremely vulnerable to the same sicknesses from which most of the Syrians and Egyptians suffered (according to the greatest medical authorities, these nations had boils, mange, and disgusting sores, their own personal plagues as it were). Moses included these, and any diseases that were more or less similar to them, under the heading of "leprosy."[402] On the other hand, when pigs have scabs or blemishes this is not a defect but a natural occurrence. So the Jews, who wanted to make sure their bodies would not be disfigured by some other kind of infection[403] (whether through eating or touching), have shunned pigs even a bit more superstitiously than God's law might ask of them, or than was customary among the other nations. And yet, how can we say that the fear these men felt made them too cautious, when the Law condemned leprosy more than any other defect? Leviticus[404] mentions the harsh edicts commanded by God when leprosy appeared not only in people but even in clothing and houses. (Though the Syrians and Egyptians of that time may have understood what sort of disease it was that could infest inanimate objects, I most certainly do not.) And though Plutarch went on to make many conjectures about the superstitions of the Jews (a number of which disagreed with or even contradicted one another), he did not invent that assertion about leprosy which I have just described.[405]

The rest of what he says—that Bacchus[406] was identical with Adonis,[407] and that he was murdered by a boar[408]—is not worth discussing. Nor can I accept his theory that the rites and secret ceremonies of the Hebrews were actually in honor of Bacchus, the drunkest of the gods:[409] he says that during one of their festivals they live in booths which they cover with palm fronds and ivy,[410] and that it is the time of year when they carry around branches and wands.[411] Plutarch also mentions the sound of trumpets,[412] and he claims that the celebration of the Sabbath (which returns every seventh day) takes its name from the rites of Liber,[413] because the word "sabus" is sometimes heard during their celebrations.[414] Then he says that the Jews drink a great deal on the Sabbath, and that the high priest appears on festival days in a headdress and boots, and a deerskin, and an ankle-length tunic with bells hanging from the edge; and that during the rites they bang cymbals together, and they never make use of honey; and that though they have many types of punishments, they believe that the most humiliating thing they can do to a guilty man is to prohibit him from drinking wine.

This description was not unique to Plutarch—others believed the same thing (though Cornelius Tacitus disputed them).[415] I have summarized it not in order to systematically refute its individual points, but to demonstrate how ingeniously the pagans misrepresented the Jewish faith: some of what they say is completely false, and though some of it is true, it has been taken in the worst possible sense by a man who was very learned but did not know the original reasons for any of these institutions. There was a reasonable explanation for why God ordered the Festival of Tabernacles to be observed; or banned honey and wax from His sacred rites; or desired the high priest to wear *bells and pomegranates*[416] on the fringes of his garment. And though our Greek author may have asked these questions, he did not find any answers. As to the Jews' drinking and overeating on the Sabbath, it is the fault of people who disgraced the most sacred of their institutions in an age of decline; in the Holy Book, God's prophets often reproach the nation for this.

Plutarch could not have made the Jews more universally despised than he did by publishing the idea that they were worshipers of Bacchus. Livy writes[417] that when the Senate set up a commission to deal with the cult of Bacchus,[418] Marcus Cato—a very important man who was given extraordinary authority to deal with the problem—addressed the people as follows:[419] *Never has there been such a threat to the state, or one connected with more people and events. Be aware that in recent years not a single act of lust, deceit, or crime has been committed which did not have its beginnings in that single cult.*[420]

.

Flavius Josephus in his *Apology Against Apion*, on the Greek historians who wrote about the affairs of other nations:

Ἄιτιον αὐτοῖς τοῦ μὲν μὴ γνώσκειν τἀληθὲς, τὸ λίαν ἀνεπίμικτον· τοῦ δὲ γράφειν ψευδῆ, τὸ βούλεσθαι δοκεῖν τι πλέον τῶν ἄλλων ἱστορεῖν.

The reason why they did not write the truth was that they had no contact at all with [the Jews]; while the reason they wrote lies was that they wanted to appear to know more about the past than the others.

—Flavius Josephus, *Against Apion* Book I, 12

BOOK III

INTRODUCTION

From Petrus Cunaeus to the great Franck van Dyck,
First Consul of Leiden

I REMEMBER, Your Excellency, that back when I was engaged in a very serious course of study, it was above all my intention to read through the authors of every age. My primary purpose was to discover clear illustrations of those matters that are relevant to the study of politics—I was of the opinion (which is in fact true) that the point was for scholars to wear themselves out with their wonderful obsessions and musings, as they pored over historical documents in order to learn about the growth and development of states and the headlong fall of empires. In this way a scholar could determine which states he and his country ought to emulate, and which ones should be avoided as having both a bad start and a bad end. I therefore applied myself many years ago to carefully examining certain works of Suetonius Tranquillus[1] and Gaius Cornelius Tacitus,[2] so that by investigating the history of the Romans I would also touch upon many of the characteristics shared by all states and republics.

It will be up to you and others like you—that is, men who are learned, wise, and experienced—to decide when if ever that work will be ready for publication. But in this book about the Hebrew Republic which I am publishing now, I have done something entirely different: it discusses the sacred people only. I have said very little here about how well or how badly the governments of other states were organized, or about the laws and institutions with which they were ruled. The reason is that there are no other states like the divine polity of Moses: it is entirely unique. It is true, of course, that many of the measures passed by the other lawgivers whom the entire ancient world greatly admired were similar to the laws of Moses, for these men made it very clear to their citizens that they were to act with virtue and courage. But the institutions they set up for performing sacred rites and worshiping God did very little to instill religious faith in the minds of men.

Moses, on the other hand, gave us a God who was one and eternal, all-powerful, the witness and judge of all man's thoughts and intentions, born of no natural process, unchanging, and beyond human sight; no art, and no craftsman, can give Him concrete form.[3] So by teaching that God sees what happens in a man's life, Moses convinced everyone of what we know to be true: that none of our actions, whether good or bad, should be considered unimportant. The inevitable result is that instead of fearing that their reputations would suffer or that others would find out what they were up to, people started to fear that they might be their own worst accusers.[4] In fact, Flavius remarks about the other ancients who gave their nations rules of behavior and laws, that they certainly knew the one true and perfect God. But since they were living among people corrupted by superstition and unquestioned dogmas, they pretended to believe exactly the same thing, "because they did not dare disclose the truth of their ideas."[5] According to Flavius, Plato himself confesses that there are certain secrets that it would be dangerous to spread in public.[6] The truth, of course, was very different. Nothing held Moses' republic together more than his religious teachings; because they were never plastered over with fables or absurd frills, they sank much more deeply into the hearts of the Hebrews than any of the Greeklings could have imagined.[7]

My task was to discover the essence of Moses' laws, their meaning, and the reasons behind them, and to compare everything within this category with the institutions and laws of the other nations. But though I tried to complete these tasks, I was held back by the sheer size of the project; so I have not yet been able to accomplish the goals I mentioned before. But be that as it may, I am not going to keep waiting forever the people who lately have been constantly pressing me to see this work. And since for the foreseeable future I am in fact going to be spending all my spare time on a commentary on all the works of Flavius Josephus—a writer who clarified this entire subject in Book 4 of his *Antiquities*[8] and again in the second book of his *Against Apion*,[9] I will have no shortage of opportunities for doing this kind of research.

Just as I hope, noble van Dyck, that my refinements on the text of Josephus will serve the needs of many readers, I am completely confident that the observations I am publishing here are so important that it would be wrong for me to pass them by. After all, even those men of our age who have bothered to write something about the Republic of the ancient Hebrews left many issues untouched. In fact, in some of my comments I am simply correcting the mistakes and fictions of other writers; and it was absolutely necessary that I refute certain men whose learning and widespread reputation long ago won them the highest acclaim. And yet I never do this willingly—it almost makes me ashamed of myself. Gaius Caesar[10] reports that Marcus Cato[11] encountered some men in the course of his early-morning duties who blushed because they had discovered him drunk; and that they actually felt not that they had caught Cato, but that Cato had caught them. I confess that as far as my book is concerned I am in the same situation: Rather than taking away from the respect in which these men are held, I am injuring my own modesty; and I criticize them in such a way that I end up singing their praises. I can only hope that I am treated as fairly by those who may one day demolish my own observations; in fact, I will regard such treatment as appropriate and admirable. I am not a person of such unrestrained arrogance that I believe I am the only man to rise above that stupidity which is part of the human condition, and that I could never have anything to apologize for. We all have foolish notions—some are serious, others are trivial—and no one has a mind so well-disciplined that it lets nothing worthwhile escape or slip by.

Besides, it is sometimes a kind of flaw never to have made a mistake. This is what Dionysius Longinus[12] said about Apollonius of Rhodes,[13] and what he meant was that even though Apollonius' work showed such perfect craft and care, it lacked the force of his personality. As soon as the mind has been inspired by the grandeur of some undertaking, it dismisses its anxious concerns. The ambitions of people who keep themselves within prescribed boundaries and limits are usually pathetic and starved. Whenever people distort their own senses and devote their energies to trivial concerns, the result is that even though they have (at great cost to themselves) spent every day for a whole year churning out a single book, they seem to us to have avoided our criticism rather than to have earned our praise. This is why Longinus, who was a man of exceptional discernment, says that though the greatest men in any age speak and write brilliantly, they are sometimes so willing to allow mistakes in unimportant matters that they may themselves point them out. It is too constricting not to make any mistakes; while someone who has accomplished this has certainly performed every task carefully according to the rules, the most one can say about him is that he has done nothing wrong. On the other hand, someone who gets through everything by a series of noble failures, and allows his impulses to run free, shows us that his very failures make him human; and since none of his ambitions is mediocre he is right behind whoever is on top. There is a kind of grandeur in failing at a great attempt.

Of course I am not doing anything nearly so grand; but even so, for me writing this book was a very great source of pleasure. After all, I was remembering the studies to which I was so incredibly dedicated as a young man. It was pleasant to recall over and again just how much pleasure I had taken in the study of Hebrew, back when I was working my way through the volumes of the Bible, the reflections of the Rabbis, and many other wise writings of the Jews. I have never had any reason at all to regret these studies; even though in later years I was distracted by the concerns of my public duties, I put as much energy into perfecting these magnificent skills (whose benefits I thought would improve everyone's lives) as other people do into visiting their friends, gambling, and the other pursuits of leisure. Reading the Bible ought to be just as pleasurable to every good man (and to learned men in particular) as it is to the theologians. So how, living as I am in respectable leisure, could I have made more serious use of my time than to become as familiar as possible with the language that God Himself once used when He thought the ancient leaders of the Church deserved His encouragement? [14]

I must be frank: the way we choose to live is reckless and negligent. We learn the languages of the Spaniards, the French, and the Italians, and ever since our ships reached the other side of the world we even speak with the Indians in their barbaric tongue. Still, for all our cleverness, there is only one language we do not understand—the only one, in fact, that it would have been worthwhile to learn. And even the people who do apply themselves to this wonderful discipline usually learn just enough to get by. Most of them reach the threshold of Hebrew studies, which is the easiest part; but they have no interest in entering the inner sancta of Aramaic and rabbinic Hebrew. And even in Hebrew studies, they cannot get a real sense of the breadth and depth of the language if they are content to learn only the words of the biblical text. And yet people who do this think they are so learned that they can even teach others; [15] but to me this seems completely wrong-headed. They must push onward, and see what the Jews—who interpreted the Bible in its own language—had to say about it so many years ago, whether or not they were right. Whoever does this is within his rights to say whatever he likes about any of the issues whose sources can be found in the Holy Book alone.

Nor should we assume that people whose positions and status oblige them to perform other kinds of duties are incapable of achieving this kind of expertise. People who are, so to speak, tied down to one minor area of study beyond which they think a mere mortal cannot possibly venture are, I think, unaware of the divine excellence of their souls. To the alert mind everything is within reach; it is constantly turning things over and reexamin- ing them, and it cannot bear to relax. Whenever it sees something beautiful, and grand, and worth knowing, it realizes that this thing is entirely within its grasp, and it usually achieves the goals it sets for itself. But be that as it may, I am still no less preoccupied by the angry feelings of people who think that I have not yet done enough to placate their outrage over the terrible crime I have committed: they are screaming that I have done something disgraceful and insufferable by crossing the border into theology, which they claim is so exclusively their own discipline that they enjoy a kind of dominion and complete jurisdiction over it. But since these men, though few in number, are also extremely hostile, the only response they will accept from me is one that readily comes to mind from the Holy Book itself: that God's wisdom, the mistress of our affairs, goes forth among the people through the medium of human speech and stands in the courtyards and at the crossroads. She summons to herself not only priests and ministers, but the common man and the unwashed masses. She does not turn people away, nor does she shut her door in the face of anyone who still hopes for better things. It is this that allows people to pick themselves up, to summon their courage, and even to consider themselves worthy before God.

Not all of today's scholars of sacred wisdom conduct their affairs in an entirely admirable way. People should weigh very carefully what these scholars have to say, if they want to present themselves before God Almighty as upright and honest citizens who show a proper amount of confidence in their own conscience, and who live their lives in holiness.[16] When I see their controversies and their disputes, which are about more than theology, I vow to serve the public good: alone with myself, far from the madding crowd, the only thing in which I really take any pleasure. And amid my duties as a teacher of political thought and jurisprudence, as well as in my spare time, I am constantly dealing with my own sort of theology: not the kind which is beholden to some faction or leader, but the unfettered, serious, and efficient kind, which is based on my education in Greek, Hebrew, and Latin literature, and which despises the consuming rage and endless brawling of other men. In fact, noble van Dyck, in this third book you will find questions about Melchizedek, the kabbalah, the faith of the ancient Hebrews, and many others of the same sort; and I have explained these questions somewhat differently from the usual way. But as you read through my explanations, please remember that I am ready to change my opinion the moment someone suggests a better one; it is not my way to turn stubborn for the sake of a theory. If I myself should ever discover my own mistakes, I will gladly offer my thanks and be the first to point them out—I would not want anyone to turn a blind eye to my shortcomings because of the enthusiasm and affection in which they hold me. But I think I will encounter very few readers of this sort; most of them will either attack statements that are completely uncontroversial, or instead of making accusations will judge me with cold indifference. I will not, however, make much of an effort to respond to the fussy complaints of such people, for it takes great eloquence to win over people who dislike you.[17] On the other hand, the great majority of them will not even give my work serious consideration: on account of a sort of congenital madness they will consider it a great disgrace to learn anything at all about Hebrew studies from me.

I am not a false prophet; all these things will happen just as I have said. But whatever the fate of my work may be, I will not put it off, nor will I shrink from what is right and good. To be moved to happiness or sadness based on the opinions of someone other than oneself is nothing less than swearing an oath to ambition, and this I have never done.[18] In a poem of Flaccus, Arbuscula (who was a very shrewd woman) said, when the crowd booed her in the theater, that it was enough for the knights to applaud.[19] I will say the same, noble van Dyck. I am happy to have only a few readers so long as they are learned. And among these readers it is you whose sense of judgment, honed by vigorous study and a great deal of training, has always (and rightly so) been most important to me. But my remarks are becoming burdensome; so I will begin what I have proposed to do.

CHAPTER 1

---

*The beginnings and growth of the Church. The tactics of
Satan. An explanation of the episode of the serpent in Genesis 1.
What is the "head of a book." The mistake of Jerome. The
fictitious Book of Enoch.*

ALL MY OBSERVATIONS about the Jewish nation fit into one of two
categories: we must deal with their Republic, which had a unique character
found in no other nation, and we must also consider what their Church
was like. Although these two issues seem to be so closely connected that
they are one and the same and cannot be separated, they are in fact very
different from one another, and the character of each should be examined
by itself. So although in my previous two books I treated the first of these
issues in such a way that I often touched on the second one (which in fact
was absolutely necessary), I will now do the best and most efficient thing
and review one at a time the various issues surrounding this Church. But my
discussion must start from a somewhat earlier point in the past: though I
have already said that it was Moses who established the sacred state, I believe
that I should now examine even earlier periods of history, and go on from
these to the age of Moses and then to the periods that followed him. It is
true that these early years and the ones right after them have been reported
so straightforwardly in the holy books that they leave me with very little
of any significance to say; but once I have gotten past them I will arrive at
more intriguing avenues of discussion.

St. Peter, whom some of the ancients correctly called "the standard-bearer
of the New Testament," says that the Church is a kingdom of priests and a
chosen race of men.[20] God Himself told Moses that though He was the ruler
of all nations and lands, it was only a special few whom He had set apart
from the rest of humanity and kept for Himself like a kind of treasure.[21]
Though to them He gave a kingdom, it was a priestly one—a kingdom that
is holy, sacrosanct, and eternal.[22] Nature has placed limits on the growth of
every great empire, and it is a law of fate that everything great collapses in
on itself, even when there are no outside forces pressing on it; and fortune

succumbs to its own burdens. The kingdom described in the holy books is the only one to become ever greater and more secure in the course of its lifetime, and to gain new strength from its old age.

The first beginnings of the Church date back almost to the beginning of the world itself, when the human race consisted of four individuals.[23] In no time at all Cain was seduced from the path of piety to that of absolute wickedness, by that perverse impulse which takes pleasure in our evil deeds. The Church was born at the very moment when God first began to distinguish the good from the wicked, and to draw His children close to Him.[24] This great shepherd was keeping a very small flock—four sheep in all the world—yet the wolf carried one of them off.[25] This was his first victory over the human race, which God had already lifted up once before from under the weight of its sins so that He might lead it to salvation.[26] It was only a short time later, when the two brothers made their offerings to God, that God made it clear He did not welcome Cain's gifts. The reason for this is obvious: Cain had a naturally evil disposition. Besides, God approves of pure hands rather than full ones; and the kind of worship most pleasing to Him is that we think wholesome and upright thoughts.

On the other hand, Flavius Josephus, an author whom I cannot praise highly enough, and whom we can trust more than anyone except for the writers of the sacred books, has not, I think, been careful enough in the way he discusses this issue. He says that God was displeased by the laborious effort with which Cain undertook to cultivate the earth;[27] but Josephus must have lost his head when he wrote this. After all, Adam, the father of the human race, farmed the land at the command of God Himself,[28] and his son followed the good example of his father. But as Josephus sometimes does, he must have been following the lead of the Rabbis; and although he was a more serious scholar than any other Jew, he could hardly have avoided every single one of his countrymen's fantasies. This is clear even from the rather uninteresting secret that he believed was hidden in the word *ehad* (*one*) in Genesis, chapter 1.[29] His explanation (which he says he will give in another book) as to why Moses said *one day* rather than *the first day* was taken from the Rabbis. There is a Jewish book called *Michlal Yofi*[30] in which the following statement is attributed to Rabbi Moses ibn Ezra:[31] *He said 'one' because one is the sign of a beginning before which there is no other.*[32] Josephus had said the exact same thing (or something similar) in his *Etiologies*, which no longer exists.[33] It is no doubt in its author's interest that this book has perished; if it had not, he would undoubtedly have become a laughingstock for using such facile arguments.

But let me return to Adam, who was the topic of our discussion. At the beginning of the world he saw his son unjustly murdered by the one person who should never have done so; and though he mourned the death of one son, he was even more distraught over the crime committed by the other. I think that at this point Adam was once again on the verge of rushing head-long into the snares of Satan and meeting his ruin. But he drew strength from a greater power; he was guided more by his hopes for the future than by anything that lay before his eyes. There is an old idea, confirmed by the general agreement of scholars, that the Messiah, the savior of the human race, was promised to our original parents when God said to the conniving serpent as follows, in the third chapter of Genesis: *I will sow hatred between you and the woman, and between your seed and hers; her seed will injure your head, and you will injure his heel.*[34] This is certainly true—Adam grasped the expectation of an eternal and heavenly life.

Since it is my goal that everything I do should be dictated by reason, I have often been surprised that the scholars whose work I have seen *insist* that they are correct rather than *proving* that they are. This is why I think we ought to look for the kind of evidence that is beyond dispute; if we want to be absolutely certain that something is true, it is not enough to rely on scholarly consensus and the majority opinion. We cannot discover the true meaning of any of the enigmas of the biblical text unless they have been explicitly pointed out elsewhere[35] under the inspiration of the Messiah, who is the best interpreter of what he means to say.[36] For the canon of the sacred scriptures was locked and sealed, but the seal was opened by the lion of Judah.[37] In fact, when I was thinking about this whole question recently, I came across an illuminating passage in the Revelation of John. It is as follows: *A pregnant woman was crying out as she gave birth, and was in torment so she could deliver; and she gave birth to a male child who will rule all the nations with an iron rod.*[38] This is the Church, and the Messiah. These two are then ambushed by the dragon, as the Apostle adds: *And that great dragon was thrown down; that ancient serpent—who is called Devil and Satan, who leads the whole world astray—it was, I say, thrown down.*[39] This ancient serpent is the same one whose head was shattered by the woman's offspring. Whatever others may have said, in my opinion this is the only reasonable source for that interpretation.[40] And yet it is more than enough; whoever relies on it is protected from attack by its great and noble reputation. I could also produce a number of arguments that would indirectly connect this interpretation with the words of St. Paul in the second chapter of his first letter to Timothy: *When the woman was led astray she became a cause of transgression; yet she will be saved by bearing children, if they remain faithful and kind.*[41] Even though this statement appears in a different context, it seems to refer to the promise God made to Eve.

This is the evidence on which the general consensus, which has long since been accepted by everyone, ought to be based. Though other proofs may be brought which have the ring of truth, on closer examination they turn out to be worthless; and I find it hard to bear when halfhearted proofs are used to support ideas that in and of themselves are definitely correct. God tells Moses a wonderful thing: *Take your shoes off your feet, because the place you are standing is holy ground.*[42] People who investigate the biblical text should pay attention to this: they should open their minds, and empty their hearts of foregone conclusions; and the person who has done the best job of weighing the truth should win out.

This is why I cannot ignore the recklessness with which Jerome passed over solid arguments in order to embrace false ones. The tenth chapter of the Letter to the Hebrews sets out David's prophecy about the Messiah:[43] *Behold, I am coming, at the head of the book it is written about me.*[44] David quotes this prophecy from the second book of Moses' law,[45] as surely everyone knows; but the divine Jerome insisted with complete confidence that this prophecy must refer to the beginning of Genesis. He says that *the head of the book means the beginning of Genesis.* I am not going to ask right now whether he was thinking of the term *reishit*, "beginning," or the promise concerning the woman's offspring[46] (he discussed both these things). It is enough that he used false testimony to prove what he wanted to say.

Now, I agree that Jerome was the most learned of all the ancient interpreters of sacred scripture because he had mastered Hebrew so thoroughly. So given that such a great man could not have made this mistake simply by accident and without a serious reason, I will try to explain the source of his delusion. Jerome himself says more than once as a reason for his opinions, *because the entire scripture is one book.* In fact, I am certain that the great man was following an ancient Jewish principle, according to which the entire Bible had at one time been *pasuk ehad* that is, *a single verse*; thus, the sacred books were not divided into sections, chapters, or even words.[47] (I remember that a friend of mine had once seen a moldy copy that the Jews had written out in this style.) Jerome, moreover, does not notice what it is that the Apostle is calling *kephalis bibliou* or *the head of the book*. For *kephalides* are what the Jews, and especially the Talmudists, call *perakim*, i.e. *the parts of books*. So the Apostle, who was himself a Jew, and was writing to his fellow Jews, naturally used this term. After all, though what I said about the biblical text a moment ago—that it was not divided up—*does* apply to the style in which it was written and to its uninterrupted narrative, this did not mean that the text was all lumped together. On the contrary, men who were superstitious to the point of ridicule had carefully learned the names, the titles, and the divisions of each part; and you could see in their hands, like so many balls of amber,[48] worn-out copies of the sacred books.

It is obvious enough by now why Jerome was misled. I have another point to add: the prophecy about the Messiah found at the beginning of Genesis would never have been understood by our original parents if God had not explained it, and revealed His hidden meanings to them out of pity. After all, if we go strictly according to the meaning of the words, the entire passage fits the serpent perfectly.[49] Those who have thought otherwise have completely misjudged the matter; for is there an idea more common in the writings of the ancients, including the pagans, than man's natural hatred of snakes? God gave the punishment he did to this animal precisely because until then it had been the most warmly regarded by human beings.[50] In the second book of Artemidorus[51] the serpent is the symbol of hatred; and in Theocritus' *Women at the Festival of Adonis* the girl says: *I have feared most of all the horse and the cold-hearted snake.*[52] See how he calls the snake the most fearsome thing of all! Livy reports that in ancient times, the inhabitants of Faliscum and Tarquinii made Marcus Fabius Ambustus flee the battlefield when their priests held up snakes and ran around in an ecstatic trance, a bizarre sight that threw the Roman soldiers into a panic.[53]

Moreover, the fact that this animal lost its legs and was made to crawl about has nothing at all to do with Satan. Aristotle, who did not know the real reason for this, has given us a very ingenious explanation drawn from Nature herself.[54] But since we have a better teacher, we know that the reason was God's anger. Nor is it unheard of that a dumb animal can understand language and respond to it.[55] Balaam's ass[56] is a famous case, and in another passage God Himself speaks to the whale.[57] Besides, the snake certainly deserved its punishment—after all, it served as the instrument through which our perverse character was guided into committing a monstrous sin. It is also very fitting that it was condemned to having its head trampled. Any injury to this part of a snake's body is fatal, and when they are threatened with any sort of danger they make an impressive effort to coil themselves up, and shield their heads with the rest of their bodies. Though Jerome gives us clear evidence of this phenomenon, I would rather not spend any more time on these questions.

I would like to examine the earliest beginnings of the Church, through all of which the awesome power of divine wisdom shines forth. Rather than using a chronological scheme, I will organize particular aspects of the subject into categories, giving each one the amount of attention it deserves. After all, I am not composing a work of history; in many cases I will skip over entire eras. The Bible says very little about the descendants of Cain because they were not part of God's chosen people, but from the very beginning it carefully records the sons, the grandsons, and the entire clan of Seth. This was the branch from which the patriarchs and the Messiah came. Seth was born about a hundred years after the murder of Abel, at a time when Cain's godless descendants had settled far and wide and government was in the hands of sinners. But because Seth himself revered God, the moment the narrator of Genesis introduces him he adds that *it was then they began to call upon the name of God*.[58] Rabbi Shlomo Yarhi misunderstood this. He says it was at this time that *avoda zara* (*idolatry*) began; and he adds that *beshemo shel hakadosh baruch hu—for this purpose they misused the name of the true God*.[59] This is ridiculous: the world was in its infancy, and knew nothing of the worship of idols, and yet most people have welcomed this interpretation with open arms.

It seems that for some time the descendants of Seth let their virtues fall by the wayside; or if any of them did possess some virtues, these were so well hidden that they were essentially the same as deep apathy. But Enoch, who was six generations later, was famous for his exceptional piety. God decided that this man would not die—He took him up to Heaven alive, with his body intact. The Jews say rather foolishly that *there are seven men who span all the ages of the world, and they are: Adam, Methuselah, Shem, Jacob, Amram, Ahiya of Shilo, and Elijah, who is still alive*.[60] This is complete nonsense. It makes at least as much sense to say that there were not seven but only two, Adam and Enoch, who was on earth for fifty-six years after Adam and buried him.[61] Although the Jews, and in particular Rabbi ibn Ezra, certainly do believe that Enoch met the same fate as the rest of us, I trust St. Paul, who says that he did not die.[62] In fact, what happened to Enoch would have happened to everyone if they had continued to lead virtuous lives. As it is, our mistake and the weight of our crimes have condemned us to our mortality, which we live out in poor health and under attack by a thousand bodily ills.

I have no doubt that Enoch was a harsh critic of his contemporaries' sinfulness, and that this encouraged some riffraff who had been struck by a foolish whim: in the hope that they might play a prank on future generations, they put their mediocre talents and limited energy to work on writing a book that they then forced on the public. And this, Lord help us, they said had been written by Enoch.[63] Of course, such a book must either have survived in one piece a flood that swept away practically everything else, or it had to have fallen from Heaven later on (which is asinine).[64] But then there is no limit to the foolish claims an idiot can make, when even the Jews say that Elijah wrote a letter to King Joram from Heaven seven years after he was snatched up there; and they add that *to this day he is up there writing the chronicles of every age.*[65] This delusion of theirs does, however, deserve some sympathy; for they have misunderstood the wording of the Second Book of Chronicles, chapter 21.[66] On the other hand, the more intelligent men of antiquity so forcefully rejected the forged prophecy of Enoch that (according to Jerome) the Letter of Jude, which is one of the seven Catholic letters,[67] was generally crossed off the list of sacred books because it quotes passages from that worthless document.[68]

CHAPTER 2

God frequently used His remarkable powers of discretion to
limit the membership of the Church more and more to one family.
Specific cases of this.

AFTER ENOCH departed the earth, the family of Seth, which God had set aside for Himself, became tainted by the poison of that age: though in the past they had been careful to seek marriages within the clan that contained the Church, now their sense of reason deserted them. They welcomed the idea of false idols, and their appetites, which favored their vices, led them to believe that the way their behavior appeared to others was more important than its actual holiness. This led to a contagion that started with the daughters of godless men[69] and from there spread to everyone. That age was at once afflicted with every kind of evil; law, integrity, and trust all disappeared, along with shame (which people are never happy to welcome back once they have gotten rid of it). Every kind of crime was tried, and there was no time to get upset over the ones that were already being committed, since new varieties were appearing all the time. A sickness this intractable required a drastic cure. The sin could not be wiped out unless the sinners went with it—the human race had to be destroyed.

The only guiltless man still alive was Noah. St. Peter calls him the "herald of justice"[70] because it was through him that God spoke in order to turn the wicked back toward sanity. They were given a hundred and twenty years to recover their senses. Unlike Flavius Josephus, who mistakenly twisted this passage into meaning something it does not,[71] we should therefore accept without hesitation what it says in the sixth chapter of Genesis.[72] Nor does it matter that the calculation of the actual amount of time that elapsed does not agree at all with the sequence of the narrative. The wisest of the rabbis, ibn Ezra and Shlomo Yarhi, took notice of this,[73] but they also added a statement that we ought to consider very carefully: *In the books of Moses' laws, events are not recorded in the order they occurred.*[74]

Because the time that God gave men to repent proved to be pointless, He made all the rivers overflow and sent down a torrent of rain, until the world was covered in water. Out of all those thousands of people only a few were left alive—God saved them for seed, so that He could make up the lost numbers of the human race with new offspring. Then Noah restored the proper worship of God, and so that he would not fear another flood, God told him to look to the rainbow and trust it as a pledge. Although at that time the Church had only a few men, God was displeased by this indiscriminate mob, so its numbers were again reduced: though Noah had produced three sons—Shem, Ham, and Japhet—the Church was restricted to the line of Shem. Some scholars have wrongly concluded from the words of Moses that Ham was the youngest, when in fact we should understand the text to refer to Ham's son.[75] In fact, Ham was a year older than Shem, as Rabbi Zacuto correctly realized.[76] Certainly Jerome felt the same way. He says that the solution to this mystery is as follows (and though it may not be true, it is nonetheless brilliant): *The older son made fun of their naked father and the younger one covered him up, just as the Jews made fun of the crucified God and the gentiles honored Him.* This formulation may be found in his essay against the Luciferians.[77]

For several years after Shem, nothing much happened worth mentioning (unless someone would like me to wax tragical about the Tower of Babel, or fill up entire volumes with genealogies; both my rational faculties and my natural character have always been incredibly resistant to this sort of activity). Finally Abraham, who was one of Shem's descendants, made himself a name among the heroes of antiquity. In his time the Church was young and growing into robust adulthood, and he was that just man whom Isaiah, the most eloquent of the prophets, says was called forth from the East.[78] He left behind the land of the Chaldeans (where he had lived at the beginning of his life), the hearth of his fathers, and all the other things men consider most pleasant, so that he could go to a strange land in which none of the places he lived could be called his own. But he had to obey God, at whose behest he was summoned to greater things.[79]

The soul of a wise man is a precious and noble thing. He never limits his thoughts to the narrow confines within which we live our lives, and he believes that he has a stake even in things that will happen many centuries from now. The divine Abraham understood that the kingdom of Canaan was fated to belong to his descendants, and this consolation helped lighten the load of his immediate troubles. On the other hand, many things were delaying his hopes of producing an heir: he himself was old, and his strength was declining with age; and his wife, who had not had children during her fertile years, was also rather elderly. Yet the great promises he had received from Heaven strengthened his resolve, and he believed that God's limitless power could accomplish something that he with his physical limitations could not. He has therefore earned his reputation as the father of all believers. He was the first to use his intellect to make manifest, and to contemplate, things that had never existed and never could have existed. Such a thing can only be accomplished by faith, which the Holy Book, in a beautiful turn of phrase, calls *confidence in things that do not exist.*[80]

Then Isaac was born; it was of course from his family that the Messiah would come. Here again we may wonder at God's plan, which, though certainly just, is no less mysterious. Abraham sired Ishmael from Hagar, and it is to him that the Saracens and the Arabs trace their origins. Keturah bore him several children as well. Though the father of all these children was a very pious old man, it was to only one of them in particular that God, the supreme judge of our affairs, pledged His good will. He wanted Isaac's family to be the only one to worship Him and to perform His rites and ceremonies. This was the same kind of selection that had already taken place a number of times; but I am not ashamed to repeat more than once things that are so worth knowing. Of Adam's children only Seth found favor and was chosen, of his line only Noah, of Noah's sons Shem, and of his descendants Abraham; finally, of Abraham's many children only Isaac was chosen, so that (for some reason beyond our understanding) his family might claim for its own—as a kind of inheritance—the name and the honor of the Church. God rejected the other nations as though they were polluted, and they remained in second place until the Messiah came to the world, threw down the wall between Jews and gentiles, and brought about what He had promised to Abraham so long before: that through His child He would give to all the nations—without distinction—the salvation for which they hoped.

CHAPTER 3

My opinion about Melchizedek is strengthened despite
the accepted consensus. The Letter to the Hebrews receives
a powerful defense.

GIVEN THE NATURE of my subject, I would like to say something about
Melchizedek.[81] In an era when the Church belonged to only one family, it
was unheard of (and practically miraculous) that there was a member of
the sinful Canaanite nation who not only worshiped God correctly, but even
prayed that Abraham, who was the leader of the Church and had recently
arrived in that region, should receive the blessings of Heaven (a prayer
that was granted).[82] I know of course what other scholars have said about
Melchizedek, but I do not hesitate to abandon their ideas. I will not blindly
follow someone else's dictates, nor does it suit my character to swear to the
truth of another man's statement. The freedom to express oneself is priceless;
anyone who considers it to be the very essence of good judgment cannot
help but agree with me.

Jerome wrote a brilliant letter to Evagrius in which he deduces from Greek
literature that Melchizedek was a real person who lived in Canaan, and was
the prince of Salem and a priest of God Almighty; and that for generations
of men he served as a sort of prefiguration of Jesus Christ, the greatest of all
who were both king and priest. Then he explains the Apostle's words on the
subject in the Letter to the Hebrews.[83] The authorities whom he names as his
sources are men of the greatest prestige: Irenaeus,[84] Hippolytus,[85] Eusebius of
Caesarea, and Emisenus;[86] he also mentions Apollinarius[87] and Eustathius,
who was appointed the first bishop of Antioch. All of today's scholars are
in complete agreement with the conclusions these men reached; for though
each has his own rationale, they all use their various arguments to arrive
at the same end. I admit that it would be wrong to dismiss offhand a claim
that has been consistently held by so many people; by doing such a thing I
risk letting my love of saying something new distort all my conclusions. But
because it seems to me that reason itself argues against the accepted opinion,
the truth ought to carry more weight than the authority of a scholar.

This is why I think that Melchizedek was not, in fact, a human being born from other human beings, but had a nature closer to God's; and that only someone greater than a man, and certainly more worthy, could have given a blessing to such a great patriarch. Evagrius had sent Jerome a book of unknown authorship which made the claim I am making here; but even though Jerome rejected this claim I don't believe he had any reason at all to do so. Every time I have read through the Letter to the Hebrews, I have been forced to conclude either that it cannot be clearly understood, or that the claim I am making against the theory of Jerome and all the others has to be right. Melchizedek is mentioned in the Old Testament in only two places—in Genesis, chapter 14, of course, and in Psalm 110. These are the sources from which scholars have tried to determine the point the Apostle was making in the sublime words of his discussion in the Letter to the Hebrews.[88] I can therefore settle this business very quickly.

The scholars who say that the city where this king held power was Salem, located in Canaan, and that we must therefore understand his kingdom to be that of a human being, are doubtless under the impression that they are supported by solid evidence. But I ask these scholars: On whose authority should we trust their opinion over that of the Apostle himself? He says very clearly: *Who according to the interpretation is called first the king of justice, and then the king of Salem, that is the king of peace.*[89] This great king is given two names in Genesis: the first is Melchizedek, and the second is Melechsalem (for this is nothing more than a proper noun).[90] The Hebrew word *melech* means *king*, *tzedek* means *justice*, and *salem* means *peace*; even first-year Hebrew students know this much. So *salem* is not the name of a city any more than *tzedek* is.[91] Or perhaps the people who are busy piling up new mistakes on top of their old ones should go ahead and add an imaginary city named Tzedek to the kingdom of Canaan; this makes just as much sense as a fiction like Salem. But this is a trivial point.

If I were not dealing with solid proof, it would certainly have been reckless of me to set out to undermine the consensus of so many learned men and so many generations of scholars; but I will hope for the best. Let me treat in turn the rest of the evidence with which the Apostle supplies us.[92] He devotes the majority of his letter to teaching us that the priesthood of the Messiah was greater and more distinguished than those of Aaron or the Levites. After all, the duties of the Levites were temporary—when one of them died he lost the honors of his priesthood and someone else took his place. But, Paul says, the priesthood of Christ is eternal just like that of Melchizedek. And to make sure that no one doubts the truth of his words, he quotes David's prophecy from Psalm 110: *You are a priest forever, like*

Melchizedek. In the Greek this[93] is rendered *kata taxin, after the order.* But the Apostle is giving the *sense* of the phrase rather than its literal meaning—what David says is *kedivrati malkitzedek*, which the learned Rabbi ibn Ezra correctly explains as *keminhag malkitzedek—in the manner of Melchizedek* or *just like Melchizedek.*[94] This is the actual meaning of the Hebrew, for the situation was as follows: Abraham had defeated the wicked kings in battle[95] and was leading his victorious army home, when the son of God happened to place himself in Abraham's path in the guise of a man, and with the bearing of a priest and king; and his tidings of good fortune gave Abraham the courage to face the most daunting challenges. And since Abraham was exhausted, he gave him bread and wine—he did not want this man who had defeated princes to lack for anything, including his sustenance.

Since Abraham realized instantly that he was experiencing something extraordinary, in his mind he worshiped what lay behind the image. And as he was face to face with the Messiah—the greatest king and priest of all, who (as Abraham knew) would one day be given to mankind—he offered him gifts and tithes.[96] Is there, I ask you, any reason we should not believe that this king of justice and peace was the very same son of God who later appeared to Abraham with his two companions at the oak of Mamre,[97] shared a meal with him, stayed with him in his house, and even spoke with him? I think that if a man suddenly encounters someone in the midst of a journey as though he had appeared from a machine,[98] and this person blesses the man and gives him food and drink, it is a much more forceful proof of that person's divine and heavenly nature than if he should enter the man's house, accept his hospitality, dine with him, and have a conversation.[99]

There is only one important difference between the two passages. Genesis 18 says explicitly that it was God who visited Abraham. It is true that the narrator of Genesis does not say this about Melchizedek: he leaves the solution of the mystery for David and Paul, who make the truth clear. And we really have nothing to fear from the fact that this immortal king and priest is called by the proper names Melchizedek and Melechsalem, because the Holy Book often applies names of this kind to God as circumstances require it. Such names are entirely symbolic, and represent the themes with which the text happens to be dealing at that moment. So in one place God is called *eheyeh asher eheyeh,* or *I am that I am,*[100] and in another *Emmanuel,* or *God is with us;*[101] and in our case, of course, He is called *Melech-salem* and *Melchi-zedek.* No one should be surprised that He who alone is All should be called by many names—He has as many as all the virtues and good works with which we associate Him. And yet who could praise every one of these virtues? However many you may list, you will leave out many more still.

Nor should it bother anyone that it is written in Genesis that *he was a priest of Almighty God*; this applies only to the *guise of a priest* that the son of God had adopted.[102] This is also true of the various other identities he assumed (such cases are well known). The most eminent theologians say that every time Immortal God has appeared to human beings, a second person has appeared alongside Him—His son. They definitely had the right idea; at any rate, when the Apostle says that *at first God often spoke through the prophets, but more recently He has spoken through His son,*[103] he is saying not that the Messiah had never appeared to the world before but that he had never taken on the task of speaking for God. Though at first this was always done by the prophets, in time he took on the task himself. I also believe that when the son of God came to Abraham on the road he had put on a likeness of the face and body that he would later wear in his earthly life, and that this is what the Apostle means by *he resembled the son of God.*[104] He could not wear the actual body that people would later see and touch in his time on earth; for this was solely the product of childbirth and did not yet exist; this is why he showed Abraham only the *image* of his body, though it was clearly the same one he would have as a mortal man.[105] I think this is also what John has in mind when he writes that *Abraham was eager to see my day, and he did see it, and rejoiced.*[106] For this happened to no one but Abraham, and it was a unique experience; about everyone else it says that *many prophets and righteous men yearned to see what you are seeing, but they did not.*[107]

It does not contradict my theory that St. Paul describes this king of justice and peace as *having neither a mother nor a father,*[108] for he was not interested here in the mystery of Christ's double nature, i.e. that while he got his divinity from his father and his humanity from his mother, neither quality came exclusively from only one parent. This question had no bearing on a time when the savior of the human race had not yet assumed human form. In any case, the Apostle believed that Christ was the product not of the natural process that requires a father and a mother, and not of lust or the joining of a man and a woman, but that he was eternal, and that (as the prophet Isaiah says in chapter 53) *nothing can be said about his birth.*[109] But there is no question that people who want to claim that Melchizedek was the prince of Salem, and a human being, have to admit that everything the Apostle said about him also agrees with the Messiah. As things now stand, the only way we can understand the Messiah to have been *without mother and father* is according to the interpretation I have just indicated.[110] I have also noticed that St. Paul defines Melchizedek's priesthood as eternal and infinite; so naturally he says that *his days had no beginning and his life has no end; he remains a priest forever.*[111] It follows from this that if we believe that the Messiah and Melchizedek were not one and the same, then there were no fewer than two priests whose office was not limited to a set term of years but lasted forever. No one has ever made such a suggestion, not even in jest—neither the ancients in their time, nor any of the more recent authorities.

Now finally I would like to discuss the one thing I consider most important of all. There is no question that even in the time of the Apostle, the Jews were possessed by some evil spirit that compelled them to make the mistake of thinking (as we may read today in their writings) that *Melchizedek was Shem the son of Noah, who was still alive in the times of Abraham and Isaac.*[112] The Apostle calls on the Jews, who were addicted to this worthless idea, to think about Melchizedek's ultimate significance; and before he goes on to say that Melchizedek was greater not only than Shem but than all other men, he prefaces his remarks with: *I have many things to say about him which are difficult to interpret.*[113] You see, he is speechless in the face of this person's greatness, and admits that he is indescribable! Paul never says this kind of thing when he discusses any of the other ancient images and symbols that had foreshadowed the reign of the Messiah. Then he adds: *It is beyond dispute that the inferior is blessed by the superior.*[114] This means that Melchizedek had a kind of divine nature and should not be considered a human being—anyone who could have blessed such a great patriarch must have been an even greater and more impressive figure. Paul also compares Melchizedek with the Levites: *In this case tithes are received by mortal men, in the other by someone of whom it is witnessed that he lives.*[115] He makes two points—first, that the Levites who were receiving tithes were *men*; and second, that they were *mortal*. On the other hand, he says that this priest to whom Abraham gave tithes was neither a man nor mortal, but one *about whom we have incontrovertible proof that he lived forever.*[116]

So what is this proof? It is no doubt Paul's quote from the words of David: *You are a priest forever, just like Melchizedek.*[117] It is just as though Paul were saying that *you are that king of justice and peace, and that priest who lives forever, whom Abraham saw, and worshiped with tithes and gifts, and called Melchizedek, because it was the greatest and most important name he could have given him.* Then again, Paul also writes that *there will appear another priest similar to Melchizedek* and different from the Levites,[118] *who is a priest not according to the dictates of the Law, which applies only to mortal men, but according to the power of eternal life.*[119] Naturally he attributes to the Messiah and to Melchizedek the very thing he says the Levites lack, *the power of eternal life.* A little before this he says that *if perfection had been attained through the priesthood of the Levites, what need would there have been for another priest to appear according to the order of Melchizedek?*[120] This must mean that the promises God had once made could not have been fulfilled by the Levite priesthood, and there was therefore a need for a more perfect priesthood, of the sort represented by the Messiah or Melchizedek.

But if, as the Jews say, he was a mortal man and the prince of Salem as well as a priest, it would be ridiculous to ascribe to his priesthood a greater level of perfection than that of the Levites; for Salem was located in Canaan, a region that (Abraham having only just arrived in that country) had not yet adopted the practices of the proper faith.[121] Even supposing there *were* some Canaanites who worshiped God Almighty, who is so ignorant as not to know that the religious rites of even the patriarchal families of Canaan were completely primitive and hideous? And that they remained so until God Himself established, by means of the Law, the order of the Levites, and set down the ceremonies and rites with which He wished to be worshiped, since until then no one at all was honoring Him as they were supposed to? If I wanted to assemble every proof of this fact I would have to write an entire book.

I have spent enough time beating my head against the wall; I want to be free of it. But I should end by discussing what both ancient and modern writers have thought about how to interpret this passage of the Apostle. They saw that it was a difficult and unclear problem which called for a daring solution—when we are faced with a fork in the road, we must plunge on ahead. So rather than taking the phrase *without father, mother, or lineage*[122] to mean that Melchizedek did not have parents, they read it as *Moses did not write down their names, either earlier or later in the text*. And they interpret in the same way *his days had no beginning and his life has no end; he remains a priest forever*.[123] They say that *of course he was born and he died; but since there is no mention of it he was thought to have been eternal, and he has stood as a sort of symbol of the Messiah's divine nature*. But they are not seeking an answer to these hidden mysteries; they are making a mockery of them. How many Levite priests can I recall, and how many holy and famous heroes of the sacred books, whose births and deaths are met with complete silence? We must therefore be very fortunate to have so many Messianic figures![124] For that matter, let the Jews believe that Jacob did not die, since in Genesis it says not *and Jacob died* but *he expired*.[125]

Now, some scholars have reported this idea in order to strengthen the general belief about Melchizedek;[126] and though its author is unknown, he was certainly a Jew. I'm sure that I remember having read it in the work of Rabbi Shlomo Yarhi,[127] though I thought it was complete and utter hogwash which we should no more tolerate than this senseless notion about

Melchizedek. People who use this kind of proof to justify their opinions are merely defending one bit of nonsense with another; and nothing is as readily available as the opportunity to say something stupid. Besides, where will this approach ultimately lead? Now I'm afraid that someone will think Tobit's dog didn't have a tail, because nothing was written about it! It is, however, Athanasius[128] who has satisfied every criterion of foolishness. He came up with a Melchizedek whose prayers could cause the earth to split asunder and swallow up his father and all his relations.[129] This, he says, is the reason that the Apostle describes him as having no parents or family. Of course, even people who are actually insane have yet to dream up something so bizarre that there is not some "scholar" who will agree with it. Marcus Terentius Varro's prediction was entirely on target—with every day that passes I am more convinced of its truth.

But enough of these games. If the Apostle had said only that Melchizedek was *without lineage* I might have been persuaded to go along with the judgment of the other scholars. But in fact he gives us a straightforward explanation of what this means: he says that *his days had no beginning and his life has no end; he remains a priest forever*. He is not talking about what Moses said or did not say, but about actual facts and how he understands them. Though none of the commentators have noticed this, everything the Apostle has to say about this question is based not on Moses' silence but on David's assertions. He says not that *Moses is silent about his death*, but rather that *David provides testimony that he lives*.[130] This is something completely different. If a person's death goes unmentioned, he may have died or he may still be alive; we can never be sure about things that have been passed over in silence, since nothing has actually been affirmed. But if it is said about someone *that he lives*, and this point is emphasized in order to draw a contrast with the Levites (who in the same phrase are called *mortal men*),[131] then the man about whom such a definite claim is made could not, I insist, have been mortal. Or if he was, the Apostle was no longer speaking to us in the language of men, but in that of the angels.[132] Now, I don't know whether it is an apparition or some kind of revelation that has made it possible for other men to learn this language, but I myself am just an average man who has not reached this level of wisdom.

On the other hand, it should be obvious to anyone what kind of "life" the Apostle is attributing to Melchizedek. David says *you are a priest forever, just like Melchizedek*. The prophet is obviously attributing to Melchizedek an eternal priesthood, and by analogy he is attributing it to Christ as well.[133] The Apostle quotes this testimony of David's, and though his wording is different the sense is the same—which is to say, *one who, according to David's testimony, lives and is a priest forever.*[134] This is the true and genuine meaning of Paul's words; any other ideas on the subject are the product of simplistic explanations of the Letter to the Hebrews.

For a long time now, I myself have wondered how it could be that there are scholars whom this letter displeases because they believe it gives credence to the errors of Novatian (though this belief is hasty and ill-conceived);[135] and that no one had ever figured out the ambiguous riddles hidden in the passage about Melchizedek because they were always explained according to the general consensus of the interpreters. Let scholars both ancient and modern examine and reexamine every aspect of the question; they will lay hold of nothing but phantoms and fancies, and be swallowed up in their own shadows.[136] I am not going to beat around the bush: when at first I was trying to solve these difficult problems with as little effort as possible, I was sure that the Latin Churches were right to have rejected this letter.[137] At the same time, I took David's statement about Melchizedek to refer not to the Messiah but to someone else. Indeed, I had accepted the explanation of the Jewish scholars, who have so often shown remarkable diligence in their interpretations of biblical texts. Rabbi ibn Ezra says that the author of this psalm was not David, but one *of the singers.*[138] This means that the words of the first verse—*God said to my lord, "Sit at My right hand, until I have turned your enemies into a stool for your feet"*—were not written by David about the Messiah, but (as ibn Ezra would have it) by the singer about David. So the sense of it is: *God told my lord David, "Have no fears, for I will so soundly defeat all your Philistine enemies that you will dance about on their heads."* After saying many other things along the same lines, the Psalmist goes on to say: *God has sworn it, and He will not renege; you are a priest forever, just like Melchizedek.* The divine spirit[139] frequently refers to kings, princes, and leaders as "priests," because they are in charge of maintaining and administering the rites and ceremonies. So *you will be a priest* is as much as to say *you will be king, and have supreme power over your citizens.* In fact, Rabbi Kimhi thinks that the term *forever* is used here because while Saul's reign had been so shameful and brief, David grew old amid happy and prosperous circumstances.

The next phrase is *just like Melchizedek.* The Jews disagree about what this means. Rabbi Abraham says that *the meaning of these words is "Israel will go to war and you will receive a tenth of the spoils, just as Melchizedek received them from Abraham."*[140] Rabbi Moses, on the other hand, did not associate the phrase with a historical event. He followed the Aramaic Targum,[141] which translates it as *You will be appointed as leader for the coming years on account of justice, for you are a just king*[142] (this is how I translate the Aramaic, which the others have misunderstood).[143] If I may return briefly to our last subject, ibn Ezra mentions other psalms of this type, in which it is not David who speaks but a singer (whoever he was) speaking about David. One of these is the twentieth psalm, *May God hear you on the day of your distress*. Then the following psalm, *Lord, the king will delight in Your strength*. The same applies to the seventy-second psalm.[144]

After I had accepted this interpretation of the problem, I was fortunate to come across a useful passage of St. Matthew, in the twenty-second chapter of his work. There Christ himself traps the Pharisees with the question: *How can David, moved by the divine spirit, call Christ the Lord? He says, "Sit at my right hand, until..."*[145] This is the only argument I need to refute the worthless fiction that the rabbis almost managed to force on me the moment I let down my guard. Throughout this entire psalm it is not, as the Jews would have it, a singer talking about David, but David talking about the Messiah. This is what the greatest teacher of all is telling the Pharisees in this gospel, and we should put our faith in it. It doesn't matter whether ibn Ezra, Rabbi Moses, Kimhi, the Aramaic Targum, and any number of other yids may say this: they are all wrong. The true meaning of this mystery is and will continue to be that David was speaking of Melchizedek, and the Apostle followed in his footsteps; his Letter to the Hebrews is therefore beyond criticism, and full of the spirit of God. In fact, I don't know whether there is any book in the New Testament (aside from the Gospel of John) which contains a deeper and more profound theology.

This is why I used to be tormented (and with good reason) by the awareness that it was only my perverse character that led me to suspend my judgment about this wonderful work, all the rest of whose content was excellent, because of a single passage whose meaning was unclear. I found it hard to believe that a text in which I was seeing such clumsily written prose could have been dictated by the divine spirit.[146] And yet we marvel at the sources of great rivers, and we experience faith in God when we see the shadowed recesses of certain forests and the height of their trees. In just this way, when I cast my eyes on other passages of the same work that surpass the mediocre talents of human beings, I decided then and there to venerate these alone until I could finally understand the others that were still eluding my grasp.[147] This has actually worked out fairly well. Though what I said about Melchizedek may not be absolutely correct, it is certainly close to the truth. It was the son of God to whom Abraham gave tithes; I reached the same conclusion about the purely historical aspect of this question.[148]

I really do not know what kind of evidence was used by the anonymous author whom Jerome condemns with such gusto.[149] He doesn't review this man's arguments or offer any response to them. It may be that (as sometimes happens) this author was defending a good cause, but did a poor job of it. His theory was in fact correct; its only flaw is that he thought it was the Holy Spirit who appeared to Abraham, when in fact it was the son of God. Though there is no need for me to mention the analyses of other scholars, nonetheless it would have helped me a great deal if we still had today the homilies of Origen, in which (according to the testimony of Jerome) he made many arguments about Melchizedek, and eventually came to the conclusion that *he was an angel*. Even though I am not completely taken with this theory because it is somewhat inelegant, still it deserves our praise more than the one embraced by Jerome and the others (both ancient and modern). I would demonstrate this if there were any need for it. Origen was, at any rate, a very gifted man and an excellent scholar, which is why Jerome was understandably drawn to his wisdom even as he envied his reputation. It's true that he was the author of some pernicious doctrines;[150] but since he was by far the best interpreter of sacred scripture, his errors had to be rejected without diminishing his great virtues. That we make mistakes and give in to our imaginations is only human; anyone who wants to live in perfection ought to look for a desert. Every man's virtues have to be weighed alongside his vices, and we must take his measure according to which side of his character is the stronger.

CHAPTER 4

The fate of the Church from the time of Abraham until the split of the Israelite kingdom, which happened after the death of Solomon. The power of prophecy given to those who are about to die. The idolatry practiced by the Israelites in Egypt. The Israelites were afflicted with Egyptian superstitions even once they were settled in Palestine. Apis. Sarapis. The worship of bulls and serpents. Did the Jews really worship an ass? Why did the Egyptians despise the ass? The baskets and straw owned by the Jews of Rome. That the history and laws of the Jews were ignored by Greek and Roman writers, and why. On Theopompus and Theodectes. The Jews' hatred of foreigners. Falsehoods told about the Jews.

NOW THAT I have successfully sailed past those rocks, it is time for me to finish what I set out to do before. I took the history of the Church as far as the time of Abraham. When God selected its members, He was concerned above all to keep it to one family and sometimes even to one individual. Isaac was Abraham's only successor, and his other children did not share in this magnificent inheritance. Likewise, though Isaac had fathered twins, Esau and Jacob, with Rebecca, Jacob's destiny was his alone. His mother had learned about it from a prophecy a long time before, while she was still pregnant;[151] and this divine prediction was ratified by his father's vision.[152] In the age of heroes[153] it often happened that as the patriarchs (who were very holy men) neared the end of their lives, they explained to their children in a solemn declaration what was going to happen to them. Clearly, as the time approached when they would be freed of the chains of their burdensome bodies and cross over to Heaven and to the land of the blessed for which they longed, their souls acquired a kind of prophetic ability. Even while still alive they were beginning to enjoy a divine quality of their own, and they were driven by a superior force. That is what happened to Isaac: when his eyes grew dim his mind was filled with light, and as death drew close it made him a prophet. It would take a long time to describe all the difficulties that Jacob had to overcome while his brother, who was hardly a devout man, was trying to ensnare him[154]—though Esau's descendants were much more wicked than he was.

At this point there was a significant change in the character of the Church's affairs: from the twelve sons of Jacob was born the people whom the Holy Spirit calls Israel.[155] So even though until then one or another family (though usually the same one) had been in charge of worshiping God, now that honor was finally given to all the Israelites. They are certainly the only people that have the right to call their origins holy, and to attribute their creation to God. It is hard to imagine the great leaps and bounds with which this nation expanded in so short a period of time; but in my chapters on the Israelite state I have amply described their lifestyle and customs, and the kind of men and values that helped them to achieve this power.

Now I would like to move on to other things. At the very start of their existence the holy people were forced to move to other lands because for a long time their own land was barren and produced nothing. They were permitted to settle in Egypt, a region that has always produced a remarkable surplus, and which is made so fertile by the Nile's floods that it has never been even slightly dependent on rainfall. For many of the years that they were in Egypt, the Israelites were completely loyal to the faith of their ancestors; but nothing lasts forever, and in the end they fell prey to the superstitions which at the time were already common among the Egyptians, and which then went on to take advantage of the Israelites' weakness.[156] Certainly Ezekiel reproaches them in the twentieth chapter of his book for having paid tribute to the idols and the filthy gods of Egypt.[157] Though this is Ezekiel's most explicit condemnation of these practices, he makes the same point (if a little less straightforwardly) in chapter 23: *O son of man, there were two women, daughters of the same mother, who prostituted themselves in Egypt. It was there that their breasts were pressed. The older was called Ahola, and her sister Aholiva. I say that they were mine, and they gave birth to sons and daughters.*[158] These symbolic names stand in for Israel and Judah.[159]

The Jews suffered for many years from the infectious idolatry they had contracted from that arrogant and self-important nation. In fact, it was entirely because of the Egyptians' false beliefs that until the days of Hezekiah the Israelites offered incense and libations to the bronze serpent that Moses had set up for a few days and for a different purpose.[160] As Marcus Tullius says of the Egyptians: *They would sooner submit to torture than dishonor an asp or an ibis.*[161] Sarapis[162] himself was represented by the serpent, which was also prominently displayed in processions of the goddess Isis; about these Ovid says as follows:

May the sluggish serpent wind its way around your presents,
And may horned Apis join you in the procession.[163]

It is very fitting that Ovid should mention Apis here, because he was a sacred bull and the supreme god of the Egyptians. Jeroboam (the king of the Israelites) imitated them by setting up gold statues of bulls in Bethel and Dan in order to maintain—and even strengthen—his hold on the people, who still remembered the superstitions of Egypt.

What more do we need to say? Every time the Jews threw out the Law of Moses and worshiped animals and images, they modeled themselves after the Egyptians. So I can't help but wonder what Plutarch and the other great authorities had in mind when they wrote that the Jews worshiped an ass as their god. Such statements are completely worthless. Not only is this not commanded in their laws, all of which we still possess today, but it could not have come from the Egyptians either, because in fact they hated this animal more than any other. For after Typhon the murderer of Osiris had died, they used to attack him with every kind of insult; and since he had reddish hair, it was their custom to throw every ass off a rock, because of the similarity in color.[164] In fact, every red-haired person was treated as a public laughingstock. Plutarch also says that the inhabitants of Busiris and Lycopis did not use horns because they thought the sound they made was similar to the braying of asses.[165] But, our authorities say, the Egyptians' greatest delight had to do with the Persian king Ochus; they always called him "the ass" because they thought it was the worst possible insult. However, he replied: *but this ass will devour your bull*, referring to Apis.[166] So even though all these writers may be in complete agreement as to what they have to say about the Jews, it is simply not true; and yet they found the temptation to invent things so overpowering that some of them even claim that every seven years the Jews would sacrifice a foreigner to this ass. Personally I think that all this was a consequence of their hatred for the holy people, which was common among the Greeks and Romans. Godlessness is naturally skilled at telling lies, and it tends to favor the products of its own invention.

But it is time to move on. I return to the Israelites, who (as I said) had settled in Egypt. Among the affairs of men, nothing is as unstable and as unpredictable as the things we possess at the bidding of others. The human mind is in a constant state of change: no one can concern himself with someone else's affairs without looking out for his own interests as well, and when the circumstances call for it, loyalties and agreements take a back seat. Certainly the Egyptians thought it was to their own advantage that the Hebrews were prospering; but as soon as they began to fear that the strangers (who had been invited in order to support the kingdom) might overwhelm them all, they changed their minds. All of a sudden and as though they had grown weary of them, they abandoned the very people they had treated with kindness for so long; and they decided to crush the Hebrews with a harsh enslavement.

Moses says that this happened after Joseph and all his brothers had died.[167] It does not matter what the Rabbis say: *While Joseph lived for a very short time, Levi lived for a very long one; and after he died the Israelites were oppressed. This is the source of the Hebrew saying that when one brother dies they all suffer, and when one colleague has passed away the entire group mourns.*[168] This is what passes for Jewish wit! I myself have always been of the opinion that most of the Hebrews' adages are flavorless and tepid. Anyone who manages to get some taste out of such "delights" must be chewing *very* slowly; they are worthless compared with the impressive power and effectiveness of the Greek and Latin adages. But this is beside the point. The same books that contain the laws of Moses tell us how cruelly that godless nation tormented the holy people—they labored under the glare of harsh overseers, and if they stopped working they were savagely whipped. The cries of these men reached Heaven. They had to bake the bricks used to construct cities, or to transport straw, or to haul away dung; but whatever the job, they all had to spend their lives doing the work of slaves.

In memory of this slavery, Jews even today eat at their Passover meal a dish that they give the special name *haroset*.[169] Remembrance must also be the reason why, according to Juvenal, the Jews of Rome always kept a basket and hay among their household possessions:

> Leaving her basket and hay outside,
> A trembling Jewess begs for alms in a whisper.
> She is an interpreter of the laws of the Solymi, and a great priestess
> Of the tree.[170]

And before this he says:

> Now the grove of the sacred spring and the shrine are rented out
> To Jews, whose possessions consist of a basket and hay.[171]

The reason they used to carry baskets and hay was in fact because in Egypt they had hauled dung and mud in little baskets, and used straw and hay to produce bricks. It was in their interest to employ such reminders in order to teach all men just how harsh and filthy were the circumstances they had endured. The only person to interpret correctly the meaning of these passages of Juvenal has been Philippus Beroaldus, who was at one time the most learned man in Italy.[172] Though I could not have quoted a more substantial witness than Juvenal, I will summon one more, whose writing has no need for ashes.[173] Martial wrote a charming epigram making fun of Gellia. Though she had turned down many perfectly respectable offers of marriage, in the end she paid for her arrogance: she married a Jew, the lowest form of life on two legs.

> While you, Gellia, were telling us about your great-grandfathers and
>   their grandfathers and their great names,
> And while you considered a knight like me to be a degrading match
> And told me, Gellia, that you couldn't possibly
> Marry anyone but a senator—you went ahead and married a *cistiferus*.[174]

Martial calls this Jew—a beggar of a man—a *cistiferus*,[175] because he made the rounds of the city with his basket and hay.[176]

No one can easily forget terrible misfortunes, and the merciless rule of the Egyptians remained deeply fixed in the Jews' minds. On the other hand, though God told Abraham that the Hebrews were going to serve the Egyptians for four hundred years, this is not what happened—He changed His plans for them for the better, clearly because He pitied them.[177] This is the point of what the Aramaic Targumist wrote: *The appointed time was shortened because of the merit of the fathers, who gathered on the mountains; and the time of servitude was reduced by one hundred and ninety years because of the righteousness of the mothers, who gathered on the hills.*

There was in that age a divine man—Moses—under whose leadership the Hebrew nation escaped from Egypt and set off on a long journey through vast stretches of desert. There was not *some Hierosolymus or Judah behind their exodus*; nor did *King Bocchoris search out and gather together this mob he thought was hateful to the gods, and exile them to another country, based on the warning of Ammon.*[178] Cornelius Tacitus and the people who provided him with this information[179] are indulging in fantasy. But it comes as no surprise to us that these writers reported such falsehoods about the Jews, since they never looked at the sacred books. God hates the pagans and condemns them to darkness; and he did not allow them to learn anything about the affairs of the holy people, including even those aspects that are common knowledge.[180] Flavius Josephus reports the reply of Demetrius[181] when Ptolemy asked him why it was that none of the historians or poets ever mentioned the laws of Moses. The reason, he said, was that they lacked the greatness of spirit necessary to take on this monumental task. He also said that God had punished Theopompus and Theodectes, who had pried into the laws: one lost his mind, the other his sight.[182]

If there *were* some pagans who wrote about the laws, they perverted the truth in several respects, and none have shown themselves to be completely trustworthy. Even though some of what they say is true, the specific details they give us are usually spattered with little lies and even deliberate malice. You will find this sort of thing wherever you may look, including the most prestigious authors. What ridiculous things did even Juvenal say when he spoke about the superstitions of the Jews:

> They are used to looking down on Roman law;
> They study, serve, and revere only Jewish law
> (Whatever Moses passed down in his secret book),
> And they show the true path only to their fellow Jews—
> They bring to the precious spring only those who have been circumcised.[183]

He mixed the truth with lies, so that it was impossible to tell one from the other. Obviously Moses was not so insane as to introduce such a barbaric law. Would there have been a better proof that he had gone from a man to a wild beast?[184] As Ennius[185] famously said,

> If a man kindly points the way to someone who is lost,
> It is as though he were lighting another's lamp from his own.
> His lamp loses none of its light by kindling someone else's.

Nature has formed us to be kind: at her command we are told to ask for and to give whatever we all hold in common. So what can we conclude from this, except that the writers who pinned this lie on Moses meant to do him an injustice?

Many years after Moses' time, however, this very attitude became for the Jews at first a bad habit and then an actual custom. Jerome was quite right to say that *they are worse now than they used to be*. From that time on they hated every nation like an enemy. They ate their meals apart from the gentiles and lived in separate quarters; they avoided them like dirt. Though they live in utter poverty they put on airs, they say that they are God's people, they boast about their ancestral religion and their ancient names, and they never do anything with moderation or sound judgment. There must have been a great deal of envy and jealousy behind the decree passed in the time of Hyrcanus and Aristobulus (which Rabbi Zacuto mentions in his book *Yuhasin*): *Cursed is he who teaches his son Greek wisdom.*[186] Their hatred of foreigners is also the reason they were so upset that the Torah was translated into a profane language in Alexandria, at the command of the great king Philadelphus.[187] They even expressed their grief over this by fasting every year on the eighth day of Tevet. This was pure unadulterated envy; the black venom of the cuttlefish had poisoned their minds.[188]

I will not need to go to great lengths to refute Tacitus' lies about the exodus from Egypt. Our Roman author goes astray, while Moses speaks on God's authority. *The proof of course is from the tablets of Jupiter.*[189] Once the Israelites left Egypt for the deserts of Arabia, God's mercy was always miraculously by their side. The Rabbis say that there were three people so pious that it was because of their merit that the people of Israel received its three greatest gifts. *They received manna because of the merits of Moses, the pillar of cloud*[190] *because of Aaron, and the well because of Miriam. When Miriam died the well vanished, but it was returned because of Moses and Aaron. When Aaron died the pillar of cloud vanished, but it was returned because of Moses. But when Moses died all three disappeared at once. For it is written, I will wipe out the three shepherds in one month.*[191] The quotation here is from Zechariah.[192]

Moreover, I believe that Jerome follows this interpretation of the Rabbis, and he adds another reason why Zechariah said they all died in the same month (though if we examine the matter closely it turns out that they died rather in the same year). In any event, it was the supreme power of God that kept the people alive for so long in very harsh conditions, after they had been exiled and had nothing at all to call their own. And just consider what happened shortly thereafter when Israel entered the land of Canaan. Everything that took place there was the product of a miracle: the enormous enemy forces were defeated by a small band of men; the Israelites crossed through the deepest rivers without getting their feet wet, as though they had never left the land;[193] and the walls of towns were thrown over without being so much as pushed.[194]

Every event of this kind is beyond the capacity of human understanding, but by far the greatest of these miracles was when Joshua, the great leader of the nation, told the sun to stop in its tracks for an entire day. The Aramaic Targum of the Song of Songs says it was then that Joshua sang the hymn that is counted as fifth in the series of ten.[195] I cannot imagine why the Jews, based on the authority of a certain Rabbi Yose,[196] report that this happened on *the New Moon of Nisan,* and that the equinox fell on that day outside of its usual season.[197] I can only imagine that the love of fantasy that is their fate has driven them to diminish the force of this miracle.[198] It would have been better if they had simply fallen silent before the awesome mystery of the thing.

But it's high time that this discussion came to an end; so after the Israelites defeated the Canaanites, the Church was for a long time the common possession of all twelve tribes. This situation did not begin to change until Solomon's death set off a monumental struggle over control of the kingdom between men who were hungry for power. At that moment the holy people was split into opposing factions: one group followed Rehoboam the son of Solomon, and the other Jeroboam the son of Nebat from the tribe of Ephraim. Judah and Benjamin stood with Rehoboam, and the other ten tribes with Jeroboam. The former held Jerusalem and the surrounding areas, the latter Samaria. So there were two kingdoms, one called Judah, the other Israel. This conflict also corrupted the faith itself. Jeroboam steered his tribes toward idolatry so that the religious differences between the two sides, who were already at odds, would make the rift between them even wider. This is why, from that time on, the Church shrank to the Judeans alone.[199] The Benjaminites were also called by this name, because of the very close bond between the two tribes; in fact, as Rabbi Elijah has written, in the Book of Esther Mordechai is called a Jew even though he was a descendant of Benjamin. This is the famous "Jewish Church"; it was worth all the effort it took me to briefly describe its fate, or rather the phases of its development. Now I will move on to other things.

CHAPTER 5

On circumcision. Which of the ancient nations were circumcised. On
the Egyptians, the Ethiopians, and the Colchians. Jeremiah's
remarks on the Egyptians are rescued from the interpretation of
certain scholars. A passage in Paul about people who restore
their foreskins, which Jerome has misunderstood. Jerome's excessive
fervor in his books against Jovinian. His fanciful interpretation
of Joshua's statement about repeated circumcision. Why circumcision
is practiced on the eighth day.

FOR A VERY LONG TIME, the holy people had nothing significant to distinguish it from any of the other nations. God knew His people because He had chosen them, and they in turn knew Him, but they were not distinguished by any signs or marks.[200] It was Abraham, to whom great things were promised, who was the first to take on a ritual whose power left him with no doubts about what the future would hold: he was commanded to circumcise the foreskins of his dependents and to pass on this practice to future generations (on whom the same law was imposed). In fact, they have been more scrupulous about this observance than about any of the others. Yet because other peoples have copied it, even some of the most careful writers have been led astray; they are completely ignorant about where circumcision originated. Herodotus says that the only people to practice it were the Egyptians, the Colchians, and the Ethiopians, but that the Syrians who were in Palestine (i.e. the Jews) learned it from the Egyptians.[201] There is (he says) no question that this is true, because the Syrians themselves admit as much. But we really ought to overlook his mistake; the origins of institutions are hard to detect because of their great age. I don't *believe* that it was Abraham who brought circumcision to all the Jews: I know it. But even in this case, Herodotus' godlike insight did not fail him entirely: he believes that the Ethiopians got the custom from the Egyptians rather than the other way around, and the Egyptians were in fact the first to imitate the Hebrews (whom they had allowed to settle in their territory). From there the practice spread to the neighboring peoples, the Colchians and Ethiopians.

Since I have been talking about circumcision among the gentile nations, I ought to refute the very learned rabbi whose book called *Aruch* still exists.[202] Anyone who has decided to search out and expose errors in rabbinic literature is taking on a daunting and monumental task; for when the Hebrews set out for us (with their exceptional erudition and natural cleverness) their opinions about the Holy Book in their ancestral language, they made many wonderful discoveries that no one else had been able to reveal despite their best efforts. And yet the Jews sometimes let arrogance or ambition lead them to interpretations that are incorrect, though they are close enough to the truth that it is very difficult for us to figure out just what is wrong with them. I am not talking now about allegories, mysteries, or fables.[203] The Jews themselves in their own writings have attacked such things without pity,[204] for they are such monstrosities that if Hercules had run into them he would have thought he'd been given a thirteenth labor to perform.[205] I am speaking rather of those interpretations in which they explain *hapashut*, that is, the *simple meaning of the text* as they call it. This is the only realm in which, whatever the other nations may say, the Jews alone hold a kind of dominion.

I do intend to speak at length somewhere else about the virtues and vices of Jewish interpretation; but for now I want to quote a passage of Jeremiah from which the author of the *Aruch* once concocted a fiction that even the most learned men of our age have embraced. In the ninth chapter of Jeremiah God says: *See, the time is almost here when I will punish all who are circumcised with the foreskin*; and then he adds about the ones he is going to punish: *the Egyptians, and the Judeans, and the Edomites, and the Ammonites, and the Moabites.*[206] The author of the *Aruch* says that *circumcised with the foreskin* refers to people who stretched out their foreskins after they had already been circumcised. He says, moreover, that this is what the Egyptians did—though they were circumcised in Joseph's time, after he died they had their foreskins stretched. The rabbi obviously means to say that the Egyptians felt such hatred for the Israelites that after Joseph died they abandoned the rite of circumcision, which they had learned from the Israelites while he was alive. In fact, he says, they used artificial techniques to restore the tissue that had been cut away. They did not want to have anything in common with a nation that they had always hated for its pastoral way of life, even though till then they had grudgingly allowed it a foothold in their kingdom, if only out of regard for Joseph.

Such is the opinion of this most excellent rabbi, who thinks that the Egyptians were no longer circumcised from the moment the Israelites left their territory and withdrew to Palestine. But this cannot be right. Herodotus and Strabo,[207] and (in a much later age) Jerome and Ambrose,[208] all remark that the Egyptians of their time were still circumcised in the traditional fashion. The Hebrew writer must have misunderstood the passage in Jeremiah, which I think is best interpreted according to the popular opinion.[209] I know, of course, that the honorable Johannes Drusius, who was once my teacher,[210] agrees with the author of the *Aruch*. But he showed how fair-minded he was by giving me his permission to express my natural candor: I am seeking complete freedom to declare, without bias for or against, whatever claims are most correct. Indeed, since the Holy Spirit calls first the Egyptians and then the Jews *circumcised with the foreskin*, the theory that this refers to rejecting circumcision cannot (as I have just shown) be correctly applied to the Egyptians. It does, though, have at least the ring of truth; whereas if we turn to the Jews whom the passage also discusses, this fanciful theory no longer works at all. For even though this people lapsed time and again into sinfulness, and learned to abandon God and to defile everything both sacred and profane, they never once abandoned the rite of circumcision; and they always took so much pride in it that they made themselves look foolish and were held up to ridicule.

But let me leave this discussion behind and return to the main reason for this holiest of institutions, which was (as I said) that the people of Israel should be marked by some distinctive characteristic. We may add to this a second reason, one that is certainly more significant and important: one of the things that prefigured the Messiah's sacrifice was the blood that was spilled by the circumcision of the foreskin; and since solid objects displace the emptiness of shadows, it was only natural that once the countenance of the Messiah had shone down upon the earth, the symbols in which the true meaning of this mystery had once been hidden would now cease to exist. So it was at this time that circumcision lost its force. Gentiles who worshiped the Messiah did not need to be circumcised in order to be initiated into the Church, while the fact that the Jews were already circumcised did not keep any who wished from joining in this worship.

There is also an instructive discussion of this issue in the seventh chapter of St. Paul's First Letter to the Corinthians: *Is someone called circumcised? He should not stretch out his foreskin. Is he called "with a foreskin"? He should not be circumcised. Circumcision is nothing, and the foreskin is nothing; only the observance of God's commands is important.*[211] At that time there were, in fact, some terribly superstitious people who were so eager to remove every trace of Jewish ritual from their bodies, when they converted from Judaism to Christianity, that as adults they restored the foreskin they had lost as infants. To achieve this end they used the services of doctors. This was certainly a neurotic approach to religion, and one the Apostle was right to condemn.

The thought has often crossed my mind, just how could the meaning of Paul's words have escaped St. Jerome when there was not a more learned man in all of antiquity? He thinks that this entire text has to do with being single or married! This is how he interprets the passage: *If you were circumcised—i.e. you were unmarried—at the moment you were summoned and you believed, do not marry, i.e. do not stretch out your foreskin, or you will weigh down the freedom of circumcision and chastity with the burden of marriage. If, on the other hand, someone is called "with a foreskin," he should not be circumcised: Did you have a wife when you came to believe? Do not suppose that faith should be the cause of dissension; for we are summoned in peace.*[212] He explains in the same way the blessed Apostle's next statement, about slaves.[213] (Jerome made these and similar comments in more than one place, but mostly in his commentary on Isaiah.) And because he wants to show us that this passage in Paul is not meant to be taken literally and cannot be explained without the use of allegory, he even says outright that *it is not within our power to draw out the foreskin after circumcision.* I will not throw in Jerome's face the consensus of famous doctors, all of whom claim that what he denies is in fact possible[214]—he can be refuted well enough by the evidence of quite a few historians. And though it actually is written in the books of the Maccabees that the sons of Tobias made themselves foreskins so that they would look like the Greeks,[215] Jerome perverts even this with an insipid interpretation. In any case, Flavius Josephus provides such reliable proof that it was so[216] that no one in his right mind should have any further doubts.

The fact is that Jerome was far too enamored of the single life: he recommended it to mankind, he rallied to its cause all the sayings of the prophets and apostles, and in many cases he forced his own interpretation on his sources. Just as people suffering from jaundice or dropsy see objects as yellow even when they are not, once a certain way of thinking has rooted itself in a person's mind it keeps him from seeing things as they truly are, and he insists that anything that stands in his way completely supports his position. In just this way, Jerome in his books against Jovinian is wildly proud and gleeful even though he has no proof worth mentioning for his claims.[217] In fact, he did something extremely unwise: though ideas of all sorts were occurring to him, he shared with the public the ones that excited his passions. He placed his reputation in such great danger that I will pass over the more extravagant of his claims in favor of virginity and against marriage. That is, he appears to be supporting Marcion[218] and Mani;[219] and while he may protect one of his flanks against Jovinian, he allows himself to be wounded on the other by the lowest sort of heretic.[220] This is why Pammachius (who was his best friend) suppressed most of the copies of this book, and why

Jerome himself wrote a defense that was, I tell you, so lovely that now not only would I tolerate this holy man's violent and passionate love of celibacy, I would even approve of it. For though most people think of this book as a severe attack on marriage, I see it as the highest form of praise.[221] I admit that we have to keep to some middle way; but since it is difficult to achieve an exact balance, it would be better if the scales fell on the side of what is more than fair.

But I have wandered farther from my subject than I should; my discussion will grow enormous unless I place stricter limits on myself from now on. Circumcision was set aside for forty years while the Hebrews were wandering in the deserts of Arabia; since they constantly had to move camp, the period of recuperation necessary after such surgery would have delayed their departures. Besides, in that vast wasteland there were no nations with whom the holy people might mix, and therefore no need for any distinguishing marks. Yet since at the same time a kind of divine grace did accompany those individuals who were circumcised, it might seem to us that those who were born in the desert and there met an untimely end were (if nothing else) very unfortunate.[222] But though I have examined the text of the Holy Book very carefully, I have found no reason why we should assume that anyone who was born in the desert actually died there. This fits with the fact that of all the people whom Moses led out of Egypt, only two entered Palestine.[223] So when the Bible tells us that after Joshua, the great leader of the nation, crossed the Jordan he had the Israelites circumcised once again,[224] this actually refers to those who had not yet been circumcised because they were born in the desert. And yet it says their circumcision was being "repeated"[225] because they were now reintroducing a custom which, though it had once been practiced in Egypt, had become intermittent and was eventually abandoned entirely.

Jerome, on the other hand, tires himself out unnecessarily and looks for a needle in a haystack when he debates the character of Joshua's repeated circumcision. He says that *if we take it literally it cannot stand on its own; for once tissue has been cut away it cannot grow back.*[226] He had to find some way out of this problem. When we cannot see the light at the end of the tunnel, the boldest plans are also the most prudent; and in this case one has to rush in headlong. So in order to free himself with a daring deed, Jerome invents *an evangelical knife*[227] for this second circumcision, which he says must have symbolized the purification of their souls. Though this is a substantial delusion, Jerome is happy to make things up. On the other hand, what I said about all the Israelites who were born in the desert reaching Palestine unharmed was nothing more than a conjecture of my own. I suggest, I do not insist. In any case, I believe that God was just as kind to those who did happen to die during the time when circumcision was not practiced as He was to those who lived out their lives before this solemn ritual had been established. We must reach the same conclusion about babies snatched from their mothers' breasts before they reached their eighth day, and deprived of their sweet lives by a sad fate. This is why the superstition practiced by the yids today is ridiculous: they circumcise before burial male infants who have died in the first week.

Since I am covering every topic (or at least would like to), I should also say something about why circumcision is performed only on the eighth day. The popular explanation, that it represents the eighth age, when the dead are going to return to immortal life, is far too much of a stretch. Only people too squeamish to experience life as it is lived by regular people have a personality suited to digging up mysteries from every simple and obvious idea, an activity that often disintegrates into feverish affectation. What impresses me is not the cleverness with which we can invent "solutions," but the importance of the questions themselves. To resume: No animal, after it is born, is listed on the tally of livestock before it is eight days old—it has been alive only briefly, and we do not yet know whether it is going to thrive. Besides, the filth that (as it is believed) still clings to it from the womb and from birth has not yet dissolved. This is why God forbade the Israelites to offer sacrifices from among such animals: He was not pleased with anything incomplete or impure. There is a law in the twenty-second chapter of Leviticus: *When an ox, a sheep, or a goat has been born, it will remain under its mother's teat for seven days; but on the eighth day and thereafter it may be offered to the Lord.*[228] Since, therefore, circumcision was just like a sacrifice through which they would consecrate to God the growing hopes they placed in their sons, it was entirely fitting that they should apply the same principle in choosing the time it ought to be performed. Moreover, the eighth day was chosen not because this number had some mystical significance, but merely because the sacred rite could not have been performed any sooner, and there was no reason to put it off any longer. If, on the other hand, it had been left up to the parents to choose any day they liked starting with the eighth, there would be good reason to fear (human inertia being what it is) that with every passing day the ritual would be less likely to take place. This is what happens in life—at first we are taken in by procrastination and the appeal of laziness, then follow contempt and neglect. Circumcision was performed even on the Sabbath if it was the eighth day after the birth, although the Jews refrained from doing any other kind of work on that day. The Messiah himself talks about this in the seventh chapter of the Gospel of St. John.[229]

I have said more or less everything there is to say on the subject of circumcision, though I suppose I might also refute Thomas Aquinas and the other important writers who say that Zipporah[230] and Joshua circumcised with a stone knife rather than a metal one, and think this symbolizes the Messiah, the source of our salvation, about whom St. Paul says, *and the rock was Christ.*[231] But I will restrain myself from scratching that itch, even though it is considered praiseworthy for commentators to linger on topics that require no explanation. Anything more I must leave to those writers who seek to make their names from disreputable kinds of work.[232]

CHAPTER 6

*On the religion of the Jews. Why the ancients thought that
the Jews worshiped the clouds or a vague sort of god. The
meaning of the phrase 'to call on the ears of Heaven' in Petronius'
'Catalects'. That it has nothing to do with Heaven-worshipers. The
Athenians' slanders against Socrates. The altar of the unknown God
in Athens. The Jews' impregnable loyalty to the worship of one
God in the time of the Second Temple.*

ALTHOUGH GOD IS EVERYWHERE and can hear the prayers of men
wherever they may be, nevertheless the Law of Moses decreed that once the
Hebrew people arrived in Canaan there would be only one city where the
sacrificial rites, both private and public, and all the rituals would be con-
ducted. It was there that all the inhabitants of the tribes and their towns
would gather for religious ceremonies; there that they would offer the first
fruits, appear before God in purity,[233] and fulfill their sacred vows.[234] Since I
have said a number of things about the Law of Moses I can hardly overlook
this issue, which was more closely connected to the law than any other. The
decree, which is in the twelfth chapter of Deuteronomy, applied only to the
Hebrews, whose weak wills were most easily encouraged to worship God
when the number of days set aside for sacrifices was no greater than the
number of locations at which they were offered. After God turned away from
Shilo, this religious center came to be at Jerusalem. At first there was only a
tabernacle where the divine presence dwelled; but eventually the auspicious
moment arrived for the wise king Solomon to build a temple of enormous
opulence. It was the place of the altar, and of the Ark that contained the
symbols of the sacred covenant.

There were also many other things added to the requirements of the faith.
People who wanted to present their wishes before God, or to obtain His help,
or to receive forgiveness for their sins would enter the Temple courtyard. God
received their prayers more warmly there than anywhere else. In the Gospel
of John a Samaritan woman says to the Messiah: *You say that Jerusalem is
the best place to offer prayers.*[235] And elsewhere it says: *Two men went up to*

the Temple to pray. One was a Pharisee, the other a tax-collector.[236] Even people who lived far away and could not travel to the Holy City were not cut off from this worship; when they prayed to God (which was the only thing they could do under the circumstances), they turned toward the Temple in Jerusalem. Anything else was forbidden. Certainly when Daniel prayed to God three times a day on bended knee, he would open the windows of his chamber and direct himself toward Jerusalem.[237] Even Solomon, in the sacred hymn with which he dedicated the wonderful structure he had built, swore it would happen that future generations would turn towards the Temple whenever they had been taken prisoner by an enemy and exiled to a foreign country, or when bad things happened to them outside their homeland. His magnificent words are in the eighth chapter of the First Book of Kings.[238] In the Book of Ezekiel God makes an angry declaration against those who used to pray facing the East with their backs to the Sanctuary.[239] The learned Rabbi Yarhi explained this passage very neatly.[240]

Moreover, no one but the high priest saw the Temple enclosure. The first Roman to see it was Gnaeus Pompey: on his way back from Asia with his victorious troops, he conquered the Jews and entered the innermost recesses of the Temple.[241] From that time on, Tacitus says, it was widely known *that the place was empty and the secret enclosure contained nothing.*[242] In fact, before that everyone had thought there was some god inside, whether Apis, Ammon, or Anubis: only the Jews knew his name, and they would never pronounce it in front of godless gentiles. But after Pompey, who enjoyed the prerogatives of the victor, threw open the enclosure, most people came to believe that all the Jews' rites and ceremonies were about nothing, because they worshiped no god in particular. This is what Cornelius Tacitus claimed, and Lucan must have meant the same thing when he wrote: *And Judea that was pledged to the worship of an unknown god.*[243]

Because of this rumor it was widely believed about the Jews that they worship the clouds and the sky. It is true that the Rabbis have ten names for God, among them *hashechina* (*Presence*), *hamakom* (*Place*), and *hashamayim* (*Heaven*). And anyone who reads what St. Matthew says in his fifth chapter cannot ignore how common it was for them to swear by Heaven; in this chapter the Messiah, the savior of men, condemns that practice.[244] On the other hand, I cannot in this instance agree with Joseph Scaliger, a brilliant man before whose astonishing competence in every branch of knowledge I must understandably bow. Since he saw that the ancient writers often mentioned a sect of Heaven-worshipers who were Christianized Jews, he thought that these were the people Petronius describes in his *Catalects*, i.e. *let the Jew worship his porcine god, and call on the highest ears of heaven.*[245]

This cannot be right—the passage has to do not with some heretical sect of the Jews, but with Jews in general. We must interpret in the same way the continuation of this passage:

> But unless he has also cut off his foreskin with a knife,
> And found some way of laying bare that head,
> He will be banned from his people and leave the holy city,
> And break the law by not fasting on the Sabbath.

This was clearly an attack on the entire community, made up by the gentiles even though it was ridiculous; the Romans did this sort of thing in order to make the Jews more despised, by suggesting that those who refused to worship the gods of all the other nations were themselves worshiping nothing but air. But they were not the first people to do so: many years before, the Athenians claimed, purely out of malice, that the gods of Socrates were clouds and fluid elements.[246] Everything Aristophanes staged in his play was taken from common rumor:

> O master, limitless Air, who holds the suspended earth;
> Bright ether and stately clouds, you goddesses of thunder and lightning![247]

And then:

> For they alone are goddesses, and all else is nonsense.[248]

This wisest of men was rejecting the gods worshiped by a city dedicated to superstition and hostile to religion; and for this the entire citizen body was ready to punish him with a disgusting show of abuse.

While I am writing about Socrates, something else occurs to me that is more in keeping with my subject. It was a particular fault of the Athenians that they were saddled with a huge number of gods, so much so that without knowing it, they even worshiped the true and ineffable God of the Israelites; for they set up an altar to *the unknown God*.[249] There is a description of this in chapter 17 of the Book of Acts—St. Paul saw this altar and felt sorry for the Athenians, so in order to help them out of their ignorance he delivered a brave speech to the citizens in the middle of the Areopagus[250] in which he said: *I am proclaiming to you the one whom you worship even though you do not know Him.*[251] The Apostle had a good reason for saying this. Once they had run out of names for all the gods they worshiped, they worshiped one they could not name; so even though there was not a single false god who did not have his own altar at Athens, there remained one—*the unknown one*—who was true. After all, I trust the word of St. Paul (who confirms that this was the wording on the altar) more than I do Jerome and the others, who write that it was somewhat different.

Tacitus despite himself gives us proof of how praiseworthy the Jewish faith was. He writes: *The Jews perceive God only with their minds, and believe He is the only one. He is supreme, eternal, unchanging, and will never fade away.*[252] No pagan could have paid Judaism a bigger compliment. Such is the grandeur of the most sacred of faiths—it receives its honors even from those who condemn it. And yet this often happens for another reason entirely: Gaius the son of Agrippa[253] was passing through Judea, but refused to bow down when he was in Jerusalem;[254] so God decided that all of Rome would suffer for what a young man of the imperial house had done wrong. The result was that the city was fraught with shortages, famine, and the highest grain prices it had ever had.[255] So Augustus, who had widely praised his grandson, learned the error of his ways. Certainly the clearest proof that he regretted his actions comes from the speech King Agrippa[256] made to Caligula, from which Philo quotes in his *Embassy to Gaius*.[257] Agrippa says that sacrifices were offered in Jerusalem every day to the supreme God of the Hebrews at Augustus' expense.[258] This was the order of an emperor who throughout his entire life had been opposed to foreign rituals of any sort! People who question Agrippa's reliability on this matter do not know what they are talking about. There is no way a Jewish man could have gotten away with a completely unsubstantiated lie in the presence of Caligula, and in that city where the memory of Augustus was still fresh in many people's minds.[259] There is an equally well-known statement about Alexander the Great reported by Flavius Josephus in the eleventh book of his *Antiquities*,[260] but I would rather not quote every single source. It would be better to mention what our Tacitus goes on to say. Among his other statements there is the following: *The Jews consider to be godless anyone who fashions humanlike images of the gods out of perishable materials; so there are no statues in their cities, let alone in their temples.*[261] Tacitus says this so earnestly that you would think he was making a point of condemning his own Romans for their stupidity. Pliny, on the other hand, shows nothing like this level of earnestness. He mentions *the Jewish race, which is well-known for its contempt for the gods*,[262] just as though he supported the usual misconceptions.

There are many laws in the books of Moses that ban the worship of idols. One was not even allowed to take gold and silver from them. We should not, however, suppose that the great king David was guilty of breaking this law when he set on his head the crown of Molech,[263] for he accepted it from Itai the Philistine.[264] The thing was therefore purified when it changed masters, and it was a foreigner and not a Hebrew who had captured it in the first place. I have often admired the unbroken spirit of the Jews, whom the Romans could not force to accept an image of Caesar. The people who ruled the world conquered not only Judea, but Asia and Africa as well, and their great empire came to be feared even by people living under another sun and other stars. And yet, only Judea dared to deny anything to its conquerors, who were used to taking by force whatever they could not obtain by request. (Power, after all, may ask politely, and it may even beg; but this makes it no less coercive.) The first test of the Jews' insistent policy took place under Tiberius;[265] but that was only a question of placing statues within the city, and the procurator[266] soon gave up the idea when he found he could not complete his plans as intended.[267] Then Gaius[268] decided to have himself set up even in the Temple, and threatened the worst when they resisted him. But Providence finally intervened: Petronius, who was governor of the province, received word of Gaius' death long before he got the letter ordering the destruction of the holy people, a letter that Gaius wrote three months before he died.[269] The Jews, of course, had made it clear to Gaius that they would rather be wiped out along with their city than accept something that would violate God's law. It was not only their leaders who were eager to die a glorious death; the common people and even the women—the weaker sex—felt the same way.

CHAPTER 7

On prophets and divine inspiration. On Elijah. Were the prophets possessed and out of their minds when they made their predictions? The dogma of Montanus, and the lunatic women he taught. On the prophets of Delphi, and the tricks and dodges they used. Making up conversations with God. On the old tricks of the heretics, and on Valens the leader of the Arians. On Isaiah and Jeremiah. The Jews' crazy notion that Daniel should not be counted among the prophets. Other scholars' pointless debates on this topic. The deliberate poverty of Crates. Elijah and John the Baptist compared.

BEFORE THE ARRIVAL of the Messiah, there were two forces that compelled the holy people to do the right thing: the threat of laws and the fear of prophecies. This is why most of the Holy Book is taken up with the laws of Moses and the writings of the prophets. In the Gospel of St. Luke, a certain rich man dressed in purple is told, *they have Moses and the prophets, and they should listen to them.*[270] I have already discussed the laws; now the subject seems to call for me to say something about the prophets as well. It was their task to inform the people of God's anger when they sinned; every one of them could perform miracles and predict the future course of events. Among these prophets, it was Elijah whose holiness and virtue set him apart as a shining beacon; he gave up his humanity so that he could be completely filled with God. And while he was living a harsh life in the desert, he had no contact with the citizens unless it was to correct their ways. It is hard to say anything about the character of most of Elijah's prophecies—there are only a few in the Books of Kings, and these do not bear witness to the Messiah. His writings (if there ever were any) must have been suppressed by Ahab, for we no longer have them.

Most of the prophets of the subsequent age wrote down their visions, and their books contain such exact predictions of events taking place hundreds of years later that we need no other proof in order to defend the divinity of sacred scripture. Such knowledge of the future could not have come from any sort of research, theory, or philosophical principle. Whatever the prophets said came from divine inspiration. What, after all, could Zechariah, Daniel, and Ezekiel have had at their disposal other than their ties with Heaven? They often envision themselves among the angels, they speak with them, they learn the fate of the nations. What has really happened to them, in essence, is that they have left their mortality behind. This is why God's addresses to them in the prophetic books often begin with *Listen, son of man*; for there was a chance they might start to take their situation for granted, and forget that they were mortal like other men.[271] The parts of our character that are trivial and silly are elevated when we experience these kinds of great and unusual things.

On the other hand, we should not even consider the idea that the prophets were transported so far beyond themselves that they lost all sense of self and did not know what they were saying. St. Paul says that *the spirit of the prophets was under their own control*,[272] which would not have been the case if this spirit had been champing at the bit, seizing the reins, and running wild. There is the famous statement of the Messiah that *many prophets yearned to see what you are seeing, and to hear what you are hearing, but they did not*.[273] Surely they could not have missed something they knew absolutely nothing about? It's true that they did not perceive these things with their eyes the way that we see events happening in the present; instead they saw with their minds things that were going to happen in the future. Luke therefore declared that John was the greatest of all the prophets,[274] because he was able to actually point to and say, "He is here," of that man whom the others knew would eventually arrive.

This is the only difference between John and the other prophets. They did not experience states of ecstasy, and their souls did not leave their bodies.[275] This was a ridiculous notion dreamed up in ancient times by Montanus, which he was trying to foist on people in order to camouflage his fraudulent schemes. He brought Maximilla and Prisca, two crazy and fanatical women, before the public eye as though he were putting them on stage, as the supporting players in his sordid little farce.[276] Violent rages and wild movements of the body are characteristic of people whose diseased minds drive them to babble like madmen, take control of their emotions, and force them to make things up (though in fact there are fewer people of this sort in any given generation than is generally believed; in most cases they are frauds and impostors).

People can easily play the part of a madman; it is even easier than being sane. The prophets of Delphi earned their living from people who were slaves to superstition.[277] They had agents all over Greece who learned about everyone's affairs and circumstances. Then when they were consulted, they gave everyone the appropriate answers; even so they inserted vague phrases into their prophecies, so that their customers would be able to interpret them in keeping with the actual outcome. When Marcus Tullius discusses why the oracles of Apollo's Pythian priestess had ceased, he puts his finger on the real reason—people had become less gullible.[278] It means nothing when they say that the power of a sacred place has waned because of its great age, since no amount of time can diminish the strength of divine power; even Demosthenes, three hundred years before Cicero, had the right idea: he said the Pythia *had gone over to Philip*.[279] There was equally little of value in the responses of Amon,[280] the lots of Praeneste,[281] and others of the sort; so I would place in the same category Montanus' crazy women. These kinds of scams were very common among the heretics. People who make up imaginary signs and wonders never succeed in their schemes unless they can summon up a *deus ex machina*: Valens the leader of the Arians[282] raised his stock much higher after he succeeded in convincing Constantius[283] that he had spoken with an angel, and he took full advantage of the emperor's gullibility. But that is enough of this topic; it is not what I wanted to discuss.

Among those prophets who wrote about the Messiah, Isaiah was especially eloquent. His prose is always learned and full of grandeur, and from it his origins emerge very clearly; for this man of noble birth, who enjoyed the distinction of being related to princes,[284] mastered every art and science that might help him improve upon his natural abilities so that that he could fulfill his great destiny. Moreover, his book seems to contain not so much prophecy as gospel. You would think he was describing things that had happened a long time ago, not ones that had yet to occur. Jeremiah, on the other hand, is so well served by his plain and simple style of speaking that all his grandeur comes from the words he chooses not to use. He says many things against the Assyrians, whom he often refers to as doves because this was the *ot degel*, the symbol of Semiramis[285] (a learned observation made by the Jewish author whose work *Me'or Einayim* survives today).[286]

On the other hand, no one had a power of prophecy like Daniel's. He tells us when the Messiah is going to arrive, and reviews the list of future kings and the lengths of their reigns. And so that nothing might be missing he even adds the signs that will foretell their coming.[287] All this is so convincing that Porphyry, who made every effort to make fun of Daniel's prophecies, did not know where to turn; since their obvious accuracy refuted any argument he might use, he was reduced to making false accusations.[288] And yet he did such a poor job of it that any intelligent people who read his work came down with a cold.[289]

I should take a moment at this point to attack the Jews' lack of discernment. St. Jerome wrote in ancient times that they did not place Daniel among the prophets, but rather among the Sacred Writings. I have come to believe that this was a very foolish decision on their part, considering all the magnificent prophecies contained in Daniel's work. In fact, this question recently led to a debate between two of the most learned men of our age: one claimed that the Jews realized Daniel was a prophet, while the other claimed exactly the opposite. This is not really such an important question: I think we should be concerned not with *what* the yids (an insane group of people) may have done once upon a time, but with how correct they were to do it. And after all, what reason do we have to approve their decision? The Jews themselves have never offered us one; or if there is one, I don't remember ever having read it. And yet people try to divine the answer and to make their guesses, as though they were dealing with some obscure question. Surely the reason the Jews believe this is that Daniel spent his days as a courtier, looking after kings—he was a public official and did not consider himself a prophet. But he did not consider himself a sacred writer either;[290] so why did they put him in that category?

Well, this is becoming tedious; I still don't understand what principle makes it impossible for Daniel to have been, at the same time, both a close friend of kings and a prophet. Even the Rabbis, the pillars of the Jews, often say that *the power of prophecy never settles on any but the wealthy*;[291] so they stab themselves with their own swords. And we know that David in his time, as well as the others who held supreme power, prophesied future events under the influence of divine inspiration. The prophets were truly unfortunate if the only way to receive this "honor" was to wander the earth carrying a stick and a pack! Aristotle has Crates, who was always eagerly seeking out wisdom, take pride in his poverty and filth, as follows: *He has a pack whose size I don't know, and a quart of beans.*[292] This, I think, was incorrect. Crates was even ready to immortalize his pack in poetry, by satirizing the verses that Homer dedicates to Crete:

> There is a land called Pera [=pack] in the midst of the wine-dark sea,
> A fair land and a rich one, very dirty, and having nothing.[293]

As if dirt really could produce wisdom or a fine intellect! One Crete was worth more than three thousand packs.

But I really shouldn't be cracking jokes in the midst of such a serious discussion. I say again that the Jews were making a mockery of their beliefs by keeping Daniel out of the company of men whom he would have honored

more than anyone else could. Now let us return to our subject. Daniel prophesied during the Babylonian Exile just like Zechariah, Haggai, and Malachi
(who was the last of them all). When these men died the Jews completely
lost the power of prophecy, until John the Baptist finally appeared. Though
he was the next to follow Malachi, he came only after a very long time. He
was both the last of the prophets and the first of the evangelists. We know
that he was a prophet from the words of the poem his father recites in the
Gospel of Luke, in a style more grand than could have come from a human mouth:[294] *But you, my son, will be called the prophet of the Most High;
for you will go before the Lord to prepare a way for Him.*[295] Malachi has a
prophecy which reads: *I will send you Elijah the prophet, before the coming
of the great and awesome day of the Lord.*[296] The Messiah (who was the finest
interpreter of these prophecies) has pointed out that this Elijah was none
other than John.[297] It was because of the many similarities between the two
men that Malachi called John "Elijah": their girdles and clothing were the
same,[298] and one upset Jezebel[299] with his unrestrained criticism, while the
other did the same to Herodias.[300] Both men lived in empty, barren regions
far from the godless crowd, so they were clearly the founders of the pious
and admirable discipline of the desert dwellers.[301] Plus, they were both moved
in the same way by the spirit of God. It was not for nothing that the angel
said, *he is going to come in the power of Elijah.*[302] In fact, when the Messiah
put on heavenly garb on a certain mountain in the presence of his disciples,
he held an intimate conversation with Elijah; this was the greatest honor he
could have given him.[303] On the other hand, the compliment he paid John
was no less impressive: he said that the man who was John's superior had
never been born.[304] Thus, the most discerning judge of our affairs gave a
wonderful testimonial to this man who had been born last of all, and yet had
begun to prophesy even before he was born.[305] John was a model of integrity,
entirely innocent and sacred; indeed, once a very holy woman named Paula
saw demons being tortured at the site of his tomb. Jerome confirms that this
definitely happened, and far be it from us to doubt his word.

CHAPTER 8

On the kabbalah, the law not commanded by Scripture. How to
untangle the knotty problems of parallel passages. How carefully we
have to make use of scriptural and mystical interpretation. On
the Karaite Jews, a group that is more intelligent than the others
and rejects their foolish notions. On their wealth.

THE JEWS have two sets of laws: one set was given in writing, while the other was issued at some time in the past by means of words alone. Now, I have already said a few things about the written laws as they occurred to me; that leaves the other laws, the kabbalah, those teachings that were handed down by Almighty God and yet were not committed to writing. The reason for this was that at the time, the Jewish masses were still trying to get through the rudimentary stages of their faith, and they were responding to the hidden meanings of the holy books with shock rather than understanding.[306] Moses had learned certain mystical interpretations of the law while he was conversing with God on Mount Horeb;[307] after his time these interpretations were entrusted to others who were moved by the sacred Spirit. Let me be clear: I wouldn't dream of using the term kabbalah here to refer to the elaborate fantasies, silly bits of foolishness, and narratives that the Jewish teachers (who were very obsessive people) passed down from one to another as though they were sacred mysteries, both before the age of Christ and for a long time after.[308] I am talking about something else entirely. What I really mean by kabbalah is the mystical understanding of the secrets hidden in the sacred books. Though this understanding had originally been in the hands of the prophets, they were forbidden to reveal it to the world. But finally the Apostles and the writers of the Gospels were granted a divine gift—they were allowed to proclaim openly to everyone what had been hidden for so long. So by kabbalah I do not mean the usual thing—"what people have handed down to others"[309]—but rather "what holy men have received from Heaven." For the meaning of kabbalah is receiving.[310] St. Paul, who had sat at the feet of Gamaliel[311] and learned everything on which the wisest men of the Jews prided themselves, had to unlearn the rabbinic kabbalah when he became an Apostle and learn the real one. Until that time he did not know that *the law is spiritual.*[312]

I should make something of an effort to clarify this issue. The Book of Numbers has certain things to say about princes and leaders, and about tribunes and centurions.[313] This is a factual narrative, and the ancient Hebrews understood it as such. But St. Paul found in these passages a more sublime meaning; and he exposed their secrets when he wrote to the Ephesians that *in Heaven there are principalities, lordships, powers, strengths, and other types of offices.*[314] After all, how could Paul (who read through the sacred books as carefully as anyone could) have said that something written in the text did not really exist? I do not hesitate in this case to agree with Jerome, who clearly felt this way. But come, let us move on to more important matters. What I now have to say is certainly not open to debate. In the thirtieth chapter of Deuteronomy, Moses, the wisest of all legislators, said as follows in his final address to the people: *The teachings I am giving you today are not hidden from you, neither are they far away; they are not in Heaven, such that you might say, "Who will go up to Heaven and bring them back for us?" Nor are they across the sea, such that you would say, "Who will cross the sea and get them?" These words are very close to you; they are in your mouths and your minds so that you may do them.*[315] This obviously means that the Hebrews did not have to look far to determine the will of God, for the Law was all around them. In the tenth chapter of St. Paul's Letter to the Romans[316] he takes this passage in a different direction—he understands it as referring to the Gospel.[317] But before he does this he looks at the words of Moses in the eighteenth chapter of Leviticus,[318] and he says, *Moses is saying about right-eousness according to the Law that those who observe it will live by it.*[319] So here he accepts the simple sense of the legislator's words as they should be literally understood.

He then adds the other passage from Deuteronomy. Though his interpretation of this passage doesn't conflict with its intended meaning, he does take it in a very different direction not only from the Hebrews, but from everyone else who had discussed it before his time: *But the righteousness based on faith says: Do not say in your heart, "Who will ascend into heaven?" or "Who will descend into the abyss?" For the word is near you, on your lips and in your heart; this is the word of faith which we preach.*[320] People who think that this is merely a play on words are very much mistaken; for the Apostle is saying that Moses created two kinds of righteousness—one based on acts, the other on faith. First he quotes Moses' testimony *al mashma'o* or *according to the literal sense*; then he gives it according to the kabbalah, *al midrasho*—i.e. it is what Moses meant, but this meaning was mystical: after quoting Moses, Paul adds, *this is the word of faith which we preach.*[321] Though I don't understand the approach behind this type of exposition,[322] I believe it is correct and truthful because it is inspired by God.

I find there is also kabbalah in the words of the second chapter of Genesis. From the passage, *a man shall leave his father and mother and join with his wife,*[323] the Apostle discovers (in the fifth chapter of his Letter to the Ephesians)[324] a sacrament unknown to humankind:[325] *This is a great mystery, and I say that it refers to Christ and to the Church.*[326] There are many things of this kind in that wonderful work—the Letter to the Ephesians is certainly full of mystical and hidden meanings, and it is exceptional in this respect. At the same time, I can hardly believe that the kabbalah is to be found only in the books of the Law; it is in fact a widespread phenomenon. Everything contained in the prophetic books and the sacred Writings has a double meaning: the plain one (which is properly called *pashut*) and another, hidden one we may call *agadeta* or *derash* because it has to be unearthed and examined. The Rabbis have an old saying for which I would prefer to render only the general sense, so that I won't have to *speak like a barbarian.*[327] *The Scripture,* they say, *always has its simple meaning. But alongside it there is a mystical meaning; and these two are always to be found together.*[328] The eighth psalm is about the excellence of human beings, who have mastery over the other creatures and are practically gods on earth;[329] but St. Paul says[330] that David was talking about the *other* world, and about Christ who rules over everything in it. This had not occurred to anyone else in all of human history, because it differs so much from the other interpretations.[331]

I would like to bring this investigation to an end. Paul's exposition is kabbalah, and that is all we need to say about it. Matthew too was thoroughly informed about these secrets. He says[332] that when the Blessed Virgin took her small boy off to Egypt because she feared Herod, and returned after the king died, she fulfilled the prediction once made by the prophet that *I have summoned my son from Egypt.*[333] But however much the learned interpreters may weary themselves with their speculations, Hosea was talking not about the Messiah but about the people of Israel whom God once led out of Egypt, and whom He calls His son and firstborn in many other places. So Matthew's explanation is entirely mystical and kabbalistic.[334] There is no reason for us to think any differently, unless we want to force our own interpretation on language that is perfectly clear,[335] or to invent some new chimeras for ourselves. Nothing would be easier for me than to produce all sorts of arguments to prove my position, but I am trying my best to be brief.

It's true that the most difficult task for any intelligent scholar is to interpret correctly the proof texts that the Apostles quoted in their writings from the

Law and the books of the prophets—it seems that many of these passages do not belong where they have been put, and that the Apostles have completely twisted the meanings intended by Moses and the prophets. Everyone who has tried to defend such passages as being anything other than mystical has met with nothing but frustration. And yet even in the past there were brilliant men who put no small effort into making everything fit together, and show a certain harmony and consistency. But with all due respect to these scholars, I have to say they have not persuaded me at all. People who want to understand these passages as nothing more than wordplay cannot see that they are only making things worse by offering feeble excuses for the Apostles. Why in fact do the latter quote the words of Moses and the prophets? Surely, if we are going to be honest with ourselves, it is because they want to give their writings more authority; but how could they have accomplished this by misusing the words of their sources, twisting their meaning, or (even worse) perverting it? Add to this that the Apostles themselves usually come right out and say that they are summoning Moses and the prophets as witnesses, and that what they had once predicted has come to pass.

I have already said in the appropriate place[336] that the canon of sacred scripture was closed until the day when its seals would be opened by the lion from the tribe of Judah. I must repeat this yet again (there is a saying that *a beautiful sentiment should be repeated two or three times*):[337] that lion was the Messiah, who used God's power and inspiration to give the Apostles a mystical comprehension of things that no one had ever understood. It is only in a state of amazement that I can revere things my feeble mind can barely grasp;[338] and whenever I am unable to find rational explanations for proofs of this sort,[339] I will call them kabbalah—not the worthless kabbalah of the Jews, but the one created by God Himself. This is the only kind of refuge I can find; otherwise all I can see are knots that cannot be undone, and complex riddles that are completely beyond my power to solve (which is not to say that I think there is anyone else capable of doing so).

I have said what I think about mystical interpretation, but let me add that it is not a common thing, or one that many people can master. It is limited to a select few, in fact to the Apostles and Evangelists, whose observations are *inspired by God*.[340] For even though the holy leaders of the Church later came to imitate this practice, this is not the same thing; we are obligated to accept only those of their ideas that make sense to us intellectually.[341] Whereas in order for human beings to understand kabbalah, a heavenly spirit has to enter their hearts; for things of such magnitude cannot exist without God.

Though Origen was certainly a great man, he allowed himself so much leeway in his scriptural interpretations that he overstepped his bounds in a very disrespectful way.[342] Augustine and Jerome, on the other hand, were more cautious, which is why their observations are usually so wonderful even though they cannot claim any sacred authority. There is, for example, a brilliant comment of Jerome's that I want to include because it has to do with the secrets of the Law that I have been discussing. He examines the wording of a passage in the twenty-seventh chapter of the Gospel of Matthew: *The curtain of the Temple was torn in two from top to bottom.*[343] Jerome says that *the fact that the curtain of the Temple is torn when Jesus cries out and gives up the ghost must be read as an anagoge:*[344] *all the mysteries of the Law were revealed, and what had previously been hidden away was now given freely to all the nations. Moreover, there were two parts to this, the Old and New Testaments.*[345] *As for* from top to bottom: *sacred history*[346] *tells us what happened at the beginning of the world when man was created, and everything that has happened since, until the world reached its consummation.*[347] *And if we ask which curtain was torn, the inner or the outer,*[348] *it seems to me that at the moment of our Lord's passion, it was the curtain located outside in both the Tabernacle and the Temple, and called the outer one, that was torn. After all, the things we see and know in our age are incomplete. When that which is complete has arrived, then the inner curtain will be torn open, and we will see all the sacraments of the House of God that are now hidden from us.*[349]

This passage is learned, and it was conceived in piety. It is certainly true that many of the interpretations of this kind written by the ancient Fathers contain more ingenuity than the facile arguments of the Jews; yet since the latter have many kinds of defenses for their learning, they have stopped at nothing.[350] Most of the joyless authorities who interpret the Law for them are constantly making fools of themselves. They plaster over one mistake with another to keep the rain from coming in, and they teach their students (at great cost to them) just one thing: *to know nothing.* The teachers who have produced the greatest number of students like themselves—that is, affected and trivial—are the most respected, and they refer to themselves very arrogantly as *marbitzei torah*, a crude expression meaning *those who knock the Law down*, i.e. who make it doze passively among them, and abide with the Jewish nation alone. Nonetheless, the Jews do have among them a more intelligent group. I mean the Karaites, who reject the teachings of men, regard the principles of the Talmud as worthless, and accept nothing but the text of the Holy Book. But other Jews reserve a special hatred for this group;[351] the result is that because there are very few Karaites they have a great deal of trouble marrying off their daughters, despite the fact that they are all rich and can offer enormous dowries. Since other people have already mentioned this, I would not have brought it up if I did not find it such a constant source of amusement: these Jews, the most perverse people in the world, have sworn off good sense to the point that they actually prefer to turn down money, which rules their lives, rather than accept a father-in-law who is not an idiot!

CHAPTER 9

What the Hebrews of the ancient Church thought and understood about the Messiah. The entire issue is carefully examined. The kind of disturbed personality that reduces everything to theories and formulas.

WHEN I SAID, earlier in the book, that after the arrival of the Messiah the Jews were rejected by God and lost their former standing, I showed that the reason for this was their complete lack of faith. And really, what better example could there be of hopeless perversity than these people who refused to have faith even in their own eyes and ears, when they had before them not witnesses and proof of what had happened, but the events themselves? Naturally they had to pay for their crimes with retribution. But I would like to return from my digression to the era when the Hebrews were aware of the Messiah's goodwill only through symbols, imagery, and the visions of the prophets. Of course, given that oracles consist of secret meanings, and that it is extremely difficult for human beings to interpret future events (let alone a foreshadowing of those events), very learned men have been debating for a long time what exactly the ancient Hebrews expected and believed about the supreme Savior. This issue has such broad significance that it is very important for the correct interpretation of the entire Holy Book, for it is a case in which St. Paul seems to contradict himself, and in other people's writings there seems to be a similar discrepancy on this point.

Although I ought to examine this issue it deserves more than a passing mention; and in the meantime I would like to leave the realm of the philologists and dwell on things of a more contemplative nature. We should go where the greatness of our subject calls us; and unless I can decide at once whose solution I should follow in this matter, I will never be able to let it alone.[352] This knot calls for someone to undo it, and I refuse to evaluate other people's opinions, for they are extremely varied. And besides, no one has said anything really convincing. Without denigrating anyone else, I will take a moderate approach and go down an open road to arrive at the truth. But first I should say about the patriarchs and the prophets that we know for a fact they believed in the Messiah with all their hearts, and knew about the greatest of mysteries. That they could be aware of such an important thing was a unique benefit they received by the grace of God. But they did not all receive it in equal measure—though they were all aware of the Messiah, some were more aware than others.[353]

Of all the men who lived at that time none had more faith than Abraham, which is why the Savior of mankind says such a magnificent thing about him: *Your father Abraham rejoiced that he was to see my day; he saw it and was glad.*[354] Could anyone think of a more wonderful thing to say? Though Abraham's mind was completely devoted to great and lofty ideas, he had no safeguards on which he could depend. He was despised because, having no children, he was found wanting; and this upset his composure. God kindly heard his prayers and promised him descendants who would rule the world.[355] But Abraham realized then and there that this promise held a deeper significance, and he understood that the Messiah was going to come from his family. That is how Paul interprets it: *Promises were made to Abraham and to his offspring. It does not say "and to offsprings," referring to many; but, referring to one, "and to your offspring," which is Christ.*[356]

I would place in the same category Jacob, David, and a few others. Whatever knowledge of this matter may have come to the rest was sketchy at best. This is the meaning of that statement of the Messiah's that I quoted above: *Many prophets and righteous men have yearned to see what you are seeing, but they did not.*[357] At the very least, they longed to be able to see the one they knew was going to come; that was the nature of their faith. Though Abraham also longed for it (this is what they all had in common), what was different about him was that he was permitted to see what the others were not. In fact, Abraham's good fortune was greater not only than that of the prophets, but greater even than that of the angels. This is what St. Peter tells us in the following passage: *The prophets inquired about this salvation, trying to determine what time was declared by the prophetic Spirit of Christ within them for the coming sufferings of Christ and the subsequent glory. It was revealed to them that they were looking—not for their own sakes but for ours—after those matters that have now been announced to you, matters into which angels long to look.*[358]

I would also, for reasons that are obvious, apply what I have said about the prophets to those leaders of the sacred nation who had visions of the future. But if we should turn our attention to the pious masses, it will take a carefully worded argument to explain what exactly they believed. I cannot allow it to seem that I am endorsing in any way the leaders of certain bizarre groups—utterly worthless men driven by the spirit of recklessness—who believe that the Jewish masses could not achieve that state to which the Messiah's virtue summoned all pious men. Obviously I feel otherwise; it is perfectly clear what the Apostle tells us in the ninth chapter of his Letter to the Hebrews: *Therefore he is the mediator of a new covenant, so that those who have been called may receive the promised eternal inheritance, since a death has occurred that redeems them from their transgressions under the first testament.*[359] He says that the sins committed by the Jews in the past have been forgiven, a point he also makes in the third chapter of Galatians: *Before faith came, we were kept under guard by the law, confined against the day when faith would be revealed.*[360] To deny this would be the very height of folly, and I am not so reckless.

While I know that the Jewish masses were blessed with heavenly gifts, there is more room for debate as to the *nature* of their faith. So first let us consider whether or not they could have received all these gifts even without any sacred faith; then, once this has been made clear, it will remain for us to show that they did have some sort of faith, and what this was like. As to the first issue, I have come to the conclusion that even if the masses had had no awareness or understanding of the Messiah, they could still have received the blessings of Heaven on account of the patriarchs, who perceived the Messiah with their minds and accepted from God this promise of a covenant: *I will be your God and the God of your descendants.*[361] This is why it happens very often in the Holy Book that when the Israelites have asked for God's forgiveness after angering Him or, more than that, for His great blessings, they are warned by a heavenly voice that they are responsible for everything that was agreed to by their forefathers Abraham, Isaac, and Jacob. This language is common in the Pentateuch and the prophetic books. Moreover, it was the Messiah who guaranteed the covenant that (as I have said) was made with the patriarchs; this is why the prophet called him *the angel of the covenant.*[362]

So the mass of Israelites received salvation, they received it because of the Messiah, and they were given this advantage because their ancestors had had faith in the great promises made to them. In fact, it would not be out of place here to point out that people think of as fortunate those babies who lose their lives just as they are born, because their parents' piety is counted towards their own salvation; so much so that according to St. Paul, children who have one sinful parent are still saved by the other one's faith. This statement is found in First Corinthians, chapter 7: *The unbelieving husband is consecrated through his wife, and the unbelieving wife is consecrated through her husband. Otherwise your children would be unclean, whereas now they are holy.*[363] I am aware of the fact that according to the writings of some very serious scholars, infants have the capacity for a certain amount of sacred faith; but this idea is so idiotic that it ought to be corrected at the end of a whip. After all, the Apostle says to the Romans that *faith comes from hearing* (to which we may add *and also from assent*).[364] But perhaps the people who believe in this fantasy ought to search as far back as they can for the memories of their own childhoods. Obviously they're not going to say that even at the age when they were first beginning to play with their little friends, they had made some remarkable discoveries about the supreme mystery of the faith; or if they do think so, then let them come to me wearing pajamas. That would be appropriate, since they are so in touch with their own childhoods.

On the other hand, it was not for nothing that I compared the Israelites to infants. God ordered Moses to give the Law in the desert of Arabia in order to establish the rituals and observances of religion, and so that the infant nation could become used to these building blocks until the Messiah promised to its forefathers should come into the world. St. Paul expresses this wonderfully in his Letter to the Galatians, as follows: *The Law was added because of sins, until the offspring should come to whom the promise was made.*[365] And a little later: *The Law has led us to Christ by the hand, like children.*[366] But the most fitting passage is in chapter 4: *When we were children, we were made slaves to the elements of the world.*[367] In the same passage he calls these elements *weak and needy*;[368] when the Messiah arrived, humanity was ordered to give them up and embrace the true and sturdy doctrine. As it was written elsewhere: *You died with Christ and were discharged from the elements of this world.*[369] This is why the Jews who are alive today are no longer children, and do not live under the supervision of a caretaker, and why they no longer enjoy the benefits that (as I have said) could once have been given to a rough and immature people for the sake of its ancestors. For the day arrived when they were required to act like men and come of age.[370]

From the passages I have quoted we can see that there were once two covenants. One was made with the patriarchs, and God sanctified it with the promises He made about the Messiah.[371] This is why Galatians says that *the promises were made to Abraham; and the law that was given four hundred and thirty years later does not annul the covenant previously confirmed by God with respect to Christ, so as to make the promise void.*[372] And in the Acts of the Apostles it says: *We bring you happy news and announce to you the promise that was made to your fathers.*[373] The other covenant was between God and the masses, and it was based on the Law. In this covenant as in the other one, God made certain promises; but because the people could not live according to the dictates of the Law, they lost hope that these promises would come to pass (although they tried, their natural weaknesses got in the way). So as the writer of the Letter to the Hebrews says in the eighth chapter: *Christ has obtained a ministry that is more excellent than the old in the same degree as the covenant for which he stands surety is better, since it is based on better promises.*[374]

Certainly in this passage, the covenant of the New Testament is being compared not with the one given to the patriarchs but with the one based on the Law, which was made much later on. But the passage is very vague, and unless I can explain it well enough to put it to rest, it will cast a shadow over the Holy Scripture. The situation is as follows: the text of the New Testament does not promise anything better than what had once been promised to the patriarchs, and it is not called "New" as though to say that it has replaced the old covenant made with Abraham. Rather, the reason is that it *did* have the authority to abolish the other covenant—based on the Law—which was made four hundred and thirty years after the first one with Abraham, and according to which promises were made to the people (though these the Apostle calls *inferior*, since the legislator had attached to them a condition no one could fulfill: *He who does these things will live in them*).[375] On the other hand, in Genesis the Holy Spirit says about Abraham, to whom the Messiah was promised in the first agreement, that *he believed, and he was reckoned to be righteous.*[376]

Since the conclusions I have drawn about this first issue may be called very probable, let me move on to the other question and prove that the pious masses once had a kind of faith. But first of all, the principles in which the whole community of the Israelites necessarily had to believe were more or less as follows: that the power of God was able to accomplish great and remarkable things; that His promises were ironclad; that He was to be worshiped not with shallow appearances (the easiest way to put on a show of piety) but with the submission of the soul; and that these are the sweetest kinds of glory and power. I could mention more things of this sort, since there are many very similar ideas, but I don't want to limit this subject with strict boundaries; it is a ridiculous superstition always to worry about definitions, for it is in the nature of certain things that they cannot be properly defined. Of course, teachers with time on their hands who turn everything into precise formulas are often painting themselves into a corner from which they cannot escape, either because they are embarrassed or because they do not want to retract what they've already said. The result is strife, anger, and a total free-for-all.[377] If the Apostles and the writers of the gospels were to enjoy a brief stay on earth and return to the company of men, they would be astonished at how many different analyses and approaches were being used to interpret their books, and how many bizarre constructions had been

assembled from the trivial notions of the sophists. Their writings have something divine about them—that awesome simplicity—and there was a time
when the more successful a person was at achieving this simplicity himself,
the closer he got to the age of the gospels. But the world has grown old,
and now that we have huddled within the shrunken space of an impover-
ished art, trivial and foolish ideas have caused the body of divine wisdom
to weaken and die.

But this is not the place for me to be making speeches. The faith that the
entire Israelite nation was supposed to place in the power and promises of
God is treated very eloquently by St. Paul (or whoever it was that wrote the
Letter to the Hebrews): *The good news came to us just as it did to them; but
the message they heard did not benefit them, because those who heard it did
not temper it with faith.*[378] His language in this passage is not at all concise.
If we are referring to the ancient Israelites, what he is calling "good news" is
the promise of a peaceful settlement, which the people who left Egypt with
Moses had understood to be in the land of Canaan. But most of them never
reached that place—people are by nature reckless, and the various disasters
and crises they suffered in the wastelands of the desert led them, time and
again, to complain and to talk of rebellion. They did not have the strength
to hold on or to conserve themselves until things could improve.

A little earlier on the divine author said: *To whom did he swear that they
would never arrive at their rest, if not to those who had disobeyed?*[379] Doubtless he is saying that it was *those who were uncooperative* who were cut off.
So the "faith" he is discussing in that passage[380] was submission, instead
of which there was disbelief, stubbornness, and an attitude of disobedi-
ence. But the nature of this disbelief emerges more clearly from the words
that the letter's author quotes from Psalm 95: *Your fathers tested Me in the
desert, and they saw My works for forty years. So I became angered at that
nation, and I said: They always sin in their hearts and they have not learned
My ways.*[381] Our author has discovered coexisting in the very same psalm a
second and better kind of "good news"; anyone who had faith in it would
have thought not of settlement in Canaan, but of the eternal and heavenly
peace that not Joshua but the Messiah, the greatest of all kings, provided
for his citizens. He says this here: *If Joshua had given them rest, God would
not have spoken later of another day. So there remains a Sabbath rest for the
people of God.*[382] In fact, he is saying that the people who came to Canaan
under Joshua's leadership did not, as a result, enjoy heavenly peace. But he
has already said that they entered Canaan through faith![383] It is therefore
obvious that faith in the Messiah was not entirely the same as the universal
faith in God's promises.

Of course, Moses himself was barred from the tranquil territory of Canaan because he doubted God's power by hitting the rock. This showed a complete lack of faith, and we are told as much in the twentieth chapter of Numbers.[384] And yet we learn just how much faith Moses had in the benefits of the Messiah from the following passage: *Moses considered the abuse he suffered for Christ greater wealth than the treasures of Egypt, for he had his eyes on the reward he would receive.*[385] So whatever the Apostle may say in chapters 3 and 4 about the disbelief of the ancient Israelites, we should accept with caution.[386] In fact, he warns the Hebrews of his own day[387] to take great care that their own disbelief does not keep them from receiving the gifts of Heaven, since their ancestors, after all, had angered God and then been exiled from the blessed region that stood as a symbol of this better, heavenly homeland. This is the simplest interpretation of that passage. I had given up hope of ever getting free of it—the entire discussion is devoted to nothing but the fickleness and foolishness of the Hebrews, whose human weaknesses were constantly leading them into grievous sin in the desert of Arabia, and who brought all their misfortunes on themselves.

The truth is, though, that there was not much strength of spirit even in the Israelites who did enter the Promised Land, and who brought with them their rites and religious observances. God had so many criticisms about this people that in the books of the prophets they fill up both sides of the ledger. If, at any rate, I should want to deal with them all, I would be overwhelmed by the sheer size of the job. This subject was, however, briefly discussed by Sulpicius Severus, a very holy bishop and, in Augustine's opinion, a man who excelled in both knowledge and wisdom.[388] His words were so fine that I want to record them here: *Whenever they were prospering, the Hebrews always forgot the gifts they had received from Heaven and bowed down to idols; when times were hard they turned to God. Since I am therefore in the habit of reckoning up the accounts of a people who were indebted to God for so many favors, and were punished with so many deaths when they sinned, and experienced both God's mercy and His wrath, but never learned from either; and who, though they were always pardoned for their sins, always sinned after they were pardoned, it comes as no surprise to me that they rejected Christ. After all, from the very start they were always being caught in the act of rebelling against their master. What is surprising is that no matter how many times they sinned, God granted them His mercy whenever they beseeched Him.*[389]

I have said enough about the faith that the entire ancient Hebrew nation ought to have placed in the word of God. Now finally I am going to discuss what is at the heart of the matter—that the pious common people of ancient times absolutely knew and believed in the Messiah before his coming.

Though this can be proven with very little evidence, it can be proven nonethe-less.[390] In the fourth chapter of the Gospel of John [391] the Samaritan woman expresses a belief that was shared by everyone, and had been accepted for a long time. She says about the Messiah, whom she did not know had arrived, *We know that the Messiah is going to come; and when he has come he will tell us everything.* The Samaritans were all that remained of the Israelites whom Jeroboam had once torn away from the Judeans, so they must have known what all the Hebrews generally felt about this issue.

In the eleventh chapter of his Letter to the Hebrews, the Apostle clearly describes the faith that he says flowed powerfully through every pious man. His description is as follows: *Faith is that through which things that are hoped for come to exist, and it proves to us things we cannot see.*[392] He then adds: *Because of it the men of old received divine approval.* After that he runs through the history of every age. Moreover, he praises for their faith not only the great leaders of the people but even the commoners among the Israelites, who left Egypt at the command of God. He says that *through faith they crossed the Red Sea as though it were dry land.*[393] Of course, we cannot suppose that these people obeyed only their bodies and their senses,[394] when they are credited with the same faith by means of which the other heroes mentioned in this chapter were able to contemplate the Messiah and the kingdom of Heaven.

In fact, this is the very passage where he says about Moses what I have already mentioned: that *he considered the abuse he suffered for Christ to be wealth.* And about others he says: *These all died in faith, after seeing what they were promised from afar, and acknowledging that they were strangers and exiles on the earth; for they were waiting for a better, that is a heavenly, homeland.*[395] He also says the following about Joseph (and with good reason): *In faith Joseph, at the end of his life, mentioned the exodus of the children of Israel and gave directions as to his bones.*[396] For Joseph knew that the Messiah was one day going to spend his youth in the territory of the Canaanites, and he wanted his bones to rest there. Otherwise it would have been very foolish for such a wise man to have gone to such trouble; for what does it matter to a person *where* he is buried, when it doesn't even matter to him whether he is buried at all? God has granted the dying this one kindness: that those who are not covered by an urn are covered by the sky. Maecenas, who in other respects was very effeminate, did say one manly thing: *I don't care about a tomb; nature buries those whom everyone else has abandoned.*[397]

I still have not mentioned the magnificent way St. Paul writes about the Israelite masses in his Letter to the Corinthians: *All our fathers ate the same spiritual food, and they all drank the same spiritual drink. For they drank from the spiritual rock which followed them, and the rock was Christ.*[398] And I could not in good conscience leave out what follows: *We must not put the Lord to the test as did some of our fathers, who were destroyed by serpents.*[399]

I thought I had already reached the finish line when I realized that I had not untied every knot; for St. Paul has an address to the Corinthians that seems to contradict everything I have said so far. It reads: *Moses put a veil over his face so that the Israelites might not see the end of what was being abolished.*[400] There is no longer any doubt at all that Moses' veil is the blindness of the Jews, and that *to katargoumenon* is *the law whose power has now ended*, while the end of *to katargoumenon* is the *Messiah*. It is about him that the Romans are told, *the end of the Law is Christ.*[401] But really this means nothing, and there is no reason for me to change my mind. For this wisest of Apostles does not say that the Jews knew nothing of Christ; he means merely that they did not know just what God intended when he introduced the Law.[402] In truth, the Law and all the rituals had to do with Christ. This was an amazing mystery, one that the Jewish masses of ancient times did not understand at all. And yet they had all learned—from the prophets if not from the Law—that the Messiah was going to come and restore their ruined state.

I am not the least bit afraid to proclaim to all and sundry whatever I have noticed in the Holy Book that has a bearing on such a complicated question. Besides, though I have not said everything there is to say, neither have I said nothing. It is not my task, or that of any sane man, to engage in tedious debates over small details, or to weave together clever theories. Heavenly wisdom does not deserve to be torn from its majestic heights and thrown into such shackles; even people who make it their business to do so don't gain much by it. All they are doing is setting up complicated mazes for themselves, which it will take them a great deal of trouble to retrace.

NOTES

PREFACE

1. I.e. the political philosophers of classical antiquity.

2. I.e. Cicero, in a fragment of Book 3 of his *Republic*.

3. Tacitus *Agricola* 30.6.2.

4. The Greek mainland.

5. Cunaeus is referring to events of the second century BCE.

6. A king of Asia Minor defeated by Rome in the first century BCE.

7. As elsewhere in his book, Cunaeus' ideas about religious conflict seem to be informed by the religious wars of his own times.

BOOK I

8. These were some of the semilegendary "lawgivers" of preclassical Greece (seventh century BCE). In this passage, and in the one which follows, Cunaeus is repeating Josephus practically verbatim.

9. A derogatory term borrowed from the Roman satirists.

10. Josephus *Against Apion* 2.16.

11. Because Cunaeus, following in the footsteps of Josephus, portrays Moses as a Greek lawgiver, he tends to describe him as the author of the laws which in the Bible he receives from God.

12. Though Cunaeus often uses this term to describe his sources for Jewish law and custom, almost everything he says about these is actually drawn from Maimonides. Claiming to have numerous sources while in practice using very few is presumably a habit Cunaeus learned from the classical authors who did the same.

13. Aristotle *Politics* 1.3.

14. The three types of state that, beginning with Aristotle, typified Greek theories of government.

15. Aristotle *Politics* 3.16.

16. Cf. Deuteronomy 4:2.

17. A reference to the *fasces*, the Roman symbol of public authority.

18. In Josephus *Against Apion* 1.22.

19. The relevant biblical texts are Leviticus 25 and Deuteronomy 15.

20. Maimonides *Mishneh Torah*, Laws of the Sabbatical Year and the Jubilee 11:15.

21. Ibid. 15:19.

22. Ibid. 11:17.

23. A Roman festival held at the end of the year, on which both citizens and slaves were free to indulge themselves and set aside the traditional strictures imposed upon them.

24. Maimonides *Mishneh Torah*, Laws of the Sabbatical Year and the Jubilee 10:14. מראש השנה עד יום הכפורים לא היו עבדים נפטרים לבתיהן ולא משתעבדים לאדניהם ולא השדות חוזרות לבעליהןים אלא עבדים אוכלין ושותים ושמחים [ושמחים] ועטרותיהם בראשיהם: כיון שהיגיע יום הכפורים תקעו בית דין בשופר נפטרו עבדים לבתיהן וחזרו שדות לבעליהן.

25. C. Licinius Stolo was a representative of the *plebs* (the common people) who, according to Roman tradition, cosponsored a law in 367 BCE that limited the holdings of aristocrats.

26. Roman citizens, regardless of their age, were not allowed to own their own property as long as they had a senior male relative.

27. Because the source for this story (Plutarch *Life of Tiberius Gracchus* 8.4) mentions that Laelius was a friend of Scipio, Cunaeus assumes it was referring to the famous Scipio Africanus, who defeated Hannibal in the late third century BCE. But the Laelius who passed the law lived fifty years after Africanus' time, and was a friend of Scipio Aemilianus.

28. Famous aristocratic families of the Roman Republic. One of the virtues which later generations attributed to such men was that they did their own farm work.

29. An agricultural writer of the later Republic.

30. Varro *On Farming* 2.1.

31. Cunaeus makes this assumption because the Mishna is divided into six sections, one of which deals with agriculture.

32. The story is found in Josephus *Jewish Antiquities* 8.5–6.

33. Josephus *Against Apion* 1.12. ἡμεῖς οὔτε χώραν οἰκοῦμεν παράλιον, οὔτε ἐμπορίαις χαίρομεν, οὐδὲ ταῖς διὰ τούτων πρὸς ἄλλους ἐπιμιξίαις. ἀλλ᾽ εἰσὶν μὲν ἡμῶν αἱ πόλεις μακρὰν ἀπὸ θαλάσσης ἀνῳκισμέναι, χώραν δὲ ἀγαθὴν νεμόμενοι, ταύτην ἐκπονοῦμεν.

34. This example is taken straight out of Josephus (*Against Apion* 1.12), who may in turn be basing himself on a similar description of Ephorus found in the geographer Strabo (4.4.6).

35. Again the story is taken from Josephus (*Against Apion* 1.22), who quotes from Clearchus' book. But unlike Cunaeus, Josephus does not dismiss offhand the notion that the Jews were in fact the offspring of Indian philosophers.

36. This comes from the same passage of Josephus as the last comment. Since ancient polemical literature was often claimed by its supporters to have been written by famous authors like Aristotle, many scholars question the authenticity of this passage of Clearchus—it praises the Jews, comes from an otherwise unknown book, and is found only in a Jewish work intended to prove Jewish claims.

37. Josephus *Against Apion* 1.12. χῶραν ἀγαθὴν νεμόμενοι, ταύτην ἐκπονοῦμεν. Although this line comes from the same passage of Josephus which Cunaeus has already quoted, he renders it somewhat differently here because (like many classical authors) he is more concerned with making his prose interesting than with providing a literal translation.

38. Aristotle *Politics* 6.4.

39. Ibid. 2.7.

40. Ibid. 4.6. πολιτεύονται κατὰ νόμους. ἔχουσι γὰρ ἐργαζόμενοι ζῆν· οὐ δύνανται δὲ σχολάζειν.

41. Josephus *Against Apion* 2.13. τὸ μὴ καινῶν εὑρετας ἔργων παρασχεῖν.

42. Aristotle *Politics* 1.13.

43. Ibid. 3.5.

44. Tacitus *Histories* 5.6.

45. Starting with the classical Greek geographers, it was a common notion in antiquity that the peoples who lived in the hot South were effeminate and those who lived in the cold North were violent.

46. Who was identified with the Egyptian god Thoth.

47. The Roman satirist.

48. Juvenal *Satires* 1:26–27. Canopus was a region of the city of Alexandria.

49. Exodus 1:9.

50. Maimonides *Mishneh Torah*, Laws of the Sabbatical Year and the Jubilee 10:3. אף על פי שלא היה יובל היה בבית שני מונין היו אותו כדי לקדש שמיטות. Although the Hebrew here says merely that the seventh year was sanctified, Cunaeus' expansion seems to be based on Maimonides' statement (in section 10:9) that the Sabbatical year continued to be kept in the Land of Israel, and loans continued to be canceled, even after the destruction of the First Temple.

51. Maimonides *Mishneh Torah*, Laws of the Sabbatical Year and the Jubilee 10:7. שנת יובל אינה עולה ממנין שני השבוע אלא שנת תשעה וארבעים שמטה ושנת חמשים יובל ושנת חמשים ויובל בכל וכן שבוע של שנים שש תחלת ואחת. In the original text Cunaeus cites this passage in Hebrew without translation.

52. A Talmudic authority who was credited, in the Middle Ages, with the invention of a reliable multiyear calendar.

53. The practice of inclusive numbering was in fact widespread. The Romans, for example, called their week—which began every eight days—the *nundinae*, or "nine days."

54. I.e. if they had begun in different months, there could at least have been a period of overlap between them to explain the confusion.

55. Maimonides *Mishneh Torah*, Laws of the Sabbatical Year and the Jubilee 10:16. יתירה שביעית על היובל שהשביעית משמטת כספים ולא יובל: ויותר יובל על השביעית שהיובל מוציא עבדים ומשמיט קרקע: יובל משמט קרקע בתחלתו ושביעית אינה משמטת כספים אלא בסופה.

56. Cunaeus seems to be reasoning that since the seventh-year cancellation of loans occurred only at the end of the year, then even if the Jubilee took place in the forty-ninth year, the fact that it did not forgive debts would not come into conflict with the fact that it was also a seventh year.

57. That is, proofs that the Jubilee was counted in the forty-ninth year.

58. Maimonides *Mishneh Torah*, Laws of the Sabbatical Year and the Jubilee 10:15. דין היובל בשביתת הארץ ודין השמטה אחד הוא לכל דבר: כל שאסור בשביעית מעבודת הארץ אסור בשנת יובל: וכל שמותר בשביעית מותר ביובל.

59. Cf. Maimonides *Mishneh Torah*, Laws of the Sabbatical Year and the Jubilee 12:15–16.

60. Maimonides *Mishneh Torah*, Laws of the Sabbatical Year and the Jubilee 13:11. יראה לי שאין הדברים אמורים אלא בארץ שנכרתה עליה ברית לאברהם ליצחק וליעקב וירשוה בניהם ונתחלקה להם: אבל שאר כל הארצות שכובש מלך ממלכי ישראל הרי הכהנים והלויים באותן הארצות ככל ישראל. Cunaeus has modified his translation to suit his interpretation of Maimonides. The Hebrew says only that "the priests and the Levites were the same as all the Israelites," without implying that they were any worse off for being allowed to own land instead of getting their food from others.

61. That is, unlike the law that adjusted the redemption price of lands in accordance with the number of years left until the next Jubilee.

62. Maimonides *Mishneh Torah*, Laws of the Sabbatical Year and the Jubilee 12:7.

63. This entire discussion is a paraphrase of Maimonides *Mishneh Torah*, Laws of the Temple 6:14–15.

64. Eusebius *Church History* 4.6.3.

65. Cf. Maimonides *Mishneh Torah*, Laws of Murder and Preservation of Life 9:4.

66. Maimonides *Mishneh Torah*, Laws of the Temple 7:23. מקום שהיה בעלייה מקוון [מכוון] על קדש הקדשים אין נכנסין לו אלא פעם אחת בשבוע לידע מה הוא עליה לחזק בדקו.

67. Josephus *Jewish Antiquities* 20.189-196.

68. Josephus *Against Apion* 1.22.

69. Psalms 30:1. ארוממך יהו-ה כי דליתני.

70. Maimonides *Mishneh Torah*, Laws of the Temple 6:11-12. Cunaeus has misunderstood Maimonides, who says that the loaves are to be taken from two *todot*, "thank-offerings." Since Cunaeus thinks the Hebrew means "songs of thanksgiving," he says not that the bread came *from* the *todot*, but that it came afterward.

71. Tacitus *Histories* 5.12.2.

72. Digest "On the Division of Properties" 9.4ff.

73. Cf. Maimonides *Mishneh Torah*, Laws of the Sabbatical Year and the Jubilee 12:12.

74. Josephus *Against Apion* 1.22. Cunaeus is misleading here. The context of Hecataeus' remark is a prohibition on idolatrous objects in the Temple, including sacred groves (*asherot*).

75. A biblical prophetess.

76. These particulars come from Maimonides *Mishneh Torah*, Laws of the Temple 7:14. As he does so often, Cunaeus is attributing to "the Talmudists" information that he has taken directly from Maimonides.

77. Maimonides *Mishneh Torah*, Laws of the Temple 7:13.

78. Josephus *Jewish War* 6.5.3.

79. Cunaeus is envisioning a system of property-based "orders" like the one in Rome, with the aristocratic senators and knights on one hand, and the plebeians on the other.

80. I.e. the Hasidim, a group of the Second Temple period which is described in 1 Maccabees as especially pious.

81. It was only in Rabbinic law that a set conversion process was developed.

82. Deuteronomy 16:2.

83. Ibid. 19:9. ויספת לך עוד שלש ערים על השלש האלה.

84. Ibid. 19:8. Cf. Maimonides *Mishneh Torah*, Laws of Kings and Wars 11:2, Laws of Murder and Preservation of Life 8:4.

85. Maimonides *Mishneh Torah*, Laws of Murder and Preservation of Life 8:10.

86. Deuteronomy 4:5, 14; 5:28; 6:1.

87. Maimonides *Mishneh Torah*, Laws of Kings and Wars 5:12. כשם שאסור לצאת מהארץ לחוצה לארץ כך אסור לצאת מבבל לשאר הארצות.

88. One of the last members of the Hasmonean dynasty.

89. Josephus *Jewish Antiquities* 15.2.2.

90. Ibid. 10.11.7. Josephus, however, says that the tower was used as a burial place for the Persian kings. Perhaps the confusion stems from the fact that in Latin, *arcanum* is "secret" and *arca* is "coffin."

91. Jeremiah 27:22. בבלה יובאו ושמה יהיו.

92. Cf. Maimonides *Mishneh Torah*, Laws of Kings and Wars 5:12.

93. Genesis 49:10.

94. The *resh galuta*, or exilarch.

95. Found in Josephus *Jewish Antiquities* 13.3.1–3.

96. A priest who fled to Egypt when his father, who was the last high priest of the Zadokite line, was replaced by King Antiochus. Despite Cunaeus' description, Onias' letter does not criticize his fellow Jews but rather the Egyptians, because they worshiped so many different gods.

97. Ptolemy VI and his sister-wife Cleopatra, who ruled together.

98. Maimonides *Mishneh Torah*, Laws of Entrance into the Sanctuary 9:14. מי שעבר ועשה בית חוץ למקדש להקריב בו קרבנו לשם אינו כבית עכום ואף על פי כן כל כהן ששמש בבית כזה לא ישמש במקדש לעולם וכן כלים שנשתמשו בהן שם לא ישתמשו בהן במקדש לעולם אלא יגנזו.

99. I.e. Jacob, who gives the prophecy about Shilo in Genesis 49.

100. Maimonides *Mishneh Torah*, Laws of the Sanhedrin 4:14.

101. Since the Latin term for "scepter" can be used either literally or metaphorically (in the sense of "political sovereignty"), Cunaeus applies it both to Jacob's prophecy in particular, and to his discussion of politics in general; so the translation will render *sceptrum* as "sovereignty" where appropriate.

102. I.e. to be called Judea. Cunaeus is at pains to show that the Jewish state of the Second Temple period was the heir of the earlier Hebrew state, because this would mean that the "scepter" of authority did in fact remain in the same hands until the arrival of Christ (to whom he thinks Jacob was referring).

103. The last king before the Babylonian Exile. See 2 Kings 24:17.

104. Who was the first of the Hasmoneans to call himself king (in 104 BCE).

105. Casaubon was an English scholar of the early seventeenth century who wrote detailed analyses of classical texts. The book to which Cunaeus refers was a refutation of the ideas of Baronius, a German theologian who had written a defense of Catholic doctrine.

106. Eusebius of Caesarea was a Church historian and commentator of the fourth century CE. He argues as follows: *"There shall not fail a prince from Judah"* cannot be referred to Judah as an individual any more than *"Judah, your brethren shall praise you"*; for there were rulers and governors of the Jewish nation at many times who

were not descended from him… [T]he only consistent interpretation of the passage is the one I have already given, that we must understand it of the tribe as a whole. The tribe most certainly was the leader of the whole nation from the very beginning, from Moses' own time. And in accordance with such headship—as being designed by God from the outset—the country is even now called Judea after the tribe, and the whole race are known as Jews.

107. Eusebius *Proofs of the Gospels* 8.1.

108. The Latin term *Judaicus* can mean either "Judean" or "Jewish," and Cunaeus uses it in both these senses. The translation will try to distinguish between the two wherever possible.

109. The terms Cunaeus is using here—*principes* and *optimates*—are characteristic of the ideological debate at the end of the Roman Republic over whether one-man rule was preferable to the traditional rule of the Senate.

110. Cicero *The Parts of Oratory* 105. I.e. even when it was an aristocracy, the real authority of the Jewish state lay in its people.

111. Livy *History of Rome* 38.11.2. Since, therefore, a "Roman people" governed by aristocrats was considered sovereign, the same applies to the Jewish people under its Sanhedrin.

112. Digest 49.15.7, "On the restoration of the legal rights of captives." In Roman law, "unequal treaties" guaranteed that the ally in question would supply military assistance to Rome without any promise of receiving it in turn.

113. The philosopher Seneca.

114. Digest 48.4.1, "On the Julian law of majesty."

115. Eusebius *Proofs of the Gospels* 8:1. ἀπὸ τε Μωσέως χρόνων καθεξῆς οὐ διέλιπον μερικοὶ μὲν αὐτῶν ἄρχοντες ἐκ διαφόρων φυλῶν ἡγησάμενοι, καθόλου δὲ ἡ τοῦ Ἰούδα φυλὴ παντὸς προεστῶσα του ἔθνος.

116. Ibid. παραδείγματι δὲ καταδέξῃ τὸ εἰρημένον. ὡς γὰρ ἐπὶ τῆς Ῥωμαίων ἀρχῆς οἱ μὲν καθ' ἔθνος ἐπίτροποί τε καὶ ἡγούμενοι, ἔπαρχοί τε καὶ στρατοπεδάρχαι, οἵ τε πάντων ἀνωτάτω βασιλεῖς, οὐ πάντες ἐκ τῆς Ῥωμαίων ὁρμῶνται πόλεως, οὐδ' ἀπὸ Ῥήμου ἢ Ῥωμύλου σπορᾶς, ἀλλ' ἐκ μυρίων, ἄλλος ἄλλοθεν, ἐθνῶν, ὅμως δὲ οἱ πάντες βασιλεῖς τε καὶ οἱ μετ' αὐτοὺς ἄρχοντες καὶ ἡγούμενοι τὴν Ῥωμαίων ἐπιγράφονται προσηγορίαν, Ῥωμαίων τε τὸ κράτος ἐπωνόμασαι, καὶ ταύτης ἐξῆπται τῆς ἐπωνυμίας, οὕτω περὶ τῶν καθ' ἑβραίους χρὴ νοεῖν πραγμάτων· μιᾶς μὲν καθόλου τῆς τοῦ Ἰούδα φυλῆς κατὰ τοῦ παντὸς ἔθνος ἐπιπεφημισμένης, τῶν δὲ κατὰ μέρος ἡγουμένων τε καὶ βασιλέων ἐκ διαφόρων καθισταμένων φυλῶν, καθόλου δὲ τῇ τοδ' Ἰούδα τιμομένων προσηγορίᾳ.

117. Casaubon.

118. I.e. that *all* the tribes were called after Judah.

119. Josephus *Jewish Antiquities* 11.5.2. ὁ δὲ πᾶς λαὸς τῶν Ἰσραηλιτῶν κατὰ χώραν ἔμεινε· διὸ καὶ δύο φυλάς εἶναι συμβέβηκεν ἐπί τε τῆς Ἀσίας καὶ Εὐρώπης Ῥωμαίοις

ὑπακούσας· αἱ δὲ δέκα φυλαὶ πέραν εἴσιν Εὐφράτου ἕως δεῦρο, μυριάδες ἄπειροι, καὶ ἀριθμῷ γνωσθῆναι μὴ δυνάμεναι·.

120. Cunaeus' assumption that the Ten Tribes were composed of commoners seems to have been influenced by the classical tradition that early in Rome's history, the *plebs* (the same term Cunaeus uses here) tried to secede from the citizen body.

121. The first king of Judah after the secession of the Ten Tribes. See 1 Kings 12.

122. Genesis 49.

123. Mark 13:30. οὐ μὴ παρέλθῃ γενεὰ αὕτη μέχρις οὗ πάντα ταῦτα γένηται.

124. The praetor was a Roman official in charge of justice, and second only to the consul; while the dictatorship was a powerful appointment used in times of national emergency.

125. Cunaeus is referring to the powerful leaders of the last century of the Republic, who paved the way for Imperial rule.

126. Presumably Moses and Joshua.

127. I.e. the Hasmoneans.

128. Cunaeus uses the Latin form of the Greek term *synedrion*, "council," as a generic term, and its Hebrew derivative *sanhedrin* to refer specifically to the Jerusalem council of the New Testament and the Talmud.

129. Cunaeus is again placing Jewish politics in a Roman context. Important aristocrats boasted when they could of ancestors who had received the honor of being elected to important public office.

130. Maimonides *Mishneh Torah*, Laws of the Sanhedrin 4:5. Despite Cunaeus' paraphrase, Maimonides doesn't suggest that Hillel was the only person to have this right, but that it was given to the *nasi* (the head of the Sanhedrin) in general.

131. Maimonides *Mishneh Torah*, Laws of the Sanhedrin 4:2. הרי את סמוך ויש לך רשות לדון אפילו דיני קנסות.

132. A Dutch classicist of the sixteenth century; the work mentioned here was a response to a book called *Trihaeresion*, which discussed the three sects—Pharisees, Sadducees, and Essenes—described by Josephus.

133. Maimonides *Mishneh Torah*, Laws of the Sanhedrin 4:1-2. הסמיכה לוא דוקא ביד כמו שעשה משה ליהושע אלא אפילו בדבור בלבד די שיאמר אני סומך אותך תהיה סמוך.

134. I.e. Scaliger thought it meant something like *except that he should say: I lay my hands*, etc.

135. Maimonides *Mishneh Torah*, Laws of the Sanhedrin 2:4. אם היה ראוי בחכמה.

136. Digest 50.1.2ff., "Municipal Law."

137. Ilium was believed to be the legendary city of Troy, so its citizenship was especially valued.

138. The assize was a circuit court for towns that did not have an established judicial system.

139. Cunaeus discusses his notion of kabbalah in Book III.

140. Maimonides *Mishneh Torah*, Laws of Rebels 3:4. זקן ממרה האמור בתורה הוא חכם אחד מחכמי ישראל שיש בידו קבלה ודן ומורה בדברי תורה כמו שידונו ויורו כל חכמי ישראל שבאת לו מחלוקת בדין מן הדיינים עם בית דין הגדול ולא חזר לדבריהם אלא חלק עליהם והורה לעשות שלא כהוראתן גזרה עליו תורת מיתה.

141. Luke 13:33.

142. Cf. Aristotle *Politics* 3.11.

143. Cf. Maimonides *Mishneh Torah*, Laws of the Wayward Woman 3:7-15.

144. See Translator's Preface, p. lxxiv.

145. Maimonides *Mishneh Torah*, Laws of the Sanhedrin 1:3.

146. Aristotle *Politics* 7.4.

147. I.e. very short or very long (a *stade* was about 600 feet).

148. Maimonides *Mishneh Torah*, Laws of the Sanhedrin 5:6-7.

149. A fourth-century descendant of the family of Gamaliel the *nasi*.

150. A Spanish rabbi and astronomer of the late fifteenth century.

151. Zacuto *Sefer Yuhasin*, section 1. ר' הלל הנשיא תקן העיבור לכל ישראל קודם שתתבטל הסמיכה עד ימי המשיח.

152. Maimonides *Mishneh Torah*, Laws of the Sanhedrin 5:6. וכל אלו סמוכים.

153. *Codex* 9.16.

154. Maimonides *Mishneh Torah*, Laws of Kings and Wars 1:1-2.

155. Tacitus *Histories* 4.17. The Batavians were a Germanic tribe whose leader, Civilis, rebelled against the local Roman forces during the civil wars of 69 CE.

156. Maimonides *Mishneh Torah*, Laws of Kings and Wars 1:3. ששאלו בתרעומת ולא שאלו לקיים המצוה אלא מפני שקצו בשמואל הנביא שנאמר כי לא אותך מאסו כי אותי מאסו.

157. 1 Samuel 8:7.

158. Ibid. 10:24.

159. Aristotle *Politics* 1.5.

160. 1 Samuel 10:25.

161. Josephus *Jewish Antiquities* 6.4.6. Josephus actually says that the book was a prophecy of the terrible things that would happen during Saul's reign.

162. Deuteronomy 17:14-20.

163. Maimonides *Mishneh Torah*, Laws of Kings and Wars 2:6. מצוה על הכהן גדול לכבד את המלך ולהושיבו ולעמוד מפניו כשיבא לו: ולא יעמוד המלך לפניו אלא כשישאל לו במשפט האורים:

אפילו נביא עומד לפני המלך משתחוה ארצה שנא' הנה נתן הנביא ויבוא לפני המלך וישתחו למלך על אפיו ארצה.

164. 1 Kings 1:23.

165. 1 Samuel 30:7.

166. Maimonides *Mishneh Torah*, Laws of Kings and Wars 2:4, Laws of the Temple 7:6. שאין ישיבה בעזרה אלא למלכי בית דוד בלבד.

167. Ibid. אם נכנס לעזרה והיה מזרע דוד ישב.

168. Maimonides *Mishneh Torah*, Laws of the Temple 7:6. בחצייה של חול. Though Maimonides is referring to the fact that part of the area in which the Sanhedrin met was sacred and part was not, Cunaeus seems to think that the latter part could only have been profane if it was part of the people's courtyard.

169. Maimonides *Mishneh Torah*, Laws of Vessels of the Sanctuary 1:1-3.

170. Maimonides *Mishneh Torah*, Laws of the Temple 4:1.

171. Zacuto *Sefer Yuhasin*, section 1. את [אש] על המזבח רובץ ככלב כי בטל כחו שחסרו חמשה דברים בבית שני ובבית ראשון היה כאריה.

172. שדבר זה מסור ביד החכמים. This issue is discussed in Maimonides *Mishneh Torah*, Laws of Vessels of the Sanctuary 1:11, and Laws of Kings and Wars 1:10. Note that Cunaeus adds the word "only" to his translation—whether intentionally or not, he is imposing on Maimonides' statement the idea that a "tradition passed down by the Sages" was not worth very much as proof.

173. Jason the Argonaut; cf. Aristotle *Politics* 3.4.

174. 1 Kings 11:28; Josephus *Jewish Antiquities* 8.7.7–8. The Bible does not call him a commander; Cunaeus may have gotten this idea from Josephus, who says Jeroboam was put in charge of the forced labor which Solomon had demanded of the tribe. In general, Cunaeus gets his description of Jeroboam as ambitious and power-hungry from Josephus and not from the Bible.

175. A ritual of purification performed every five years at the end of the census.

176. I.e. the worship of the golden calf. See Exodus 32.

177. The Shishak of the Bible. See 1 Kings 14:25–26 and 2 Chronicles 12.

178. Although Cunaeus borrows this criticism from Josephus (*Jewish Antiquities* 8.10.3), Herodotus doesn't actually say that Sesostris set up columns of this sort.

179. 2 Chronicles 17–18.

180. 2 Kings 24:17–25:8.

181. Berossus was a Babylonian priest who wrote about his people's history and traditions. His work survives only in secondary quotations, a few of which are found in Josephus. This is Cunaeus' only source for him; but however trustworthy the information itself may be, Cunaeus embellishes it by adding that it was the Temple's wealth that paid for the temple of Bel.

182. I.e. the high priests of the Persian and Hellenistic periods, and the Hasmonean kings.

183. I.e. Persian.

184. An ironic comment—the priest was supposed to sprinkle the blood of the sacrifices.

185. He was a Samaritan who was appointed governor of Samaria in the last years of Persian rule.

186. The last Zadokite high priest, also known as Menelaus.

187. Onias' brother, Jason, had been high priest but was removed by the king. He was now trying to get his office back.

188. That is, *nasi*, the generic biblical term for a ruler.

189. The son of Epiphanes, who was now king.

190. That is, the rebellion against Antiochus Epiphanes.

191. Cunaeus associates Onias' immorality with the rebellion because according to Josephus (*Jewish Antiquities* 12.9.7) it was Onias who started the trouble in the first place by persuading Antiochus to prohibit Jewish practices.

192. Since Seleucus had been Antiochus Epiphanes' older brother and was king before him, Demetrius killed Antiochus Eupator and took the throne for himself.

193. Aristobulus was the grandson of Simon and the son of Jochanan. Cunaeus' entire account of the high priests and Judah Maccabee comes from Books 11 and 12 of Josephus' *Jewish Antiquities*, though he does add his own observations.

194. In 37 BCE.

195. Josephus does not say that they were not Jews; but unlike him, Cunaeus seems to reject the idea of conversion to Judaism. This is not surprising, given that he wants to emphasize the continuities between the Israelites of the Bible and the Jews of later times.

196. Cf. Josephus *Jewish Antiquities* 14.9.4. Some scholars identify this Sameas with the Mishnaic authority Shammai; Cunaeus may be doing the same, as he calls Shammai "Sameas" earlier in the book.

197. To whom he had fled for protection. (This is Hyrcanus II, a descendant of the Hyrcanus mentioned earlier on the page.)

198. Josephus *Jewish Antiquities* 15.8.1. ξενικοῖς ἐπιτηδεύμασιν ὑποδιέφθειρε τὴν πάλαι κατάστασιν, ἀπαρεγχείρητον οὖσαν· ἐξ ὧν οὐ μικρὰ ἢ πρός τε αὖθις χρόνον ἠδικήθημεν, ἀμεληθέντων ὅσα πρότερον ἐπὶ τὴν εὐσεβείαν ἦγε τοὺς ὄχλους.

199. 2 Samuel 7:12–13.

200. Luke 1:33. τῆς βασιλείας αὐτοῦ οὐκ ἔσται τέλος.

201. Isaiah 9:6–7: *For to us a child is born, to us a son is given, and the government will be upon his shoulder... Of the increase of his government and of peace there will be no end, upon the throne of David and over his kingdom, to establish it.*

202. The medieval commentator Rashi (Rabbi Solomon ben Isaac), who was later called Yarhi by Christian scholars who confused him with Rabbi Solomon of Lunel (both Yarhi and Lunel are related to the word *moon*). This quote, however, comes not from Rashi but from the medieval Spanish exegete ibn Ezra, whose comments, like Rashi's, appear in the margins of standard printed editions of the Bible.

203. דרך דרש הסופרים שהמ"ם סגור בחוך המלה. In the Masoretic text of the Bible, the word *lemarbeh* ("of the increase," v. 7) is written with the form of *mem* normally used only at the ends of words.

204. That is, they felt the need to use subtle interpretation to solve this problem, which for Cunaeus is always a sign of desperation.

205. Since the verse in Isaiah has to do with a redeemer who will come in the future, the Talmud associates it with the Messiah (Sanhedrin 94a). Cunaeus seems to be implying that the Rabbis had admitted that it referred specifically to Jesus, but would not say so openly.

206. Maimonides *Mishneh Torah*, Laws of Kings and Wars 11:4.

207. Cf. ibid. 11:8–9. Though Maimonides, of course, describes the Messiah as a *future* king, Cunaeus may be trying to play down this problem. Since the Latin of the phrase "though the last king of that line..." avoids using any verbs, he does not have to choose between the past tense of Jesus and the future tense of Maimonides' Messiah.

208. Maimonides *Mishneh Torah*, Laws of Kings and Wars 12:1.

209. So, for example, the statement that "the wolf shall lie down with the lamb" (Isaiah 11:6) should be understood allegorically. As before, Cunaeus wants to use Maimonides as proof of the Second Coming. If the Messianic Age need not be essentially different from the world as it is now, then the Messiah may already have arrived.

210. A French rabbi of the twelfth century who wrote a detailed (and often critical) commentary on the *Mishneh Torah*, which appears in the standard printed editions.

211. Leviticus 26:6. השבתי חיה רעה מן הארץ. Rabbi Abraham takes this as proof that the course of nature will change.

212. Ezekiel 43–46.

213. Babylonian Talmud Menahot 45a. As he seems to have done throughout his book, Cunaeus has gotten this reference to the Talmud from the *Kesef Mishneh*, a commentary on the *Mishneh Torah* published by Rabbi Joseph Caro in the late sixteenth century, which appears on the page in printed editions of Maimonides. In general, Cunaeus limits himself to noting the section of a Talmudic tractate to which Rabbi Caro's comments refer; he does not discuss the comments themselves. Nor is there

anything to indicate that Cunaeus ever saw the text of the Talmud himself—his discussions invariably follow those of Maimonides, whether he mentions him or not.

214. The Hebrew specifies not *shelamim*, "peace offerings," but *milu'im*, which were offered at the dedication of the Tabernacle and the Temple and were therefore special sacrifices.

215. Maimonides *Mishneh Torah*, Laws of Manner of Offering Sacrifices 2:14. כל שיעורי הנסכים האמורים בספר יחזקאל ומנין אותן הקרבנות וסדרי העבודה הכתובים שם כולם מילואים הן ואין נוהגין לדורות אלא הנביא צוה ופירש כיצד יהיו מקריבין המילואים עם חנוכת המזבח בימי המלך המשיח כשיבנה בית שלישי.

216. I.e. because it is not the same temple as Solomon's building.

217. Maimonides *Mishneh Torah*, Laws of the Temple 1:4. בניין שבנה שלמה כבר מפורש במלכים. וכן בניין העתיד להבנות אף על פי שהוא כתוב ביחזקאל אינו מפורש ומבואר ואנשי בית שני כשבנו בימי עזרא בנוהו כבניין שלמה ומעין דברים המפורשים ביחזקאל.

218. Quoted in turn by Augustine *City of God* 7.17.

219. Cicero *On Divination* 2.5.

220. I.e. of the Old Testament.

221. Jeremiah 17:1.

222. Matthew 27:25.

223. Romans 11:25.

224. In Exodus 34:33–35, Moses places a veil on his face to protect the people from the light that shines from it after he has spoken with God; but here and in the following quotation from Paul, the metaphor of the veil is applied to the Jews themselves, who are unable to see the light of salvation.

225. 2 Corinthians 3:16. ἡνίκα δ᾿ ἂν ἐπιστρέψῃ Ἰσραὴλ πρὸς κύριον, περιαιρεῖται τὸ κάλυμμα.

226. Romans 9:4–5.

227. Homer *Odyssey* 17.320.
Ἥμισυ τῆς ἀρετῆς ἀποαίνυται εὐρύοπα ζεὺς
Ἀνέρος, εὖτ᾿ ἄν μιν κατὰ δούλιον ἦμαρ ἕλῃσι.

Eumaeus, who was Ulysses' herdsman, had been enslaved since childhood.

228. Josephus *Jewish Antiquities* 18.3.5.

229. Josephus *Jewish War* 7.3.1.

230. גזרו שמד שלא יקראו בתורה.

231. I.e. the lump of dough from which "first fruits" were taken as an offering before the bread was baked. The Jews, then, are the stuff from which the Christians have been set aside for a holy purpose.

232. Romans 11:16.

233. That is, the Church Fathers who wrote in either Greek or Latin.

234. Origen was a Greek-speaking Church scholar of the second century CE, who lived in Caesarea (then the capital of the province of Judea). Jerome was the author of the Vulgate, the Latin translation of the Bible.

235. I.e. Abraham Zacuto.

236. Cunaeus sometimes calls Palestine "Syria," because Roman Judea had once been part of the province of Syria.

237. In Spain.

238. I.e. the seventh century CE. While according to the Hebrew, Zacuto saw *some of the copies* corrected according to Hillel's original, Cunaeus translates him as saying that he had seen some of the original itself, and found it to be nine hundred years old. This mistranslation (whether deliberate or not) suits Cunaeus, because he wants to prove that the Masoretic text we have today comes from the early Middle Ages rather than the Second Temple period.

239. Rabbi David Kimhi, the thirteenth-century biblical commentator.

240. Numbers 15:40.

241. במלכות ליאון הוציאו ספר הארבעה ועש' אשר נקרא הביבליא שכתב אותה ר' הלל ומשם היו מגיהים כל הספרים ואני ראיתי חלק מהם שנמכרו באפריקא ובזמני היה ט' מאות שנה שנכתבו והקמחי אמר בחלק הדקדוק בפסוק למען תזכרו שהחומש היה בטולטולא.

242. Such as the passage of Isaiah mentioned above.

243. Palestinian Jewish scholars of the early Middle Ages who fixed what is now the standard text of the Bible.

244. The vowel and cantillation signs.

245. המסרה סיג לתורה. Cf. Mishna Avot 3:17.

246. The fifth century BCE.

247. Cunaeus never explains what this argument is.

248. An Aramaic translation of the Bible.

249. I.e. that the Masoretic notes were written by Ezra.

250. Midrash Numbers Rabba 22:9. עשו העקר טפל והטפל עקר. In context this statement refers to the two and a half tribes who preferred receiving good land on the other side of the Jordan to being with the rest of the people.

251. A slave whose job was to lead children from one place to another.

252. Seneca *Moral Letters* 5.50.

BOOK II

1. Cf. for example Mishna Avot 4:17.

2. Cunaeus has already referred to the father of this Onias as the *fourth* Onias, a confusion that ultimately stems from the conflict between Josephus, who says that this man was the son of the previous high priest (Onias III) but was also known as Menelaus, and 2 Maccabees, which only calls him Menelaus and does not suggest that he was the son of an Onias. According to Josephus, then, the father of the Onias who went to Egypt was Onias IV, while according to Maccabees he was Onias III.

3. The sons of Aaron, whose descendants were priests, as opposed to the other Levites, who served as their assistants.

4. Josephus *Jewish Antiquities* 20.10 in modern editions. Josephus says there that Alcimus was "of the stock of Aaron, but not of that family of Onias," which Sigonio took to mean that he was therefore from one of the non-priestly Levite houses. But as Cunaeus says here, of the twenty-four priestly families descended from the sons of Aaron only one supplied high priests. It was therefore from one of the others that he thinks Alcimus came.

5. Cunaeus makes the distinction between "high priest" and "other priests" clearer than it is in English (or Hebrew) by using two different Latin terms—*pontifex* ("bridge-builder," an important Roman priesthood) for the high priest, and *sacerdos* (a more generic term) for the others.

6. Maimonides *Mishneh Torah*, Laws of Vessels of the Sanctuary 4:15.

7. A grandson of Herod to whom Claudius had given a kingdom in Lebanon.

8. From the Latin for "shoulder."

9. In classical literature, the heart is the seat of both emotion and thought.

10. A Latin translation of the part of the *Jewish War* that describes the fall of Jerusalem and the Temple; cf. Josephus *Jewish War* 5.5.7.

11. ταύτην τὴν ἐσθῆτα οὐκ ἐφόρει ὁ ἀρχιερεὺς τὸν ἄλλον χρόνον, λιτοτέραν δὲ ἀνελάμβανεν, ὁπότε δὲ εἰσίοι εἰς τὸ ἄδυλον. εἰσῄει δὲ ἅπαξ κατὰ ἐνιαυτὸν μόνον ἐν ᾗ νηστεύειν ἔθος ἡμέρα πάντας τῷ θεῷ. The standard editions of this text differ from Cunaeus' version: instead of *monon* ("only, sole"), which would refer to the Day of Atonement as being the only occasion on which the priest entered, they read *monos*, referring to the high priest as the only person to go in on that day. This is significant because in chapter 4, Cunaeus will insist that the priest went in alone not just on the Day of Atonement, but all the time.

12. Leviticus 16:4.

13. Maimonides *Mishneh Torah*, Laws of Vessels of the Sanctuary 8:3. בגדי לבן הם ארבעה כלים ששמש בהן כהן גדול ביום הכפורים וארבעתן לבנים ומן הפשתן לבדו הן: כתנת. ומכנסים. ואבנט. ומצנפת.

14. A band of wool worn around the head by Roman priests, to which Cunaeus is comparing the priestly *mitznefet*.

15. I.e. completely burned.

16. Leviticus 16:2–4.

17. Leviticus 16:32.

18. I.e. embroidered.

19. In the classical world, an especially expensive kind of flax.

20. τὴν ἱερὴν ἐσθῆτα.

21. Josephus *Jewish Antiquities* 15.11.4.

22. An important Roman priest, who wore a distinctive kind of headdress.

23. Maimonides *Mishneh Torah*, Laws of Vessels of the Sanctuary 8:2.

24. The Hebrew name for the hat—*migba'at*—would therefore come from the same root as *giv'a*, "hill" (though Maimonides doesn't actually say this).

25. Joseph Caro, the sixteenth-century authority who also wrote the *Shulhan Aruch*.

26. מחוסר בגדים.

27. Maimonides *Mishneh Torah*, Laws of Vessels of the Sanctuary 10:5.

28. I.e. about the future.

29. Presumably the *shechina*, or divine Presence, found in Jewish thought.

30. Maimonides *Mishneh Torah*, Laws of Vessels of the Sanctuary 10:10.

31. This sentiment is actually a partial paraphrase from the Roman poet Vergil, *Aeneid* 10.502.

32. Maimonides *Mishneh Torah*, Laws of Vessels of the Sanctuary 10:10–12.

33. A traditional Jewish practice, performed upon learning of the death of a close relative.

34. Maimonides *Mishneh Torah*, Laws of Vessels of the Sanctuary 5:6.

35. Cunaeus is referring to a comment of the *Kesef Mishneh*.

36. The high priest at the time of Jesus' trial.

37. Matthew 26:64–65: Jesus implies that he is the Messiah, and Caiaphas calls him a blasphemer.

38. The law therefore served the purpose of further distinguishing the high priest from the others.

39. A prohibition which was applied to all Jews only in the Middle Ages.

40. Maimonides *Mishneh Torah*, Laws of Vessels of the Sanctuary 5:10.

41. Ibid. 5:7. ‫לשכת כהן גדול‬.

42. Ibid. As opposed to the outlying districts.

43. Perhaps the most important Roman priesthood. The pope is called "pontiff" by analogy, and Cunaeus himself uses *pontifex* as the translation of "high priest." The office of *pontifex* was filled by members of important political families, which is why in this instance it went from Lepidus to Augustus, both of whom were members of the powerful Second Triumvirate at the end of the Roman Republic.

44. Who would later be known as Augustus, the first Roman emperor.

45. For the story, cf. Dio Cassius *Roman History* 54.27.3.

46. Paul.

47. Letter to the Hebrews 9:7. εἰς τὴν δευτέραν σκηνὴν ἅπαξ τοῦ ἐνιαυτοῦ μόνος ὁ ἀρχιερεὺς εἰσῄει οὐ χωρὶς αἵματος.

48. Maimonides *Mishneh Torah*, Laws of the Temple 7:19. ‫בית קדש הקדשים מקודש‬ ‫מבין ההיכל שאין נכנס לשם אלא כהן גדול ביום הכפורים בשעת העבודה‬.

49. The *kaporet*, sometimes translated "mercy seat."

50. Leviticus 16:2–8. As before, Cunaeus quotes some of the same text he has already quoted elsewhere, but he translates it somewhat differently.

51. The Holy of Holies.

52. Hebrew *kodesh*, "holy."

53. Exodus 30:1, 6–7.

54. A reference to the classical theory of four humors, according to which an excess of phlegm makes a person sluggish.

55. It is actually verse 5.

56. Exodus 40:26.

57. A Hellenistic Jewish philosopher of the first century CE, whose work became an important influence on Christian Neoplatonist thought.

58. About the location of the incense altar.

59. ὁ νόμος προσέταξε δύο κατασκευασθῆναι βωμοὺς ἢ ταῖς ὕλαις, καὶ τοῖς τόποις, ἢ ταῖς χρείαις διαφέροντας. ὁ μὲν γὰρ ἐκ λίθων λογάδων ἀτμήτων ἀνῳκοδόμηται, ἢ ἐν ὑπαίθρῳ παρὰ ταῖς τοῦ νεὼ προβάβεσιν ἵδρυται καὶ γέγονε πρὸς χρείαν τὴν τῶν ἐναίμ ων. ὁ δὲ χρυσοῦ μὲν κατεσκεύασται, ἵδρυται δ᾽ ἐν ἀδύτῳ εἴσω τοῦ προτέρου καταπετάσματος, ὃς οὐδενὶ τῶν ἄλλων ἔστιν ὁρατὸς ὅτι μὴ τοῖς ἁγνεύουσι τῶν ἱερεων· καὶ γέγονε πρὸς χρείαν τὴν τῶν θυμιαμάτων. The passage actually comes from Philo's work *On the Special Laws* (1:273–274), but Cunaeus calls it by the title it bears in a contemporary printed edition of selections from this work.

60. Luke 1:9.

61. The father of John the Baptist.

62. Luke 1:10. πᾶν τὸ πλῆθος τοῦ λαοῦ ἦν προσευχόμενον ἔξω, τῇ ὥρᾳ τοῦ θυμιάματος.

63. Luke 1:21. ἦν ὁ λαὸς προσδοκῶν τὸν Ζαχαρίαν. καὶ ἐθαύμαζον ἐν τῷ χρονίζειν αὐτὸν.

64. Philo *On the Special Laws* I.72. ὁ νεὼς παντὸς λόγου κρείσσων, ὡς ἐκ τῶν περιφαινομένων ἔστι τεκμήρασθαι. τὰ γὰρ ἐντὸς ἀόρατα παντί τῳ, πλὴν ἑνὶ τῷ ἀρχιερεῖ.

65. Ibid. καὶ τούτῳ μέντοι δι᾽ ἔτους ἐπιτετραμμένον ἅπαξ εἰσιέναι πάντ᾽ ἔστιν ὁρατὰ.

66. Cunaeus is bothered by the fact that although this statement begins with the word *tamen*, "yet," it does not seem to be making a contrast: if the priest could go in, why *wouldn't* he be allowed to see everything?

67. καὶ τούτῳ μέντοι δι᾽ ἔτους ἐπιτετραμμένον ἅπαξ εἰσιέναι, πάντ᾽ οὐκ ἔστιν ὁρατὰ. Here Cunaeus adds the word "not" to the Greek text of Philo.

68. πυρεῖον μὲν γὰρ ἀνθράκων πλῆρες καὶ θυμιάματος εἰσκομίζει. πολλῆς δὲ ἀναδιδομένης, ὡς εἰκὸς, ἀτμίδος κατέχεται τὰ ἐν κύκλῳ πάντα. καὶ ἡ ὄψις ἐπισκιάζεται, ἢ ἀνακοπήν ἴσχει, πρόσω ἀδυνατοῦσα.

69. Cunaeus presumably means the time right after the exiles returned from Babylonia, which was marked by conflict with the Samaritans and disagreements within the community.

70. 1 Maccabees 4:47.

71. 1 Maccabees (which is written in Greek) is now thought to have been based on a Hebrew original of the second century BCE.

72. Exodus 30:10.

73. Leviticus 16:18.

74. Maimonides *Mishneh Torah*, Laws of Vessels of the Sanctuary 10:11.

75. Judges 1:1–2, 20:18.

76. 1 Samuel 10:22. These texts actually say only that the people consulted God.

77. Deuteronomy 34:10.

78. Maimonides *Mishneh Torah*, Laws of Service on the Day of Atonement 1:2.

79. By contact with a ritually unclean person or thing.

80. Cunaeus is assuming that the word *matkinin*, "arrange," means (as it often does) "make a change in the law."

81. In the techniques of the rituals.

82. Which the high priest would have to perform himself.

83. Which it was feared might happen while he was in the Holy of Holies.

84. Maimonides *Mishneh Torah*, Laws of Service on the Day of Atonement 1:3. מתקינין לו כהן גדול אחר שאם יארע בזה פיסול יעבוד האחר תחתיו. בין שאירע בו פיסול קודם תמיד של שחר בין שאירע בו פיסול אחר שהקריב קרבנות זה שנכנס תחתיו אינו צריך חינוך. עבר יום הכפורים הרי הראשון חוזר לעבודתו והשני עובר. ואם מת הראשון זה שני מתמני [מתמנה] תחתיו. *They arrange another high priest for him so that if this one accidentally becomes invalid, the other one will serve in his place. Whether he becomes invalid before the daily morning sacrifice or after he has made his offerings, his substitute does not need any training. Once the Day of Atonement has passed, the first one returns to his duties and the second moves on; and if the first one dies, the second is appointed in his place.*

85. Josephus *Jewish Antiquities* 17.6.4 in modern editions.

86. Though neither Josephus nor Cunaeus say so explicitly, the Rabbis were generally concerned that the high priest might have an emission which would make him impure. Josephus says (perhaps out of respect) that the high priest was dreaming about his own wife.

87. Maimonides *Mishneh Torah*, Laws of Vessels of the Sanctuary 4:16.

88. From the Greek *katholikos*.

89. I.e. the Sanhedrin.

90. *And he will take a brazier full of coals from the altar, from before the Lord... and he will bring it within the veil; and put the incense on the fire before the Lord, so that the cloud of the incense may cover the mercy seat which is upon the testimony, lest he die.* Cf. Maimonides *Mishneh Torah*, Laws of Service on the Day of Atonement 1:7.

91. Leviticus 16:2. בענן אראה על הכפרת.

92. Maimonides *Mishneh Torah*, Laws of Service on the Day of Atonement 1:7. משביעין אנו עליך במי ששכן את שמו בבית הזה שלא תשנה דבר מכל דבר שאמרנו לך.

93. Since this last comment does not come from Maimonides, it is not clear what Cunaeus is referring to here; he may have in mind the fact that the high priest was read to from the Bible to keep him from falling asleep.

94. Maimonides *Mishneh Torah*, Laws of Service on the Day of Atonement 3:7.

95. Ibid.

96. Cunaeus seems to be bothered by the degree to which the practices associated with the scapegoat in Rabbinic law have no explicit basis in the Bible.

97. מתרבה בגדים.

98. מתרבה משחה.

99. ריבוי בגדים ומשחה.

100. Though Maimonides, whom Cunaeus is summarizing here, doesn't mention the people, Cunaeus seems to be importing the idea from the biblical source for the priest's sin offering (Leviticus 4:3).

101. Leviticus 4:3.

102. Maimonides *Mishneh Torah*, Laws of Vessels of the Sanctuary 4:12–13. וממנין
כהן גדול הוא ראש לכל הכהנים ומושחין אותו בשמן המשחה. ומלבישין אותו בגדי כהונה גדולה. ואם אין שם
שמן המשחה מרבין אותו בגדי כהונה גדולה בלבד. כשם שמתרבה בשמן המשחה כך מתרבה בבגדים: כיצד
מרבים אותו בבגדים. לובש שמנה בגדים ופושטן וחוזר ולובשן למחר שבעת ימים יום אחר יום. וכשם שריבוי
בגדים שבעה כך משיחה בשמן שבעה יום אחר יום.

103. Maimonides *Mishneh Torah*, Laws of Vessels of the Sanctuary 4:14. אין בין כהן
משוח בשמן המשחה למרובה בגדי' אלא פר שמביא כהן המשוח אם שגג באחד מן מצו' שחייב עליהן חטא.

104. Cunaeus brought the previous two quotes in Hebrew without translation.

105. The sons of Aaron.

106. Josephus *Jewish Antiquities* 7.14.7.

107. A saying found in the Roman satire called *Apocolocyntosis*, which is full of improbable events.

108. Maimonides *Mishneh Torah*, Laws of Vessels of the Sanctuary 4:4–5.

109. Cf. Luke 1:8.

110. As usual, Cunaeus is repeating the reference to the Talmud he has found in the *Kesef Mishneh*.

111. Literally, "hewn stone."

112. Cunaeus presumably means the *bet av*, one of the twenty-four groups of priestly families descended from two of the sons of Levi.

113. Josephus *Jewish War* 5.5.7.

114. Maimonides *Mishneh Torah*, Laws of Entrance into the Sanctuary 6:11–12.
בית דין הגדול היו יושבין בלשכת הגזית ועיקר מעשיהם התדיר שהיו יושבין ודנין את הכהונה ובודקין הכהנים
ביוחסין ובמומים: כל כהן שנמצא פסול בייחוסו לובש שחורים ומתעטף שחורים ויוצא מן העזרה: וכל מי שנמצא
שלם וכשר לובש לבנים ונכנס ומשמש עם אחיו הכהנים: מי שנמצא כשר בייחוסו ונמצא בו מום: יושב בלשכת
העצים ומתלע עצים למערכה וחולק בקדשים עם אנשי בית אב שלו ואוכל.

115. Cunaeus quotes the original without translation.

116. Josephus *Jewish Antiquities* 14.13.10.

117. The Parthians had taken him captive and made his brother Antigonus high priest.

118. Maimonides *Mishneh Torah*, Laws of the Sanhedrin 2:1.

119. Josephus *Jewish Antiquities* 4.8.17. πρασσέτω δὲ μηδὲν ὁ βασιλεὺς δίχα τοῦ ἀρχιερέως καὶ τῆς τῶν γερουσιαστῶν γνώμης. This idea does not appear in the text on which Josephus is basing himself (Deuteronomy 17:13–20), but Josephus (like Cunaeus after him) has been influenced by the classical idea that the best form of government is aristocracy, and if there is a king he should at least be advised by aristocrats like the Sanhedrin.

120. Exodus 19:6.

121. 2 Chronicles 19:11. Though this term was originally a Persian title for the governor of a province, Cunaeus presumably has in mind something much more modest. The passage in Chronicles has here "officers."

122. 1 Chronicles 26:30.

123. 1 Chronicles 26:31–32.

124. 1 Chronicles says they were members of the family of Hevron, who was one of the grandsons of Levi.

125. I.e. the Judeans.

126. Cunaeus is combining two critiques of one-man rule: a Roman one, in which *superbia* (arrogance) causes a leader to place himself above the other citizens; and a Jewish one, in which only God can be the true ruler (i.e. the "theocracy" he says existed in the time of the Bible).

127. Cunaeus presumably means "people" in the sense of the non-Levite masses, while "community" would include the aristocrats of the priestly class and the Sanhedrin.

128. Cunaeus is using "Israelite" here not as he has elsewhere, but as Maimonides does—to refer to Jews who are neither priests nor Levites.

129. It is not clear where Cunaeus has gotten this idea. He may be extrapolating from the rule that those who could not go to Jerusalem had to gather in their own towns.

130. All the above comes from Maimonides *Mishneh Torah*, Laws of Vessels of the Sanctuary 6:1–2 (though Maimonides says that the problem was not that the people had to travel great distances, but that they could not all fit into the Temple courtyard).

131. Ibid. 6:3. שלא יצאו מעונג שבת לצום.

132. Ibid. 6:4–6. The Torah was read in public on these occasions.

133. Though this rhetorical device ("see for yourself") was often used by classical authors, it should not be taken to mean that such primary sources were actually available to the reader, or even that the author himself had seen them.

134. Cunaeus is presumably thinking of the common expression "the sons of Aaron, the priests."

135. Cf. 1 Chronicles 15:16–22, which does not however say that there were twenty-four families of these.

136. Gibeon was a Canaanite city that tricked Joshua into making peace; rather than break this treaty the Israelites decided to turn its inhabitants into conscripted laborers. See Joshua 9.

137. Literally "subjects."

138. Maimonides *Mishneh Torah*, Laws of Forbidden Intercourse 12:22–23.

139. Maimonides *Mishneh Torah*, Laws of Vessels of the Sanctuary 3:8.

140. Ibid.

141. Ibid. 3:9–11. Unless the Bible specified otherwise, the violation of such a negative commandment was to be punished by lashes.

142. Josephus *Jewish Antiquities* 8.3.

143. Plutarch *Moralia* 819e.

144. Maimonides *Mishneh Torah*, Laws of the Temple 7:2. לא יכנס אדם להר הבית במקלו או במנעל שברגליו או באפונדתו ובמעות הצרורין לו בסדינו.

145. Mark 11:16. ἵνα μή τις διενέγκη σκεῦος διὰ τοῦ ἱεροῦ.

146. As in classical texts, "Asia" is today's Asia Minor.

147. The midrash known as *Pirkei deRabbi Eliezer*, which the *Kesef Mishneh* mentions as the source of this opinion in his comment on the passage from which Cunaeus has taken it, Maimonides *Mishneh Torah*, Laws of the Temple 2:2.

148. Midrash Genesis Rabba 2:7.

149. These references come from the same comment of the *Kesef Mishneh*. However, the tractate of the Jerusalem Talmud to which Cunaeus refers has no twenty-third chapter; he has misread the letters כ"ג, which stand for *kohen gadol* (high priest)—the name of one of the chapters—as their numerical equivalent.

150. Maimonides *Mishneh Torah*, Laws of the Temple 2:2. שנברא ממקום כפרתו.

151. Cunaeus seems to mean that even though the Jews admit that Jerusalem is the spot where their sins were forgiven, they refuse to believe that this was accomplished by the Crucifixion.

152. Josephus *Against Apion* 2.8.

153. Josephus *Jewish War* 6.9.3. This is misleading—Josephus is describing the Passover sacrifice made by the entire people at once, on the eve of the festival; in fact, Josephus mentions it as a means of calculating the size of the nation.

154. Maimonides *Mishneh Torah*, Laws of the Daily Offerings and Additional Offerings 2:4. ראשונה מערכה גדולה שעליה מקריבין התמיד עם שאר הקרבנות: שנייה בצדה קטנה שממנה לוקחין אש במחתה להקטיר קטורת בכל יום: שלישית אין עליה אלא לקיים מצות האש שנאמר אש תמיד תוקד.

155. This detail is not found in Maimonides; perhaps Cunaeus has added it to strengthen his claim that the incense altar was placed outside the Holy of Holies.

156. Leviticus 6:6.

157. Josephus *Jewish War* 2.17.6.

158. I.e. they brought enough wood to last the entire year.

159. The reason Cunaeus suggests there were twenty to thirty families at a time is presumably that—assuming each family had about ten or twelve people—he can then arrive at the figure of 120,000 which he has already mentioned as the population of Jerusalem.

160. A sacrifice which was burned entirely on the altar.

161. Cunaeus seems to have read Maimonides, who says (see below) that "this is" the wood offering, as though he had said "this is the reason for it."

162. I.e. to perform the practices associated with mourning, such as sitting on the ground.

163. Maimonides *Mishneh Torah*, Laws of Vessels of the Sanctuary 6:9. זמן קבוע
היה למשפחו' לצאת ליערים להביא עצים למערכ': ויום שיגיע לבני משפחה זו להביא העצים היו מקריבין
עולות נדבה וזהו קרבן העצים והיה להם כמו יום טוב.

164. Maimonides *Mishneh Torah*, Laws of the Temple 7:3.

165. Ibid. 7:4.

166. That is, whether they were found in the Torah and were not an innovation of the Rabbis.

167. The issue, according to Maimonides, was that the cubit of floor space taken up by the wall could have come from either (or both) of the two rooms it was dividing.

168. Maimonides *Mishneh Torah*, Laws of the Temple 4:2.

169. Ibid. 8:1–6. Cunaeus seems to be saying that the preferential treatment given to the priests was (as with the separate courtyards in the Temple) a proper expression of piety.

170. One of the most famous Hellenistic poets.

171. Callimachus *Hymns and Epigrams* 4.286. γηλεχέες θεράποντες ἀσιγήτοιο λέβητος. The priests attended the Pythia, a woman who gave oracles while suspended in a vat which hung over a cleft in the rock.

172. Maimonides *Mishneh Torah*, Laws of the Temple 8:2–3. Maimonides cites these verses to support specific features of the law on watches, but he does not feel the need to offer any biblical proofs for the institution itself.

173. Numbers 3 describes the duties of the Levites in the Tabernacle, to which Cunaeus is comparing the Talmudic description of their Temple duties.

174. And therefore (as Cunaeus has already pointed out) very unlike the portable Tabernacle.

175. As he has done before, Cunaeus is contrasting the written law of the Torah with the rulings of the Rabbis, which he considers worthless.

176. Maimonides *Mishneh Torah*, Laws of Vessels of the Sanctuary 7:1.

177. Ibid. 7:14.

178. The Roman satirist.

179. Juvenal *Satires* 6.397. The job of the *haruspex* was to interpret the future from the shape and appearance of the organs removed from sacrificed animals, and by observing the heavens.

180. I.e. his Seleucid successors.

181. The political leader of the returnees from Babylonia. See Haggai 1.

182. Cunaeus is presumably thinking of Josephus' critique of the Zealots, whom he blamed for stirring up pointless resistance and turning the Jews against each other. If not for them, Cunaeus is saying, the Jews would have defeated the Romans.

183. A Jewish work of the early Middle Ages which assigned specific dates to the events of the Bible and the Second Temple period.

184. Rabbi Yose ben Halafta, the Talmudic authority who is traditionally considered the author of *Seder Olam*.

185. היה ר' יוסי אומר מגלגלין זכות ליום זכות וחובה ליום חובה שנמצאת שנחרב הבית בראשונה אותו היום מוצאי שבת היה ומוצאי שביעי היתה ומשמרתו של יהויריב היתה ותשעה באב היה וכן שנייה ובזה ובזה הלוים עומדים על דוכן ואומרים שירה. וישב עלהם את אונם [עונם].

186. According to Josephus, Titus never meant for the Temple to be destroyed, and even tried to prevent it.

187. I.e. the Jewish state.

188. An aphorism of the Roman comic writer Publilius Syrus.

189. The destruction of a city was a favorite source of pathos for classical historians (including Josephus) who liked to make their work dramatic.

190. Matthew 24:2. οὐ μὴ ἀφεθῇ ὧδε λίθος ἐπὶ λίθον, ὅς οὐ μὴ καταλυθήσεται.

191. The Sabines were an ancient Italian people, the first to be taken over by the early Romans, whose disappointed hopes had become proverbial.

192. Emperor 117–138 CE.

193. The Jupiter whose cult was on the Capitoline Hill in Rome.

194. Cunaeus presumably means ancient authorities like Josephus.

195. Cf. 2 Kings 17:24.

196. The region north of the Black Sea.

197. The Persian state that bordered the Roman Empire to the East.

198. The Hellenistic poet Theocritus, in *Idylls* 14.48–49.

199. οὔτε λόγω τινὸς ἄξιοι, οὔτ' ἀριθμητοί,
     δύστανοι μεγαρῆες ἀτιμοτάτῃ ἐνὶ μοίρᾳ.

The point seems to be that the inhabitants of Megara (in Greece) were, like the Samaritans, an entire people held in contempt.

200. I.e. *Seder Eliyahu Rabba.*

201. ‏למה היה דוד המלך דומה לכותי המחזיר על הפתחים‎.

202. The king of the Philistine city of Gath; cf. 1 Samuel 21:10–15.

203. This comment implies that the Samaritans were so pitiable because by leaving their own communities, they had lost their rights as citizens (the states of classical antiquity were reluctant to extend such rights to immigrants).

204. Cunaeus is referring to the legislation of the Christian emperor Justinian (sixth century CE).

205. Apparently a legal device that allowed them to use their own procedures.

206. The "arrogance" mentioned in *Novella* 129 seems to refer to the frequency with which Samaritans who had ostensibly become Christians kept their traditional practices, such as observing the seventh day as the Sabbath.

207. 2 Kings 17:30–31.

208. In classical society, cooperation between states often centered on mutually respected cults.

209. 2 Kings 17:24–29.

210. "Superstition" was the standard Roman term for unfamiliar foreign religions.

211. Who was a contemporary of Alexander the Great.

212. This description of the sects is based on Josephus *Jewish War* 2.8.14; but though Josephus does criticize the Sadducees, he also praises the Pharisees for their legal interpretations.

213. Cunaeus seems to think that the Essenes were the last of the three sects to develop, presumably because Josephus mentions them last; but Josephus never attempts to date the origins of any of the sects. His order (Pharisees, Sadducees, Essenes) is based on the relative size and importance of each group.

214. Josephus emphasizes their purity, simplicity, and abstinence, which he admired a great deal.

215. Cunaeus' feeling that such disputes were worse than idolatry presumably had something to do with his experience of the religious conflicts of the seventeenth century.

216. Cunaeus presumably means not that there were no well-educated men, but that there was no one who had the divine inspiration needed to give the laws their deeper meaning; this is why he emphasizes that the scholars of the time were "mortal" and "human." As he explains in III.8, this situation continued until Christ gave the Apostles the ability to understand the mysteries of the Bible.

217. This is how Cunaeus characterizes the entire process of Rabbinic interpretation and the Oral Law which it served, just as he has already attacked the Rabbis for drawing conclusions not found in the text of the Bible itself.

218. Maimonides says this in the preface to his *Commentary on the Mishna*. According to tradition, when Elijah returns to announce the Messiah he will settle all the unresolved controversies of the Rabbis.

219. As opposed to being discussed in groups.

220. The Rabbinic tradition explains such disputes as the product not of interpretation *per se*, but of the carelessness with which students preserved the explanations they had received from their teachers, in a line of transmission going back to Moses.

221. The Nazirites were Israelites who took vows of abstinence (Numbers 6); the Kenites and the Rechabites were originally foreign tribes (and possibly one and the same tribe) that were incorporated into the Israelite nation.

222. By "recent times" Cunaeus means everything after the First Temple period.

223. Josephus *Life* 2.

224. Ibid.

225. Josephus *Jewish War* 2.13.4.

226. Followers of a man from the Golan named Judah, who refused to pay Roman taxes.

227. All this is essentially Josephus' view of things.

228. 44–46 CE.

229. Josephus *Jewish Antiquities* 20.5.1.

230. This man, whose name is not known, is also referred to as "the Egyptian" in the New Testament (Acts 21:38).

231. Josephus *Jewish Antiquities* 20.8.6.

232. Procurator 55–60 CE.

233. Josephus *Jewish Antiquities* 20.8.5. ληστηρίων ἡ χώρα ἀνεπλήσθη, καὶ γοήτων ἀνθρώπων, οἱ τὸν ὄχλον ἠπάτων. δείξειν ἔφασαν ἐναργῆ τέρατα ἢ σημεῖα κατὰ τὴν τοῦ Θεοῦ πρόνοιαν γενόμενα· καὶ πολλοὶ πεισθέντες, τῆς ἀφροσύνης τιμορίας ὑπέσχον.

234. Cf. Cicero *On Behalf of Murena* 22.

235. I.e. the seven nations, whom Cunaeus has already described as completely devoid of human decency.

236. Cf. Josephus *Against Apion* 1.22.

237. Though Cunaeus wants to prove the Jews' bravery as soldiers, the stories in Josephus to which he refers actually talk about their resistance to changing their customs even under threat of punishment.

238. ἔα αὐτούς στρατεύσιν τοῖς πατρῴοις ἔθεσιν ἐμμένοντας, καὶ κατὰ ταῦτα ζῶντας. This passage actually comes from *Jewish Antiquities* 11.8.5, a mistake that implies either that Cunaeus was consulting not the text of Josephus but a selection

of passages from his various works; or that Cunaeus himself had first copied down passages from different places and only then inserted them into his text (which could also explain why he sometimes misquotes or misspells the Greek).

239. In 479 BCE.

240. A fifth-century BCE poet who wrote an epic about the Persians.

241. The passage comes from a description of the various armies, each from a different nation, which took part in Xerxes' invasion of Greece.

242. Josephus *Against Apion* 1.22.
Τῷ δ' ὄπιθεν διέβαινε γένος θαυμαστὸν ἰδέσθαι,
Γλῶσσαν μὲν φοίνισσαν ἀπὸ στομάτων ἀφιέντες.
Ὤικεε δ' ἐν Σολύμοις ὄρεσι πλατέῃ ἐνὶ λίμνῃ,
Αὐχμαλέοι κορυφάς, τροχοκούριδες· αὐτὰρ ὕπερθεν
Ἵππων δαρτὰ πρόσωπ' ἐφόρουν ἐσκληκότα καπνῷ.

243. Like some other classical authors, Josephus equates "Solymi" with "Hierosolyma," i.e. Jerusalem, which he takes as a Greek name (*hieros* means "holy" in Greek). The mountains would then be the Judean hills.

244. τροχοκούριδες. I.e. like a monk's tonsure.

245. Leviticus 19:27. As he often does when quoting Latin and Greek texts as clauses within one of his own sentences, Cunaeus has adjusted the grammar of the biblical quote; here he changes it from second to third person: שלא יקפו פאת ראשׁ|ם.

246. Poseidon.

247. Homer *Odyssey* 5:282–84.
Τὸν δ'ἐξ αἰθιόπων ἀνίων κρείων ἐνοσίχθων
Τηλόθεν ἐκ Σολύμων ὀρέων ἴδεν· εἴσατο γὰρ οἱ
Πόντον ἐπιπλείων.

248. Pisidia was a country in southwestern Asia Minor.

249. Cunaeus seems to be thinking here of Aramaic rather than Phoenician as such.

250. Maimonides *Mishneh Torah*, Laws of Kings and Wars 5:1. מלחמת המצוה היא מלחמת שבעה עממים ומלחמת עמלק ועזרת ישראל מיד צר שבא עליהן.

251. This reference is incorrect; and though these peoples are mentioned in chapters 23 and 33, God says there (and in Deuteronomy 7) that he himself will destroy them. Only Deuteronomy 20:17—which is the one source Maimonides does quote—tells the people themselves to do so.

252. Deuteronomy 7:1.

253. Ibid. 25:17–9.

254. Maimonides *Mishneh Torah*, Laws of Kings and Wars 5:1. מלחמת הרשות היא המלחמה שנלחם המלך עם שאר העם להרחיב גבול ישראל ולהרבות גדלתו ושמעו.

255. Maimonides *Mishneh Torah*, Laws of Kings and Wars 6:1–4.

256. That is, the age of monotheism. Cf. Maimonides *Mishneh Torah*, Laws of Kings and Wars 6:1.

257. Though Maimonides does not say this, it does suit Cunaeus' ideas about natural law.

258. Maimonides *Mishneh Torah*, Laws of Kings and Wars 9:1.

259. Cunaeus is not using the term "kabbalistic" in its modern sense; he is simply echoing Maimonides, who says that the six precepts were a *kabbalah*—a tradition—from Moses.

260. Cunaeus has slightly misunderstood the point of Maimonides, who says (see note 262 below) that though intuition may tell us this is so, it is also commanded explicitly by the text of the Torah.

261. Genesis 9:4.

262. Maimonides *Mishneh Torah*, Laws of Kings and Wars 9:1. על ששה דברים נצטווה אדם הראשון על עכום ועל ברכת השם ועל שפיכות דמים ועל גילוי עריות ועל הגזל ועל הדינים: אף על פי שכולן הן קבלה בידינו ממשה רבינו והדעת נוטה להן מכלל דברי תורה יראה שעל אלו נצטווה: הוסיף לנח אבר מן החי שנאמ' אך בשר בנפשו דמו לא תאכלו: נמצאו שבעה מצוות: וכן היה הדבר בכל העולם עד אברהם בא אברהם נצטווה יתר על אלו במילה.

263. Maimonides *Mishneh Torah*, Laws of Idolatry and Heathenism 1:1.

264. Maimonides suggests that at first men worshiped the stars only because they saw that God had given them a place of honor.

265. Since Maimonides doesn't draw any distinction between the worship of stars and of planets, it may be that Cunaeus is singling out the latter as an even lower form of religion (as well as drawing on the association between the planets and the Greco-Roman pantheon).

266. Maimonides *Mishneh Torah*, Laws of Idolatry and Heathenism 1:3.

267. According to the Midrash, Nimrod the king of Ur imprisoned Abraham for ten years and tried but failed to kill him.

268. Maimonides *Mishneh Torah*, Laws of Idolatry and Heathenism 1:2. עמודו של עולם. Though Maimonides is calling him "the pillar of the world," Cunacus (as he does in other places) interprets *olam* "world" to mean "age," as it does in certain Hebrew phrases.

269. I.e. the practice of idolatry before the time of Abraham.

270. While the Rabbis thought such a city should be destroyed for its impiety, Cunaeus seems to think it was guilty of violating natural law, which also governed the relations between nations. He says that Maimonides' discussion of idolatry "sheds light" on this issue because if, outside of Abraham's community, all cities were idolatrous, they were therefore violating at least one of the seven precepts and had to be treated accordingly.

271. Joshua 11:19-20.

272. Fetials were Roman priests in charge of the rituals of warfare and diplomacy; Cunaeus is comparing them to the Israelites who went ahead of the army to offer peace.

273. Though they would have become slaves of the Israelites.

274. Joshua 9.

275. Assuming, of course, it is true that even though they were Canaanites they could still reach a settlement.

276. Cunaeus seems to be conflating the end of Joshua, chapter 8 (where Joshua reads all the laws to the people), with the beginning of chapter 9 ("When... the Hittites, the Amorites, the Canaanites, the Perizzites, the Hivites, and the Jebusites heard of this," i.e. Joshua's victories) and concluding that it was the law of destroying the seven nations that they had heard about.

277. In Maimonides *Mishneh Torah*, Laws of Kings and Wars 6:5. Maimonides, however, says that the Gibeonites were afraid because they did *not* know the law, which would in fact have given them another chance.

278. Since neither the Bible nor Maimonides mention the idea of expiation in a voluntary war, Cunaeus may be inferring it from the statement (Deuteronomy 20:18) that the Canaanites had to be destroyed so that they would not cause the people to sin.

279. Thus, as in the case of the seven Noahide laws, the nation to be destroyed has violated natural law.

280. It is because the sins listed here are all some form of incest that Cunaeus describes the Canaanites as unnatural.

281. Leviticus 18:25.

282. Deuteronomy 23:4-7.

283. These actions are similar to those of the Canaanites in the sense that they also show a disregard for the natural rights of others.

284. The Israelites.

285. The seven nations.

286. Maimonides *Mishneh Torah*, Laws of Kings and Wars 6:6. אף על פי שאין שואלים בשלומם אם השלימו מעצמם תחלה מקבלין אותן.

287. Maimonides *Mishneh Torah*, Laws of Kings and Wars 7:1. אחד מלחמת הרשות ואחד מלחמת המצוה ממנין כהן לדבר אל העם בשעת המלחמה ומושחין אותו בשמן המשחה וזהו הנקרא משוח המלחמה.

288. Deuteronomy 20:3-4.

289. Maimonides *Mishneh Torah*, Laws of Kings and Wars 7:2-3.

290. Maimonides actually says that the priest recites the words at the border; but Cunaeus has misread the word *sefar*, "border," as *sefer*, "book."

291. Deuteronomy 20:5-9.

292. 1 Samuel 11:6-7.

293. A number of emperors were considered gods after their deaths.

294. The knights were a social class ranked just below the Roman Senate.

295. Suetonius *Augustus* 24.

296. Digest 49.16.4.12.

297. Josephus *Against Apion* 2.34. περὶ γε τοῦ μήτε χλευάζειν, μήτε βλασφημεῖν τοὺς νομιζόμενους θεοὺς παρ" ἑτ'ροις αὐτῆς ἕνεκα προσηγορίας τοῦ θεοῦ.

298. I.e because they were called God.

299. Exodus 22:27. אלהים לא תקלל.

300. Josephus *Against Apion* 1.22.

301. Maimonides *Mishneh Torah*, Laws of Kings and Wars 6:11. שצרין על עיירות כותים בשבת ועושין עמהם מלחמה בשבת.

302. Cf. 1 Maccabees 2:39-41.

303. A historian of the Hellenistic period.

304. Josephus *Against Apion* 1.22.

305. The daughter of the Seleucid king Antiochus I.

306. One of Alexander's generals, and the first Greek ruler of Egypt.

307. Cunaeus is presumably relying on *Jewish War* 2.16.4, where King Agrippa says that Pompey was able to besiege the Jews successfully because he made his preparations on the Sabbath. However, it is clear from *Antiquities* 14.4.2-3 that the Jews did in fact respond to direct attacks on that day; but since Pompey knew that they would ignore anything less than an attack, he made sure to build his siege works on the Sabbath, when the Jews would not try to tear them down. Cunaeus, who was presumably aware of this, chooses to ignore it in order to strengthen his point.

308. Cunaeus may have in mind the self-sacrifice with which the Maccabees and their followers were later associated, and which made them models for the Christian martyrs of the Roman Empire.

309. Josephus *Against Apion* 1.22.

310. Augury—watching the sky and the direction in which birds flew—was a traditional form of Roman prophecy.

311. This is a paraphrase of Cicero *Letters to Friends* 6.6.

312. Pliny *Natural History* 28.17.

313. Deuteronomy 22:5: *A woman shall not wear the appurtenances of a man, and a man shall not wear women's clothing; for all who do this are an abomination to the Lord.*

314. Josephus *Jewish Antiquities* 4.7.43. φυλάσσετε μάλιστα ἐν ταῖς μάχαις, ὥστε μήτε γυναῖκα ἀνδρικῇ σκευῇ χρῆσθαι, μήτε ἄνδρα στολῇ γυναικείῳ.

315. That is, they were made to wear the toga. Although this was the traditional garment of Roman men, it was also worn by prostitutes, who spent their time in the public places frequented by men, where decent women would not go.

316. Martial *Epigrams* 10.52. The joke is that a eunuch wearing a toga looked like a woman (Thelys means *female*) who was being forced to wear one.

317. Xenophon *Education of Cyrus* 8.40.

318. As in his description of the Egyptians in I.5, Cunaeus is referring to the classical theory that people who live in warm southern climates (like Egyptians and Jews) are too soft, and those who live in cold northern ones (like Germans and Britons) are too hard.

319. His name was actually Lucius.

320. Seneca *To Helvia on Consolation* 7.1. Seneca was a Roman thinker in the court of Nero (first century CE), who wrote an essay in which he used philosophy to comfort his mother Helvia during the time of his exile from Rome.

321. Since Alexander and his army were Macedonians, this refers to the colonies he founded in the East.

322. A region of Greece.

323. The Phoenician colony of Carthage, in modern Tunisia.

324. These were Carthaginians who established communities on the Spanish coast.

325. In classical geography, "Asia" is Asia Minor and "Africa" is North Africa above the Sahara.

326. Josephus *Against Apion* 2.4.

327. The second Ptolemy to rule Egypt, in the third century BCE.

328. Ptolemy VI and his sister-wife.

329. Josephus *Against Apion* 2.5: They were put in charge of the army.

330. Augustus' friend and military commander.

331. Proconsul of Asia, 31–27 BCE.

332. Proconsul of Asia in 4 BCE.

333. Josephus *Jewish Antiquities* 16.6.1–7.

334. Cunaeus may mean to imply that because these communities were so cut off, they did not know they had already sent the Jerusalemites more than enough money.

335. John Hyrcanus, the Hasmonean ruler.

336. The son of Demetrius, who was in turn the nephew of Antiochus Epiphanes.

337. Josephus *Jewish Antiquities* 7.15.3. The dating (which is very inaccurate) belongs to Josephus. The Greek talent is equal to about 26 kg.

338. Ibid.

339. This story is found in Herodotus *Histories* 1.187, though it is told about Nitocris, who like Semiramis was a legendary queen of Assyria.

340. 1 Kings 10:22: *Once every three years the fleet of ships of Tarshish used to come bringing gold, silver, ivory, apes, and peacocks.*

341. Josephus *Jewish Antiquities* 8.7.4. ὅτι τοῦ ἀργυρίου τοσοῦτον ἐποίησε πλῆθος ἐν Ἰεροσολύμοις ὁ βασιλεὺς, ὅσον ἦν καὶ λίθων.

342. That is, the right to try their own civil cases.

343. Cf. Maimonides *Mishneh Torah*, Laws of Kings and Wars 5:9. When Cunaeus calls the law "harsh" he is presumably referring to the statement that one may not leave the land unless there is such great famine that the price of wheat has doubled.

344. Maimonides *Mishneh Torah*, Laws of Kings and Wars 5:12. כל הדר בחוצה לארץ כאילו עובד עכום.

345. 1 Samuel 26:19.

346. Maimonides *Mishneh Torah*, Laws of Kings and Wars 5:9.

347. Ibid. 5:8. מפני שמעשיה מקולקלים יותר מכל הארצות.

348. Ibid. 5:7. שאלסכנדריאה בכלל האיסור.

349. That Maimonides feels the need to specify Alexandria may well have to do not with the behavior of its Jews, but with the fact that it was on the coast of Egypt and had never been considered a part of the country proper (whose borders he gives in the same chapter).

350. I.e. the fighting between Alexander's successors over the territory between Syria and Egypt.

351. Josephus *Against Apion* 1.22. Josephus attributes this information to Hecataeus, and there is no other evidence for a high priest with this name.

352. This is an odd proof of persecution. By "undisturbed," the text means "given an exemption from their civic obligations" (in this case guardianship of a minor). Cunaeus may be influenced here by the fact that in the late Roman Empire, people often measured their status by their ability to get out of just such civic obligations.

353. It was a Purim custom to burn Haman in effigy; though the crosses mentioned here could be the gallows on which Haman planned to hang Mordecai and was then hanged himself, the law itself assumes they are anti-Christian symbols.

354. This presumably refers to the restrictions placed on the marriages of priests, and of people who were somehow related to each other.

355. *Codex* 1.9.7, "On Jews and Heaven-worshipers."

356. II.3.

357. 2 Samuel 12:8.

358. Leviticus 18:18.

359. Cf. Luke 16:18; Mark 10:11–12.

360. Cunaeus mentions these three specific emperors (from the late fourth and early fifth centuries CE) because they are all mentioned in the above passages of Justinian's *Codex* as authors of the rules on Jewish marriage and litigation.

361. It is not clear whether Cunaeus is ignoring the development of rabbinic civil law because he considers it illegitimate, or because he thinks of the Talmud as a repository of biblical interpretation rather than a source of contemporary legal procedure.

362. I.e. civil as opposed to religious law.

363. I.e. the Ten Commandments.

364. Cicero.

365. I.e. so that everyone can rest from their labors.

366. *Seder Eliyahu Rabba*, section 2.

367. That is, the six days of creation preceding the first Sabbath represent six millennia of labor, to be followed by a seventh millennium of peace.

368. Tacitus *Histories* 5.4.4.

369. In the same passage Tacitus reports a belief that the Jews originally came from Mount Ida in Crete, and that their name was corrupted from *Idaioi* (Ideans) to *Ioudaioi* (Jews). If the Ideans worshiped Saturn, then naturally they would have honored the seventh day.

370. In his comments on Exodus 20:13.

371. That is, the last nine of the Ten Commandments; ibn Ezra omits the first ("I am the Lord your God...") because the number one is, like God, the unchanging source of all the others, and therefore beyond the natural world.

372. I.e. the Sun, the Moon, Mercury, Venus, Mars, Jupiter, Saturn, the Zodiac, and the Prime Mover (which turned the other spheres). The command to rest on the Sabbath, then, corresponds to the sphere of Saturn.

373. That is, we are to rest on the Sabbath because only then are both these un-lucky planets dominant—one at night, and one during the day. For the rest of the week they rule on different days.

374. A paraphrase of Horace *Satires* 1.10, which makes fun of bad writers.

375. In his comments on Exodus 20:7.

376. The prophet.

377. 2 Kings 4:23.

378. In antiquity, Pythagoras was thought to have been the founder of a sect that lived according to his teachings.

379. The legendary second king of Rome, who was said to have founded its re-ligious institutions.

380. According to Plutarch's *Life of Coriolanus* 25.2, Numa decreed that a her-ald would be appointed to make sure the official who performed the rites was not distracted.

381. Pliny *Natural History* 31.24.

382. Horace *Satires* 1.9. The line is spoken by a man who tells his friend he won't accompany him that day because it is a Sabbath, and he is a Jewish sympathizer. Cunaeus is implying that Pliny's gullibility puts him in the same category.

383. Horace *On the Art of Poetry* 10.

384. This comment is actually made by Rabbi Moses ben Nachman, on Deuteronomy 32:26. Cunaeus may have read it in a later Hebrew text, and confused the abbrevia-tions Rambam (Maimonides) and Ramban (Nachmanides).

385. Josephus *Jewish War* 7.5.1. Josephus says that Titus saw a river in Syria which was dry for six days and ran on the seventh (i.e. the opposite of Pliny's stream) and was therefore called "sabbatical," though it had no connection to the Jews as such.

386. Author of a collection of all the omens and supernatural events mentioned in Livy's history of Rome.

387. Pliny did not write about "history" in the modern sense, but about "natural history," in particular, biology, botany, and geology.

388. That is, why the Ten Commandments had to be supplemented by the rest of the Torah.

389. Cunaeus presumably has in mind the "anxious superstitions" with which he associates Rabbinic Judaism.

390. When, that is, even the inferior societies of the gentiles had inexplicable practices.

391. The chief officials of Sparta.

392. This entire passage is based on Plutarch *On the Postponement of Divine Vengeance*, 550.

393. Plutarch *Table Talk* 4.5 ("Whether the Jews abstain from pork because of their reverence or aversion for the pig").

394. The point seems to be that since superstitious people react to the appearance of things rather than their deeper significance, they would not normally consider worshiping an animal with disgusting habits.

395. Possibly a turtle.

396. Horace *Epigrams* 1.12.21.

397. Juvenal *Satires* 15.10.

398. Petronius fragment 37.

399. I.e. that the Jews worshiped the pig. It was also believed that the Holy of Holies contained the image of a pig's head.

400. That is, instead of *porcinum numen adoret* he was reading *porcinum nomen abhorret*.

401. I.e. it cannot be translated into Latin.

402. Which in the Bible is sometimes a punishment for sin.

403. That is, one that they might catch innocently from pigs, but that would resemble leprosy and therefore shame its victims.

404. Leviticus 13.

405. Perhaps Cunaeus means that since Plutarch offers naturalistic explanations of Jewish practices, he would appreciate the theory that they avoided the pig because it spread disease. Such a theory could also coexist with Plutarch's belief that the Jews worshiped pigs.

406. Dionysos, the god of wine.

407. A Semitic harvest god.

408. Plutarch *Table Talk* 4.5.3.

409. Ibid. 4.6.2. The idea that the Festival of Tabernacles was in honor of Bacchus was not original to Plutarch; it was found in Greek literature long before his time (the first century CE).

410. Which was associated with Dionysos.

411. I.e. the *thyrsos*, also associated with Dionysos. Thus the four species associated with the Festival of Tabernacles are actually symbols of Dionysiac worship.

412. I.e. as though they were the *shofar* associated with the New Year.

413. A Roman god identified with Dionysos.

414. That is, the celebrations of the Bacchants.

415. Tacitus *Histories* 5.5: *While Liber established festive rites, the customs of the Jews are absurd and shabby.*

416. κώδωνας καὶ ῥοΐσκους.

417. Livy *History of Rome* 39.16.2.

418. In 186 BCE, the Senate—fearing that the worshipers of Bacchus in Italy were a secret society which threatened the safety of the state—outlawed the cult and punished a number of its members.

419. The speaker is actually not Cato, but one of the two consuls for that year.

420. Despite Cunaeus' comment, the participants in this cult were not generally abused even in Italy, let alone in the Greek world; and though classical writers gave a number of reasons for disliking Jews, they did not accuse them of being followers of Dionysos.

BOOK III

1. Author of biographies of the first twelve emperors.

2. Author of (among other works) histories of the emperors of the Julio-Claudian dynasty, and of the "year of the four emperors" in 69–70 CE.

3. Cf. Josephus *Against Apion* 2.17.

4. Modern anthropologists draw the same distinction between "shame cultures" and "guilt cultures."

5. Josephus *Against Apion* 2.17. ὅτι τὴν ἀλήθειαν τοῦ δόγματος ἐξενεγκεῖν οὐκ ἐτόλμησαν. Josephus is actually talking about philosophers like Plato, rather than legislators.

6. Josephus *Against Apion* 2.32.

7. That is, though the Greeks thought civic values could be taught by means of the traditional myths, they would have created a stronger state if, like Moses, they had taught the simple truth about God. Plato likewise did not think these myths should be used as a source of spiritual education.

8. Josephus *Jewish Antiquities* 4.8–49, a review of Moses' legislation.

9. Josephus *Against Apion* 2.15–42, a comparison of biblical and Greek laws and beliefs.

10. I.e. Julius Caesar. The story is in Pliny *Letters* III.12.

11. A contemporary of Caesar and his political rival.

12. The name traditionally given to the author of *On the Sublime*, a book about literary theory.

13. A Hellenistic poet of the second century BCE, author of the *Argonautica*.

14. By "ancient leaders of the Church," Cunaeus presumably means the patriarchs of the Hebrew Bible (see his discussion in III.1).

15. There are at least two reasons to think that Cunaeus himself studied with Jewish exiles from the Spanish Expulsion: he is familiar with the Hebrew/Aramaic terminology of rabbinic texts, and he sometimes transliterates Hebrew terms according to the Sephardic pronunciation used by the exiles.

16. That is, by relying too much on the judgments of others we risk abdicating our responsibility for our own thoughts.

17. Like Socrates in Plato's *Apology*, Cunaeus claims that his rhetorical skills are poor.

18. I.e. by allowing the judgments of his readers to sway his feelings about his work.

19. Horace *Satires* 1.10.

20. Cf. 1 Peter 2:9.

21. Cf. Exodus 19:5.

22. As he has said earlier in this work, Cunaeus does not think that Jewish sovereignty ended with the monarchy.

23. Adam, Eve, Cain, and Abel.

24. I.e. when God accepted Abel's offering and rejected Cain's. Though Cain had not yet killed his brother—the act that earned him his mark—Cunaeus believes that because God is aware of our true natures, he condemned Cain from the start.

25. I.e. Satan. The one "carried off," then, was not Abel—who died pure—but Cain, who was seduced.

26. The story of the Garden of Eden, which Milton, in *Paradise Lost*, likewise portrays as God's victory over Satan.

27. Josephus *Jewish Antiquities* 1.2. Josephus blames Cain for inventing farming, which was an unnatural process achieved by force (unlike shepherding, which depended on the natural behavior of animals), and for doing so in order to satisfy his own selfish desires.

28. Cf. Genesis 3:17–19.

29. In Genesis 1:5, the first day of creation is called *ehad*, or "one."

30. A sixteenth-century Spanish commentary on the Bible, which Cunaeus presumably learned about from the exile community in Holland (a later edition was published there).

31. A Spanish poet and philosopher, and a relative of the biblical commentator.

32. ‏אמר אחד לפי שהאחד הוא סימן להתחלה אשר אין תחלה קודמת לה.‏

33. Josephus never actually wrote this book. In *Antiquities* 1.1.1 he says that he will explain why Genesis 1 uses the phrase "one day" when he comes to write his book of "reasons" (*aitiai*); and Cunaeus assumes that he did eventually do so.

34. Genesis 3:15. This verse was taken to refer to the coming of Christ and his battle with Satan, because the "seed" is described in the singular rather than the plural; he is the child of a woman rather than a man; and the snake (as Cunaeus will go on to explain) is linked in the New Testament with Satan.

35. I.e. in the New Testament.

36. I.e. difficult passages in the Old Testament must be explained by reference to the New Testament. The phrase "inspiration of the Messiah" seems to include not only those statements actually made by Jesus himself, but also those made by the writers of the Gospels and by the Apostle Paul.

37. So that the New Testament became as much a part of the biblical canon as the Old.

38. Revelation 12:2, 5. γυνὴ ἐν γαστρὶ ἔχουσα, ἔκραζεν ὠδίνουσα καὶ βασανιζομένη τεκεῖν· καὶ ἔτεκεν υἱὸν ἄρρενα, ὃς μέλλειν ποιμαίνειν πάντα τὰ ἔθνη ἐν ῥάβδῳ σιδηρᾷ.

39. Ibid. 12:9. καὶ ἐβλήθη ὁ δράκων ὁ μέγας, ὁ ὄφις ὁ ἀρχαῖος, ὁ καλούμενος Διάβολος καί ὁ σατανᾶς ὁ πλανῶν τὴν οἰκουμένην ὅλην, ἐβλήθη εἰς τὴν γῆν.

40. I.e. that the passage in Genesis refers to Christ and Satan.

41. 1 Timothy 2:14–15. ἡ γυνὴ ἀπατηθεῖσα ἐν παραβάσει γέγονε. σωθήσεται δὲ διὰ τῆς τεκνογονίας, ἐὰν ἐπιμείνωσιν ἐν πίτει καὶ ἀγάπῃ.

42. Exodus 3:5.

43. In Psalms 40:8.

44. Hebrews 10:7. ἰδοὺ, ἥκω· ἐν κεφαλίδι βιβλίου γέγραπται περὶ ἐμοὺ.

45. Perhaps Cunaeus has in mind Exodus 19:9: "Behold I am coming to you in a thick cloud…"

46. Whether, in other words, Jerome means that the term "head" is identical with the term "beginning" used in Genesis 1:1, or is instead referring to the story of the serpent, which is found more or less at the beginning of the book.

47. If this is so, then the head of this "book" can only be Genesis.

48. This simile comes from Juvenal *Satires* 6.573, where it refers to a superstitious woman who clutches an astrological chart in her hands like other women carry around amber (a fashion at the time).

49. And therefore has nothing to do with Satan. Cunaeus' point in the discussion that follows is that as far as Genesis is concerned, the snake was punished because of its character and its behavior in the garden, and not because it was the manifestation of Satan. *That* fact was revealed separately by God to the Church, at first in secret and later through the New Testament.

50. Perhaps Cunaeus is remembering that the serpent was the only animal in the Garden of Eden to speak with people.

51. The author of a guide to dream interpretation.

52. Theocritus *Idylls* 15.58. Ἵππον καὶ τὸν ψυχρὸν ὄφιν τὰ μάλιστα δέδοικα.

53. Livy *History of Rome* 7.17.

54. Aristotle's argument is that no animal with a bloodstream has more than four points with which to move its body, and snakes are far too long to be able to get by on four feet; they therefore have four points along their bodies which they use to undulate (*On the Gait of Animals* 8).

55. Again, something that we might expect to happen only if the animal were being possessed.

56. Numbers 22:28-31.

57. He tells the whale who has swallowed Jonah to spit him up. See Jonah 2:11.

58. Genesis 4:26.

59. Since the Hebrew means simply "in the name of God," Cunaeus seems to be reading Rashi in light of Maimonides' comments about the development of idolatry.

60. ששבעה בני אדם שקפלו את העולם כולו ואלו הן אדם הראשון ומתושלח ושם ויעקב ועמרם ואחיה השילוני ואליהו ועדיין הוא קיים. That is, each one lived into the lifetime of the next, and at least one was alive at any given moment of history. Cunaeus is quoting from the midrash *Seder Olam*, chapter 1.

61. Since, as Cunaeus goes on to explain, Enoch did not die, the two men could be said to cover all of history.

62. Hebrews 11:5.

63. I.e. the Apocalypse of Enoch.

64. I.e. it was written there after Enoch was taken up.

65. *Seder Olam*, chapter 1. ועכשיו הוא כותב מעשי כל הדורות כולם.

66. In 2 Chronicles 21:12-15 Joram receives a letter from Elijah around seven years into his reign; but according to the order of the narrative in 2 Kings, chapters 1-2, Elijah went up to Heaven in the second year of Joram's reign.

67. Seven letters included in the Catholic New Testament canon, which were associated with Jesus' followers. Jude was a brother of Jesus.

68. Jerome *On Famous Men* 4.

69. Cunaeus may be alluding to Genesis 6:1-4, where the daughters of men marry the "sons of God" and give birth to the Nefilim.

70. 2 Peter 2:5.

71. According to *Jewish Antiquities* 1.3.2, which implies that the flood came almost immediately, one hundred and twenty years was the lifespan given to all succeeding generations.

72. Genesis 6:3: *Then the Lord said, "My spirit shall not abide in man forever, for he is flesh, but his days shall be a hundred and twenty years."* Cunaeus takes this to mean that the generation of Noah was given a period of time in which to repent.

73. The problem noticed by the commentators is that if the one hundred and twenty years was a period of probation before the flood, then the Torah should not have said, only a few verses before (Genesis 5:32), that Noah had his sons when he was five hundred, because this was only a hundred years before the flood began.

74. אין מוקדם ומאוחר בתורה. See Rashi on Genesis 6:3. Cunaeus means that though God's warning occurs in the text at the time Noah's sons were born, it had actually been issued twenty years before.

75. Which means that Genesis 9:24, "When Noah awoke from his wine and knew what his youngest son had done to him," refers to *Ham's* youngest son, Canaan. This interpretation is meant to explain why, in verses 25 and 26, Noah reacts by cursing Canaan rather than Ham.

76. The reasoning (found in the Talmud, Sanhedrin 69b) is that if the three sons were born starting when Noah was five hundred years old, Shem had to be the youngest, because according to his genealogy he should have been born when Noah was five hundred and two.

77. Lucifer was a Catholic bishop known for his intolerance of the nonorthodox Arians.

78. Isaiah 42:2.

79. Cunaeus' description of Abraham is strongly reminiscent of the Roman poet Vergil's description of his hero Aeneas, who likewise left his home and went to foreign lands because he felt bound to obey the will of God.

80. ὑπόστασιν τῶν μὴ ὄτων.

81. Described in Genesis as a "priest of Almighty God" who blesses Abraham.

82. The story appears in Genesis 14:18–20.

83. Hebrews 7.

84. Second-century bishop of Lyon and theologian.

85. Third-century theologian and commentator.

86. Fourth-century Syrian commentator.

87. Fourth-century scholar and bishop of Laodicea.

88. Cunaeus' problem is that while Paul discusses Melchizedek as a significant figure, he does not explicitly define his relationship to Christ.

89. Hebrews 7:2. πρῶτον μὲν ἑρμηνευόμενος βασιλεὺς δικαιοσύνης, ἔπειτα δὲ καὶ βασιλεὺς σαλήμ, ὅ ἐστι βασιλεὺς εἰρήνης.

90. Since in the Hebrew of Genesis 14:18 these two words follow one after the other, Cunaeus is taking them together as one long name.

91. That is, since Melchizedek could be translated "king of justice" but should instead be understood as a proper name, we can say the same for Melechsalem.

92. In the following paragraphs, Cunaeus enters into the specific phrasing of Paul's argument about Melchizedek in Hebrews 7, which reads as follows:

1: For this Melchizedek, King of Salem, priest of the Most High God, met Abraham returning from the slaughter of the kings and blessed him;

2: and to him Abraham apportioned a tenth part of everything. He is first, by translation of his name, king of righteousness, and then he is also King of Salem, that is, king of peace.

3: He is without father or mother or genealogy, and his days had no beginning and his life has no end, and he resembled the son of God; he remains a priest forever.

4: See how great he is! Abraham the patriarch gave him a tithe of the spoils.

5: And those descendants of Levi who receive the priestly office have a commandment in the law to take tithes from the people, that is, from their brethren, though these also are descended from Abraham.

6: But this man who has not their genealogy received tithes from Abraham and blessed him who had the promises.

7: It is beyond dispute that the inferior is blessed by the superior.

8: In this case tithes are received by mortal men, in the other by someone of whom it is witnessed that he lives.

9: One might even say that Levi himself, who receives tithes, paid tithes through Abraham,

10: for he was still in the loins of his ancestor when Melchizedek met him.

11: Now if perfection had been attained through the priesthood of the Levites, what need would there have been for another priest to appear according to the order of Melchizedek rather than one named after the order of Aaron?

12: For when there is a change in the priesthood, there is necessarily a change in the law as well.

13: For the one of whom these things are spoken belonged to another tribe, from which no one has ever served at the altar.

14: For it is evident that our Lord was descended from Judah, and in connection with that tribe Moses said nothing about priests.

15: This becomes even more evident when another priest appears similar to Melchizedek,

16: who is a priest not according to the dictates of the Law—which depend on family descent—but according to the force of unending life.

17:   For it is witnessed of him, "You are a priest forever, after the order of Melchizedek."

93. I.e. the word *like*.

94. Ibn Ezra on Psalms 110:4. The Hebrew text actually reads, עַל דברתי מלכיצדק.

95. The kings who had captured the people of Sodom, including Abraham's nephew Lot (Genesis 14:1–17).

96. Genesis 14:20. Since Cunaeus believes that the highest form of worship is purely intellectual, he can use this to explain how Abraham could have encountered the Messiah without sacrificing to him as he would to God.

97. Genesis 18:1–15. Although we are told there that God appeared to Abraham, it is by means of three men, none of whom is singled out from the others. The idea that one of them was Christ may have to do with the fact that in Genesis 19, only two of these messengers arrive in Sodom to carry out God's will.

98. I.e. like the *deus ex machina*, the god sometimes lowered onto the stage at the end of a Greek tragedy to set things in order.

99. Cunaeus seems to have two things in mind here: that only God could intercept a person in the middle of his journey, and that the spiritual character of the Melchizedek story makes it a more suitable illustration of Christ's interest in Abraham.

100. Exodus 3:14.

101. Isaiah 7:14.

102. πρὸς τὸ σχῆμα τοῦ ἱερέως. The issue is presumably that he is called "priest of God" rather than "son of God."

103. Hebrews 1:1–2.

104. Hebrews 7:3. ἀφωμοιώμενος τῷ υἱῷ τοῦ θεοῦ.

105. One is again reminded of the story of Aeneas, who (like Odysseus before him) encountered his divine protector on the road in the guise of a human being.

106. John 8:56.

107. Matthew 13:17; Luke 10:24. In these verses "you" actually refers not to Abraham but to the Apostles, whom Cunaeus also considers to be prophets.

108. Hebrews 7:3. ἀπάτωρ καὶ ἀμήτωρ.

109. At 53:8 Isaiah says (of the "suffering servant"): *who will describe his generation?*

110. I.e. that as the noncorporeal image of Christ, Melchizedek has no parents.

111. Hebrews 7:3. μήτε ἀρχὴν ἡμερῶν, μήτε ζωῆς τέλος ἔχων, μένει ἱερεὺς εἰς τὸ διηνεκές.

112. Cf. Nachmanides on Genesis 14:18.

113. Hebrews 5:11. περὶ οὗ πολὺς ἡμῖν ὁ λόγος, καὶ δυσερμήνευτος λέγειν.

114. Hebrews 7:7. χωρὶς πάσης ἀντιλογίας τὸ ἔλατον ὑπὸ τοῦ κρείττονος εὐλογεῖται.

115. Hebrews 7:8. καὶ ὧδε μὲν δεκάτας ἀποθνήσκοντες ἄνθροποι λαμβάνουσιν, ἐκεῖ δὲ, μαρτυρούμενος ὅτι ζῇ.

116. Cunaeus is paraphrasing Paul's statement, "someone of whom it is witnessed that he lives," because he wants to draw a complete contrast with his statement about the Levites. Paul, of course, does not explicitly equate Melchizedek and Christ (he says he "resembles the son of God"), or claim that Melchizedek was immortal.

117. Psalm 110:4.

118. Cunaeus' expansion.

119. Hebrews 7:15–16. κατὰ τὸν ὁμοιότητα Μελχισεδὲκ ἀνίσταται ἱερεὺς ἕτερος, ὃς οὐ κατὰ νόμον ἐντολῆς σαρκικῆς γέγονεν, ἀλλὰ κατὰ δύναμιν ζωῆς ἀκαταλύτου.

120. Hebrews 7:11.

121. I.e. monotheism.

122. Hebrews 7:3. ἀπάτωρ, ἀμήτωρ, ἀγενεαλόγητος.

123. Hebrews 7:3. μήτε ἀρχὴν ἡμερῶν, μήτε ζωῆς τέλος ἔχων, μένει ἱερεὺς εἰς τὸ διηνεκές.

124. Cunaeus, then, believes that when a biblical figure's lineage is omitted it is for reasons of expedience, and only in the case of Melchizedek does it have any theological significance.

125. Genesis 49:33.

126. I.e. that he was a mortal man. The point seems to be that for these scholars, Paul's statement that Melchizedek has no birth and death should not be taken to mean he was immortal, because if this were true we would have to draw the same conclusion for every figure whose death was not explicitly recorded.

127. On Genesis 49:33 ("And Jacob expired...").

128. A fourth-century theologian and bishop of Alexandria.

129. Cunaeus is referring to the "History of Melchizedek," a fanciful story that came to be associated with Athanasius.

130. ὁ μαρτυρούμενος ὅτι ζῇ. This is another paraphrase of verse 8.

131. ἀποθνήσκοντες ἄνθροποι.

132. I.e. he is incomprehensible, like a person "speaking in tongues."

133. Even though the Psalms is not traditionally considered a prophetic book, it is in the interest of Cunaeus' argument that he calls David a prophet who is anticipating the life of Jesus.

134. ὁ μαρτυρούμενος ὅτι ζῇ. This paraphrase borrows not just from verse 8, which is the source of the Greek, but from verse 17, "you are a priest...".

135. Novatian was a third-century Christian leader who rejected a newly installed pope and declared himself to be the legitimate head of the Church. One of the points of contention was theological: Novatian did not accept the principle that Christians who had become idolaters during periods of persecution should be readmitted to the Church, a position that seems to be strengthened by Hebrews 6:4–6: *It is impossible to restore again to repentance those who... have become partakers of the Holy Spirit, and have tasted the goodness of the word of God... if they then commit apostasy, since they crucify the son of God on their own account and hold him up to contempt.*

136. Cunaeus seems to be criticizing these scholars just as he does the rabbis, whom he often attacks for their obtuseness and overly clever solutions.

137. That is, as a genuine letter of Paul's. In the West, the letter was at first unknown, considered anonymous, or associated with some other author.

138. Ibn Ezra on Psalms 110:4. מהמשוררים.

139. I.e. the inspiration that dictated the exact wording used by the authors of the Bible.

140. Ibn Ezra on Psalms 110:4. הטעם שישראל ילחמו ואתה תקח המעשר כאשר לקח מלכיצדק מאברהם.

141. The Aramaic translation.

142. Targum to Psalms 110:4. דאנת מתמני לרבא לעלמא דאתי בגין זכותא דחויתא מלך זכאי.

143. The phrase *alma de'ati* actually means "the world to come," but as in other places Cunaeus is taking "world" to mean "age." In this case, though, he has a particular incentive, because he wants to emphasize the eternity of Melchizedek's/Christ's priesthood in *this* world.

144. *Lord, give Your justice to a king, and Your righteousness to a king's son; He will judge your people with righteousness and your poor with justice.*

145. Matthew 22:43–44. πῶς Δαβὶδ ἐν πνεύματι κύριον καλεῖ Χριστὸν; λέγων, εἶπεν ὁ κύριος τῷ κυρίῳ μου, κάθου ἐκ δεξιῶν μου, ἕως ἄν, etc. The full quote (Psalms 110:1) is: *The Lord says to my lord: "Sit at my right hand, till I make your enemies your footstool."* In other words, according to Jesus David is talking about the Messiah, whom he calls "my lord."

146. Because its style and content differ in many ways from those of the other Pauline letters, the authorship of the Letter to the Hebrews has always been disputed.

147. I.e. just as we presume the existence of God from His visible creations, Cunaeus will presume the spiritual significance of the obscure passages from the ones he can clearly understand.

148. That since Jesus the man lived much later, he appeared to Abraham only as an image of his corporeal form.

149. In his letter to Evagrius.

150. He subscribed to the Platonic belief in the superiority of ideas over physical substance, and he interpreted the events of the Bible allegorically.

151. God speaks to her at Genesis 25:23.

152. Both God's statement to Rebecca and the blessings Isaac later gives to his sons say that Jacob will be Esau's master. See the verse referred to in the previous note as well as Genesis 27:29, 37 and 40.

153. This is strictly speaking a Greek idea, but since it refers to a time of myth when extraordinary events were common, Cunaeus is applying it to the age of the patriarchs.

154. This presumably refers to Jacob's flight from his family after he took Esau's blessing and Esau determined to kill him. See Genesis 27:41-45.

155. As in the story of the angel who wrestled with Jacob and then renamed him. See Genesis 32:25-29.

156. I.e. their spiritual weakness.

157. For example, Ezekiel 20:6-7: *On that day I swore to them that I would bring them out of the land of Egypt into a land that I had searched out for them... and I said to them, Cast away the detestable things your eyes feast on, every one of you, and do not defile yourselves with the idols of Egypt.* And Ezekiel 20:18: *And I said to their children in the wilderness, Do not walk in the statutes of your fathers, or observe their ordinances, or defile yourselves with their idols.*

158. Ezekiel 23:1-4.

159. Ezekiel himself says so in verse 4.

160. I.e. to cure the Israelites who had been bitten by the snakes God sent as a punishment. Cf. 2 Kings 18:4 and Numbers 21:6-9.

161. Cicero *Tusculan Disputations* 5.78.

162. A deity created by Hellenistic Greeks living in Egypt, which borrowed from the characteristics of several Egyptian gods.

163. Ovid *Loves* 13.

164. Plutarch *Isis and Osiris* 362.

165. Ibid.

166. Ibid. 363. ὁ μέντοι ὄνος οὗτος ὑμῶν κατευωχήσεται τὸν βοῦν.

167. Cf. Exodus 1:6-8.

168. *Seder Olam*, chapter 3. אין לך בכל השבטים שקצר ימי' פחות מיוסף ואין לך בכל השבטים שהאריך ימים יותר מלוי וכל זמן שהיה לוי קיים לא נשתעבדו ישר' למצרים ומשמת לוי התחילו המצרים לשעבדם: מכאן אמרו אחד מן האחים שמת ידאגו כל האחים אחד מן החבירה שמת תדאג כל החבירה.

169. *Haroset*, the mixture of fruit, nuts, and wine made to resemble mortar.

170. Juvenal *Satires* 6.542–45.

171. Ibid. 3.13–14.

172. He was a late-fifteenth-century scholar who produced editions of some of the classical texts that were then being printed for the first time.

173. I.e. for scouring things clean—a Roman expression for a harsh and cutting wit.

174. Martial *Epigrams* 5.17.

175. *Basket-carrier.*

176. It is not at all clear from his poem that Martial is in fact referring to a Jew.

177. Though four hundred years is the figure given at Genesis 15:13, and four hundred and thirty at Exodus 12:40, the Rabbis thought this period should be dated from the time that God told Abraham this would happen, and that the Israelites were therefore slaves for only two hundred and ten years.

178. Tacitus *Histories* 5.3.

179. In fact, Tacitus says he is doing nothing more than summarizing earlier authors' theories about the Jews.

180. Cunaeus is being disingenuous. Before the Christian era, classical authors showed no sign of knowing that the Bible even existed.

181. The royal librarian of King Ptolemy Philadelphus, who appears in the story of the translation of the Torah into Greek as told in the fictional "Letter of Aristeus," which Josephus paraphrases in Book 12 of *Jewish Antiquities*.

182. Josephus *Jewish Antiquities* 12.2.14.

183. Juvenal *Satires* 14.100–104.

184. Cunaeus has already said that people who don't respect natural law are like animals, and here he is adding to this category those who don't share their wisdom with foreigners.

185. An early Latin poet.

186. Zacuto *Sefer Yuhasin*, section 1. ‏ארור מי שילמד לבנו חכמה יונית‎.

187. Cunaeus is referring to the rabbinic statement that when the translation was finished, three days of darkness descended on the world. See *Shulhan Aruch*, Orah Hayim 580:2.

188. A paraphrase of Horace *Satires* 1.4.

189. ἐκ τῶν διὸς δέλτων γὰρ ὁ μάρτυς. A quote from the satirist Lucian.

190. Which led the Israelites through the desert during the day. See Exodus 40:36–38.

191. *Seder Olam*, chapter 10. 'מן בזכות משה עמוד ענן בזכות אהרן באר בזכות מרים מתה מרי
נסתלקה הבאר וחזרה להן בזכות משה ואהרן ונסתלק עמוד הענן חזר להן בזכות משה מת משה
נסתלקו שלשתן ולא חזרו שנית שנאמר ואכחיד את שלשת הרועים בירח אחד.

192. Zechariah 11:8.

193. In Joshua 3–4 the waters of the Jordan part so that the priests carrying the Ark can walk through.

194. A reference to the conquest of Jericho in Joshua 6.

195. According to the Midrash there were ten songs (such as the song at the Red Sea) sung by the heroes of the Bible. This one appears at Joshua 10:12.

196. See p. 244 n. 184.

197. *Seder Olam*, chapter 11.

198. I.e. by trying to find a rational explanation for it.

199. As in Book I, Cunaeus is blurring the distinction between Judeans and Jews proper.

200. Cunaeus is referring to the period from Adam, whom he considers the first member of the Church, to Abraham.

201. Herodotus *Histories* 2.104. Though Cunaeus is relying on Herodotus to make the point that the ancients confused the creators of circumcision with its imitators, it is not at all clear that Herodotus is even referring to the Jews since he never mentions them by name.

202. The *Aruch* was an eleventh-century glossary which explained many of the terms found in rabbinic literature.

203. I.e. Midrash.

204. Cunaeus may be thinking of Maimonides' critique of Midrash (which suggests that we should not take Midrash literally when it contradicts the laws of nature), or he may refer to the more serious criticisms of Azariah de Rossi, whom he mentions elsewhere.

205. One of his labors was to kill the hydra, a creature that grew two new heads for every one he cut off.

206. Jeremiah 9:25–26.

207. A writer of geography and ethnography in the early Roman Empire.

208. Bishop of Milan, fourth century.

209. I.e. that they were uncircumcised only in their hearts.

210. Drusius was a professor of Semitic languages at two Dutch universities in the late sixteenth century.

211. 1 Corinthians 7:18–19. περιτετμημένος τις ἐκλήθη; μὴ ἐπισπάσθω. ἐν ἀκροβυστίᾳ τις ἐκλήθη; μὴ περιτεμνέσθω. ἡ περιτομὴ οὐδέν ἐστιν, ἀλλὰ τήρησις ἐντολῶν Θεοῦ.

212. Jerome, Letter 48 (to Pammachius).

213. 1 Corinthians 7:21–23. Jerome's interpretation would sound less arbitrary than it does if Cunaeus had told us that the passages both before and after this one deal with the virtues of marriage as compared with virginity and widowhood.

214. To say what one is not going to say is a rhetorical strategy typical of Cicero.

215. 1 Maccabees 1:15.

216. Cf. Josephus *Jewish Antiquities* 12.5.1.

217. Jerome attacked Jovinian for suggesting that the Church should respect wives and widows as much as virgins, and for supporting the idea that after Mary gave birth to Jesus as a virgin, she had other children with Joseph as a married woman. In the course of his attack Jerome criticized the institution of marriage in general, and the vanity and selfishness of women.

218. Marcion was a second-century theologian who was considered heretical because he thought Christianity should have nothing to do with Judaism or the Old Testament. The members of his church practiced celibacy.

219. Mani was the founder of a Persian religion that believed the world was in the grip of equally powerful forces of good and evil. Those at the highest levels of the Manichaean hierarchy were supposed to remain unmarried.

220. I.e. although he represented himself as a reactionary in his attack on Jovinian, his views on marriage left him open to charges of radicalism.

221. Although this work was meant as an apology which had good things to say about marriage, some considered it another attack on Jovinian's position.

222. Cunaeus seems to be drawing an implicit analogy with non-Christians who died before they could be baptized.

223. Joshua and Caleb.

224. Joshua 5:2–8.

225. Cf. Joshua 5:2: *The Lord said to Joshua, "Make flint knives and circumcise the people of Israel again the second time."*

226. Jerome *Against Jovinian* 1.21.

227. In this context, "evangelical" presumably means something like "symbolic of Christ."

228. Leviticus 22:27.

229. John 7:21–23: *Jesus answered them, "I did one deed, and you all marvel at it... You circumcise a man upon the Sabbath. If on the Sabbath a man receives circumcision,*

so that the Law of Moses may not be broken, are you angry with me because on the Sabbath I made a man's whole body well?"

230. Moses' wife, who circumcised their son (Exodus 4:25).

231. 1 Corinthians 10:4. ἡ δὲ πέτρα ἦν ὁ Χριστός. The reference is to the rock from which Moses drew water in the desert.

232. I.e. by wasting their time on minutiae instead of tackling important questions.

233. On the three pilgrimage festivals.

234. The voluntary sacrifices they had vowed to make.

235. John 4:20. ὑμεῖς λέγετε, ὅτι ἐν Ἱεροσολύμοις ἐστὶν ὁ τόπος ὅπου δεῖ προσκυνεῖν.

236. Luke 18:10. ἄνθρωποι δύο ἀνέβησαν εἰς τὸ ἱερὸν προσεύξασθαι, ὁ εἷς Φαρισαῖος, καὶ ὁ ἕτερος τελώνης.

237. Daniel 6:10.

238. 1 Kings 8:46–50.

239. Cf. Ezekiel 8:16, though here he is criticizing not people who faced the wrong direction as such, but those who were actually praying to the sun.

240. Rashi says that the word in this passage which means "to bow down" also comes from the root meaning "to destroy," because this was what these worshipers were doing to the Temple.

241. In 63 BCE. He was returning from his successful campaign against the eastern king Mithridates.

242. Tacitus *Histories* 5.9.

243. Lucan *Pharsalia* 2.592–593.

244. Matthew 5:33–35: *Again you have heard that it was said to the men of old, "You shall not swear falsely, but shall perform to the Lord what you have sworn." But I say to you, "Do not swear at all, either by heaven, for it is the throne of God, or by the earth, for it is His footstool, or by Jerusalem, for it is the city of the great King."*

245. The second part of the verse is what is relevant here.

246. Aristophanes wrote a play, the *Clouds*, in which Socrates and his school have replaced the traditional gods with natural phenomena. Socrates himself never advocated this, and he was not particularly interested in nature. He did criticize certain aspects of Greek religion, and claimed that there was an invisible kind of power that warned him when he was about to do something ill-advised.

247. Aristophanes *Clouds* 266–267:

Ὦ δέσποτ' ἄναξ ἀμέτρητ' ἀήρ, ὅς ἔχεις τὴν γῆν μετέωρον,
Λαμπρός τ' αἰθὴρ σεμναί τε θεαὶ νεφέλαι βροντησικέραυνοι.

248. Ibid. 365. Αὗται γὰρ τοι μόναι εἰσὶ θεαὶ, τἄλλα δὲ πάντ᾽ ἐστὶ φλύαρὸς.

249. ἀγνώστῳ θεῷ.

250. The "hill of Ares," where a prestigious Athenian court met.

251. Acts 7:23. ὃν ἀγνοῦντες εὐσεβεῖτε, τοῦτον ἐγὼ καταγγέλλω ὑμῖν.

252. Tacitus *Histories* 5.5.

253. Gaius was a grandson of the emperor Augustus, whose daughter was married to the general Agrippa; until his death he was considered a potential emperor, since Augustus had no sons of his own.

254. Suetonius *Augustus* 93.

255. Though Suetonius says nothing here about a famine, Cunaeus may be inferring this connection from the fact that he does mention one, though without dating it, in chapter 70.

256. Agrippa II, who as a descendant of Herod was given a small kingdom in Judea.

257. Philo's account of the Jewish delegation with which he went to Rome to ask the emperor Caligula to intervene against Greek attacks on the Jewish community of Alexandria.

258. Philo *Embassy to Gaius* 317.

259. Augustus had in fact died over twenty years before.

260. In *Jewish Antiquities* 11.8.5, Alexander comes to Jerusalem to offer sacrifice after discovering that the high priest was the man he had seen in a vision predicting his victory over the Persians.

261. Tacitus *Histories* 5.5.

262. Pliny *Natural History* 13.46–47.

263. The god of Ammon.

264. According to Rashi and Kimhi on 2 Samuel 12:30, David put on the crown only after Itai (who was an ally of his) had taken it himself in order to remove its taint of idolatry.

265. Emperor, 14–37 CE.

266. Pontius Pilate, who was then the governor of Judea.

267. According to Josephus (*Jewish War* 2.9.2–3 and *Jewish Antiquities* 18.3.1) Pilate tried to bring the army's standards, on which were images of the emperor, into Jerusalem, but the people's reaction changed his mind.

268. Caligula, who ruled from 37–41 CE.

269. I.e. since the letter had been written so long before, by all rights it should have arrived first.

270. The story to which Cunaeus refers is found in Luke 16:19–31: A wealthy man dies at the same time as the poor man who begged outside his door and is sent to Hell, from where he can see the poor man nestled in the lap of Abraham. When the rich man asks that the poor one be returned to earth to warn his surviving brothers of their own fate, Abraham replies that they should already know it from Scripture.

271. Cunaeus seems to be thinking of the Roman custom of placing a slave in the chariot in which victorious generals rode through the city in triumph, to whisper in the general's ear that he was after all only a man.

272. 1 Corinthians 14:32.

273. Luke 10:24.

274. Though Luke doesn't say this explicitly, Cunaeus seems to have two verses in mind—1:76: *And you, child, will be called the prophet of the Most High; for you will go before the Lord to prepare His ways*; and 7:28: *I tell you, among those born of women none is greater than John.*

275. The point seems to be that just as John was no less a prophet because he identified Jesus without using any supernatural or mystical methods, neither did the earlier prophets need such methods to foresee his eventual arrival.

276. Montanus was a second-century Christian who developed a following when he and the two women who accompanied him claimed to be receiving ecstatic visions from God and Christ. They were banned by the Church because of their method of prophecy, and because unlike earlier prophets, who only brought God's message, they said that God spoke through them directly.

277. They were supposed to interpret as divine messages the ravings of the oracle of Apollo, a woman known as the Pythia, who went into trances.

278. Cicero *On Divination* 2.118.

279. φιλιππίζειν. According to Cicero, Demosthenes had accused the oracle of being paid to give prophecies favorable to the side of Philip of Macedon, who was in the process of conquering the independent states of Greece.

280. The sanctuary of Amon in the Egyptian desert had been consulted by Greeks including Alexander the Great.

281. This Italian city had a Temple of Fortune in which lots were cast to foretell the future.

282. A church popular among the northern European peoples that differed with the Catholics on some important theological questions.

283. A Christian emperor of the mid-fourth century CE.

284. According to the Midrash, he was related to the Judean king Amaziah.

285. A legendary Assyrian queen.

286. This was Azariah de Rossi, an Italian Jewish scholar of the sixteenth century who was among the first to use classical and modern texts in order to interpret Jewish ones.

287. Cf. the vision in Daniel 2 of the statue made of four substances, each of which represented a future kingdom.

288. Porphyry was a Platonist philosopher of the third century who argued in favor of classical culture and against Christianity; one of his observations (still accepted today) was that the content of the Book of Daniel implied that it had been written only in the time of the Maccabean revolt.

289. This is a play on the Latin word *frigidus*, which means both "feeble" and "freezing."

290. Nor did the authors of Ruth, Ecclesiastes, and the other books of the Hagiographa.

291. Kimhi on Jonah 1:3. ‏שאין הנבואה שורה אלא על אדם עשיר‎.

292. οὐκ οἶδα, πήρη δύναμιν ἡλίκην ἔχει, θέρμον τε χοίνιξ. Since Aristotle and Crates were not contemporaries, Cunaeus must have some other author in mind; and the quote does resemble one in Diogenes Laertius' biography of Crates, in his *Lives of the Eminent Philosophers*.

293. πήρη τις γᾶι᾽ ἐστι μέσῳ ἐνὶ οἴνοπι τύφῳ,
    Καλὴ καὶ πίειρα, περίρρυτος, οὐδὲν ἔχουσα.

This satire is found in Diogenes Laertius. For the original, cf. Homer *Odyssey* 19:172–174.

294. Because Cunaeus wants to use this text as infallible proof, he claims (as he has done before) that it was the product of the divine spirit.

295. Luke 1:76. καὶ σὺ παιδίον προφήτης ὑψίστου κληθήσῃ. προπορεύσῃ γὰρ πρὸ προσώπου κυρίου, ἑτοιμάσαι ὁδοὺς αὐτοῦ.

296. Malachi 3:23.

297. Cf. Matthew 11:13–14, 17:12–13; Mark 9:13.

298. Compare 2 Kings 1:8: *They answered him, "He wore a garment of haircloth, with a girdle of leather about his loins," and he said, "It is Elijah the Tishbite"*; and Matthew 3:4: *John wore a garment of camel's hair and a leather girdle around his waist.*

299. The wife of Ahab, king of Israel. See 1 Kings 19:1–2.

300. The daughter of Herod's son and the wife of Herod Antipas, the ruler of the Galilee.

301. Living on one's own in the desert was an early form of Christian monasticism.

302. Luke 1:17.

303. Cf. Matthew 17:3; Mark 9:4. Cunaeus has distorted the sense of these passages. Jesus is actually speaking with both Elijah and Moses, and it appears that *they* are honoring *him*.

304. Luke 7:28.

305. Cf. Luke 1:15: *He will be filled with the Holy Spirit, even from his mother's womb.*

306. Remarks like this imply that Cunaeus sees the Hebrew state as an expression of the Platonic ideal—its leaders are spiritually precocious people like Abraham and Moses, who are able to arrive at the truth on their own; they must then pass it on to the masses, whose inferior spirits can only be improved through education.

307. I.e. Sinai.

308. It is hard to say from this whether Cunaeus is referring strictly to homiletical Midrash as opposed to legal interpretation. Certainly in other passages he has been just as dismissive about the value of rabbinic expansions of biblical law.

309. Which is how Maimonides uses the term.

310. Cunaeus seems to want to preserve the Jewish idea that kabbalah is essential without having to concede any importance to the Jewish traditions that the term represents.

311. The head of the Sanhedrin in the years before the destruction of the Second Temple.

312. Romans 7:14. ὁ νόμος πνευματικὸς ἐστι.

313. Though Cunaeus is using the names of Roman military offices, he seems to have in mind the heads of the tribes mentioned in Numbers 30:2, the "captains of thousands and hundreds" in 31:14, and the "heads of fathers' houses" (a division of the tribes) in 31:26.

314. Though this passage does not actually appear in Ephesians, it might be based on 3:8–10, which mentions both the revelation of secrets and the government of heaven: *To me... this grace was given... to make all men see what is the plan of the mystery hidden for ages in God who created all things; that through the church the manifold wisdom of God might now be made known to the principalities and powers in the heavenly places.*

315. Deuteronomy 30:11–14.

316. Romans 10:5–10.

317. In the generic sense of the "good news."

318. Leviticus 18:5: *And you shall observe My laws and statutes, which a man shall do to live by them.*

319. Romans 10:5.

320. Ibid. 10:6–8.

321. Since Cunaeus is quoting the passage from Romans selectively, it is difficult to follow his point here, which is that Paul alternates between the text of the Deuteronomy passage as written, and his own theological interpretation of its meaning.

322. I.e. switching back and forth between an Old Testament passage and its interpretation.

323. Genesis 2:24.

324. Ephesians 5:32.

325. As opposed to the sacrament of marriage.

326. The husband and wife, respectively.

327. βαρβαρίζειν.

328. אין מקרא יוצא מידי פשוטו: אבל יש לו פשוטו עם מדרשו ואינו יוצא מידי כל אחד מהן. Cunaeus' translation is actually very close in meaning to the original. His remark seems to refer not to the *sense* of the passage, but to its pithy and idiomatic style. Where he writes *has its simple meaning* and *alongside it there is a mystical meaning*, the Hebrew has *does not leave the hands of its simple meaning* and *it has its simple meaning with its interpretation*.

329. Cf. Psalms 8:6–9: *You have set him a little below gods, and crowned him with glory and honor. You have given him rule over Your creations, and put everything beneath his feet—all the sheep and oxen, and the beasts of the field.*

330. Hebrews 2:5–8.

331. As he has already done earlier in the chapter, Cunaeus makes two important assumptions in this passage: that the rabbinic distinction between simple meaning and interpretation is a real one, and that nevertheless it has to do not with creating such interpretations and accepting them from others, but with receiving them directly from God and without any personal contribution to the process (a possibility granted only to the Church).

332. Matthew 2:15.

333. Hosea 11:1.

334. Because there was no basis for it in the prophetic passage itself.

335. I.e. Hosea's language.

336. III.1.

337. δὶς καὶ τρὶς τὸ καλὸν.

338. I.e. like the simple Hebrews mentioned at the beginning of this chapter, who were not ready to learn the higher meanings of Scripture.

339. The obscure biblical citations in the New Testament.

340. θεόπνευστοι.

341. Hence the freedom Cunaeus feels in attacking even Church Fathers like Augustine.

342. Cunaeus is presumably referring to Origen's love of allegorical interpretation.

343. Matthew 27:51.

344. I.e. the allegorical interpretation of a scriptural text.

345. Corresponding to the two halves of the curtain.

346. The narratives of the two Testaments.

347. I.e. the crucifixion of Jesus.

348. Cf. II.14.

349. Jerome, Letter 120 (to Hedibia).

350. I.e. the only reason the Church Fathers did not beat the Jews at their own game was that they would not resort to any means in order to win.

351. In Cunaeus' time the Karaites, though technically regarded as Jews, were essentially a separate community.

352. The sense of this passage seems to be that even though Paul and the later writers made some (apparently) contradictory statements about whether or not the Hebrews believed in the future Messiah, and the language of these statements therefore needs to be analyzed, Cunaeus would rather discuss a larger philosophical issue—the nature of their belief.

353. This is presumably Cunaeus' explanation of why some prophets alluded to Christ and others did not.

354. John 8:56.

355. Cf. Genesis 15, the "covenant among the pieces."

356. Galatians 3:16.

357. See III:7, this edition, p. 202.

358. 1 Peter 1:10–12.

359. Hebrews 9:15.

360. Galatians 3:23.

361. Cf. Genesis 17:7.

362. Cf. Malachi 3:1: *I am going to send My messenger, and he will clear the way before Me. And the Lord, whom you seek, will suddenly come to His Temple; and the messenger of the covenant, in whom you delight, behold he is coming.* (In Hebrew the same word means both "messenger" and "angel.")

363. 1 Corinthians 7:14.

364. Romans 10:17. ὅτι ἡ πίστις ἐξ ἀκοῆς.

365. Galatians 3:19.

366. Ibid. 3:24.

367. Ibid. 4:3. Paul is using "slaves" here in the sense of the strictures imposed on children by their legal guardians, which in Roman law were very broad. Likewise, the term "elements" refers to the basics of childhood education.

368. Galatians 4:9.

369. Colossians 2:20.

370. I.e. the Jews were told to put aside the Law which had prepared them as children to come to Christ, but even once freed from the restrictions of childhood, they have refused to accept their adult responsibilities.

371. I.e. its validity hinged on faith in Christ rather than on the laws spelled out in the Bible.

372. Galatians 3:16–17.

373. Acts 13:32.

374. Hebrews 8:6.

375. Leviticus 18:5, quoted above. Cunaeus is presumably referring here to the Pauline principle that one dies through the Law and lives through faith.

376. Genesis 15:6.

377. I.e. scholars prefer to fight with their colleagues rather than to accept any changes in their particular formulation.

378. Hebrews 4:2.

379. Ibid. 3:18.

380. Ibid. 4:2.

381. Psalms 95:10. According to this interpretation, the "ways" that the Jews have not learned are those of Christ.

382. Hebrews 4:8–9. Paul is referring not to the Sabbath of the Bible, but to the Second Coming.

383. This seems to be a conclusion drawn from 3:19: *So we see that they* (the Israelites who died in the desert) *were unable to enter because of unbelief.*

384. Numbers 20:12: *Because you did not believe in Me and sanctify Me before the children of Israel, you will not bring this assembly to the land I have given them.*

385. Hebrews 11:26.

386. I.e. we should not assume that he is talking about explicit faith in the Messiah, which brought with it complete salvation.

387. I.e. the Jewish Christians to whom the letter was addressed.

388. Sulpicius was a Christian writer of the fourth century, though not a bishop (Cunaeus has confused him with a later figure of the same name).

389. Severus *Chronicles* 1.24.

390. An ironic comment on scholars who give us more information than is necessary.

391. John 4:25.

392. Hebrews 11:1.

393. Ibid. 11:29.

394. Which would have made them reluctant to enter the sea.

395. Hebrews 11:13, 16.

396. Ibid. 11:22.

397. Quoted in Seneca *Moral Letters* 95.27. Maecenas was a friend of Augustus and a leading figure in the cultural circles of aristocratic Rome.

398. 1 Corinthians 10:3–4.

399. 1 Corinthians 10:9. The point here seems to be that this verse says, "*some* of our fathers," while the previous one says, "*all* of our fathers."

400. 2 Corinthians 3:13. εἰς τέλος τοῦ καταργουμένου.

401. Romans 10:4. τέλος νόμου Χριστὸς. If, then, the Jews were deliberately blinded to the truth by the Law, how can we say that they had faith in the coming of Christ?

402. I.e. they thought it was an end in itself rather than an educational device.

INDEX OF SOURCES

HEBREW BIBLE

Genesis

1:5	162 n.29
2:24	208 n.323
3:15	163 n.34
3:17-19	*257 n.28*
4:26	166 n.58
6:1	*259 n.69*
6:3	168 n.72
9:4	128 n.261
14:1-17	173 n.95
14:18	172 n.90
14:18-20	*260 n.82*
14:20	173 n.96
15	*275 n.355*
15:6	216 n.376
17:7	214 n.361
18:1-15	*262 n.97*
25:23	*265 n.151*
27:29	*265 n.152*
27:37	*265 n.152*
27:40	*265 n.152*
27:41-45	*265 n.154*
32:25-29	*265 n.155*
49	45 n.122, *226 n.99*
49:10	35 n.93
49:33	176 n.125

Exodus

1:6-8	*265 n.167*
1:9	*223 n.49*
3:5	164 n.42
3:14	173 n.100
19:5	*257 n.21*
19:6	*241 n.120*
19:9	*258 n.45*
22:27	134 n.299
30:1	89 n.53
30:6-7	89 n.53
30:10	92 n.72
34:33-35	*233 n.224*
40:5	89 n.55
40:26	89 n.56
40:36-38	*266 n.190*

Leviticus

4:3	*239 n.100*
6:6	*239 n.100*
13	149 n.13
16:2	95 n.91
16:2-4	81 n.16
16:2-8	88 n.50
16:12-13	95 n.90
16:4	*235 n.12*

16:18	92 n.73
16:32	81 n.17
18:5	207 n.318, 216 n.375
18:18	142 n.358
18:25	131 n.281
19:27	126 n.245
22:27	194 n.228
25	*222 n.19*
25:21	28
26:6	*232 n.211*

Numbers

6	*246 n.221*
15:40	74 n.240
20:12	218 n.384
21:6-9	*265 n.160*
22:28-31	*259 n.56*
30:2	*275 n.213*
31:14	*275 n.213*
31:26	*275 n.213*

Deuteronomy

4:2	*222 n.16*
4:5, 14	34 n.86
5:28	34 n.86
6:1	34 n.86
7:1	127 n.252
15	*222 n.15*
16:2	*225 n.83*
17:14-20	58 n.162, *240 n.119*
19:8	33 n.83
19:9	33 n.84
20:3-4	131 n.288
20:5-9	133 n.291
20:10-16	127-128
20:18	*249 n.278*
22:5	136 n.313
23:4-7	131 n.282

25:17-19	127 n.253
30:11-14	207 n.315
34:10	*238 n.77*

Joshua

3-4	*267 n.193*
5:2	*268 n.225*
5:2-8	*268 n.224*
6	*267 n.194*
9	*241 n.136, 249 n.274*
10:12	*267 n.195*
11:19-20	130 n.271

Judges

1:1-2	92 n.75
20:18	92 n.75

1 Samuel

8:7	57 n.157
10:22	92 n.76
10:24	57 n.158
10:25	*229 n.159*
11:6-7	*250 n.292*
21:10-15	*245 n.202*
26:19	140 n.345
30:7	58 n.165

2 Samuel

7:12-13	*231 n.199*
12:8	*253 n.357*

1 Kings

1:23	58 n.164
8:46-50	197 n.238
10:22	*252 n.340*
11:28	*230 n.174*
12	*228 n.121*
14:25-26	*230 n.177*

19:1-2	*272 n.299*

2 Kings

1-2	*259 n.66*
1:8	*272 n.298*
4:23	145 n.377
17:24	*244 n.195*
17:24-29	*244 n.209*
17:30-31	*244 n.207*
18:4	*265 n.160*
24:17	*226 n.103*
24:17-25:8	*230 n.180*

Isaiah

7:14	*262 n.101*
9:6-7	68 n.201
42:2	169 n.78
53:8	174 n.109

Jeremiah

9:25-26	190 n.206
17:1	71 n.221
27:22	35 n.92

Ezekiel

8:16	197 n.239
20:6-7	182 n.157
20:18	182 n.157
23:1-4	182 n.158
23:4	182 n.159
43-46	69 n.212

Hosea

11:1	208 n.333

Jonah

2:11	*259 n.57*

Zechariah

11:8	187 n.192

Malachi

3:1	214 n.362
3:23	205 n.296

Psalms

8:6-9	208 n.329
20:2	179
21:2	179
30:1	31 n.69
40:8	*258 n.43*
72	179 n.144
95:10	217 n.381
110:4	175 n.117, 178-179

Daniel

2	203 n.287
6:10	197 n.237

1 Chronicles

15:16-22	*241 n.135*
26:30	102 n.122
26:31-32	102 n.123

2 Chronicles

12	*230 n.177*
17-18	*230 n.179*
19:11	102 n.121
21:12-15	167 n.66

CLASSICAL SOURCES

Aristophanes *Clouds*

266-267   198 n.247

365   198 n.248

Aristotle *On the Gait of Animals*

8   165 n.54

Aristotle *Politics*

1.3   12 n.13

1.5   57 n.159

1.13   22 n.42

2.7   21 n.39

3.4   61 n.173

3.5   22 n.43

3.11   51 n.142

3.16   13 n.15

4.6   22 n.40

6.4   21 n.38

7.4   53 n.146

Callimachus *Hymns and Epigrams*

4.286   113 n.171

Cicero *On Behalf of Murena*

22   *246 n.234*

Cicero *On Divination*

2.5   70 n.219

2.118   203 n.278

Cicero *Letters to Friends*

6.6   *250 n.311*

Cicero *The Parts of Oratory*

105   40 n.110

Cicero *Republic*

fragment of   4 n.2
Book 3

Cicero *Tusculan Disputations*

5.78   182 n.161

Codex

1.9.7   142 n.355

1.9.11   142 n.353

9.16   55 n.153

Digest

9.4ff   31 n.72

27.1.15.6   142 n.352

48.4.1.1   40 n.114

49.15.7   40 n.112

49.16.4.10-11ff   133 n.293

49.16.4.12   *250 n.296*

50.1.2ff   50 n.136

Dio Cassius *Roman History*

54.27.3   *237 n.45*

Diogenes Laertius *Lives of the Eminent Philosophers*

      272 n.292

Ennius   186 n.185

Herodotus *Histories*

1.187   *252 n.339*

2.104   189 n.201

Homer *Odyssey*
5:282-284   126 n.247
17.320   72 n.227
19:172-174   *272 n.293*

Horace *On the Art of Poetry*
10   146 n.383

Horace *Epigrams*
1.12.21   148 n.396

Horace *Satires*
1.4   *266 n.188*
1.9   145 n.382
1.10   *254 n.374, 257 n.19*

Juvenal *Satires*
1:26-27   23 n.48
3.13-14   184 n.171
6.397   114 n.179
6.542-545   184 n.170
6.573   *258 n.48*
14.100-104   186 n.183
15.10   148 n.397

Livy *History of Rome*
7.17   165 n.53
38.11.2   40 n.111
39.16.2   150 n.417

Lucan *Pharsalia*
2.592-593   197 n.243

Martial *Epigrams*
5.17   185 n.174
10.52   137 n.316

Ovid *Loves*
13   183 n.163

Petronius
fragment 37   148 n.398

Pliny *Letters*
III.12   *256 n.10*

Pliny *Natural History*
13.46-47   199 n.262
28.17   136 n.312
31.24   145 n.381

Plutarch *Isis and Osiris*
362   *265 n.164*
363   *265 n.166*

Plutarch *Life of Coriolanus*
25.2   *254 n.380*

Plutarch *Life of Tiberius Gracchus*
8:4   *222 n.27*

Plutarch *Moralia*
819e   108 n.143

Plutarch *On the Postponement of Divine Vengeance*
550   147 n.392

Plutarch *Table Talk*
4.5.3   149 n.408
4.6.2   149 n.409

Seneca *To Helvia on Consolation*
7.1   138 n.320

Seneca *Moral Letters*

5.50	75 n.252
95.27	*277 n.397*

Strabo

4.4.6	*223 n.34*

Suetonius *Augustus*

24	*250 n.295*
93	*270 n.254*

Tacitus *Agricola*

30.6.2	5 n.3

Tacitus *Histories*

4.17	56 n.155
5.3	185 n.178
5.4.4	144 n.368

5.5	149 n.415, 199 n.261
5.6	23 n.44
5.9	197 n.242
5.12.2	31 n.71

Theocritus *Idylls*

14:48-49	118 n.198
15.58	165 n.52

Varro *On Farming*

2.1	18 n.30

Vergil *Aeneid*

10.502	*236 n.31*

Xenophon *Education of Cyrus*

8.40	137 n.317

PHILO

Embassy to Gaius

317	199 n.257

On the Special Laws

1:273-274	90 n.59
1.72	91 n.64

JOSEPHUS

Against Apion

1.12	20 n. 33, 152, *223 n.34*
1.22	14 n.18, 31 n.68, 125 n.236, 126 n.242, 134 n.300, 135 n.304, *223 n.35, 225 n.74, 250 n.309, 252 n.351*
2.4	*251 n.326*
2.5	*251 n.329*
2.8	111 n.152

2.13	22 n.41
2.15-42	156 n.9
2.16	12 n.10
2.17	156 n.5
2.32	156 n.6
2.34	133 n.297

Jewish Antiquities

1.1.1	162 n.33
1.2	162 n.27

1.3.2	168 n.71	16.6.1-7	139 n.333
4.7.43	137 n.314	17.6.4	95 n.85
4.8-49	156 n.8	18.3.1	*270 n.267*
4.8.17	102 n.119	18.3.5	*233 n.228*
6.4.6	57 n.161	20.10	*235 n.4*
7.14.7	99 n.106	20.5.1	*246 n.229*
7.15.3	*252 n.337*	20.8.5	124 n.233
8.3	108 n.142	20.8.6	*246 n.231*
8.5-6	*222 n.32*	20.189-196	*225 n.67*
8.7.4	140 n.341		
8.7.7-8	*230 n.174*	*Jewish War*	
8.10.3	63 n.178	2.8.14	*245 n.212*
10.11.7	*226 n.90*	2.9.2-3	*270 n.267*
11.5.2.	44 n.119	2.13.4	123 n.225
11.8.5	199 n.260	2.17.6	111 n.157
12.2.14	186 n.182	5.5.7	*235 n.10*
12.5.1	192 n.216	6.5.3	32 n.78
12.9.7	*231 n.191*	6.9.3	111 n.153
13.3.1-3	*226 n.95*	7.3.1	*233 n.229*
14.9.4	*231 n.196*	7.5.1	146 n.385
14.13.10	100 n.116		
15.2.2	*226 n.89*	*Life*	
15.8.1	67 n.198	2	123 n.223
15.11.4	83 n.21		

NEW TESTAMENT AND APOCRYPHA

Matthew		27:51	210 n.343
2:15	*274 n.332*		
3:4	*272 n.298*	**Mark**	
5:33	197 n.244	9:4	*273 n.303*
11:13-14	*272 n.297*	9:13	*272 n.297*
13:17	174 n.107	10:11-12	*253 n.359*
17:3	*273 n.303*	11:16	109 n.145
17:12-13	*272 n.297*	13:30	46 n.123
22:43-44	179 n.145		
24:2	116 n.190	**Luke**	
26:64-65	85 n.37	1:8	99 n.109
27:25	71 n.222	1:9	90 n.60

1:10	90 n.62
1:15	*272 n.305*
1:17	*272 n.302*
1:21	90 n.63
1:33	68 n.200
1:76	205 n.295, *271 n.274*
7:28	*271 n.274, 273 n.304*
10:24	174 n.107
13:33	50 n.141
16:18	*253 n.359*
16:31	*271 n.270*
18:10	197 n.236

John

4:20	196 n.235
4:25	219 n.391
7:21-23	194 n.229
8:56	174 n.106, 213 n.354

Acts

7:23	*270 n.251*
13:32	215 n.373

Romans

7:14	207 n.312
9:4-5	72 n.226
10:4	220 n.401
10:5	207 n.319
10:5-10	207 n.316
10:6-8	207 n.320
10:17	215 n.364
11:16	73 n.232
11:25	71 n.223

1 Corinthians

7:14	214 n.363
7:18-19	191 n.211
7:21-23	192 n.213

10:3-4	220 n.398
10:4	*269 n.231*
10:9	220 n.339
14:32	202 n.272

2 Corinthians

3:13	220 n.400
3:16	72 n.225

Galatians

3:16	213 n.356
3:16-17	215 n.372
3:19	215 n.365
3:23	214 n.360
3:24	215 n.356
4:3	215 n.357
4:9	215 n.358

Ephesians

3:8-10	*273 n.314*
5:32	208 n.324

Colossians

2:20	215 n.369

1 Timothy

2:14-15	163-164 n.41

Hebrews

1:1-2	174 n.103
2:5-8	*274 n.330*
3:18	217 n.379
4:2	217 n.378, n.380
4:8-9	217 n.382
5:11	175 n.113
6:4-6	*264 n.135*
7	171 n.83, 172 n.92
7:2	172 n.89

7:3	174 n.103, 176 n.122-123
7:7	175 n.114
7:8	175 n.115
7:11	176 n.120
7:15-16	175 n.119
8:6	216 n.374
9:7	87 n.47
9:15	214 n.359
10:7	164 n.44
11:1	219 n.392
11:5	*259 n.62*
11:13, 16	219 n.395
11:22	219 n.396
11:26	218 n.385
11:29	219 n.393

1 Peter

1:10-12	213 n.358
2:9	*257 n.20*

2 Peter

2:5	168 n.70

Revelation

12:2	163 n.38
12:5	163 n.38
12:9	163 n.39

1 Maccabees

1:15	192 n.215
2:39-41	*250 n.302*
4:47	92 n.70

CHRISTIAN SOURCES

Augustine *City of God*

7.17	*233 n.218*

Casaubon *Baronian Exercises*

	39 n.105

Eusebius *Church History*

4.6.3	*224 n.64*

Eusebius *Proofs of the Gospels*

8.1	39 ns.106-107, 42 ns.115-116

Jerome *On Famous Men*

4	*259 n.68*

Jerome *Against Jovinian*

1.21	193 n.226

Jerome *Letter*

48	192 n.212
120	210 n.349

Severus *Chronicles*

1.24	218 n.389

RABBINIC SOURCES

Mishna Avot
3:17   *234 n.245*
4:17   *235 n.1*

Babylonian Talmud Shekalim
114

Babylonian Talmud Yoma
81, 82, 85, 94, 97

Babylonian Talmud Ta'anit
104

Babylonian Talmud Yevamot
109

Babylonian Talmud Menahot
69 n.213

Babylonian Talmud Hullin
107

Babylonian Talmud Middot
100

Jerusalem Talmud Nazir
109-110

Midrash Genesis Rabba
2:7   109 n.148

Midrash Numbers Rabba
22:9   75 n.250

Targum to Psalms
110:4   178 n.142

Ibn Ezra on Exodus
20:7   145 n.375
20:13   145 n.370

Ibn Ezra on Psalms
110:4   178 n.138, n.140, 179

Kimhi on Jonah
1:3   204 n.291

Nachmanides on Genesis
14:18   *262 n.112*

Nachmanides on Deuteronomy
32:26   *254 n.384*

Rashi on Genesis
4:26   166 n.59
6:3   *260 n.74*

Seder Olam
chapter 1   166 n.60, 167 n.65
chapter 3   184 n.168
chapter 10   187 n.191
chapter 11   *267 n.197*

Seder Eliyahu Rabba
section 2   *253 n.366*

Zacuto *Sefer Yuhasin*
section 1   54 n.151, 60 n.171,
             186-187 n.186

Shulhan Aruch, Orah Hayim
580:2   *266 n.187*

MAIMONIDES *MISHNEH TORAH*

Laws of Idolatry and Heathenism

1:1	129 n.263
1:2	129 n.268
1:3	129 n.266

Laws of the Wayward Woman

3:7-15	*229 n.143*

Laws of Forbidden Intercourse

12:22-23	*242 n.138*

Laws of the Sabbatical Year and the Jubilee

10:3	25 n.50
10:7	26 n.51
10:14	16 n.24
10:15	28 n.58
10:16	27 n.55
11:15	15 n.20
11:17	15 n.22
12:7	*224 n.62*
12:12	*225 n.73*
12:15-16	*224 n.59*
13:11	30 n.60
15:19	15 n.21

Laws of the Temple

1:4	70 n.217
2:2	110 n.150, *242 n.147*
4:1	*230 n.170*
4:2	113 n.168
6:11-12	*225 n.70*
6:14-15	*224 n.63*
7:2	109 n.144
7:3	*243 n.164*
7:4	*243 n.165*
7:6	59 n.168
7:13	*225 n.77*
7:14	*225 n.76*
7:19	88 n.48
7:23	31 n.66
8:1-6	*243 n.169*
8:2-3	114 n.172

Laws of the Vessels of the Sanctuary

1:1-3	60 n.169
1:11	*230 n.172*
3:8	*242 n.139*
3:9-11	107 n.141
4:4-5	*240 n.108*
4:12-13	98 n.102
4:14	98 n.103
4:15	80 n.6
4:16	95 n.87
5:6	*236 n.34*
5:7	86 n.41
5:10	*236 n.40*
6:1-2	*241 n.130*
6:3	105 n.131
6:4-6	*241 n.132*
6:9	112 n.163
7:1	*243 n.176*
7:14	114 n.177
8:2	83 n.23
8:3	81 n.13
10:5	*236 n.27*
10:10	*236 n.30*
10:10-12	84 n.32
10:11	*238 n.74*

Laws of Entrance into the Sanctuary

6:11-12	100 n.114
9:14	36 n.98

Laws of Manner of Offering Sacrifices

2:14	69 n.215

Laws of Daily Offerings and Additional Offerings

2:4	111 n.154

Laws of Service on the Day of Atonement

1:2	94 n.78
1:3	94 n.84
1:7	96 n.92, *239 n.90*
3:7	*239 n.94*

Laws of Murder and Preservation of Life

8:4	*225 n.84*
8:10	*225 n.85*
9:4	*224 n.65*

Laws of Sanhedrin

1:3	53 n.145
2:1	102 n.118
2:4	49 n.135
4:1-2	49 n.133
4:14	37 n.100

4:2	49 n.131
4:5	49 n.130
5:6	54 n.152
5:6-7	54 n.148

Laws of Rebels

3:4	50 n.140

Laws of Kings and Wars

1:1-2	56 n.154
1:3	57 n.156
1:10	*230 n.172*
2:4	59 n.56
2:6	58 n.163
5:1	127 n.250
5:7	141 n.348
5:8	141 n.347
5:9	*252 n.346*
5:12	34 n.87, 35 n.92, 140 n.344
6:1	*248 n.256*
6:1-4	127 n.255
6:5	131 n.277
6:6	131 n.286
6:11	135 n.301
7:1	131 n.287
7:2-3	132 n.289
9:1	128 n.262, *248 n.258*
11:2	*225 n.84*
11:4	*232 n.206*
11:8-9	69 n.207
12:1	69 n.208

GENERAL INDEX

Aaron 60, 79, 81-82, 88-89, 92, 106, 172, 187, 235, 240-241, 261

Abraham 31, 109, 116, 128-129, 169-171, 173-176, 178, 180-181, 185, 189, 213-216, 248, 260, 262, 264, 271

Adam 109-110, 162-163, 166, 170, 257, 267

agrarian law 14-15, 17-19, 25

    in the Bible 14-15, 17-19, 25-26

    at Rome 17-18

Agrippa, King 31, 80, 139, 199, 250, 270

Alcimus (high priest) 66, 79, 235

Alexander the Great 14, 20, 118, 125, 199, 245, 271

Alexandria 138, 141, 187, 223, 252, 263, 270

anointment 98

    of kings and priests 97-98

    sacred oil of 59-60, 97-98

Antigonus II (Hasmonean prince) 67, 100, 240

Antiochus Epiphanes (Hellenistic king of Syria) 66, 79, 115, 139, 226, 231, 250, 252

Apion (Hellenistic Egyptian writer) 8, 11, 20, 156, 221-223, 225, 242, 246-247, 250-252, 256

Apostles 192, 206, 208-209, 215-216, 220, 245, 262

Aramaic 158, 178-179, 185, 187, 234, 247, 257, 264

Aristobulus (Hasmonean king) 39, 67, 186, 231

Aristotle 12-13, 21-22, 51, 53, 57, 59, 61, 165, 204, 221-223, 229-230, 259, 272

Ark of the Covenant 60, 84, 88-89

Athens 39, 198

Augustine 38, 73, 87-88, 90, 92, 210, 218, 233, 275

Augustus (emperor) 139, 199, 237, 250-251, 270, 277

Babylonia, Babylonian 35, 44, 68, 73, 113, 138-139, 238, 244

    Exile 35, 45, 63-64, 68, 238

    and Jewish sovereignty 37-38

Balaam 68, 131, 165

Benjamin, tribe of 102, 188

Berossus (Hellenistic Babylonian writer) 64, 230

Bertram, Corneille (Renaissance philologist) 7, 107

Cain 162, 166, 257

Caligula, Gaius (emperor) 199, 270

Canaan 3, 12, 14, 23, 25, 28-29, 34-37, 42, 44, 47-48, 53, 56, 61, 63-64, 75, 112, 118-119, 122, 125-126, 129-130, 138-141,

169, 171-172, 176, 181, 187, 189-190, 193, 196, 217-218, 234, 260

Canaanites 43, 127, 131, 176, 188, 219, 249

Casaubon, Isaac (Renaissance philologist) 39, 226-227

Cato, Marcus (Roman censor) 150, 157, 256

Cicero 203, 221, 227, 233, 246, 250, 253, 265, 268, 271

circumcision 66, 128, 189-195, 267-268

cities of refuge 33

courts of twenty-three 53-54

covenant 29, 33, 60, 72, 196, 214-216, 275

Daniel 20, 197, 202-205, 269, 272

David, King 32, 35, 38, 45, 58-59, 62, 64, 68-69, 79, 83, 99, 102, 106-107, 114, 119, 138-140, 142, 164, 172-173, 175, 177-179, 199, 204, 208, 213, 232, 234, 263-264, 270

Day of Atonement 16, 80, 87-88, 94-95, 235, 238-239

desert, Israelites in 3, 34, 114, 125, 185, 187, 193-194, 215, 217-218, 266, 269, 276

Diaspora, status of 34, 138-143

Egypt, Egyptians 23-25, 61, 79, 119, 138-141, 146, 182-185, 187, 189-191, 193, 217-219, 226, 251-252, 265

farmers in 24, 147

Israelites in 23-24, 182-185, 187, 189-190, 193, 208

shepherds in 24

elders 51, 54, 67, 79

Eleazar (son of Aaron) 79, 99

Elijah 60, 122, 166-167, 201, 205, 246, 259, 272-273

Enoch (ancestor of Noah) 129, 166-168, 259

Essarhaddon (king of Assyria) 63, 119

Essenes 121, 123, 228, 245

Eusebius 39, 42-43, 45, 99, 117, 171, 224, 226-227

Eve 164, 257

Ezekiel 69-70, 72, 182, 197, 202, 265, 269

Ezra 29-30, 44, 69-70, 74, 97, 234

faith 113, 122, 146, 155, 159, 170, 199, 207-208, 212-219, 276-277

of the patriarchs 212-216

of the people 212-220

Flavius Josephus 11-12, 14, 21-22, 31-32, 44, 47, 51, 57, 63-64, 79, 81, 83, 95, 99-100, 102, 108, 111-112, 123-126, 133-134, 136, 139-140, 152, 156, 162, 168, 185, 192, 199

fortune 4, 35, 47, 61-62, 103, 115, 136, 140, 161-162

Gabinius, proconsul of Syria 54-55

Gerizim, Mount 66, 118

Gibeonites 107, 130-131, 249

Greeks 11, 14, 21, 47-48, 64, 66, 73, 87, 109, 137, 147, 183, 192, 256, 265, 271

Hadrian (emperor) 30, 116

Ham (son of Noah) 169, 260

Hasmoneans 39-40, 67-68, 83, 226, 228

Heaven, worship of 148, 197, 269

Hebrew, importance of 73-74, 88, 158-160, 164, 172

Hebrew manuscripts of the Bible 73-74, 165

Hebrews see also Israelites, Jews 3, 14, 20, 24, 38, 42, 44, 47, 63,

144, 147-148, 156, 183-185, 189, 193, 196, 207, 218-219

Hecataeus of Abdera (Greek historian) 14, 31

Herod, King 35, 39, 67-68, 80, 83, 100, 115-116, 139, 208, 235, 270, 272

Herodotus (Greek historian) 63, 189-190, 230, 252, 267

high priest 31, 33, 49, 56, 58, 65-67, 79-88, 90-92, 94-95, 97-103, 107, 141-142, 149-150, 197, 226, 231, 235-240, 242, 252, 270

   functions and duties of 80, 85-86

   garments of 80-84, 97-98, 149-150

   oracle of 58, 84

   and the service on the Day of Atonement 80-81, 85, 87-88, 91-92, 94-96

Hillel the Elder 73, 228, 234

Hillel IV 54

Holy of Holies 30, 80-83, 85, 87-92, 95, 111, 113, 197, 237, 239, 242, 255

   layout of 82, 88-91, 113

Hyrcanus II (Hasmonean prince) 35, 67, 100, 186

ibn Ezra, Abraham (medieval Bible commentator) 145, 166, 168, 173, 178-179, 232, 253, 262, 264

idolatry 62-63, 119-123, 128-129, 166, 168, 182-183, 188, 199-200, 218, 245, 248, 259, 270

incense altar 88-92, 111, 237, 242

interpretation of scriptural mysteries 68, 163-165, 206-210

Isaac 116, 170, 181, 232, 265

Isaiah 36, 68-69, 74, 169, 174, 203, 262

Israel, kingdom of 60, 133, 149, 187-188, 219, 272

Israelites see also Hebrews, Jews 12, 24, 40, 43, 56, 118, 127-128, 130-131, 145, 182-183, 187-188, 190, 193, 214-219

Ithamar (son of Aaron) 79, 99

Jacob 29, 38, 116, 166, 176, 181-182, 213-214, 226, 263, 265

Jeremiah 35, 71, 190-191, 203

Jeroboam (king of Israel) 4-5, 43, 61-62, 183, 188, 219, 230

Jerome (Church father and Bible translator) 164-165, 167, 169, 171-172, 179-180, 186-187, 190, 192-193, 199, 204-205, 207, 210, 234, 258-259, 268, 275

Jerusalem 4, 20, 30-33, 35-36, 40, 44, 48, 50, 53-55, 62-64, 66, 80, 86, 96, 99, 102, 104-109, 111, 114-115, 118, 124, 135, 139-141, 188, 196-197, 199, 228, 235, 241-243, 247, 269-270

"Jewish Church" 158, 161-163, 165-166, 169-171, 181-182, 188

Jewish scholarship, delusions of 27, 29, 51, 70, 74, 110, 116, 166-167, 175-176

Jews see also Hebrews, Israelites 11, 13-14, 20-23, 25-40, 43-48, 58, 60, 65-75, 81, 83-85, 87-88, 90, 94-96, 99, 108-110, 112-113, 115-121, 123, 125-130, 133-135, 138-150, 152, 158, 164, 166-167, 169-170, 175-176, 178-179, 181-187, 189-191, 194, 196-201, 204-206, 209-212, 214-215, 220, 223, 226-227, 231, 233, 236, 241-242, 244, 246, 250-256, 266-267, 275-277

   and the ban on idols 128-129, 182-183, 197-200

   pagan misconceptions about 20-22, 145-150, 183, 185-186, 189, 197-199

John the Baptist 205, 237

John Hyrcanus (Hasmonean ruler) 67, 118, 252

Joseph 184, 190, 219

Joshua 14, 29, 47-49, 107, 130, 187, 193, 195, 217, 228, 241, 249, 267-268

Josiah, King 56, 59-60, 84, 97

Jubilee 14-16, 19, 25-30, 222-225

Judah (tribe and kingdom of), Judeans 4, 32-33, 35, 40, 42-45, 50, 54, 63-64, 67, 69, 102-103, 114, 118-119, 139, 145, 182, 188, 190, 209, 219, 226-228, 241, 261, 267

Judah Maccabee 66-67, 79, 99, 231

Judah, son of Baba 49

Judea (Roman province) 60, 65, 123, 197, 199-200, 234, 270

judges 3, 37, 47-48, 50, 53-54, 84

Juvenal (Roman satirist) 184-186

kabbalah 50, 159, 206-210, 248, 273

Karaites 210, 275

Kimhi, David (Bible commentator) 74, 178-179, 234, 270, 272

kings 31, 39-40, 47-48, 50-51, 56-60, 62, 67-69, 84, 102-103, 114, 133, 139, 171-173, 178, 231
  dignity of 57-59
  duties of 31, 48, 57-58, 84, 133

law 4, 11-13, 15, 30-37, 49-50, 58, 66, 75, 80, 84-86, 103, 107, 119, 121-122, 128-131, 142, 147, 183, 186, 199, 206-207, 221, 243, 245, 248-249, 253, 266, 273, 276
  "The Law (of Moses)" 57, 66, 72-74, 79-80, 85, 92, 105, 122, 127, 133, 144-145, 147-148, 175-176, 183, 206-210, 215-216, 220
  natural 21, 131, 248-249, 266

Letter to the Hebrews, authenticity of 87, 164, 178-179, 264

Levites 29-30, 32-33, 39-40, 43-44, 49, 58, 64-65, 67-68, 99, 102-104, 106-107, 113, 116, 122, 172, 175-177, 224, 235, 241, 243, 261, 263
  divisions of 104, 113
  duties of 58, 102-103, 106, 113-114
  property of 29-30, 32-33
  status of 106-107

Maimonides 7, 15-16, 19, 25-31, 34-35, 37-38, 48-50, 53-54, 56-60, 68-69, 80-81, 83-84, 86, 88, 94-96, 100, 102, 107, 109, 112-114, 127-132, 135, 140-141, 146, 221, 223-225, 228, 232, 239, 241, 243, 246, 247-250, 252, 259, 267, 273

Manasseh (fourth-century high priest) 65-66, 102, 118

Martial (Roman satirist) 137, 185, 251, 266

Masorites 74

Mattathias (father of the Hasmoneans) 66, 135

Melchizedek (biblical priest) 159, 171-180, 260-264
  compared with Levites 172, 175-177

meshuah milhama (priest anointed for battle) 59, 95

Messiah 29, 33, 39, 45-46, 50, 54, 68-71, 85, 109, 116, 142, 163-166, 170, 172-176, 178-179, 191, 194-197, 201-203, 205, 208-209, 212-220, 232, 236, 246, 258, 262, 264, 275-276
  arrival of 33, 39, 46, 54, 69-71, 217, 220, 232

Moses 8, 11-15, 17-19, 21, 25, 30, 32-34, 37-40, 42, 47-49, 51, 72, 79, 92, 99, 121, 128, 133, 144-146, 155-156, 161, 164, 182,

185-187, 193, 206-207, 215, 217-221, 228, 233, 246, 248, 256, 269, 273

Nebuchadnezzar (Babylonian king) 44, 63-64, 115
Nile   23-24, 147, 182
Noah   109, 129, 147, 168-170, 260
Noahide laws   12, 128-129
Numa (Roman king)   137, 254

omens   136, 145, 254
Onias III   235
Onias IV   66, 235
    Temple of   36, 79, 139
oracles   145, 203, 212, 243
    Apollo at Delphi   113, 202-203
    Jewish   31, 58-59, 84, 92, 145
Origen (early Christian philosopher) 38, 73-74, 180, 209, 234, 275

Palestine *see Canaan*
Passover   111, 148, 184, 242
patriarchs   29, 72, 116, 166, 181, 212, 214-216, 257, 265
Paul   71-73, 166, 172-175, 178, 198-199, 206-208, 212-215, 258, 260, 263-264, 274-276
Petronius (Roman satirist)   148, 197, 200, 255
Pharisees   121, 123, 179, 228, 245
Philo (Hellenistic Jewish philosopher) 90-92, 199, 237-238, 270
pigs   117, 144, 147-149, 255
Plato   70, 156, 256
Pliny the Elder (Roman naturalist) 136, 145-146
Plutarch (Greek writer)   108-109, 147-150, 183, 255
    his misconceptions about Jews 147-150, 183
Pompey the Great (Roman general) 50

priests   30, 40, 48-49, 51, 58-59, 65, 71, 79-81, 83, 85, 87, 90-92, 94-95, 99-100, 102, 104, 106-107, 111-114, 161, 176, 178, 224, 235, 241, 243, 253, 267
    divisions of   99-101, 104, 113
    duties of   49, 51, 58, 80, 85, 94, 100, 111-112, 114
    garments of   81, 83
    officials of   95, 101, 114
prophecy   35, 38-40, 45-46, 58, 68-70, 164-165, 172, 181, 201-205, 226, 271
prophets   28, 32, 50, 58-60, 66, 72, 104, 121-124, 150, 174, 201-206, 212-213, 220, 262, 271, 275
Ptolemy I Lagus (ruler of Egypt)   135, 138, 141
Ptolemy II Philadelphus (ruler of Egypt)   139, 187, 266
Ptolemy VI Philometor (ruler of Egypt)   36, 139, 226, 251

Rabbis   37, 59, 74, 79, 88, 115, 125, 158, 162, 179, 184, 187, 197, 204, 208, 232, 239, 243, 245-246, 248, 264, 266
Rashi (medieval Bible commentator) 68, 166, 168, 176, 197, 232, 259-260, 269-270
Rome, Roman   5, 14, 17-18, 24, 31, 39-42, 44, 47, 54-55, 62, 67, 83, 92, 106, 115-116, 119, 133, 137, 142, 145, 148, 155, 165, 183-184, 198-200, 221, 225, 227-228, 234, 244-245, 252, 254, 256, 259, 270, 277
    authority in Palestine   31, 54-55, 142-143

Sabbath   105, 116, 135, 144-146, 149-150, 194, 198, 217, 245, 250, 253-254, 268-269, 276
    warfare on   135, 250
Sabbatical year   20, 25-28, 223-224

remissions of 25-28

sacrifices 29-30, 32, 36, 54, 58, 69, 80, 90-91, 94, 97, 99-100, 104, 109, 111-112, 141, 145, 162, 191, 194, 196, 199, 225, 231, 233, 239, 269

sacrificial altar 60, 65, 69, 80, 90-92, 96, 99, 111-112, 196

Sadducees 95, 121, 123, 228, 245

Salem 171-172, 174, 176, 261

Samaria (capital of Israel) 4, 43, 62, 66, 118-119, 188, 231

Samaritans 20, 118-121, 196, 219, 231, 238, 244-245

Samaritan temple 66, 118

Sambatyon (river) 145-146

Sanballat (Samaritan leader) 65-66, 118, 120

Sanhedrin (or Senate) 16, 30-31, 37, 40, 47-51, 53-54, 59, 67, 95, 100, 102, 227-228, 230, 240-241, 273

Satan 163, 165, 257-258

Saul, King 57, 59, 133, 140

Scaliger, Joseph (Renaissance philologist) 49, 99, 197, 228

scepter of authority 38-40, 45-46, 226

Scipio Africanus (Roman general) 18, 62, 222

sectarianism 6, 121-124

semicha (laying on of hands) 48-49, 54, 228

Semiramis (legendary queen of Assyria) 64, 140, 252

serpents, snakes 163, 165, 259, 265

Seth (son of Adam) 166, 168, 170

Shammai (early Rabbinic authority) 49, 67, 122, 231

Shem (son of Noah) 129, 166, 169-170, 175, 260

Shilo 35-36, 45, 48, 166, 196, 226

Sigonio, Carlo (Renaissance philologist) 7, 79, 87-88, 90-92, 107, 235

Socrates 198, 257, 269

soldiers, Jewish 72-73, 125, 134, 136, 138-139, 246

sota (woman suspected of infidelity) 51

Sufacus (Egyptian pharaoh) 63

superstition 5, 24, 112, 119-122, 135-136, 145, 147-149, 156, 182-183, 186, 194, 197-198, 202

Tabernacles, festival of 150, 255

Tacitus, Cornelius (Roman historian) 23, 31, 144-145, 149, 155, 185, 187, 197, 199, 223, 253, 266

Talmudists see Rabbis

Temple 3, 25-26, 31-32, 36, 39, 46, 48, 53, 56, 58-60, 63-66, 69-70, 74, 80-81, 83-89, 91-92, 95-97, 99-100, 103-109, 111-116, 138-139, 141-142, 196-197, 199-200, 210, 225, 230, 233, 235, 241, 243, 244, 269

First 25, 60, 84, 97, 113, 115-116

Second 60, 70, 84, 92, 97, 113, 115

Ten Commandments 144, 146, 253-254

Ten Tribes of Israel 44, 62-63, 188, 228

theocracy 12, 241

Tiberius (emperor) 72, 200, 222

tithes 29, 173, 175, 178-179, 261

Titus (emperor) 25, 29, 73, 115-116, 244, 254

Twelve Tribes 5, 40, 42-43, 133, 188

Ulpian (Roman jurist) 31, 40-41, 49-50

Urim and Tummim 31, 60, 84, 92

Varro, Marcus (Roman writer) 70, 177

Vespasian (emperor) 4, 51, 139

wood   91, 100, 107, 111-112, 242

Yarhi, Rabbi *see Rashi*

Zacharias (father of John the Baptist)
    90, 99
Zacuto, Rabbi Abraham (sixteenth-

century writer)   60, 73-74, 169,
    186, 229-230, 234, 266
Zealots   121, 123, 244
Zechariah (prophet)   187, 202, 205,
    267
Zedekiah, King   43, 63, 67
Zerubabel (Second Temple leader)
    115